CHINA'S TWENTIETH CENTURY

CHINA'S TWENTIETH CENTURY

CENTURY

Revolution, Retreat and the Road to Equality

WANG HUI

Edited by Saul Thomas

VERSO

London • New York

First published by Verso 2016
Introduction translation © Saul Thomas 2016
Chapter 1 translation © Chen Xiangjing 2016
Chapter 2 translation © Anne Chao 2016. An earlier version of this chapter was previously
published in English as "The Transformation of Culture and Politics: War, Revolution, and
the 'Thought Warfare' of the 1910s," *Twentieth-Century China* 38, no. 1 (January 2013)
Chapter 3 translation © Gao Jin 2016
Chapter 4 translation © Gao Jin and Yin Zhiguang 2016; an earlier version of this
chapter was previously published in English as "The Crisis of Representativeness
and Post-Party Politics," *Modern China* 40, no. 2 (March 1, 2014)
[...] Saul Thomas 2016
Chapters 6 [...] Christopher Connery 2016
Appendix translation © Tani Barlow and Saul Thomas 2016

UK: 6 Meard Street, London W1F 0EG
US: 20 Jay Street, Suite 1010, Brooklyn, NY 11201
versobooks.com

Verso is the imprint of New Left Books

ISBN-13: 978-1-78168-906-6 (PB)
ISBN-13: 978-1-78168-905-9 (HB)
eISBN-13: 978-1-78168-908-0 (US)
eISBN-13: 978-1-78168-907-3 (UK)

British Library Cataloguing in Publication Data
A catalogue record for this book is available from the British Library

Library of Congress Cataloging-in-Publication Data

Names: Wang, Hui, 1959– author. | Thomas, Saul, editor.
Title: China's twentieth century : revolution, retreat, and the road to
equality / Wang Hui ; edited by Saul Thomas.
Description: Brooklyn, NY : Verso Books, 2016. | Includes bibliographical
references and index.
Identifiers: LCCN 2015030497 | ISBN 9781781689066 (alk. paper)
Subjects: LCSH: China—Politics and government—20th century. |
China—History—20th century.
Classification: LCC DS775.7 .W33713 2016 | DDC 951.05—dc23
LC record available at http://lccn.loc.gov/2015030497

Typeset in Fournier by Hewer Text UK Ltd, Edinburgh, Scotland
Printed in the US by Maple Press

Contents

Introduction

In 1907, well before the 1911 revolutionary process was underway, the twenty-six-year-old Lu Xun, using an obscure and antiquated style of classical Chinese, expressed his expectations for the newly arrived century thusly:

> This writer would venture the opinion that [since] cultures tend to gain perspective as they develop and the human mind is never at ease with a static and unchanging state of affairs, the civilizations of the twentieth century will most assuredly be characterized by depth and dignity and their proclivities will diverge markedly from those of the nineteenth. Will not the advent of a new life put an end to hypocrisy and cause the inner life to gain in profundity as well as in strength? Will not the radiance of spiritual life come to flourish and thrive? Cannot an awakening from the illusory world of objectivity enhance the growth of a life of subjectivity and self-awareness? If the inner-life is strengthened, the significance of human existence will consequently be deepened and the value of the integrity of the individual become more clear; then a new spirit may indeed inform the twentieth century—one which can enable it to withstand the rages of wind and sea, and rely upon the strength of the human will to carve out a new path for a different mode of existence.[1]

Lu Xun used two phrases to summarize what he called the "new spirit of the twentieth century": "cut away the material and expand the spirit, and rely on the individual and reject sheer numbers."[2] The "material" mentioned here referred to the "material civilization" of the nineteenth century brought about by England's industrial revolution—that is, the capitalist economy. The "sheer numbers" pointed to the "political civilization" of the nineteenth century initiated by the French Revolution—that is, constitutional democracy and the parliamentary party system. Lu Xun declared that the creative power of the nineteenth century had declined by the century's end, and that economic and political innovations that had initially seemed to symbolize freedom and equality were turning into new forms of despotism not entirely unlike the despotism of the past. China's task for the newly arrived century was thus to transcend the two earlier European revolutions (the "dual revolution," as Hobsbawm put it—the bourgeois democratic and industrial revolutions) and their consequences, and establish a "country of humans" in which every person would have the freedom to develop.[3]

This is one of the earliest pronouncements on "the twentieth century" that can be found in China. To contemporary Chinese people, the concept of the "twentieth century" was an "alien thing" (*yiwu*) which had seemingly appeared out of nowhere—for before this, China had not known a "nineteenth century" or "eighteenth century." This was at a time when 1907 was known as the *dingmo* year of Guangxu, that is, the thirty-third year of the reign of the Qing emperor Guangxu, the ninth emperor since the Manchus had come down from the north. In Lu Xun's essay, the "the nineteenth century" set against the "twentieth century" did not point to China's past, but to the historical period initiated by the revolutions in France and England. For Lu Xun, however, we in China could only achieve "self-awareness" if we took this alien element of the "twentieth century" as our mission. Why was this the case? Because the dual revolution of the nineteenth century had been the old goal established by the tide of reform and revolution in the late Qing period. Beginning in 1860, under the shadow of the defeats suffered in the First and Second Opium Wars, China began a "Westernization Movement" (*yangwu yundong*) aimed at enriching the country and strengthening its military. After China's loss in the first Sino-Japanese War (1894–95), this movement to "study the advanced techniques of the barbarians to control the barbarians" morphed into a political reform movement exemplified by the Hundred Days' Reform of 1898, one of the key aspects of which was an attempt to imitate European constitutional politics, establish a parliament and change the dynastic kingdom into a "modern state." The failure of this movement to reform the government marked the arrival of the era of national revolution. In the raging tide of revolution, the republic gradually rose on the horizon. The forces driving the birth of this new China were the arrival of Europe's nationalism, market economics, material civilization and political systems. Because of this, even though China did not have a nineteenth century in the same sense as Western Europe or Russia, the "twentieth century" became the way for China to achieve its mission of moving beyond the late Qing goal of reform and revolution, and became its opportunity to achieve "self-awakening."

In a sense, the concept of the twentieth century was not merely one "alien thing," but many. The promoter of constitutional monarchy Kang Youwei wrote *Datong shu* (The great unity) during this period, a work whose concepts and vision—generated from an amalgam of Confucian, Buddhist and utopian communist ideas—not only surpassed the constitutional monarchy he himself supported, but transcended the entire content of the "nineteenth century." The radical nationalist revolutionary Zhang Taiyan used a theory of "the equality of all things" to make sharp criticisms of nineteenth-century statism, racism, party politics, constitutional democracy and formal democracy, and as such, Zhang became an internal "alien thing" within the revolutionary movement. Even the leader of the 1911 Revolution, Sun Yat-sen, attempted to combine two different and opposed revolutions—the nineteenth-century revolutionary nationalist movement to increase the wealth and power of the state, and the twentieth-century social revolution—into a single revolution. If state sovereignty, national identity, party politics, civil society, industrial revolution, urbanization, state planning, market economics, and the corresponding educational system and media culture together constituted the main content of China's social transformation during this period, then the truly alien elements of the twentieth century remained latent within it. To put it another way, while most of the content of China's twentieth-century transformation were extensions of or derived from the "long nineteenth century," latent within these transformations were their opposites or negation. To reiterate Lu Xun, "a new spirit may indeed inform the twentieth century, one which can enable it to withstand the rages of wind and sea, and rely upon the strength of the human will to carve out a new path for a different mode of existence." "Will" expresses a sort of conscious activity, a power that can transcend objective conditions and carry out creative action. This type of creative power is not simply subjectivity, but rather a product of bringing the goal of a particular struggle into a broader framework.

Twentieth century China was characterized by numerous phenomena produced by political processes consciously driven by new subjectivities in formation. Creating a single sovereign republic on the basis of a multiethnic empire and at the same time allowing this sovereign state to encompass a type of institutional pluralism, defining a new politics by way of a cultural movement that repudiated existing political parties and the state and in so doing creating a form of politics different from that of nineteenth-century political parties and states, using the mode and techniques of people's war to carry out land reform, party construction and cyclical movements between the party and the masses to form a super-political party with supra-party elements, and pushing forward a class movement that strived for socialism in a society in which neither the proletariat nor the bourgeoisie were mature, to turn politics and initiative into the main content of the concept of class—in all, not only creating class politics, but creating a socialist revolution within a multiethnic agrarian empire—none of these phenomena could have been predicted or derived from an investigation of the actually existing material conditions of the time. Rather, they can only be understood as the products of politicizing processes.

In 2004, I wrote in the preface to *The Rise of Modern Chinese Thought*, "In the 'long twentieth century,' the Chinese Revolution radically changed the basic structure of Chinese society. We cannot simply rely on the continuity of the category of 'China' to explain the problem of modern Chinese identity. I hope that further historical research can provide new insight into this issue."[4] I would like to supplement this idea here: The twentieth century brought "China" into an era that was not possible to predict or derive from its past, and for this reason any account of "China" must contain an explanation of this century.

This collection of essays begins where *The Rise of Modern Chinese Thought* ended. It carries out an investigation of twentieth-century China and its political processes. During the past ten years, my view of the twentieth century was revised from "long" to "short." The century's core was the "long revolution" from the 1911 Revolution to the end of the Cultural Revolution in the mid-1970s. In this century, although politicization and depoliticization were mutually intertwined and recurring phenomena, we can say that each became dominant in different periods. Thus it might be useful to consider politicization, depoliticization and repoliticization as themes with which we can focus our investigation.

I consider twentieth-century China's politicization chiefly through an examination of three different processes: *political integration, culture and politics*, and *people's war*. These three themes were born of an era of revolution and war, but they appeared in different forms in other historical periods. The attempt to find a form of the state that could integrate China politically turned into a competition, not only between different political forces, but also between different political principles. The state that was born of this process was highly politicized. Attempting to explain the "state" or "nation-state" in the abstract fails to comprehend the importance of the relationship between state and political process. The continuing cultural movement renewed the participants' understanding of politics and redefined the realm of the political, creating a new generation of people. People's war not only fundamentally changed the relations between the countryside and the cities and catalyzed the political mobilization of national identity, it also transformed and restructured such familiar political categories as class, political party, state and people. Without considering these complex processes of politicization, we have little chance of grasping the historical meaning of these categories within the context of the twentieth century.

These three processes of politicization saturated every aspect of China's twentieth century. They were expressed in radical revolution and in strategic compromise, as well as through many issues categorized as "cultural" questions: in the questions of how to view the youth, women's liberation, labor and laborers, language and literature, the cities and the countryside, and so forth, making politics a realm of creativity. They were also expressed in the people's war, which brought together military struggle, land reform, the construction of governmental power, and the united front into a single process. They were also manifest in the way in which people's war transformed every political category after the nineteenth century. For example, the line between the political party and the masses became blurred, political power came to inhere in something different from the traditional idea of a state apparatus, and the idea of a fixed class became supplanted by processes of becoming a class (in the way in which the peasants became a proletarian political force), and so forth. And although the realm of international politics is usually thought of in terms of the normative concepts of sovereignty and national interest, from the 1950s to the 1960s the War to resist U.S. Aggression and Aid Korea and the debate between the Chinese and Soviet Communist Parties provide examples of politicization in the realm of international military and political affairs.

The political innovations of the twentieth century were intimately connected with protracted war, revolution and upheaval. With the global changes that took place from 1989 to 1992, the socialist movement represented by the Chinese and Russian revolutions ended in failure. The tragic end of the "short century" has provided some people with a lens through which they could judge the twentieth century negatively, with the process of politicization itself appearing as the root of the tragedy. Such a view aims to repudiate all of the political concepts directly related to this century—including class, political party, national liberation, masses and mass line, the people and people's war, and so on. But rather than dismiss these concepts, it is worth asking when and in what sense were these concepts politicized, and under what conditions did they become depoliticized? Take the concept of class as an example. While class played a huge role in the political mobilizations of the twentieth century, class mobilization contained within it two possibilities. First, even though from the standpoint of identity or property rights one may not have belonged to a given class, it was still possible to become an agent or soldier for that class. For example, intellectuals from peasant or ruling-class backgrounds became proletarian subjects and even leaders. Second, class background later became an ossified institutionalized marker of identity, and became the key marker by which enemies were distinguished from allies. Both of these possibilities could mobilize people, but the first should be regarded as politicizing, and the second as depoliticizing. To take the political party as another example, under the conditions of people's war the Party was intimately connected with the mass line, with the practice of bringing ideas "from the masses, to the masses," generating an immense and vital force. But the Party in power often became estranged from the masses and degenerated into a typical political machine. I refer to this phenomenon as the statification of the Party—that is, the depoliticization of the Party. Thus, unlike those who wish to search for a new politics outside of these categories, I aim to analyze these categories themselves along with their evolution, and undertake a theoretical investigation of the causes and logics of both politicization and depoliticization. Even though these categories first emerged in an earlier century, I hope to find the alien elements within them, as it is these very different elements that may ignite within these old categories powerful new energies.

In this sense, I argue that searching for a new politics cannot depart from an engagement with these "alien things." From an explanation of the politics of culture to a consideration of people's war and its evolution, from tracing the origins of post-party politics to a study of "the equality of all things," each chapter in this volume undertakes an exploration of the internal "alien elements" of twentieth-century political practice and the possibilities they may contain. Like the "hope" Ernst Bloch wrote of, these suppressed elements may well arise in new forms and relations different from those in the past to reappear again in our era.

2015年4月8日星期三于清华园
Wednesday, April 8, 2015, at Qinghua
University Park

1

Revolution and Negotiation (1911–13)

"The Awakening of Asia" at the Beginning of China's Twentieth Century

China's "Short Twentieth Century": Two Characteristics

As the twentieth century came to an end, Eric Hobsbawm, articulating a particularly European standpoint, defined the "short twentieth century" as the period from 1914 to 1991, beginning with the outbreak of the First World War and ending with the collapse of the Soviet Union. Hobsbawm termed this period "the age of extremes," in contrast to what he called "the age of revolution" between 1789 to 1848, implying that the twentieth century, though filled with violence, lacked the creative historical legacy of the earlier "dual revolution" (France's revolution and Britain's industrial revolution). Counter to that, I have defined the period in China from 1911 to 1976 as the country's "revolutionary century."[1] It was an age that was both extreme and revolutionary. The 1911 Chinese Revolution initiated this "long revolution" as not only the beginning of China's "short twentieth century" but also the most significant of the chain of events marking the "awakening of Asia." Comparing these two perspectives on the "short twentieth century" allows us to discern two unique characteristics of modern China during that period.

First, the continuity between empire and nation established in the revolutionary state-building process is particularly notable during a period marked by nationalist movements and constitutional democracy. The Russian Revolution of 1905, the Iranian Constitutional Revolution of 1905–7, the Turkish Revolution of 1908–9, and the Chinese Revolution of 1911 were central to the "awakening of Asia." The

Chinese Revolution of 1911 quickly led to the founding of Asia's first republic, endowing the revolution with the significance of a true beginning. The 1905 Russian Revolution earned its significance in two ways. First, it was triggered by Russia's defeat in the Russo-Japanese War, a war that took place within the borders of China. Second, it precipitated the outbreak of China's national revolution (the Chinese Revolutionary Alliance [*Tongmenghui*] was founded the same year), triggering fierce debates between republicans and constitutionalists, and inspired the Iranian and Turkish revolutions as well.

The "awakening of Asia" and the outbreak of the First World War signified the age of the collapse of empires. Though the Russian Revolution of 1905 failed, it revealed symptoms of decay in the huge multiethnic Russian empire, which ultimately collapsed through wars and revolutions. The Russian socialist revolution and the growing power of nationalism marched forward together, and the principle of self-determination gained thousands of adherents in Russian border regions such as Poland and Ukraine. Although most of these border regions later joined the larger body of the Soviet Union as federated republics, the disintegration of the USSR in 1991 revealed that its structure was profoundly connected with the nationalist principle. In 1919 the Austro-Hungarian Empire established in 1867 collapsed and Hungary and Austria each established its own republic while the smaller nations formerly part of the empire acquired the status of independent nations. The Austrian Social Democratic Party's plans to enact revolutions and reforms consistent with Otto Bauer's theory within the domain of the Austro-Hungarian Empire resulted in utter failure. The Ottoman Empire had a wide territory and a large population; its rise was an internationally significant world historical event that had prompted the age of European naval exploration. In the smoke of the First World War, that empire, a survivor of previous revolutions, limped toward collapse; the newborn Turkey relinquished its institutional pluralism for a smaller territory and a less complex structure. In the collapse of these three empires, nationalism, constitutional reform and the disintegration of complex institutional pluralism were different facets of the same event. In 1918, the "fourteen points" of Woodrow Wilson placed the national principle above the imperial in the name of national self-determination; nation, nationalism and nation-state would come to dominate the political logic of the entire twentieth century.

The Qing Empire at first seemed doomed to collapse like its neighbors: A regional uprising in 1911 triggered the breakdown of the entire imperial system, and the winds of separatism and independence spread through the empire. On the philosophical level, ethnic nationalism resonated strongly in areas with Han, Mongolian, Tibetan and Uyghur majorities. Zhang Taiyan, moreover, an intellectual leader of the revolutionaries, had compared the Qing to the Austro-Hungarian and Ottoman empires.[2] Surprisingly, however, in spite of violent turmoil, fragmentation and foreign invasions, the precarious republic ultimately managed to remain unified, maintaining the territory and population of the previous empire.[3] How can we explain the unique continuity between the multiethnic empire and the sovereign state?

Modern China's second unique characteristic is the continuity between revolution and post-revolution at the end of the short twentieth century. Beginning with the Russian Revolution of 1917, nationalist revolutionary movements allied not only with bourgeois constitutional democracy, but also with social revolutions and state-building movements influenced by socialist ideas. The October Revolution of Russia was a product of European wars, but it echoed the Asian revolutions, and particularly the 1911 Chinese Revolution, in its combining of national revolution with a socialist economic program and state-building project. Lenin first took notice of the distinctive characteristics of the Chinese Revolution in 1912–13. On the one hand, he argued, "the socialist revolution . . . will be a struggle of all the imperialist-oppressed colonies and countries, of all dependent countries, against international imperialism."[4] On the other hand, a socialist state and program of action (a socialist movement without a proletariat) needed to be established in order to develop capitalism in a backward agrarian country (capitalism without a bourgeoisie).[5]

The socialist aspect of the 1911 Chinese Revolution was embodied in the fact that Sun Yat-sen's state-building program entailed not only a nationalist political revolution, but also a social revolution that aimed to overcome the weakness of capitalism. Its main tactics to accomplish this were to equalize land ownership and tax increases in land value, a policy influenced by Henry George's theories. Linking the national movement to socialist nation-building and international revolution was the key feature distinguishing the 1911 Chinese Revolution from the Russian Revolution of 1905, the Iranian Revolution of 1905–7 and the Turkish

Revolution of 1907–9. This feature presaged the radical difference between the twentieth-century revolutions and those of the eighteenth and nineteenth centuries, as exemplified by the American and the French revolutions. The 1911 Revolution was the turning point for the sequence of revolutions occurring after 1905 and constituted the real beginning of the revolutionary "short twentieth century" (which points to much more than an "age of extremes").

The short-lived 1911 Revolution was a clarion call for the long Chinese Revolution. The Chinese Revolution of 1911, the Russian Revolution of 1917, and the establishment of the socialist camp remade the global landscape that had until then been dominated by the one-way expansion of capitalism. We cannot understand the overall world order after the nineteenth century, therefore, without the perspective of "revolution."

After the Cold War ended, the Soviet Union and Eastern European socialist states disintegrated one after another, and the national principle and the market-democracy capitalist system gained a double victory. In the West, this change was compared to the disintegration of earlier empires and was viewed as a moment of liberation for nations and peoples from the despotic Soviet empire and a step toward constitutional democracy. In Russia and Eastern Europe, the rupture between the ages of revolution and post-revolution was readily apparent. But, while these radical changes in the Soviet Union and Eastern Europe stemmed indirectly from Beijing's 1989 social upheaval, China itself has not only maintained the integrity of its political structure, population composition and size after the end of the "age of extremes," but has also completed, or is on its way to completing, a market-oriented economic transformation directed by its socialist state system. Why?

The first question concerns the relations between empire and nation and between the imperial system and republican system. The second concerns the relations between market economy and socialism. After 1989, no one expected that China would develop its economy so quickly while still maintaining its old political structure. Similarly, no one in the turbulent years following 1911 had any idea where the social upheaval of the day would lead. Modern China's political structure is the product of the nation-building project of 1949; its size and sovereign relations, however, date back to the continuity established between the Qing dynasty and the newly born Republic after the 1911 Revolution. In other words, both "revolution" and "continuity," considered as issues in themselves as well as together as "ruptures within continuity," provide important insights into China's "short twentieth century." Whether we wish to interpret China's twentieth-century history or to discuss contemporary China and its future, we cannot proceed without a basic understanding of these issues.

The Invention of Revolution and Continuity

The link between revolution and continuity was neither a historical inevitability nor the necessary product of some "cultural norm"; it was born in the unfolding of specific historical events, produced by different participants in these events and conditioned by such invisible forces as ideas, values, customs and traditions. Without the outbreak of revolution there would be no issue of continuity to discuss, but continuity cannot be treated simply as the natural outcome of revolution. After the Wuchang Uprising of 1911 and the subsequent disintegration of the authority of the Qing government, a loose inter-provincial revolutionary alliance subsequently formed in the South, but it lacked the power necessary to complete the state-building project across the entire country. On February 12, 1912, after rival forces in the South and the North reached agreement in their peace negotiations, the Qing emperor issued his edict of abdication. Meanwhile, the revolutionaries, constitutionalists and militarists led by Yuan Shikai unexpectedly reached a compromise under the banner of the "Republic of Five Nationalities" (*wuzu gonghe*).[6]

The initial revolutionary nation-building movements that ensued unfolded in a chain of complicated, tumultuous and tangled events. How should we evaluate this chain of events? Ariga Nagao, a Japanese constitutional law scholar, was the first person to expound on the influence of the Qing emperor's imperial edict of abdication and the North–South peace negotiations with regard to the question of the transfer of sovereignty between the Qing dynasty and the Republic of China. In his 1913 essay "The full story of the transfer of power in the revolutionary age," Ariga directed the question of sovereignty away from the revolutionary movements themselves (the Wuchang Uprising and the establishment of the Nanjing Provisional

Government) and toward the North-South peace negotiations and the edict of abdication, claiming that the sovereignty of the Republic of China was "bestowed" by the emperor. Ariga was Yuan Shikai's constitutional advisor, and his theory thus had the clear political goal of justifying Yuan's ascension to the presidency. He later participated in Yuan's campaign to restore the imperial monarchy.

In the revolutionary narrative, the peace negotiation between the North and the South, the abdication of the Qing emperor and the election of Yuan Shikai to the presidency were symptoms of an unfinished and ultimately failed revolution. In fact, after the Qing emperor abdicated and Yuan Shikai was "commissioned with full power to organize the Provisional Republican Government" in command of domestic politics and diplomatic relations, Sun Yat-sen openly declared that "the power to organize the Republican Government cannot be commissioned by the Qing emperor."[7] Later, in the Manifesto of the First National Congress of the Nationalist Party, he reflected on his having to "seek compromise with the counterrevolutionary despotic class."[8] However, the compromise between the North and the South on the principle of the "Republic of Five Nationalities" can serve as a lens through which to view how the continuity between the Republic of China and the Qing dynasty was "created." With the establishment of the principle that "sovereignty resides in the people," this compromise constituted one part of the continuity of sovereignty.

In the "long revolution" of the "short twentieth century," new struggles would unfold along the central questions of who constituted "the people," how they were to be defined, and who represented them—all central problems of modern revolution. But the effects of the compromises and negotiations described above were sweeping: In the subsequent domestic and international struggles—including the attempts to restore the monarchy, the May Fourth Movement, the First National Revolution, the War of Resistance against Japan, the struggles between the Nationalist Party and the Communists, and the struggle by the People's Republic of China to obtain official recognition in international affairs—the continuity of sovereignty was always reconstructed, renewed, and never abandoned, such that it acted as an implicit premise for all of the disparate contending political forces. Even during the National Protection War against Yuan Shikai's imperial rule, the provinces declaring "independence" never sought complete separation, but premised their struggles on the demand to rebuild a unified republic. While the Habsburg, Hohenzollern, Romanov and Ottoman empires were disintegrating one after another, the various old and new political forces in China were all predicating their varied political goals upon the unification of the state.

Empire and State, North and South

Hobsbawm noted that a suitable theme for the nineteenth century would be the rise of the nation-state. After the First World War, the nation-state replaced empire to become the major story of the twentieth century. Nationalism, popular sovereignty, constitutionalism, the centralization of sovereignty, treaties and agreements were at the forefront of the postwar nationalist narrative. Opposed to these were empire, the power of the monarch, despotism, multipolar or distributed sovereignty and suzerain relationships, the tributary system and military domination. In the narrative of nationalism, "the march toward the republic" denotes a political process of transforming from empire to nation-state. In the realm of international politics, sovereignty is a category deeply related to and that in fact often normatively assumes the existence of a nation-state. In the field of historical studies, nation-building, nationalism, mass mobilization and the public sphere are all intimately related with the category of "nation-state."

However, one of modern China's primary characteristics—the continuity between empire and nation-state formed through the revolution, as described above—complicates the narrative. As discussed, while many empires fragmented into multiple smaller nations after the First World War or joined large unions as separate republics, the 1911 Chinese Revolution enabled the transfer of sovereignty from the Qing dynasty to the Republic of China through a "great compromise" under the banner of the "Republic of Five Nationalities." The continuity of sovereignty became the normative premise for domestic political struggles. After the Soviet Union collapsed, China was the only pre-twentieth-century agrarian empire to carry this continuity into the twenty-first century.

Secondly, the transformation from empire to nation-state had several historical preconditions. The construction of empire and of the state overlapped in various ways during the history of Qing dynasty, yet these overlaps cannot be treated as the natural evolution of an empire into a state. From the Manchu intrusion south of the Great Wall in the seventeenth century and the formation of the universalistic empire system in the eighteenth century to the institutional reforms in the latter half of the nineteenth century resulting from imperialist invasions and the signing of unequal treaties, the domestic and foreign relations of the Qing dynasty were constantly changing. Some behaviors usually seen as characteristic of the modern nation-state, such as demarcating administrative authority within borders as well as granting permits for trade and regulating its volume, had long existed in Qing diplomatic relations, especially with the Northern peoples, and were constantly developing. The establishment of Xinjiang Province in 1884 was also an organic part of this process. The imperial system was not static and had multiple centers of authority, even if a certain centralization of sovereignty was born in the process of the empire's self-strengthening.

With regard to the nation-state, modern China not only inherited the ethnic, religious and geopolitical relations of the Qing dynasty and legitimized them through the transfer of sovereignty, but also, in its later institutional designs, preserved multicentered arrangements through such policies as "regional autonomy for ethnic minorities" (*minzu quyu zizhi*). From the revolutionary perspective, the social content of this institutional design (the different paces and patterns of land reform in different regions, for example) was also a "necessary compromise." China's resumption of sovereignty over Hong Kong in 1997 and Macau in 1999 marked the official end of the European colonial system, yet the institutional design of the "Special Administrative Regions" can be seen as a modern variation on imperial-style suzerain relations in the era of the nation-state. Just as we should not view the centralizing tendency within the imperial system as containing the seeds of the nation-state but should treat it as a part of the imperial structure, we should not deem "regional autonomy for ethnic minorities" the natural legacy of empire, but should understand it as a reinvention of a historical tradition under the modern principle of sovereignty and national equality. Even a hundred years after the fall of the Qing, the conflicts between the central government and the semiautonomous regions of the northwest and southwest and the Special Administrative Regions of Hong Kong and Macau have historical links with the complicated relationship between empire and state.

These phenomena therefore suggest that empire and state cannot be demarcated as two distinct political entities. If the continuity of sovereignty between the Qing Empire and the Republic of China signifies the uniqueness of China, then the mutual penetration of empire and nation-state is a widespread phenomenon. We can find elements of "empire" in the United States, Russia, India and many other "nation-states" in terms of their systems of organization and modes of behavior. In the twenty-first century, the power of what was once regarded by Lenin as the "best possible political shell" for nineteenth- and twentieth-century capitalism—that is, the nation-state—is becoming more and more limited, with the world of capitalism now depicted as "empire." As the twentieth century ended, historians discovered that the narrative of "from empire to nation-state" was an oversimplification; in fact, empire and nation-state share many aspects. Characteristics often attributed to empire not only exist in the past and the present, but are becoming more and more manifest as a new political form in the ongoing project of European regional integration. In this sense, the forms of empire and nation-state cannot be judged at face value, but must be interpreted according to their political and historical context. In other words, neither a relatively homogeneous ethno-national nor a multiethnic national form of a polity in themselves merit a positive or negative characterization on either moral or political grounds; the grounds on which to judge a polity is always historical and political.

The continuity between empire and nation born against the backdrop of revolution was the product of a complicated drama. Each force on the stage—Southern revolutionaries, Northern powers headed by Yuan Shikai (including military cliques, the Mongolian aristocracy and Northern provinces that did not approve of the Republic), the imperial household and constitutionalists—had their own interests, demands and political goals, but they all agreed on the premise of "uniting Han, Manchu, Mongol, Uyghur and Tibetan lands as one nation and their peoples as one people," as laid out in the imperial edict of abdication. Even when the North and the South were at war with each other, this principle never lost its legitimacy. How do we explain this phenomenon, and how do we understand the relations of the "continuity of sovereignty" amid "revolution and counterrevolution"?

To explain this problem, we must first look at two conceptions of "China" that unfolded along the division of North and South, inland

and sea in the late Qing and early Republican period. The difference between the two conceptions was not only regional, but also political: The former was a multinational body centered on the territory and population of the Qing dynasty, and its political expressions included the constitutional monarchy and "great nationalism" oriented toward "competition with the outside." The latter was a Han Republic centered on the more constricted territory and population of the Ming dynasty, and based its legitimacy on opposing the Manchu rulers, Han nationalism oriented toward competition "from within" and the theory of "sovereignty of the people" proposed by revolutionaries in the late Qing period. While these revolutionaries' opposition to the Manchus was rooted in a demand for political revolution not necessarily or completely equal to "Han nationalism," there is much historical evidence showing that these revolutionaries were motivated by a vague conception of a Han Republic.

Historiography of the revolution has always centered on the South and the coastal regions, largely because the Chinese Revolutionary Alliance and its precursors were most active in these areas. In the 1980s, historians debated whether the center of the Chinese revolution lay in Southeast Asia (*nanyang*)[9] or in China in the provinces of Hubei, Hunan and Zhejiang.[10] Viewed from a broader perspective, the second conception of China not only fit in with the landscape of the Ming dynasty as was often imagined by the overseas Chinese, but also echoed the ocean-centered modern historiography. Scholars in China have done much research on topics such as the "Self-Strengthening Movement," the development of commerce and industry, the flourishing of cities and towns in coastal areas and the newly emerging classes and other social groups in the late Qing period. If we connect this work with research on the activities of Chinese revolutionaries in the Americas, Japan and Southeast Asia, then support for revolution along geographical lines—namely, in the South and the coastal regions—becomes manifest.

The ocean-centered view is closely related to the global expansion of capitalism. As the overseas Chinese suffered racial discrimination, their conception of "China" was intertwined with their demand to "Oppose the Qing, Restore the Ming." Yen Ching-hwang has suggested that, "if the Chinese government was composed of Han Chinese instead of Manchus, the massive participation of overseas

Chinese in the 1911 Revolution probably would not have happened."[11] This echoes with Sun Yat-sen's nationalist slogan to "expel the Tartar barbarians, restore China" (*Quchu dalu, huifu Zhonghua*). After the revolution, the revolutionaries quickly adjusted their anti-Manchu nationalist demands to lay claim to the slogan of the "Republic of Five Nationalities," but it is not difficult to perceive their intention to break away from the Qing dynasty and establish a Han Republic, as encouraged by such revolutionaries as Zou Rong, Chen Tianhua, Zhang Taiyan, Sun Yat-sen, Wang Jingwei and Zhu Zhixin, among others. After the 1911 Wuchang Uprising, the newly founded Hubei military government appealed to the support of the "eighteen provinces"— those mostly inhabited by Han—in its official statements and telegrams, thereby easily producing the impression that the revolution aimed to build an independent Han nation-state according to the territory of the Ming dynasty. Moreover, judging from the actual distribution of political forces, the seats in the Nanjing provisional government and senate were mostly occupied by Han or representatives from the eighteen provinces. This ethnic distribution seems to correspond perfectly with the pattern formed by the two governments in the North and the South.

National Self-Determination and the "Backward North"

Whether from the perspective of the Southern supporters of the 1911 Revolution or from Lenin's argument that capital's political demand is for a "complete democracy and the demand for a republic,"[12] it would seem that a bourgeois republic and independent nation-state should have constituted the "political shell" for the development of capitalism. There are several factors which prevented this shell from forming: the fragmentation of China by imperial powers, the conservative forces in China's rural areas, and the "backward North" represented by the Qing court and the Northern warlords. The "backward North" was a term used by Lenin in 1912 in comments on the North-South struggle: "Yuan Shikai's parties are based on the backward north of China," comprising "reactionaries, namely, bureaucrats, landowners and reactionary bourgeoisie" of the most backward regions.[13] As early as 1912, he had foreseen the possibility of Yuan Shikai's restoration of monarchy and related it to "the problem of the North" facing the Chinese revolution. Lenin's understanding of the "backward North" was rooted in class analysis, especially his analysis of the interest groups that Yuan Shikai represented, and therefore neglected the regional, ethnic and religious aspects of "the most backward regions" that deterred development of capitalism. Judging from Lenin's later theory of national self-determination, he viewed the nation-state as "the rule and the norm" of capitalism, with complex multiethnic empires as obstacles to the development of capitalism. Guided by Lenin and as a natural extension of his political analysis, the Bolsheviks supported the independence of Ukraine and Poland based on the principle of national self-determination.

But why did Lenin, when speaking of Chinese revolution, not only speak highly of Sun Yat-sen's program, but also withhold support for the independence of Mongolia, Tibet or Xinjiang, and yet declare the "backward North" an obstacle to revolution? Methodologically, Lenin's attitude toward the national question was not based on "legal definitions deduced from all sorts of 'general concepts' of law," but instead on "a historico-economic study of the national movements."[14] The economic basis of national movements was "the complete victory of commodity production," therefore "the bourgeoisie must capture the home market, and there must be politically united territories whose population speak a single language, with all obstacles to the development of that language and to its consolidation in literature eliminated." It is on this ground that "the tendency of every national movement is towards the formation of national states, under which these requirements of modern capitalism are best satisfied."[15]

It is from this standpoint that Lenin not only rejected Austrian Social Democrat Otto Bauer's concept of "cultural-national autonomy," but also criticized Rosa Luxemburg for opposing Poland's bid for independence. Luxemburg's main mistake, according to Lenin, was that she "lost sight of the most important thing—the difference between countries where bourgeois-democratic reforms have long been completed, and those where they have not." After the European democratic revolutions between 1789 and 1871, Western Europe "had been transformed into a settled system of bourgeois states, which, as a general rule, were nationally uniform states. Therefore, to seek the right to self-determination in the programs of West-European socialists at this time of day is to betray one's ignorance of the ABC of Marxism." However,

> In Eastern Europe and Asia the period of bourgeois-democratic revolu-
> tions did not begin until 1905. The revolutions in Russia, Persia, Turkey
> and China, the Balkan wars—such is the chain of world events of our
> period in our "Orient." And only a blind man could fail to see in this
> chain of events the awakening of a whole series of bourgeois-demo-
> cratic national movements which strive to create nationally independent
> and nationally uniform states. It is precisely and solely because Russia
> and the neighbouring countries are passing through this period that we
> must have a clause in our programme on the right of nations to self-
> determination.[16]

Therefore, for Lenin, the national principle was not absolute; whether
to endorse national self-determination depended on its potential benefit
to the development of capitalism in the backward regions as well as the
specific geopolitical situation of the country in question. For example, in
Austria, there was

> a striving on the part of the Hungarians and then of the Czechs, not for
> separation from Austria, but, on the contrary, for the preservation of
> Austria's integrity, precisely in order to preserve national independence,
> which might have been completely crushed by more rapacious and
> powerful neighbours! Owing to this peculiar situation, Austria assumed
> the form of a dual state, and she is now being transformed into a triple
> state (Germans, Hungarians, Slavs).[17]

In Russia, however, the "alien" peoples were the majority of the total
population (composing up to 57 percent of the whole population), most
of them inhabiting Russia's border regions. The oppression of these
"subject peoples" in the Russian Empire was much stronger than in the
states surrounding Russia, and, as Lenin points out, not merely the
"European states alone." The level of capitalist development and liter-
acy in non-Russian-inhabited border regions, furthermore, was usually
higher than in central regions. "Lastly, it is in the neighbouring Asian
states that we see the beginning of a phase of bourgeois revolutions and
national movements which are spreading to some of the kindred nationalities within the borders of Russia."[18]

Based on this analysis, we can deduce Lenin's basic attitude
toward the question of China's border regions. First, like Hungarians

and Czechs in Austria, China's border regions, if seeking independence, would likely fall under the rule of "more rapacious and powerful neighbors" such as the Russian Empire. From the Sino-Japanese War to the "Triple Intervention" by Russia, Germany and France, and from the combined effort to put down the Boxer Uprising to the Russo-Japanese War fought largely in and over territory in China, we can see that Russia, Japan, England, France and other European powers were continuing their efforts to carve out and control significant portions of China. Secondly, not only did China's central region have a more advanced "development of capitalism and general level of culture" than the frontier areas, but a "bourgeois revolution and nationalist movement" had already begun to develop there. Preserving the integrity of China would thus benefit the development of the revolution (and, in turn, the development of capitalism). It is in this sense that Lenin termed Yuan Shikai and his Northern allies "the backward North"—that is, an obstacle standing in the way of the developing revolution that needed to be overcome or eliminated. The reason that Lenin did not argue that Chinese revolutionary radicals had made a compromise that betrayed their revolutionary goal was possibly due to his politico-theoretical vision. The compromise indicated that the "backward North" had triumphed over the Southern revolutionaries in the negotiations, but also that the revolution did not rely on separatism to develop capitalism—both revolution and capitalism in China grappled with the "Northern problem." Judging by this historical genealogy, it is hard to explain the continuity of sovereignty between the Qing dynasty and the Republic of China.

The so-called "North" referred to in the "Northern problem" not only referred to Northeast China, Mongolia and North China under the rule of the Beiyang (Northern) warlords, but also regions inhabited by four of the five major nationalities in the "Republic of Five Nationalities," including those in the Northwest and Tibet in the Southwest, both of which had close relationships with the above regions. Even after the founding of the People's Republic of China, land reform in Mongolian and Tibetan areas progressed much more slowly than in other regions, demonstrating that relations with the "North" would require continuing "compromises" over the entire course of the Chinese revolutionary process. Sun Yat-sen, in his

Inaugural Statement as Provisional President of the Republic of China on January 1, 1912 (as well as in the Provisional Constitution of the Republic of China), discussed the concept of the "Republic of Five Nationalities": "The foundation of the country lies in the people. To unite the lands of the Han, Manchus, Mongols, Uyghurs and Tibetans into one country is to unite the Han, Manchu, Mongol, Uyghur and Tibetan nations into one person. This is national unification."[19] Compared to his earlier concept of nation, the "Republic of Five Nationalities" no longer confined the new republic to the Han-inhabited regions of the Ming dynasty, but developed on the territory of the unified Qing Empire, thus opening up ample space for more diverse approaches in the "march toward a republic." In this respect, Sun accepted the concept of China earlier advocated by the constitutionalists, but replaced constitutional monarchy with a republic.

Scholars such as Murata Yujiro, Yang Ang and Chang An have pointed out that the concept of a "Republic of Five Nationalities" had a much earlier origin as "a product of the debates, struggles and dialogues on the concept of nation between constitutionalists and republicans in the late Qing period."[20] Kang Youwei, Liang Qichao, Yan Fu and Yang Du contributed to this concept in various ways, but they all treated a "Constitutional Monarchy of Five Nationalities" as the foundation for the unification of China—monarchy was always the precondition for the unification of the five nationalities. Thus, before the 1911 Revolution, the "Constitutional Monarchy of Five Nationalities" was the antithesis to the anti-Manchu revolution and Han nationalism. After the 1911 Revolution, the Republic became the new consensus, and Sun Yat-sen began to summon people under the banner of the "Republic of Five Nationalities."

However, aside from the above documents, Murata Yujiro points out that Sun Yat-sen "barely mentioned the 'Republic of Five Nationalities' except in the presence of Mongolian, Tibetan and Manchu representatives."[21] As the Qing court declined and the monarchy became unsustainable, constitutionalists who had advocated for a "Constitutional Monarchy of Five Nationalities" before the revolution now turned to the "Republic of Five Nationalities."[22] This transformation laid the foundation for modern egalitarian politics in China, but it also gave rise to the challenge of balancing conservative religious-political traditions (such as the politico-economic system in the religious society of Tibet) with radical class politics through law, institution and practice.

After the Republic of China was founded and the concept of the "Republic of Five Nationalities" had been invented, the North–South problem did not disappear. Responding to the demand for the founding of a Han republic, Urga (Ulan Bator) first declared independence, followed by Tibet issuing orders to expel Han Chinese from of the region. During the North-South peace negotiation, the Mongolian nobility held an extremely suspicious attitude toward the idea of a republic, complaining that "the intellectuals of the South often coerce us with the theory of republic."[23] They emphasized that Urga's independence "did not mean to betray the emperor, but because we lack a thorough understanding of 'what a republic is,' we are concerned that rumors of 'democracy' cannot produce the unification of China."[24]

These words resonated with the arguments of intellectuals such as Kang Youwei, Liang Qichao, Yang Du and others before the revolution. Yang Ang and other scholars have demonstrated that Mongolian nobles identified more with a "Constitutional Monarchy of Five Nationalities" than a "Republic of Five Nationalities" because a transformation of the political system would affect the interests of the Mongolian aristocracy and the structure of Mongolian society itself. This was a struggle between egalitarian politics and traditional politics. In their letter to representative for the South Wu Tingfang, the Mongolian nobles emphasized that for Manchus, Mongols, Tibetans and Uyghurs, "the customs of the people determine that they know only their monarch, and know nothing about what a 'republic' is, and what they fear further is a republic despotically ruled by a small group of elites." They asked, "Will the polity of 'republic' you proposed apply to just the eighteen provinces of the Han, or will it integrate the Manchu, Mongol, Tibetan and Uyghur areas?"[25]

In the broader Northern area, the struggle of monarchy and republic did not reach consensus, and the slogan of a "Constitutional Monarchy of Five Nationalities" had not yet been revised into the "Republic of Five Nationalities." If a "great compromise" had not occurred to take in the opinions of various forces, enable a smooth transfer of sovereignty and "integrate regions that do not participate in revolution or approve of a republic into the territory of the Republic of China," the map of China would have greatly changed. The three Northeast provinces where the Manchus originated, the four provinces of Hebei, Shandong, Shanxi and Henan which did not approve of the Republic or declare independence, the ten leagues of Inner and Outer Mongolia and the Chahar, Uriankhai and Kazakhs who Ariga Nagao claimed "know only their duty to the Qing emperor and nothing of democracy and republic" could not have become part of the Republic of China.[26] When preparing for the national congress in the middle of the peace negotiation, provincial representatives were summoned by the Southern and Northern governments. The Nanjing Provisional Government was in charge of summoning representatives from the provinces of Jiangsu, Anhui, Jiangxi, Hubei, Hunan, Shanxi, Shaanxi, Zhejiang, Fujian, Guangdong, Guangxi, Sichuan, Yunnan and Guizhou. The Qing court was in charge of summoning representatives from the provinces of Hebei, Shandong, Henan, Gansu, Xinjiang and the three Northeast provinces. Representatives of Mongolia and Tibet were jointly summoned by the two governments. In order to hold the national assembly in Beijing, Yuan Shikai claimed that the Mongol and Uyghur representatives did not want to come so far south as Shanghai.

The imperial edict of abdication of the Qing emperor adopted the same rhetoric as Sun Yat-sen's inaugural speech and the "Provisional Constitution" on the question of the polity, stating that "the authority to rule belongs to the entire country as a constitutional republic," and "In hope that people live in peace without unrest within the borders, therefore I unite Han, Manchu, Mongolian, Uyghur and Tibetan lands as one territory, constituting a grand Republic of China."[27] However, the form of transferring sovereignty through abdication, as well as the political arrangement to "commission Yuan Shikai with full power to organize the Provisional Republican Government to coordinate with the army and people to unify the country," was clearly designed to appease the Northern forces. Without this unstable negotiation and the form of "transfer" which laid down the continuity of sovereignty, as well as the ensuing revolutions and struggles that would reinforce this consistency of sovereignty, the modern-day geographical regions of Central Asia, Central Eurasia, Inner Asia, Inner Eurasia—the broad areas extending from the Volga River eastward to the Xing'an

Mountains—and the Himalayan plateau would have been completely different.

Though the relationship between Mongolian, Uyghur and Tibetan lands and the Central Plains in the heart of China dates far back, we must still explain the revolution and continuity in relations between these regions during the transition from empire to republic in order to understand the particular configuration of modern China. From the perspective of Inner Asia, the compromise made with the Chinese revolution was similar to that which developed with the Qing from the seventeenth century onward. Since the 1980s, many scholars have considered Inner Asia an important region of the Eurasian continent rather than a marginal area isolated from the centers of civilization. In their opinion, peoples of Inner Asia were the driving force for great changes on the Eurasia continent between the fifth and fifteenth centuries, including the Mongolian Empire's development into the largest inland empire in world history in the thirteenth and fourteenth centuries. Mongolian supremacy ended after the fifteenth century due to a combination of factors: changes in trade routes, the rise of other agrarian empires (such as the Grand Duchy of Moscow, the Ottoman Empire in Turkey, the Mughal dynasty in India, the Safavid dynasty in Persia, and the Ming and Qing dynasties in China) assisted by technological and military advantages and religious factors. Ultimately the nomadic culture of the Mongols "ended either by cooptation or subjugation under the Qing . . . The last Mongol people to strive for renewal of Mongol unity, strength, and glory, the Zunghar Oirats, were squeezed out between two great empire-builders—Czarist Russia and Qing China—which then divided the steppe region between them."[28]

The fall of the Mongolian empire had tremendous geopolitical consequences: "The elimination of a powerful, independent Mongol-nomadic state in the steppe was a world-historical event. The closure of the steppe frontier meant the end of an age of fluidity, ecumenical exchange, fighting, and shifting of boundaries, and the division, dispersal, and extermination of the Mongols, who are now scattered from the Volga River to North China, one of the widest involuntary diasporas to occur on the continent."[29]

Historians have also pointed out the different manner in which the Qing dynasty dealt with maritime and inland affairs and that the Qing's

Inner Asian policy was more successful. Sino-Russian relations of the seventeenth and eighteenth centuries resonated strongly with the international law and diplomatic relations of nineteenth-century Europe, which inspired the Qing in its dealing with Mongolians and other peoples on the Sino-Russian border areas.[30] On one hand, from the seventeenth century onward, the Mongols' legal, economic, military and other factors consistently acted upon the internal structure of Qing society (for example, the banner system); on the other hand, Mongolians were also assimilated into the agrarian culture of the Central Plains through interaction with Manchus.

Thus Lenin, from the perspective of this trend in capitalism's development, termed the area the "backward North." Sun Yat-sen, however, operating from the perspective of the integration of China, a phenomenon that had become increasingly significant since the seventeenth century, gradually gave up the concept of the "Republic of Five Nationalities" and turned to the concept of a new and single "Chinese nation" (*zhonghua minzu*). In 1920, Sun delivered a speech at the Nationalist Party Conference in Shanghai criticizing the slogan of the "Republic of Five Nationalities" as being "very improper," saying, "Don't we have more than five nationalities in our country? In my opinion, we should unite all nationalities in China into one Chinese nationality (as in America, which was originally composed of various ethnic peoples from Europe, but now has grown into one American nation, the most glorious nation in the world), and we should turn the Chinese nation into a most civilized nation. That is when 'nationalism' will be realized."[31]

In spite of this, from the debate on the "Republic of Five Nationalities" in 1912 to the "regional autonomy for ethnic minorities" established within the framework of the Constitution of the People's Republic of China after 1949, the concept of the "Chinese nation" still retained traces of the complicated relationship between the North and the South. As the sea powers rose in the nineteenth century, and as industry, commerce and urban towns developed in coastal areas, new conflicts between different modes of production once again became manifest.

Two Types of Political Integration and Revolution: Multi-Party Parliamentary System, Administrative Integration and Revolutionary State Building

The policy of "regional autonomy" (*difang zizhi*) promoted by the late Qing government provided the political conditions for the tendency toward separatism in the early republican era. The central government faced severe military and financial difficulties and lacked the ability to effectively deploy military forces within the country or force provincial governments to deliver the taxes they had collected to the center. At the same time, the revolution had caused the old bureaucratic system to lose efficacy. These problems, coupled with the separatist trend on the frontiers and the worsening international situation, directly impeded the construction of the constitutional government. The temporary compromise formed after the 1911 Chinese Revolution had set off a new round of political divisions, military conflicts and regional separatism. The Northern Beiyang government attempted to achieve centralization with military and political power, while the Southern forces and the Chinese Revolutionary Alliance, now organized as the Nationalist Party (*guomindang*) and occupying the majority of seats in the assembly, tried to centralize power within the parliament. In 1912, after Yuan Shikai was selected as provisional president, the Nanjing parliamentarians drafted the Provisional Constitution of the Republic of China in an attempt to limit the power of the president. In 1913, with the Nationalist Party dominating the national assembly, members produced a "Temple of Heaven Draft Constitution" which promoted a "super-parliament." After Song Jiaoren's assassination and the ensuing "Second Revolution," Yuan Shikai responded to this bid for a super-parliament by organizing a constitutional group to pass the "Constitution of the Republic of China," which formed the constitutional framework for a "super-president" and reduced the parliament to a mere consulting agency.[32] In 1915, just a few years later, Yuan Shikai would restore the monarchy.

If we put "political integration" at the center of the historical picture, we see that it emerged in two opposing modes around 1912. The first mode was constitutional democracy centered on new "open parties" and parliamentary politics. In March 1912, Song Jiaoren held a convention in Nanjing for provincial representatives from the Chinese

Revolutionary Alliance, and proposed changing the Alliance from an underground revolutionary organization to an above-ground "open party," which would enlarge the party organization, allow it to participate in a national election and attempt to form a cabinet. The political programs he proposed included unifying the administrative system, promoting regional autonomy, encouraging ethnic assimilation, enforcing state social policy, popularizing compulsory education, supporting equality between men and women, implementing military conscription, reforming the fiscal system, standardizing the taxation system, striving for international equality, and encouraging immigration to and cultivation of land in the border areas. Starting after the North–South peace negotiation in 1912, the announcement of national elections caused new political parties of every variety to sprout across the entire country, and parliamentary party politics flourished. But after Song Jiaoren was assassinated on March 20, 1913, and the subsequent attempt to oust Yuan Shikai and form a new government (the "Second Revolution") failed, the democratizing trend centered on the spread and activity of parliamentary parties to promote national integration came to a close. It must be said, however, that the idea that the growth and activity of parliamentary parties could bring about political integration is not without precedent, for such parties have displayed an important integrating function within European democracies.[33]

In place of political integration centered on parliamentary-party politics rose integration centered on administrative or executive power. On January 1, 1912, Sun Yat-sen gave his inauguration speech as provisional president, describing the duties of the provisional government in this way: "The citizens believe that internally there is no institution which unifies the country and that we are without a sovereign body to deal with international affairs. The task of constructing this institution cannot be delayed any longer, therefore they entrust me with the duty of organizing a provisional government."[34] Given the diversity of opinions, goals and interests within a society, political integration by means of centralized administrative power can have the effect of maintaining political unity and promoting effective administration. In the modern era, bureaucratic administration under a parliamentary system is not the only institutional arrangement considered legitimate. Centralized administrative and executive authority continues to this day to be widely recognized as a legitimate form of government.

By February 1912, however, executive power was usurped by the Northern forces represented by Yuan Shikai, and the Chinese Revolutionary Alliance and Nationalists were forced to turn to parliamentary politics. In an attempt to prevent Yuan from attempting to bring about political integration under his own centralized executive power, the Nationalists in parliament drafted a constitution that reduced the executive branch to the enforcement agency of a bureaucratic system under parliament's control. In this complicated political situation, some of the early constitutionalists who had long doubted the effectiveness of parliamentary politics now recast their earlier preference for constitutional monarchy into a new theory of political integration under centralized executive authority, designating it "sovereignty of the state." But even while they highlighted the importance of executive power, their foregrounding the concept of the "state" was an attempt to limit the power of any possible future monarch. During the late Qing dynasty, Kang Youwei and Liang Qichao had advocated statism (especially German statism, which represented the state as an organic body) precisely in order to provide constitutional support for limiting the monarch's power.

The primary target of late Qing statist theory, therefore, was first and foremost unchecked monarchical authority, and only second the revolution. After the 1911 Revolution, however, and especially after the Qing emperor's abdication in 1912, the constitutionalists' slogan "sovereignty lies with the state" was aimed at constraining the swiftly expanding power of the parliament. Kang Youwei questioned whether the conflict-ridden parliament would be capable of representing the collective will of all citizens, and he implied that the government itself should take on the responsibility of representation, integration of the citizens' goals, and enforcement. Kang's theories, therefore, sought to strengthen the political integrating function of centralized administrative power. Kang and Sun Yat-sen were opposed to each other politically, but Kang's opinions on the sovereignty of the state and Sun's hopes for the provisional government shared some common ground, in that they both thought that centralized administrative power should take up the responsibility of integrating the country politically.

The two antithetical political positions, favoring parliament or centralized administrative authority, represent different concepts of the state. To view the parliament or party system as the representative of the citizens—as that which issues political will—is to view administrative power as a nonpolitical (and nonrepresentative) instrumental power and purely bureaucratic, the most formally rational type of authority. This is the theory of Max Weber, who defined administrative power as a nonpolitical instrument. This principle characterizes the general political view of modern liberalism.[35] In contrast to this, Kang and Liang hoped to fortify the governmental power in the name of "sovereignty of the state." The governmental power they envisioned was apparently different from that of a state in a bureaucratic system.[36] Kang Youwei's "sovereignty of the state" was a variation on the theory of the "sovereignty of the people," which held that the "state" would represent the collective will of all citizens. Thus, centralized administrative power, as a representative of the "state," was no longer a nonpolitical bureaucratic system but a political power—the integrator of society's goals.

"Sovereignty of the state" was, therefore, not just a theory of sovereignty, but a political theory of political integration. Lacking systematic theoretical support on the relationship between administrative power and political integration, Kang's theory thus appealed directly to the concept of "sovereignty." If we put the debate of 1913 in the context of the struggle between the president and the parliament, we can discern the difference between the two: While the former aimed at shifting power from the monarch to the state, the latter saw public administration as a political integrator. Kang Youwei repeatedly analyzed the terms and rules regarding relations between the president and the prime minister, and hoped to use a national religion (Confucianism) as a spiritual source for political integration. He hoped to integrate the diverse and often conflicting interests and demands of the central and local governments and the North and South by applying effective governmental power.

If we connect the demand for "sovereignty of the state" to the debates about land reform, we can find another dimension of early republican political integration in the relationship between land ownership and the state. Kang Youwei opposed the political concept of "united autonomous provinces" (*liansheng zizhi*) or the federal system; instead, he supported a certain level of autonomy at the grassroots level of society in the unit of the locality (*xiang*). His theory of the "sovereignty of the state" integrated local autonomy (*jiceng zhengzhi*), collective land ownership and a "great unified state" (*da yitong guojia*), with public administration as a mechanism of political integration rather than a bureaucratic, formalist and nonpolitical enforcement apparatus.

The ambiguity of the theory that "sovereignty resides in the state" may derive from state theory itself. The German scholar of public administration Wolfgang Seibel has expressed an interesting observation: Even though Hegel and Weber have provided important insights to twentieth century political theory, what prevails in actual German politics is a non-Hegelian, non-Weberian theory. According to Seibel, Hegel

> conceived the state, and thus government and administration, as the incarnation of reason as long as it justly applied the law and as long the individual members of the governmental apparatus—read: the bureaucrats—were committed to that universal idea. This corresponded to Weber's concept of bureaucracy as the materialization of the rule of law . . . Hegel connected legitimate state power to the abstract notion of the representation of a universal common good, while Weber focused on the legitimizing effect of formal legality . . . Hegel and Weber were representatives of the 'rationalist' school of thought in public administration, which neglected the "organicist" perspective on the state as an organizational phenomenon . . . Accordingly, the actual quality of German public administration in achieving not only organizational effectiveness and coherence but also the political integration of challenging societal groups was beyond their theoretical grasp.[37]

According to this theory, the state administration, through its interaction with the public and cooperation with various interests, generates "symbolic sense making" and "the creation of patterns of identity." In Germany public administration "served as a political integrator long before parties and parliaments emerged. It was even conceived as such as an alternative to constitutional government in the early nineteenth century."[38]

The emergence of the theory of administration as an integrator was intimately tied to the state of disunity Germany experienced since the early modern period. After the Thirty Years' War, the need to organize standing armies as well as provide revenue spurred the development of a comprehensive and efficient government which could integrate competing social groups into a unified polity. One of the goals was to mitigate the conflicts between the royal standing armies and the aristocracy which frequently took place in Europe. In the late nineteenth century, the central proponent of this theory of administration, Lorenz von Stein (1815–90), explained it in terms of "the working state"—"a living organism rather than a tool of government," allowing the state to be conceived of as an entity embedded within society: "Just as Hegel's notion of the state as the actual materialization of reason served as a reintegrative myth that was helpful for organizing the coherence of a decentralized and territorially dispersed administrative structure, Lorenz von Stein's notion of the working state serves as the keyword of non-Weberian rhetoric in German administrative science." Von Stein borrowed Hegel's concept of "the juristic personality" to suggest that the actual life of the state was like the actual life of a person, in that its activity can be divided into "deeds" and "work." "Deeds" consist of such formal acts as propagating laws and making official judicial and other decisions. But the actual life of the state cannot be characterized by the sum of individual decisions. Just as a person's actual life is characterized by carrying out decisions grouped in the form of work, the actual life of the state is characterized by work carried out in the form of administration. Administration is thus the "actual life of the state as a working state."[39]

Others in this non-Weberian tradition of theorizing the relation between administration and politics include Otto Hintze (1861–1940), who in the midst of his account of the necessity of bringing the landed aristocracy into the royal army emphasized the idea that the integrative capacity of public administration was a precondition for a modern stable German government. Rudolf Smend (1882–1975) made a further contribution by emphasizing the mutual interaction between administrative decisions and public spirit, and from this perspective described the entire state apparatus as having an integrative function.[40]

The connection raised here between administrative decision making and public spirt is somewhat reminiscent of Kang Youwei's promotion of a national religion. All of these theories point in a single direction: that public administration is a mechanism for political integration, not a bureaucratic, formalistic, nonpolitical executive apparatus. Seeing administrative power as a political integrator also implies that administrative power is in reality a mediator between the state and society. Like the German theory of "public administration as political integrator," the theory of state sovereignty was also produced from a situation of disunity. The commonality between these two theories is that they give the state or public administration a role in political integration. In this sense, "sovereignty lies with the state" is not an accurate expression. Kang and Liang's use of the phrase "sovereignty lies with the state" bore the marks of late Qing statism, and it did not accurately express their hope that public administration could perform the function of political integration. "Political integration" is a process. It attempts to bring divided social forces and interests together within a single organic administrative apparatus. Only in this sense is public administration not merely formalistic and bureaucratic, but also political. Through its function of integration it manifests the existence of the will of the entire nation's people. Lacking a system of checks and balances, liberals have reason to worry that such a system can take an authoritarian turn (such as Yuan Shikai's attempt to declare himself emperor), and democrats have reason to fear that under this principle the idea that "sovereignty lies with the people" will die out. But they both overlook its "integrative" political function and the conditions for its creation. "Political integration" cannot be achieved through a solely top-down process.

Comparing "the theory of state sovereignty" and "administration as public integrator," we can see that the "state" in the former is abstract, similar to Hegel's notion of the state as telos. Kang and Liang were not able to find an appropriate governmental power to implement political integration. The idea that political integration could be achieved through the activity of the state was born of China's situation of rupture and division. Political integration is a political process which integrates diverse social forces, social interests and demands into the organic operation of an administrative system. In the early republican period, the conflict between the parliament and the executive was also the conflict between the South and the North, the military force and the political force, and the remnants of the old regime and the revolutionary forces. It seemed impossible to defuse any of these conflicts through formalist procedures. The Qing emperor's Imperial Edict of Abdication could be said to have provided the greatest possible of legal continuity from the old state to the new, but it had left multiple problems in its wake. After

Yuan Shikai became president, he made frequent appeals to the need for "unification"; aside from having some minor effect in the border regions and in the realm of diplomatic relations, he was able to construct real integration neither with the Southern revolutionaries nor even the rival military cliques in the North. The tension between the central government and local governments remained the same, and the vast rural areas were utterly ignored in the sovereignty claims of both the North and the South. In this context, the question of how to carry out political integration and on what basis was a pressing one.

It was in this sense that Kang Youwei and Liang Qichao hoped that the public administrative system could act not only as a formal bureaucratic apparatus, but also as a political one that could represent the collective will of the entire country through political integration. Yet the symbol of the central administrative power was the head of government (the president or prime minister), which meant that the theory of "sovereignty of the state" became somewhat like a monarchist theory without the monarch. Without proper checks and balances, liberals had good reason for their concern that the system could develop into personal authoritarianism (with Yuan Shikai as the prime example). Democrats were also justified in their worry that under this principle, the idea of "sovereignty of the people" could be reduced to a facade. Aside from their mistaken faith in certain powerful individuals, the most important mistake of the statists was their failure to understand that political integration could not be created from the top down. Without participation and recognition by the people from the bottom up, there could be no real "political integration." After 1913, with the continuing political confrontation between the North and the South and the inability of any governmental force to mobilize society, centralized administrative power was unable to fulfill the task of political integration. The decline of this theory was natural.

By the twentieth century, the "modern prince" was not the "state" or the "administration," but the political party that sought to command state power and integrate social demands and goals. What appeared after the First World War was no longer a party in the first mode of political integration, that is, a European-style parliamentary party of the sort represented by Song Jiaoren. This was a new type of force. After a dramatic series of revolutions, compromises, parliamentary struggles, the super-presidency and the restoration of monarchy, what emerged was not a "political party" of the nineteenth-century type, but a political innovation of the twentieth century which also went by the name of "political party." As this new force came to occupy the political stage it greatly changed the nature of the bureaucratic state. While this special type of political party—which included both the Nationalist Party and the Communist Party—would from time to time engage in parliamentary struggles, it focused much more on direct social mobilization, promoting political integration by means of confrontational politics. For this political organization, leadership or "hegemony" (including "cultural hegemony") was bound up and integrated with the formation of the popular will, and its legitimacy derived from "revolution."

Mao Zedong, in his "Report on an Investigation of the Peasant Movement in Hunan," famously said of the 1911 Revolution: "The national revolution requires a great change in the countryside. The Revolution of 1911 did not bring about this change, hence its failure."[41] This conclusion came from the perspective of new revolutionary movements, but it also revealed the fundamental reason why the theory of the "sovereignty of the state" had failed politically. When Mao published this report, new-style political parties were already leading social movements and creating political integration from the bottom up. By the time that the principle of "sovereignty of the people" had gained universal acceptance, it was not the "state" that Kang Youwei and Liang Qichao had envisioned but the "revolution" which they feared and from which they felt most alienated that was propelling integration.

This integration, furthermore, was not administrative integration by the state but a complete restructuring of the state itself through social mobilization. In these movements the party formed an organizational force for political integration under specific conditions of political identification (the revolutionary process of war and social struggle). No longer subject to the conditions of the early republican parliamentary-party system, it was a political group that sought to directly command political power by integrating the social will. The restructuring of the Nationalist Party and the emergence of the Chinese Communist Party (CCP) both reflected this new political change, and their divergence and confrontation unfolded in a new round of historical struggles. During the Northern Expedition, the political party was the organizer, participant and political integrator of social mobilization, and it was through this function of political integration that the party gained control of state power. However, in its ensuing political development, the Nationalist Party gave up its involvement in social movements and turned to the more bureaucratic party-state system. The CCP, on the other hand, insisted on integrating the party, the state (including the soviet governments in the border regions) and large-scale social mobilization based on land reform.

In the terminology of this political organization, "national citizen," "peasant," "working class" and "the laboring masses" were neither neutral nor descriptive terms, but instead new political categories invested with political meanings. In the context of the 1911 Revolution, the enemies of the revolution were the Beiyang warlords and the so-called "old" or "feudal forces" composed of elites in the urban and rural areas. In the political context of Nationalist-Communist confrontation, the movement for peasant revolution and the liberation of other oppressed classes set as their political opponent the Chinese bureaucratic class, which was composed of state officials degenerated from the previous revolutionary movement into a counterrevolutionary force, as well as the feudal and bureaucratic comprador forces that they represented.

In his famous 1926 essay "Analysis of the Classes in Chinese Society," Mao Zedong, with the aim of distinguishing between "friends" and "enemies," divided Chinese society into the "landlord class" and the "comprador class" which "depended upon imperialism for their survival and growth," the "middle bourgeoisie class" which "represents the capitalist relations of production in China in town and country," the "petty bourgeoisie class" consisting of the "owner-peasants," the "master handicraftsmen," and the "lower levels of the intellectuals," the "semi-proletariat class" comprising the "semi-owner peasants," the "poor peasants," the "small handicraftsmen," the "shop assistants and the peddlers," and finally the "modern industrial proletariat" and the "fairly large lumpen-proletariat." Among these groups, the warlords, the bureaucrats, the comprador class and the big landlord class, all groups which directly or indirectly depended on the imperialist powers, were "our enemies," the industrial proletariat was "the leading force in our revolution," and the semiproletariat and the petty bourgeoisie were "our closest friends."[42] The most important concept here is the "we," which recurs frequently and without which there could not be "enemies," "friends" or even the "leader of revolution." This "we" was the revolutionary political party.

Mao's analysis of classes in Chinese society was not a static classification, but a strategic analysis made from the standpoint of a social movement propelled by a revolutionary party. Every category was a political one, in that this was a political categorization created with the aim of achieving political integration. For example, in actual mobilization, terms such as "peasant," "worker" and "urban petty bourgeoisie" were used to describe people who farmed, people who were hired by others and people who did business. These concepts, however, like concepts such as the "masses" or the "united front," were from the beginning categories in the realm of political mobilization. The concept of "the people" in the Chinese revolution was based on these political categories, or, rather, produced through the integration of these political categories.

The revolutionary party and the governments under its leadership followed the organizational line of "from the masses, to the masses." On the one hand, they enlarged the united front (through political integration); on the other, they consolidated the leading role of their party and revolutionary governments in the rural areas. Through military struggle and land reform, they sought to realize the demand to "equalize land ownership" that had been proposed in the early phase of revolution. All of these can be seen as means and strategies adopted by the party for the purpose of political integration. The primary function of the revolutionary party was to create "the people," their revolution and their war ("people's war") through various forms of mobilization and struggles. "The people" was not a simple agglomeration of ordinary workers, peasants and other laborers, but a political category that implied an "enemy-friend" relationship. Thus, such practices as building the party organization, organizing workers, mobilizing peasants, carrying out land reform, engaging in military struggle, and building base areas were part of the process by which "enemies," "ourselves" and "friends" were discerned, and by which workers, peasants, students, youth and women were reconstructed as "the people."

Politicization was the central feature of this era. In fact, both the Nationalist Party restructured after 1920 and the Communist Party born in 1921 followed the principle of "ruling the state with the Party" (*yi dang zhi guo*) and directly intervened in the state's administration functions at various levels. Public administration thereby ceased to observe a typical bureaucratic logic; instead the parties' organizational branches gained increasing influence within the social body. The outcome of the competition between the Nationalist and Communist parties was largely decided by the different degrees to which their efforts toward political integration successfully reached into society. Both parties combined "political integration" with public administration, each party acting as intermediary between the state and the people (society), both representing the people and acting as the dominating force of state administration. Through the interaction between the party and the state, especially as the party directly intervened in administration, the state became a public administration system undertaking the function of political integration. This, in turn, created a new party-state system distinct from the multiparty parliamentary system. Because this type of state led by a party organization has the two functions of political integration and public administration, perhaps we can refer to it as a "public administration system which serves as the mechanism for political integration."

With the "long revolution" and its changing strategies suited to different historical circumstances, the integrating function of the party and the state reached an unprecedented level, unmatched by any other bureaucratic state. The mobilizing ability and integrating function of the new party state unfolded within the framework of confrontational struggles (national struggle and class struggle); it combined the two characteristics of "democratic dictatorship"—"democratic" in that it had a vast capacity for political integration and representation, and "dictatorial" in that this political integration was exclusive and violent. If we view this unique political process through the lens of the "continuity of sovereignty," we see that the emergence, renewal and completion of this continuity in the course of the Chinese revolution and state-building process was accompanied by the birth of a new political subject and its ever-increasing capacity for political integration. This political subject, unlike the Beiyang government, did not primarily rely on international recognition to confirm its continuity of sovereignty. On the contrary, the new party-state was denied recognition by other states, in violation of the generally accepted norms and standards of international relations. Instead, its international standing was formed amidst international struggle and the political unfolding of a united front. Even compared to the Soviet Union and Eastern European socialist states, the political (non-bureaucratic) character of the socialist state structure which emerged out of the Chinese revolution is especially prominent. If we want to answer the question of why the Chinese political system still retains a certain degree of stability even after the "age of extremes" has ended, then we must not ignore this unique political legacy. This is not to say that the political system is free from bureaucracy; in fact, as soon as a political party moves from participating in social movements to integrating with the state, various degrees of bureaucratization become inevitable. In the age of marketization and legal codification, the political organization gradually became or is trending toward a bureaucratic system that carries out administration according to law, while its role in political integration gradually diminishes.

I described this process as the transformation from "party-state" to "state-party" in my book *The End of the Revolution*.[43] In order to prevent the integrative state from oppressing citizens' rights, some people today advocate further increasing the distance between the state and citizens in the hope of turning the state from an integrative state, perceived as oppressive, to a bureaucratic one ruled by law. However, with the decline of the previously existing mechanisms of political integration, the representational function of public administration has come into crisis, such that some people are calling for a revival of the "mass line" and broad and meaningful public participation in governance at all levels.[44] The above contradictory demands point in the direction of two other related phenomena: On the one hand, the supposed expansion of "political freedom" and the "rule of law" have failed all across the world to save representational politics from crisis; on the other hand, as China's public administration has shifted its role from political integrator to a nonpolitical bureaucratic system, the party-state has inevitably suffered a breakdown of representation. This is a complex issue that merits further discussion; suffice it to say here that neither the "sovereignty of the people" nor the "continuity of sovereignty" achieved by China during the "short twentieth century" can be understood without an analysis of the new political organization—one quite distinct from a nineteenth-century-style parliamentary party—which refashioned both the society and the state. Nor can we recognize what spiritual resources and power may yet be found in the experience of China's twentieth-century "political integration."

As soon as the legitimacy of "sovereignty of the people" was established, political integration in the form of revolution became inevitable and irreversible. We should pay attention to two features of the "revolutionary condition" thus set in motion: First, the continuing radical "cultural revolution" that lasted from the May Fourth Movement of the 1910s until the 1970s, and second, the unfolding of "people's war" from the Northern Expedition to the founding of revolutionary base areas, and from the War of Resistance against Japan to the War of Liberation. Here, "people's war" is not a military struggle in the general sense, but a revolutionary process accompanied by land reform and the refashioning of the peasant class. I shall treat the topics of "culture" and "war" in twentieth-century China in the chapters that follow.

2

The Transformation of Culture and Politics

War, Revolution and the "War of Ideas" in the 1910s[1]

The Age of "Awakening"

A full ninety years have passed since the May Fourth Movement, and its significance in Chinese history, like that of most important historical events all over the world, becomes harder and harder to describe definitively. Scholars have demonstrated that many of the themes once thought to uniquely characterize the movement, such as science, democracy, republicanism and vernacularization, cannot be considered its original creations. Looking solely at the historical evidence, it is possible to trace the origins of these important elements of the May Fourth Movement to the various currents of the late Qing dynasty. But I pose a different question: Can the meaning of the May Fourth Movement be grasped through a strictly evidential or positivistic interpretation? How can we understand the innovations of the May Fourth Movement?

Over the past twenty years, two influential but opposing narratives have arisen to describe the movement. One traces the origins of modern Chinese literature and intellectual tradition to the late Qing dynasty, thereby refuting the orthodox scholarly demarcation of the movement as the beginning of modern Chinese history. The other narrative frames the Self-Strengthening Movement, the Hundred Days' Reform, the 1911 Revolution and the May Fourth Movement as different stages within the same process, thereby highlighting the transformation and evolution of the focus of intellectual discussion from questions of how to improve China's backward weapons and technology, to the question of modernizing its political and social institutions, and finally to the debate on whether it was necessary to overhaul the bases of Chinese thought itself.[2] Each narrative stresses a different complexity: The former casts doubt on the traditional historical definition of the May Fourth Movement, reiterating the importance of the movement as a continuity of the late Qing dynasty, while the latter emphasizes the pioneering significance of the movement in modern Chinese history. This "pioneering" nomenclature, however, actually derives from the standard narrative of modernization; when comparing it with the orthodox view that the May Fourth Movement constituted the "comprehensive initiation of China's march toward modernity,"[3] we find that this historical narrative does not offer much new insight.

Using progressively instrumental, institutional and conceptual perspectives to locate the May Fourth transformation in a linear development descending from the late Qing dynasty does not faithfully capture the sense of "directional change" implied in the concept of the "May Fourth cultural turn." What propelled the May Fourth Movement's "cultural turn" was not only the progressive concept of advancing instrumental and institutional change, but also the "enlightenment" of a cultural recreation. During World War I and China's republican crisis, the model of eighteenth- and nineteenth-century European modernity was in a profound crisis, as the bourgeois nation-state, the freely competitive capitalist economy and their associated set of values suddenly lost their previously self-evident progressiveness. The republican crisis and national peril were no longer blamed solely on Chinese tradition, but increasingly considered products of the modern civilization of the nineteenth-century West.

As a result, the questions of how to evaluate the republic as a governmental system, how to assess the political, economic and social systems of the late nineteenth-century West which from that time Chinese intellectuals had taken as a model, and, stemming from this, how to evaluate Chinese tradition, together became the fundamental concerns of the "May Fourth cultural turn." This "turn" was catalyzed not only by the Republican crisis, but also the changing image of the West as a result of the European war and subsequent revolutions. A comparison between Liang Qichao's *Discourse on the New Citizen* (*Xin min shuo*), written from 1902 to 1906, with his later work *Inner Reflections on European Travels* (*Ouyou xinying lu*), written during the European war, makes apparent that the former presented an idealized image of the West, while the latter drew attention to the myriad flaws of Western civilization. The "self-awareness of the Chinese people" that Liang then discussed was no longer predicated on Western civilization, but instead derived from introspection based on the crisis in which the West found itself.[4] In "The reconciliation of Eastern and Western civilizations after the war," published in April 1917, Du Yaquan wrote: "There is no longer any doubt after the war that humanity must undergo a drastic change. The age of reform is imminent."[5] The war, furthermore, "revealed significant flaws in Western civilization"; people became "enlightened" to the realization that "modern life in neither the East nor the West can be considered perfect," that "the modern civilization of neither the East nor the West can be considered as exemplary" and that therefore, "the birth of a new civilization, born of people's awakening, hastens to arrive."[6]

Was this need for a "cultural turn" perceived solely by the "conservatives"? Clearly not. In his analysis of the writings of Huang Yuanyong, Ted Huters unequivocally concluded that "*Youth* magazine [*Qingnian zazhi*, later known as *New Youth* (*Xin qingnian*)] most certainly adopted its bold and unyielding editorial voice straight from the renowned magazine *Eastern Miscellany* (*Dongfang zazhi*)."[7] The fundamental political agenda of *New Youth* was to affirm the foundation for genuine republicanism by not only attacking the political motivation for monarchical restoration, but also uncovering the social basis of monarchy itself. It would have been impossible, however, to ignore the crisis of the European war, and the Russian and German revolutions provided them an opportunity to look anew at the history of the West. Chen Duxiu wrote in an article titled "The year 1916" that "if we want to create a new civilization for the twentieth century, we should not be restricted by the legacy of nineteenth-century civilization." He declared that under the influence of the European war, military affairs, politics, scholarship, and intellectual trends "would undergo a drastic change, greatly diverging from the past." China, having experienced the monarchical restoration and its failure in 1915, "must reflect and repent in order to start anew . . . and to make 1915 the beginning of a new era, relegate all that came before to ancient history."[8]

At the outbreak of the Russian February Revolution a year later, Chen asserted that "this great war is unparalleled in history. The reforms and advancement in political knowledge and institutions after the war will be unrivaled in history. I predict a radical change in the understanding of European history after the war. To extrapolate global conditions after the war by adopting a pre war historical perspective would be meaningless."[9] Two years later, Li Dazhao declared: "The French Revolution in 1789 not only symbolized a change in the hearts of the French people, in reality it represented a change of heart by the people of the world in the nineteenth-century. The Russian Revolution of 1917 is not only indicative of the change in the minds and hearts of the Russian people, but in reality it represents a twentieth-century change of heart by people around the world."[10] While the New Culture Movement, faithful to republican values, raised the banners of "science" and "democracy" and launched a full-fledged attack on Kang Youwei and his cohort for their advocacy of monarchical restoration, the rhetoric of these New Culture Movement writers was no longer merely a refrain of older nineteenth-century themes—instead, they increasingly intertwined their affirmation of the French Revolution and its values with an underlying desire to renounce the political and economic systems of the nineteenth century.

Radical Chinese politics could not have arisen without the desire to break from the nineteenth-century political and economic model. Similarly, the cultural theory known as "conservatism" could not have been formed without this intent to make a clean break. This set of attitudes toward the "nineteenth century" was far from immediately evident, but with the progression of the war, both sides of the culture debate increasingly engaged in deep reflection on the issue. By situating the "May Fourth cultural turn" in the context of the thunderclap to humanity brought about by World War I, we can better appreciate the general significance of this "change in consciousness." This was an age of "self-awakening" (*juexing*), an age when new politics was stimulated by this "self-awakening," an age where opposing types of "self-awakening" generated debates and grounded the theory behind every position.

The terms "self-awakening" and "awakening" (or "enlightenment" *juewu*) abound in the various publications of the time. The first three issues of the first volume of *Youth* magazine in 1915 serialized Gao Yihan's "The republic and the self-awakening of youth."[11] In October of the same year, *Eastern Miscellany* published Du Yaquan's "My people's present and future self-awakening."[12] In February 1916 Chen Duxiu published "Our final awakening" in *Youth*.[13] In October of the same year, Liu Shuya published "The European war and youth's awakening" in *New Youth*.[14] In April 1917, *New Youth* carried Chen Duxiu's "The Russian Revolution and the awakening of our citizens."[15] In August of the same year, Du published "The enlightenment of our present and future political situation" in *Eastern Miscellany*.[16] Toward the end of 1917, *Eastern Miscellany* carried Zhang Shizhao's "European intellectual trends and my awakening."[17] A year later, in December 1918, Zhiyan (Chen Duxiu) published "The postwar awakening and demands of the Eastern peoples" in *The Weekly Review*.[18] In January 1919, Du's "The state of our people's awakening after the Great War" appeared in *Eastern Miscellany*.[19] In the same year, amid the tumult of the May Fourth Movement, the Tianjin Student Association established the "Enlightenment Society" and started a journal titled *The Enlightenment*. Meanwhile, a supplement to Shanghai's *Republican Daily* also titled *The Enlightenment* appeared, soon becoming one of the four most famous newspaper supplements of the May Fourth period.

All of these "self-awakenings" or "enlightenments" stemmed from the European war and the republican crisis; the former demolished the near-perfect image of the West constructed by Chinese intellectuals since the late Qing dynasty, while the latter extinguished the illusion that republican politics by itself could save China from calamity (despite different persuasions of self-awareness taking drastically different approaches to republican values). In short, new politics had to be established on the basis of a new "self-awakening." But what in the end was the relationship between politics and self-awakening? I think it involved the identification of a break between politics and history. Politics, according to this theory, should no longer be considered the natural extension of history, but rather born from the awareness of a historical rupture. "Conservatism" posited the rupture as the basis on which to discuss historical continuity, while "radicalism" considered it a lens through which to envision a brand new world.

*   *   *

Culture and politics are both fundamental attributes of human life; there is no inherent distinction between the two. Against the political backdrop of the crisis of war and republicanism, then, why did the May Fourth cultural movement intentionally distinguish between the cultural and political spheres? Why was this movement, propelled by obviously political motivations, understood as a cultural shift? Before we delve into an analysis of the historical materials, there are several aspects of the way the ideological agenda of the May Fourth cultural movement was shaped that are important to explore. I will take the position carved out by *Youth* as a starting point from which to outline a few questions.

First, under what circumstances did the May Fourth cultural movement distinguish culture from politics? The "Correspondence" column of the first issue of *Youth* published an exchange between Wang Yonggong and "a journalist" (Chen Duxiu) that reveals how this was accomplished. Wang's letter commented on the discussion of statehood and monarchical restoration by the Chou-an Society (Peace Planning Society), and requested that the magazine directly intervene. In response Chen firmly refuted the society's explanation of the restoration, but revealed that *Youth* would not engage in this discussion:

> The heaven-endowed mission of our journal is to reform the thinking of the youth and to guide the youth's self-cultivation. Critiquing current political events is not its mission. The thinking of our people has not undergone a fundamental awakening, which is why it is difficult to rule the country. The government's actions in the past year have been completely driven by an attempt to follow ways of China and the teachings of the first kings to preserve the national essence. What a vexing problem for the government! Can we alert the people of the ambitions of our neighboring countries? Our citizens do not want to engage in politics. Japan's ultimatum was not a strong enough warning, let alone one article from this magazine.[20]

Referencing the opening article, "The manifesto of our journal," he declared, "The decline of our national fortune, the erosion of morality and collapse of learning will ultimately be problems shouldered by the youth. The purpose of our publication is to discuss with our youth how to practice self-cultivation and conduct good governance in the future."[21] The political motivation for the founding of *Youth* was clear; this political action, however, could be successful only after a distance had been established from the political sphere, through stating intentions to "reform the youth's thinking and guide the youth's self-cultivation" and to quicken "the complete awakening" of the citizens. "Culture" and its "movement" provided the strategy to accomplish this political endeavor.

Why was *Youth* magazine compelled to interject itself into politics in this indirect manner? Although politics are ubiquitous in human life, a unique characteristic of contemporary politics is its close relationship with the state, with the term "politics" an effective stand-in for actions involving the state or political parties. In other words, politics confined to state activities have come to define the most basic character of modern politics. But the fundamental self-awakening of the May Fourth era not only emerged from the consciousness of a failed republican state, but also from disillusionment with eighteenth- and nineteenth-century Western modernity as a whole. As a result, the movement to recreate politics had to be predicated on renewing this peculiar model of "politics."

In his speech "My agenda for fixing Chinese politics," Chen argued, "We do not ignore political issues; rather, because the political system handed down from the eighteenth century is bankrupt, we want to create a new politics from the foundation of society. It is not that we do not want a constitution; rather we want to create the real social conditions which naturally call for a new constitution. Discussing formal conditions in the abstract is pointless." Politics are everywhere; "human beings cannot escape politics." The eighteenth-century nation-state-centered political model and the the post-republican power struggle were all "pretend politics"[22]; a state-centered politics or "statism" constituted "depoliticized politics." Chen's repeated call "to create a new politics from the foundation of society" was the task of the cultural movement. This assessment was also applicable to Chinese party politics, which likewise were not predicated on society, but confined to the state. "Politics is repressive politics, parties are private cliques," "the majority of the people do not interact with them. Our publication's main goal is the education of youth, with the expectation that our citizens will reach a complete awakening, and therefore we hope to vastly improve upon a still awaited-for party politics."[23]

What was this "culture" that was separate from politics and yet could recreate politics? Both in classical Chinese as well as Latin, the root form of "culture" denotes an active process. The root of "culture" in Latin is *colere*, meaning to cultivate the ground; it later expanded to refer to the nurturing of one's interests, spirit and intellect. The Chinese concept of "culture" came together from the words *wen* and *hua*. *Wen* refers to natural patterns[24] as well as the order of rites and music.[25] *Hua* connotes the developmental stages of *wen* (birth, transformation, change). As with the concept of "politics," the modern concept of "culture" is intimately connected with the state—according to the Marxist conception, the "superstructure" is formed on top of the capitalist forces of production, and culture is a function rooted in this superstructure. The New Culture Movement aimed to use "culture" to stimulate politics (the politics of the "fundamental awakening"). Its program for social transformation involved building enthusiasm for completely new systems of state and party politics; "culture" and its "movement" would create a new people ("youth") from the ground up, and also reverse the trend of depoliticization of the state and political parties with this new people and their "fundamental awakening." These concepts of culture and politics were born of the disillusionment with and rejection of the state politics of the eighteenth and nineteenth centuries. From this perspective, the New Culture Movement was a quintessentially "twentieth-century" phenomenon.

Clearly, twentieth-century politics did not completely depart from the basic paradigm of the eighteenth and nineteenth centuries; the state and the parties remained the main vehicles for "politics." Revolutionary politics was similarly defined. The direct product of the May Fourth cultural and political movement was the formation of a new party politics—from the founding of the Communist Party and the restructuring of the Nationalist Party to the birth of the Youth Party and other political groups. "Culture" therefore sustained two crucial missions: one to invent and nurture a new political subject from the foundation of society, the other to use the broad process of contradiction and struggle within and between the state and political parties (or, the "revolution") to bring about the rebirth, development and fundamental transformation of politics.

The fate of this twentieth-century "culture" was to continually shift outside and inside of state politics; the May Fourth cultural movement is an example of the former, and the ceaseless "cultural revolution" that took place between and within the political parties and the state is an example of the latter. Whether "outside" or "inside," methods of engaging and stimulating politics by way of "culture" became one of the distinctive phenomena of twentieth-century China. From this perspective, the May Fourth cultural movement was one of the most important starting points for the new post-nineteenth century politics.

Here I refer to the "May Fourth cultural movement" to differentiate it from the concept of the New Culture Movement. In January 1920, in his "Letter to overseas comrades of the Guomindang," Sun Yat-sen wrote:

> Ever since the students of Peking University initiated the May Fourth Movement, patriotic youth all over have been preparing for new revolutionary activities with radically new thinking, and they are full of vitality and eager to share their views. The opinions of disparate sectors of our country have achieved a consensus . . . All sorts of new publications, founded by enthusiastic youth, have appeared in response to the needs of the time . . . As corrupt and debased as this fake government is, it nevertheless dares not attempt to suppress this movement. This sort of new cultural movement truly represents an unprecedented sea change in the thinking of our country. Tracing its origin, it began with the advocacy of only one or two enlightened thinkers in the publishing world which then produced a magnificent flowering in the realm of public opinion, a wave of student movements permeating the country, an awakening of people's conscience, and a patriotic movement to which people pledged their lives. If our party wishes to benefit from the success of this revolution, we must rely on the change in thinking. Exhortations from *The Art of War* to "attack the heart and mind" and *The Analects'* to "reform the heart and mind" all refer to this. That is why this type of new cultural revolution is truly the most valuable of occasions.[26]

Sun Yat-sen's fundamental aim was for the party "to benefit from the success of this revolution"; thus a "change in thinking" was one of the preconditions. Therein lay the motive to merge the cultural movement with party politics. Sun used the phrase "New Culture Movement" to include the intellectual tide launched by *New Youth*, *Renaissance* (*Xin chao*) and other publications. In so doing he not only gained the recognition of both old and new activists such as Chen Duxiu, Hu Shi, Fu Sinian, Luo Jialun and others, but also demonstrated the unavoidable interaction between this movement and the new party politics. In scholarship on the "war of ideas" of the May Fourth period, the term "New Culture Movement" refers specifically to the above publications and the cultural tide that engulfed their followers. The publications that opposed or engaged in debate with them, however, are usually not included in this category. Cultural movements are formed through confrontation and debate, their political nature rooted in confrontation and the intermingling of thought and values. Without thoroughly examining the opposing positions, debates, alliances and divisions, it is impossible for us to truly understand the nature of any "cultural movement." By framing the May Fourth cultural movement as an object of investigation rather than a known event, we foreground the rise, formation, development and transformation of the struggle and debate between parties, opinions and attitudes. This allows us to observe how "culture" became the nucleus of the "new politics" in this vibrant movement.

In the 1970s, first in North America and later in China, a consensus gradually formed that defined the May Fourth cultural movement as an intellectual movement characterized by "radicalism." The famous formulation of the "dual transformation of enlightenment and salvation" dissected the historical entanglement of enlightenment and nationalism while lamenting the tragic fate of the Chinese liberal enlightenment movement.[27] Benjamin Schwartz's tripartite categorization of liberalism, conservatism and radicalism[28] likewise directly pointed its intellectual spearhead at May Fourth radicalism. By contrast, Lin Yu-sheng argued that intellectuals' attempt in the "May Fourth cultural turn" to "use cultural thought to solve problems" was (as a form of unconsciousness predisposition) deeply rooted in traditional Confucian culture. As a result, Lin argued, the May Fourth Movement's antitraditionalism and radicalism were a modern manifestation of a traditional form of thought; all of this comprised "the crisis of Chinese consciousness."[29] But if this were the case, the how should we interpret the political innovations of the May Fourth cultural movement? If this cultural movement formed the nucleus of and prelude to radical politics, then how should we account for the unique transformations of culture and politics in twentieth-century China? How does one explain the cultural nucleus of this politics? None of these questions receive adequate explanation in the two analyses described above.

Some forty years ago, Maurice Meisner placed the May Fourth Movement in the same sequence of thought as China in the 1960s. He pointed out that both movements, though they transpired half a century apart, were "cultural revolutions" aimed at the "transformation of consciousness."[30] This was a very meaningful observation, but it did not receive sufficient recognition. Schwartz, apparently granting Lin Yu-sheng's assertion that emphasis on "culture" was an essentially Confucian preoccupation, attempted to link the conclusions of Meisner and Lin Yu-sheng: "No doubt, Mao would insist that the cultural revolution could only affect reality when it transformed itself into a political revolution. Yet the fact remains that if 'culture' was crucial in 1966, it probably was also crucial in 1919."[31] In accepting the notion that the origin of the May Fourth's "cultural turn" can be traced to the traditional Confucian mode of thinking, Schwartz resituated the "ruptured consciousness" of the May Fourth Movement back into the depths of history, and as a result, he buried Meisner's insistence on the unique role played by "culture" in twentieth-century Chinese politics as well. The central question is this: From where did the rupture in consciousness inherent in the May Fourth Movement's "cultural turn" come, and why was twentieth-century Chinese revolutionary politics closely linked with "cultural revolution"?

The May Fourth cultural debate was far-reaching in scope, so I must limit the selection of materials under discussion. This chapter will be divided into three parts to explore the formation and transformation of the May Fourth cultural movement. The first part centers on *Eastern Miscellany*, and explains why Chinese intellectuals turned their political-economic analysis of the European war and the crisis of the republic into a discussion of cultural issues. The second part focuses on *New Youth* and *Renaissance*, and analyzes the relationship between the cultural politics of the New Culture Movement and the May Fourth–era political movement. The third part centers on the political movements of the early twentieth century, especially the formation of a new form of party politics, and discusses the relationship between the cultural movement and party politics in order to explain the decline and transformation of the New Culture Movement.

From the "Clash of Civilizations" to the "Reconciliation of Civilizations"

The September 1918 issue of *New Youth* published editor-in-chief Chen Duxiu's essay "Query to the journalist of *Eastern Miscellany*— on the Question of *Eastern Miscellany* and the Issue of Monarchical Restoration."[32] Three months later, *Eastern Miscellany*'s editor-in-chief Du Yaquan published "In response to the query of the journalist of *New Youth*."[33] Two more months passed, and Chen issued "Further query to the journalist of *Eastern Miscellany*."[34] Du (the pen name of Wei Sun [1873–1933], known as Du Yaquan after 1900, and later Cang Fu and Gao Lao) did not respond, but a great ideological debate surrounding the question of "whether or not the culture of the East and the West can be reconciled" had already begun. At the end of 1919, Du wrote the essay "On the vernacular language" in *Eastern Miscellany*, laying out a critique of the two important branches of the New Culture Movement—the vernacular language movement and the new literature movement[35]—and foreshadowing a new, offensive strategy. However, the struggle ended soon after it had begun. One month later, under both internal and external pressure, Du quietly resigned from his editorial position at *Eastern Miscellany*. At the time, the leadership of *New Youth* in the intellectual movement and in the realms of language and literary reform had already created huge waves and pushed in new directions. After Du stepped down, the editorial direction of *Eastern Miscellany* turned toward "emphasiz[ing] real and practical problems," signaling its departure from attempts to guide public opinion.[36]

The "reconciliation of Eastern and Western civilization" was not a passing notion of Du's, but a lasting topic of interest for *Eastern Miscellany*.[37] To clarify the cause and effect of this raging debate, it is necessary to investigate *Eastern Miscellany* itself, and to analyze the historical forces and ideological trends that guided the discussion on civilization. Founded on March 11, 1904, *Eastern Miscellany* was published by the Shanghai Commercial Press. It ceased publication in December 1948, totaling forty-four volumes with three short suspensions (December 1911 to March 1912, February 1932 to December 1932 and November 1941 to March 1943), spanning a period of forty-five years. The first editor-in-chief was Jiang Weiqiao, the next Qian Xuke, who took the position before the fifth volume, and the next Meng Sen from volume three, issue seven, on August 21, 1908. Once published as a simple compilation of literary digests, the journal's appearance changed significantly in 1911, starting with the first issue of volume eight. Du officially assumed the position of editor-in-chief with the first issue of volume nine on July 1, 1912, but had taken on full editorial responsibility as early as the fifth issue of volume six on June 12, 1909, after Meng Sen's election to the Jiangsu Provincial Assembly; the journal's changing format was Du's handiwork. It was on his watch that the question of "Eastern and Western civilizations" gradually took shape as an important topic, leading eventually to a debate between *Eastern Miscellany* and *New Youth*.

Even though there had already been a heated debate on "Chinese knowledge as the essence and Western knowledge for practical use" during the late Qing dynasty, the debate on Eastern and Western civilizations in the May Fourth period was significant for entirely different reasons. Broadly speaking, this debate emanated directly from the reaction of the Chinese intellectual world to two important events: World War I and the crisis of republicanism in China. It addressed how the causes and consequences of the First World War should be interpreted, and how the crisis of the early Republic, in particular Yuan Shikai's attempt to restore the monarchy, should be understood. The "debate on Eastern and Western civilizations" began with a focus on civilization, culture and ideas, but a political subtext was implicit in these issues. In January 1919, Du published "The state of our people's awakening after the Great War" in volume sixteen, issue eleven, of *Eastern Miscellany*. He lamented:

> Observing the current state of affairs, we cannot help but become somewhat enlightened, and that is, after such a catastrophic struggle and great

sacrifice, across the world mankind will have to undergo some form of great material and spiritual reform. No country on earth can escape the impact of this great change. Any of our countrymen who have paid the slightest attention to the affairs of the world would agree. As demonstrated in the war between the North and the South in our country, some were fooled into joining the war, but having suffered its consequences they withdrew soldiers and halted the war. Thus we can know that our countrymen have become somewhat enlightened. But the degree of enlightenment has a great deal to do with how our country can adapt to the great reforms the world will undergo in the future. Thus I greatly desire to convey to my countrymen the impact of the Great War in order to hasten their awakening."[38]

Here, he posits that World War I and China's North-South Civil War were intrinsically related events, and that therefore it was necessary to advance "our countrymen's awakening."

What was implied by this "awakening"?

Since the founding of the Republic, *Eastern Miscellany* had consistently been concerned with the political crises of the republican period. During the war, discussions about the republican crisis gradually merged with concerns about the crisis of civilization triggered by the war. Between 1914 and 1919, every issue of the magazine presented major news events concerning China and foreign countries, producing a great volume of analyses of international politics and military affairs. Its analysis of the differences, conflicts and reconciliation between Eastern and Western civilizations were shaped by its analysis of the European war. Du's pre war writings suggest that had World War I not taken place, *Eastern Miscellany* would likely have continued the fundamental positions of the late Qing enlightenment;[39] had there been no republican crisis, *Eastern Miscellany* likely would have continued to promote the early republican optimism toward democratic politics.

The war fundamentally transformed the appearance and themes of the magazine. The announcement of Du's resignation from *Eastern Miscellany* stated: "It has been seventeen years since the birth of this magazine. And this seventeenth year is also the first year after the end of the European war. The world situation has changed, and the magazine world, too, must be aware of the changing times in order to keep up with the world."[40] In other words, Du's resignation and the change in direction of *Eastern Miscellany* all stemmed from one single fact: that the ideological and cultural "postwar period" had begun.

Eric Hobsbawm argued that the "short twentieth century" began in 1914 with the outbreak of World War I and ended in 1991 with the dissolution of the Soviet Union and the Eastern bloc. His theory implies that the entire history of the twentieth century was heavily intertwined with the First World War and the revolutions it precipitated, ending with termination of the historical paradigm inspired by this war.[41] Like other significant historical events that altered the course of historical evolution and created new values and paradigms (such as the French Revolution, the Russian Revolution, World War II and the Chinese revolution), the European war triggered a series of outcomes in various arenas and societies, with China's republican crisis among them. However, these historical developments transformed the course of history not only because of their magnitude, but also because they ended the preceding historical paradigms, such that what followed was no longer the natural progression of a previous model, but the sequential unfolding of a new model created by the event.

The historical interpretation of an event depends on the recognition, judgment and feelings it triggers, as well as the actions produced by them. *Eastern Miscellany* and *New Youth* together endured the twin crises of war and republicanism, but deviated greatly in the way each constructed its historical narrative. The former closely followed the development of the war and the republican crisis and reflected on the relationship between war and modern civilization. The latter used revolutions as signposts (first the French, then the Russian Revolution) in an effort to break away from war and republican crisis through the historical changes and value realignment wrought by the revolutions. *Eastern Miscellany* reevaluated the meaning of Chinese "civilization" in this crisis, emphasizing the modern potential of tradition, while *New Youth* favored "youth" and "youthfulness," using "new culture" and "new thoughts" to beckon the "new mainstream," and in so doing paved the way for the creation of an era of the third kind, differing from both Chinese civilization and the nineteenth-century West. As a result, different constructions of the relationship between the self and historical events produced two types of cultural politics. Along with

Du's resignation came a shift in the influence of *Eastern Miscellany* and *New Youth* on thought and speech, which in turn assisted the transformation of the central problem of Chinese politics and thought in the postwar period.

The European war and the crisis of Chinese republicanism not only overlapped chronologically, but they were also closely related to each other. On July 28, 1914, the Austro-Hungarian Empire, with the encouragement of Germany, declared war against Serbia, triggering a multinational war. More than a month later, on September 20, 1914, the famous German biologist and creator and advocate of monism Ernst Haeckel (1834–1919) published an article in the *Indianapolis Star* and became the first to introduce the term "First World War."[42] This war was a product of the gradual formation of the German-Austrian alliance and its arms race and colonial disputes with the British, French and Russian "Entente" countries after the Franco-Prussian War (1870–1). As the war progressed, Russia, Japan, the United States, Italy and twenty-eight other countries successively declared war against one another, resulting in an unprecedented state of warfare in the world. During the war and at the end of 1915, with the assistance of the Peace Planning Society and other political forces (as well as Yuan Shikai's own schemes), Yuan declared himself the founding emperor of a new monarchy, giving himself the reign name "Hongxian."

This state of affairs differed from previous political crises: While the restoration was clearly a product of the republican crisis, the ensuing debates on the question of national unity were closely tied to the uniqueness of World War I—that of war between nation-states. After the outbreak of war, Japan declared war against Germany under the pretext of honoring its obligation in the Anglo-Japanese alliance treaty and its mission to keep peace in East Asia. On August 27, 1914, the Japanese military sealed off Jiaozhou Bay and sent troops into Shandong in an attack against Qingdao. On January 18, 1915, Japan presented the "Twenty-One Demands" to Yuan's government, demanding the leasing of Shandong, Southern Manchuria, Mongolia, the Hanyeping mining complex, coastal harbors and islands. Japan also imposed conditions giving itself political, financial, military and other powers that would allow it to gain complete control of China.

On May 7, it issued an ultimatum and demanded that China respond within forty-eight hours.

The rapid downfall of the monarchy was closely linked to Yuan's acceptance of these "Twenty-One Demands." But hidden sympathy toward the monarchy among the populace did not immediately vanish with Yuan's death, for the simple reason that sympathy toward the monarchy was not the same as sympathy toward Yuan. Sympathy for the monarchy not only stemmed from the early Republic's political chaos and crisis of legitimacy (the Mongolian and Tibetan issues were seen as symptoms of the change in political systems), but also from Chinese intellectuals' reflections on modern European polities during the war. After the failure of Yuan's attempt to declare himself emperor, a standoff around the issue of China entering the war occurred between the pro-war Duan Qirui cabinet and the antiwar President Li Yuanhong. This conflict between the presidency and the cabinet resulted in an attempt by General Zhang Xun to restore the deposed Manchu emperor to the throne in June 1917.[43] From Yuan Shikai's attempt to establish himself as emperor to Zhang Xun's effort to restore the Qing dynasty, China's struggles over its political system were intertwined with questions of international political strategy during World War I.

Also in 1917, the February and October revolutions erupted in Russia. Lenin subsequently signed the Treaty of Brest-Litovsk with Germany, withdrawing Russia from the war. In 1918 Germany witnessed the November Revolution, in which the Social Democratic Party formed a provisional government and the German Republic came into being. In the process of analyzing the cause and effect of the war, Chinese intellectuals gradually shifted their emphasis from war to revolution, thereby inciting new reflection and debate. The most immediate cause of the May Fourth Movement in 1919 was the perceived betrayal of Chinese interests at the Paris Peace Conference and the Treaty of Versailles, but this crisis also had its roots in the struggle of Japan and Germany over sovereignty of Shandong as well as Germany's defeat in the war. In this sense, the May Fourth Movement directly resulted from World War I. The end of the war and the establishment of the Soviet Union provided new opportunities for China's ongoing cultural movement and political reform. The founding of the Chinese Communist Party, the restructuring of the Guomindang and the launch of the Northern Expedition, all major events that occurred within a short span of time, were interrelated even as they appeared to be entirely distinct.

In this cataclysmic transformation, how did "Eastern versus Western civilization" become the central question in the Chinese intellectual domain, and why did it gradually subside after the May Fourth Movement? To answer this, we must carefully study the emergence, development and evolution of the "Eastern and Western civilization" problem.

The Nationalistic Response to the European War

Without the historical occasion supplied by the First World War, China's intellectual world could not have reflected on such a multitude of events. As early as 1911, *Eastern Miscellany* had begun publishing articles on the European political situation and the foreign policies of the various countries after the Franco-Prussian War, predicting that Europe would suffer a great calamity within its borders that would spread to Asia as well, given that the Anglo-Japanese Pact was to expire in 1915, potentially giving rise to Japanese, British and Russian rivalries in Manchuria and Mongolia. A premonition that "the next fifteen years would be critical for the survival of the European and Asian continents" gradually emerged.[44]

On the eve of the outbreak of war in Europe, the July 1, 1914, *Eastern Miscellany* published "Diplomatic dealings between the U.S. and Mexico," "Upheavals in Japanese politics," "New situation in the issue of Ireland" and other commentaries on foreign relations that closely followed and analyzed the current international situation. Countering a proposal by the Japanese prime minister Okuma Shigenobu for an Anglo-Japanese alliance, Qian Zhixiu argued for the necessity of an Anglo-Chinese alliance in his essay "On the Anglo-Japanese alliance against China." The essay predicted that harm would be done to Chinese interests by Japan's participation in the war on the side of the Allied nations. Another article, "Chronicling the British monarch's visit to France," discussed "the serious problems in the entente between the three countries" of Britain, France and Russia.[45] On the eve of the outbreak of the Great War, Qian and other Chinese intellectuals already sensed the inescapable tie between China and the war in faraway Europe. In this broad context, *Eastern Miscellany* shifted the locus of the post-republican political crisis from "politics" (constitution, parliament and political parties) to "state" (sovereignty, unity and independence). In view of the magazine's complete embrace of the regime-changing "revolutionary war" and the republican constitutionalism in 1911,[46] the shift in political cognitive focus was highly significant.

Du's article "Continuism" was published in the first issue of volume eleven, on the eve of the eruption of the war in Europe. He argued that "a country is not built in a single short period," but implicitly involved the past, present and future. "An abrupt interruption would lead to weakening the nation's foundations . . . because old customs would be abandoned, and individual opinions will diverge," making it impossible to arrive at any consensus. The state and its continuity implicitly pronounced a judgment against the revolution and its weakening of the nation's foundation. Based on this judgment, he advocated the necessity of "conservatism" and "continuity from the old to the new":

> Applying "continuism" in running the country would necessitate the observation and maintenance of conservatism. "Conservatism" does not refer to restoring the old ways but to not busily changing everything. Once the nation suffers disruption, a portion of the old polity will be damaged; if continuity could support the wounded system, and not further destroy it, then the broken system could heal on its own. However if the destruction is too great and continuity is halted, then the only solution would be to apply cosmetic repair, to rearrange and to continue what cannot be continued. If one then insisted on reviving the old system and destroying the new polity, it would mean inflicting a second destruction after the original destruction, thus further weakening the nation's foundation . . .
>
> The maintenance of the nation's continuity and its prevention from disintegration cannot be restricted only to the nation's law. One must rely on popular morality to sustain it. The nation is made up of the sum of individuals. But an individual and the nation are not the same; as a result the goal of the nation is naturally not the same as that of an individual. The morality in our citizen's political behavior lies in the sacrifice of the individual's goal for the nation's goal.[47]

"Continuism" requires two contextual explanations to understand. On the one hand, after the 1911 Revolution, the provisional government was forced to seek recognition from various countries—since the revolution involved a rupture, it was only natural to reclaim recognition. However, was post-revolutionary China not a continuation of Chinese orthodoxy? Did seeking recognition imply an admission that the nation itself had fractured? While in the above context, continuism's reclaiming of the nation's continuity implied a criticism and a revision of the revolutionary notion of posing an opposition between republicanism and monarchy, its real motivation was to protect Chinese sovereignty.

With the collapse of the Qing, the situation in China's border regions deteriorated by the day. Outer Mongolia first sought independence under the influence of Russia. Surrounding the question of investiture and other issues, the disagreement between the Kulun government in Outer Mongolia and Yuan Shikai's government directly implicated China's sovereignty. Secession even emerged as an issue in the Hailar region outside of Outer Mongolia, with the latter forming an alliance with Russia in which both parties denied China's suzerainty. After the 1911 Revolution, internal strife and mutiny arose within the Qing troops garrisoned in Tibet, leading to severe opposition from the Tibetans. In 1912, with mediation by the Nepalese, the Qing troops in Tibet disarmed en masse; with the help of funds from the Kashgar government, all Qing troops and officials returned to China proper by way of India. This was the so-called "Renzi Incident." For some time after this, the relationship between the central government and Tibet was in a state of neglect or even suspension.[48]

In January 1913, the thirteenth Dalai Lama sent his Russian tutor, Buryat Mongol Agvan Dorzhiev, to Kulun to sign the "Mongol-Tibetan Agreement," in which the two nations recognized each other as "independent states." In October 1913, during the Simla Conference between China, Britain and Tibet, the Tibetan representative Shatra Pal-jor Dorje with British encouragement presented the demand for "Tibetan independence." Toward the end of 1915, the "China-Britain Conference on Tibet" opened in London, with the principal objective of revising the treaties and appendices of 1905. Article Five of the original 1905 treaty stated that "senior Tibetan officials respect directives from the Beijing government and deeply desire to revise Tibetan laws to resemble laws of other countries." At the same time Britain agreed to relinquish extraterritoriality in China as well as in other countries. But after the founding of the Republic, Britain used the pretext that "Chinese laws, in particular with regard to Tibet, have not completely reformed" as an excuse to "postpone the treaty revision for ten years" and to cancel this article. Instead Britain demanded that China open up Lhasa.[49]

The question of national continuity that "continuism" sought to solve was quite a profound one. Qing imperial power was a multifaceted and ambiguous style of representation, encompassing the emperor of China, the Great Khan of Mongolia, the clan elders of Manchuria, representatives of the Confucianism, the followers of Lamaism, and many others, thereby assembling the complex society of "China" into a vast imperial polity of assorted ties. The Republic of China succeeded the Qing, but its political culture underwent dramatic transformation; the devolution of Mongolia, Tibet and other surrounding regions became perennial crises threatening this new nation. In the winter of 1911, Kang Youwei wrote in his essay "On the republican polity" that "if the late Qing perishes, Mongolia and Tibet cannot be preserved." From January to March 1913, he reiterated this point in his "Eulogy for Mongolia and Tibet" in volumes one and two of *Buren* magazine, concluding, "Although the issue of Mongolian and Tibetan independence came from the revolution the year before . . . one cannot place all the blame on the current government."[50] His pronouncements on republicanism and the imperial restoration along with his advocacy of Confucianism were closely related to the crisis described above.

The cultural debate in the May Fourth era increasingly presented the problem of the political system as an opposition between authoritarianism and republicanism, while eliding the inevitable question since the outbreak of revolution of the multiple representative nature of imperial authority. Integral to resolving this issue was the question of whether any continuity existed between the two forms of government. When "Continuism" was published, the Mongolian question had already surfaced and the Tibetan question was forming. While diplomatic recognition directly hinged on the completeness of China's sovereignty, Du's exposition on the continuity of the state was a clear response to this historical state of affairs. The concept of "continuism" emphasized the dependence of the nation's continuity on the voluntary submission of the individual to the will of the state. As a result, the political succession problem had a close relationship with the moral state of the citizenry. The problem of the political system ultimately touched on moral issues, and this point underpinned the shift in *Eastern Miscellany*'s emphasis from politics to issues of civilization or culture.

The second issue of volume eleven of *Eastern Miscellany* appeared on August 1, 1914, the first issue to appear after the outbreak of war. Aside from publishing photographs of the Senate and the meeting of the Constitutional Council, it also included pictures of the new heir of the Austro-Hungarian Empire, the Archduke Ferdinand and his wife who had been assassinated in Serbia, as well as British and French warships. Chinese publications rarely used photos to follow the development of a war, its protagonists or events, but *Eastern Miscellany* insisted on doing so for many years. The cover story of the issue featured an article by Du (using the name Gao Lao) titled "On resisting passivity"; it argued, mirroring "Continuism," that "prompted by external circumstances . . . our people" should overcome passivity and bravely assume social responsibility. Following this piece, another article by Du, titled "The great European war begins," traced the development of the European war before July 31. Toward the end the author pointed out that

> This war will affect all European and Asian countries . . . Japan is an ally of Britain in the East; if Britain and Germany have engaged each other in war, then fighting will spread to their possessions in East Asia. It is not difficult to predict that Japan will attack Germany to aid Britain. With rumors of fighting spreading, the ports of Hong Kong, Qingdao and Saigon are hurriedly preparing their defense. Since our country does not maintain special relationships with any of the Great Powers, we remain completely neutral. Which country has not entertained the thought of exploiting the situation, gaining advantages, usurping power and violating the interest of the neutral country. How can we not prepare to protect ourselves?[51]

In the same issue, Xu Jiaqing's "The proceedings of the exchange between Russia and Mongolia" described in detail the "Orange Book" issued by the Russian Foreign Ministry to describe its diplomatic dealings with Mongolia, and publicized Russia's displeasure with the Dalai Lama's intention to "shun Russia and ally with China."[52]

Aside from continued discussions on issues related to Manchuria, Mongolia, Shandong and other contested regions, from the outbreak of the war in 1914 to the signing of the peace treaty in 1919, no other magazine scrutinized every incremental development of the European war and its significance as closely as *Eastern Miscellany*, with its voluminous analyses and commentaries. Coming closest was the magazine *New Youth*, founded in 1915, which emulated *Eastern Miscellany*'s practice of publishing "Chronicles of Major Chinese and Foreign Events." The lead story in the third issue of volume eleven of *Eastern Miscellany*, published in September 1914, was Du's article "The Great War and China": "The great war among the European countries today is indeed the greatest change in one hundred years, while its effect on China will be a minor change of ten years." The article placed imminent changes in China within the general scheme of the European war, arguing that if the nationalistic conflicts in Europe resulted in a complete victory for one side, China would face even more serious challenges and unprecedented pressure. Supposing a hypothetical victory of the German-Austrian axis, Du conjectured:

> The Holy Roman Empire of the Middle Ages would reappear in Europe. Russia's southern drive in Eastern Europe would be stopped, and it would have no choice but to turn its attentions to Asia, so that it could advance in the east. Consequently the British would be eagerly focusing their attention on the defense of India. The Dutch colonies in the South Sea such as Borneo, Sumatra, Java, Celebes and others possess a surface area several times that of Japan. If the Netherlands was subsumed by Germany, then the parts of Qingdao and the Pacific islands belonging to Germany would unify and surpass the power of Japan, Britain, Russia, and France in East Asia. In order to preserve the balance of power in East Asia these nations would most likely negotiate with each other, extracting all sorts of rights to counterbalance one another, and our country would be besieged from all sides. But if Germany and Austria succumbed completely, then the three Entente countries of Britain, Russia and France . . . would have no opposition in Europe . . . and would be able to freely expand their influence in East Asia.[53]

Because of the Jiaozhou Bay issue, China favored the Entente countries in the war; even so, years before the outbreak of the war, *Eastern Miscellany* analyzed the balance of power in Europe after the Franco-Prussian War and found that the eruption of the European crisis was directly linked to the struggle over spheres of influence. For example, tensions had flared between France and Germany over the Morocco issue in 1911. When Italy signed a pact of alliance with Turkey in 1912, war immediately broke out between the Balkan states and Turkey, leading to interference by the Great Powers. In the Asian region, Britain occupied India, Russia ruled Siberia, France invaded Annam, Britain and Russia fought over Afghanistan and Persia and in Korea and the Manchurian region, the Russo-Japanese competition was already tilting toward Japan.[54] In sum, the apprehension that the European war would lead to both parties encroaching on other regions was not one-sided.

Generally speaking, the Chinese intellectual sphere had three different interpretations of World War I. The first saw the European war as a conflict between ethnic nation-states (of the same "race" but different nationalities). This, in turn, led to two goals: one to strengthen China's position as a nation-state, and the other to reach beyond the Western model of nation-states and form a new political body. The second interpretation considered the war a conflict between democracy and authoritarianism, in which the United States and Britain were the democratic republics and Germany and Russia the autocracies. In this scenario the war became an opposition between democracy and authoritarianism, open politics and secretive politics, republicanism and monarchism. The third interpretation arose after the Russian and the German revolutions and regime changes, as both Russia and Germany withdrew from the war and signed a peace treaty. It explained the origins and aftermath of the war as products of class struggle and class warfare. During the first phase of the war, intellectuals' main concern was the relationship between war and the political system of nation-states. In the view of many, it was under this system that national identity superseded racial identity, leading to wars of unprecedented horror between the political systems of mismatched racial and national identities. In order to avoid the fate of occupation or partition, it was necessary to arouse the racial identity and national consciousness of the Chinese people (as articulated in "Our Countrymen's Patriotism" and "Our People's

Self-Awareness"). These were Du's and *Eastern Miscellany*'s first responses to the European war.[55] Consequently, to advocate for the continuity of the nation by way of "Continuism" implied a shift in the political debates before and after the 1911 Revolution, a leap from the question of the political system to that of the nation.

Transnationalism, the Clash of Civilizations and Race-Based Nationalism

"The Theory of the Alliance of the White Race" and "Pan Asianism"

At the initial outbreak of the war, *Eastern Miscellany*'s analysis of the conflict between various European countries yielded another perspective that transcended relations between nations to gauge the outcome of the war and its tendencies. The European war induced reflections on nationalism by Europeans, who wondered whether Europe, posing as a monolithic race and civilization, could put an end to war and ultimately unite. This logic relied on racism to overcome the strife between nation-states. Chinese intellectuals, in turn, wondered what situation China would face if this trans-state and transnational unified civilization appeared. Qian Zhixiu's "The grand alliance of the white race" can be viewed as the inception of this discourse. Referring to Major Stewart Murray's article in *The Nineteenth Century*, Qian commented,

> Murry's article refers to the prediction Napoleon made on St. Helena, which was that "the European powers, when forced by circumstances, would of necessity form some sort of alliance." It explained that due to the desire of the white man to achieve hegemonic rule over the whole world, [whites] such as the British Anglo-Saxons and those in Europe and in the United States of America would have to become one unified entity . . . According to Murray, once a great war erupted in Europe, the various continental countries, as well as Great Britain, would have no base in the Pacific. This would present an opportunity to Japan, and China would become Japan's supply base. As a result, when insurrection starts in Africa, Asia could send troops . . . [Quoting Murray]: "There is not a single Chinese man or woman who is not married; and in the fifty years from 1750 to 1800, the population has already doubled. How can

we be sure that it will not double again in the next fifty years? Imagine how we can defend against these 800 million Chinese? How important is it to think about the next fifty years?"

After exploring the idea of a great alliance of the white race and the notion of European unity, Qian briefly mentioned the view of the "president of the Royal Academy in London, Dr. Caldecott," on "the alliance of the human race." This view epitomized the method of "gauging to what extent the entire human race could accept the teachings of Christianity."[56] While "the alliance of the white race" incorporated the theory of "the clash of civilizations" to quell internal dissent in the West, the theory of "the alliance of the human race" would propound the universality of Christianity as its core—one was a discourse of conflict, the other of harmony. However, with (Western) "civilization" as their foundation, the two theories were quite identical in their discussions of East-West relations.

The concept of "civilization" encompassed the notions of race and religion, but transcended nation-states. The European war was fought between nation-states, and some antiwar efforts attempted to use the concepts of civilization and a unified Europe to supersede nationalism. But judging from the logic of the "alliance of the white race" and the theory of "the alliance of the human race," even if a vision of Europe centered on civilization could solve the conflict between nation-states or Christian countries, it could not eliminate conflict itself. Instead, it would point conflict to a new paradigm—the clash between civilizations.

In 1911, Du translated former British Governor-General of India George Curzon's theory of the East and West. One article defined the "meaning of the East" by saying that "the East is to the West in effect a name for opposition," and foretold clashes between the East and the West in Afghanistan, Persia, the Arab region, Asia Minor, Turkey and elsewhere.[57] In November 1915, Xu Jiaqing published "The theory of the United States of Europe (Translated from the *Diplomatic Times*)" and warned, "Deducing from history, Europe's union was strongest when threatened by a powerful enemy state . . . As a result, although the formation of a United States of a Europe could preserve peace internally . . . unlike the mantra of some pacifists, it would not be the best way to guarantee world peace. It only shifted and changed the unit of competition, and inevitably would foster new calamities."[58]

The concept of a European union was grounded in "race," and this is seen most clearly from the Asian perspective. Liu Shuya's article "The European war and youth's awakening" in *New Youth* and relevant commentaries from *Eastern Miscellany* reinforced each other. The second of a list of principles of the "Consciousness of Our Youth" cited by the author was that "the yellow and white races are opposed to each other."[59] Why would *New Youth*, which advocated "French Civilization," also express a similar opinion?

Near the beginning of the war in Europe, French General Charles Mangin, faced with invasion and pressure from Germany, launched a propaganda campaign proposing the drafting of 500,000 subjects in the French colonies to join the military. There were also politicians who advocated "recruiting Japanese soldiers to support fighting on the Western front." But these proposals produced a huge outcry from the French public: "It would truly be a great humiliation for the superior European race to seek help from the yellow people."

At the same time, two famous German intellectuals, Rudolf Eucken (1846–1926, 1908 winner of the Nobel Literature Prize) and Ernst Haeckel, jointly declared opposition to the British in allowing the "yellow race" to participate in the war, labeled the Russians a "semi-Oriental, semi-barbaric race," and urged the British not to "ally itself with a barbaric race to slaughter its own people."[60] Both Eucken's philosophy, which combined Eastern thought with his own reflections on war and civilization, and Haeckel's monist philosophy, which attempted to reconcile spirituality and materialism with the binary between Nature and God, were highly influential in China in the 1910s and early 1920s.[61] But this declaration attested to the fact that Eucken's conception of "spiritual life" and the "internal struggle of life" and Haeckel's so-called "theology of God's omnipotence" not only supported nationalism, but were also directed to the white race. "If they saw the East Asian race as dogs, sheep and felines, then we can see their very low opinion of East Asia and the yellow race. Alas! If such educated scholars hold such views, would their military men and politicians regard East Asians as human beings?"[62] Liu asked further,

If in the midst of a life and death struggle France still refused to seek help from the yellow race for fear of being humiliated, how low do they normally regard the yellow race? Their pronouncements such as "the Asian situation should be resolved with Asian blood," and "Asians should be our slaves," often appeared in British and London papers. Judging from the way each country treated its prisoners of war, the latter's treatment varied depending on their race, and colored people were treated as animals. Although all were prisoners . . . the kind and harsh conditions varied as day and night. Does that race view the East Asian people as humans?

He thus concludes: "When the European war ends it will be the 'time when the white and yellow races will engage in a life and death struggle.'"[63]

In the European court of public opinion, the discourse on creating a "European Union" to quell the crisis of war was inevitably intermingled with the oppositional struggles of Europe against Asia and the "white race" versus "yellow race." With this as background, in January 1916, Zhang Xichen published "The future great war between Europe and Asia" (based on the original work of a German author), predicting that a new form of conflict between civilizations would follow from the clash between nations:

After the great European war is over, the next problem will not be the struggles and conflicts between the various nation-states, but those of one civilization against another, of one race against another. In other words, it will be the conflict and struggle of Europe against Asia.

East Asia forms a unique sphere of civilization. At its center is unequivocally China, while Indian culture and Japanese political clout add depth and nuance. Thus, Japan is the arm of East Asian civilization and China its brain.

Today's East Asian condition is one of turmoil and internal strife. But once war ends in Europe and the peace treaty is signed among warring states, then the various East Asia nations will most likely form an alliance to build a strong coalition, and the civilizations representing the yellow and white races respectively will surely engage in a tremendous struggle.

The resulting war will be unprecedented in the history of the world. The reason the war will be unlike any other is because it will not be caused by military or industrial factors, but by a clash between two worldviews, two religious outlooks and two conflicting national spirits.[64]

As is widely known, "the clash of civilizations" was a popular topic after the final years of the Cold War. According to Samuel Huntington's analysis, at the conclusion of the Cold War, with the demise of the conflict between ideology and nation-states, the new paradigm of conflict will be based on civilizations.[65] Yet the "clash of civilizations" is not a modern discovery, rather it has been a question considered by Europeans for hundreds of years. The theory of a "war between Europe and Asia" was a manifestation of the theory of the clash of civilizations during World War I. Like the impact of today's theory of the clash of civilizations on post–Cold War thought, this earlier version of the clash of civilizations arose from explorations of the postwar political situation. Through reflection on the European war, the theory of the clash of civilizations demonstrated a transnational way of thinking, and a "post-nation-state" (despite the continuing prevalence of nationalism) way of thinking about the format of international clashes.

The theory of the clash of European and Asian civilizations and the topic of "pan-Asianism" became increasingly relevant from the late Qing dynasty onward. *Eastern Miscellany* was founded in 1904 during the Russo-Japanese War; the title page of the first issue happened to advertise two publications of the Shanghai Commercial Press—the *Chronicle of the Russo-Japanese War* and *Russia*—with illustrations of the Russian and Japanese imperial households and photographs of Russian generals. The lead article in the first issue was titled "Principles of the New *Eastern Miscellany*" and claimed that the periodical "aimed to inspire the citizenry and to liaise with all of East Asia." *Eastern Miscellany* of this period not only aspired to "collaborate with Japan, to fully regain Eastern autonomy in order to achieve all things under heaven,"[66] but also at times carried discussions of "yellow-race" nationalism.[67] However, not only did Japanese "pan-Asianism" and the European theory of a "clash of civilizations" maintain a complementary relationship,[68] both also harbored elements of imperialistic discourse.

After the Russo-Japanese War, *Eastern Miscellany* was deeply humiliated by the government's strict neutrality with regard to the question of the "restoration of Manchuria"[69] and anxious over the British and Russian competition over Tibet, the Japanese and Russian struggle for China's Northeast and the German and Japanese contest over Jiaozhou Bay. On the one hand it understood the need for Sino-Japanese-Korean cooperation in the face of the "escalating contest between the white and yellow races."[70] On the other, it felt that Japan had designs on China like the other great powers, and concluded that a "plan to recover national sovereignty," instead of any alliance on the part of the yellow race, was the best way to save the country.[71]

After 1905, the pan-Asianism that centered on the yellow race and was predicated on a Sino-Japanese alliance receded.[72] In its place came an expansionist strategy by autocratic countries, including Japan, which modeled itself after the Western imperialists.[73] Along this trajectory it was only natural that a political nationalism based on the defense of national interests would follow suit.

Under conditions very similar to those following the Russo-Japanese War, Japan's declaration of war against Germany in August 1914 caused the Shandong question to become the focal concern of Chinese public opinion. In November 1915 rumors circulated about China's joining the Allied Powers without an obligation to send troops, and subject to four conditions: to expel all German influence from China, to defend against Japanese invasion of China, to provide military supplies to the Allied Powers, and to refute "all instigations" by imperialists in the vicinities of India and Russia. These conjectures caused a backlash in Japanese public opinion; talks regarding China joining the war were swiftly suppressed by Japan.[74]

On August 14, 1917, acting president Feng Guozhang finally declared war against Germany and Austria; one of the motives for doing so was to borrow money from Japan in order to fight the southern Revolutionary Party. As the European war approached an end, the realization that China would become the battleground for postwar economic warfare gradually arose in Europe, the United States and Japan. Chinese intellectuals' suspicion of Japan's role in the postwar peace settlement grew deeper by the day.[75] When the Treaty of Versailles was signed at the Paris Peace Conference in 1919, Germany's rights in Shandong and its territorial lease in Jiaozhou Bay were completely transferred to Japan. Under these circumstances, the Chinese public lost all interest in the Japanese version of "pan-Asianism" and became more concerned with its imperialist underpinnings.[76]

Eastern Miscellany contributed heavily to the questions of Sino-Japanese relations and "pan-Asianism." For example, Gao Lao's "The case of Japanese demands," published in the fourth issue of volume twelve, Zhang Xichen's "Resolving the case of Japanese demands" published in the sixth issue of volume twelve (a translation of "Japan's Militarism" appeared in the same issue) and Xu Jiaqing's "The Position of the powers in the postwar Far East" (translated from the *Sun Journal*) in the tenth issue of volume thirteen commented on the process of Sino–Japanese negotiations from different angles and gave in-depth analyses of the Jiaozhou Bay question.[77]

As a result it was hardly unexpected that three months after publishing "The future great war between Europe and Asia," Zhang Xichen wrote "The fate of pan-Asianism" to supplement his previous work. He criticized "pan-Asianism'" as vague and lacking in solid planning, and found obstacles to the "future of Pan-Asianism" from seven angles: "the Allied Powers still maintain a presence," "the present and future weakness of the foundations of Asian countries," "the lack of institutions for implementation," "the mutual suspicion among the Asian nations," "the divergence in goals of the Asian states," "the inequity of interests" and "the absence of ideology." He therefore concluded: "So-called pan-Asianism can only rile opposition from parts of the world but not achieve anything. Its advocates thought deeply and opted to broadcast this pipe dream for a fleeting thrill."[78]

A year and a half later, Du translated "Internationalism for the international citizen" from the Japanese *Diplomatic Times*. From the dual perspectives of the assimilation of races and the freedom of investment and immigration, he discussed the limitations of theories of unity of the white race, of pan-Americanism and of pan-Asianism when based on race and geopolitics. He advocated instead a form of "internationalism for the international citizen."[79] Du was one of the few who studied the problem of postwar immigration and its impact; his theory of the reconciliation between civilizations was closely related to his research on the economic flow and human migration of the modern world.[80] In November 1918, he again translated and published Ukita Kazutami's (1859–1946) article "New Asianism," clearly still interested in ways of thinking about a certain degree of transnational civilizational polity.[81]

"Pan-Asianism" was not only discussed in *Eastern Miscellany*, but proved to be a common topic of concern in the intellectual world at the time. In 1919 Li Dazhao published two articles, "Pan-Asianism and new Asianism" and "Reassessing Asianism," in the magazine *Citizen*, which echoed the discussions in *Eastern Miscellany*. Li Dazhao believed that Japanese "pan-Asianism" was "greater Japanism" derived from an Asian form of the Monroe Doctrine; its nature was "not pacifism but aggression; not national self-determination, but imperialism that conquers the weak, not Asian democracy, but Japanese militarism, not an institution that adapts to world institutions, but one which subverts international institutions."[82] For this, he proposed a "new Asianism" with two key principles: "One is that before Japanese pan-Asianism inflicts any harm, our weak nations of Asia should unite together to sabotage this pan-Asianism; the other is that when Japanese pan-Asianism is destroyed, all of the people in Asia should come together and join a world organization—such an organization can be formed at that time."[83] Evidently Li Dazhao focused less on national alliances and the theory of the clash of civilizations and more on the unity of "all people." Consequently, according to his argument, a regional or international organization must represent a "great union of the people" predicated on a social movement or revolution.

Reconciliation of Civilizations and Transcending Modern Western Civilization

The Chinese intellectual critique of "pan-Asianism" had one effect that, unlike Japanese public opinion's use of "Asian civilization" (in actuality Japan-centered "Asian civilization" or "East Asian civilization") contrasted with the West, and aimed toward reconciling civilizations by modifying and revising the theory of the clash of civilizations. Li Dazhao's political stance differed greatly from that of *Eastern Miscellany* but agreed with its advocacy of a reconciliation of civilizations. Regardless of the concrete assessment, the hypothesis that included European and Asian civilizations either clashing or reconciling had become one of the "parameters of discussion" at the time.[84] At the beginning of 1915, Qian Zhixiu in "The Sino-Western cultural thesis of Wu Tingfang" introduced Wu's theory on Chinese and Western cultures.[85] Wu emphasized the superiority of Asian culture in his discussion:

> The West's social system is unfamiliar to many in Asia. The influence of religion on Western civilization is minimal, but religion forms the basis of all Asian civilization. As a result, the pragmatic white men use economic concerns as [a] foundation while the colored men set the foundation on morality. In my opinion, white men do not understand contentment. Why? Because they do not have time to enjoy contentment. The white men regard the accumulation of wealth as life's goal, while our people consider morality as the goal. In terms of filial relations, colored peoples have stronger filial relations than the irresponsible white men. Consequently the sense of society is more acute [in Asia] and individuals suffer less.[86]

The basic conceptual divide between Europe and Asia was rooted in racial discrimination between the white and colored races while social systems, religions and other lifestyle differences reinforced this racial division.

But as with Tagore's propagation of Eastern civilization, this binary of Eastern and Western civilization was not predicated on clash and antagonism, but directed toward conquering the crisis of modern civilization. Tagore's 1916 visit to Japan was a momentous event. At the end of the year, *Eastern Miscellany* published Hu Xueyu's "The Speech of famous Indian Tagore in Japan":

> We Asians need not envy Western civilization, but instead would do well to preserve our Eastern traditional civilization, to develop and broaden upon it. Our Eastern civilization is apolitical and society-oriented; it is not aggressive or mechanistic, but spiritual. Its principles are founded on humanistic relations. As we in the East today determine the world's direction, certainly we must consider the world's problems as our problems, and to spread Eastern civilization in order to harmonize with the history of every nation on earth.[87]

Tagore's analysis of the European war and modernity from the perspective of religion and spiritual civilization greatly stimulated Chinese intellectuals' reflections on civilization.[88] Liang Qichao's "inner reflections on European travels," Du Yaquan's "Tranquil civilization and active civilization," Liang Shuming's *Eastern and Western Cultures and Their Philosophies* and numerous other works responded to and echoed Tagore, thereby producing several volumes of discourse on Eastern and Western civilizations that shared the theme of overcoming the crisis of modernity.[89]

Eastern Miscellany spent years studying the differences between the East and West from the standpoint of civilization,[90] using the divergence in civilizations as an intellectual tool to reject worship of the West and to pave the way for "civilizational self-awareness." For *Eastern Miscellany*, "self-awareness" was, first and foremost, a way to redress the tendency to blindly follow the West (or modernity). It was also a tool for combating blind rejection of China (or tradition). This posed a position diametrically opposed to that of *New Youth*. Qian Zhixiu summed up the intellectual trend of worshipping the West and denigrating China as an antipatriotic "envy-nationalism," and in political terms attempted to build on Du Yaquan's "continuism":

> Sensing the sentiment of our people lately, things are not quite what they seem. From the larger concerns of institutions and systems, to the smaller issues of dress and hobbies, all prefer European and American practice. When it comes to their own country, they express a deprecatory and demeaning view, saying that being Chinese was not adequate. Comparing with extreme patriotism, the two look in opposite directions, but both think in the same way and reach an extreme of denial. I have heard of no name for this, therefore coin it "envy-ism toward other countries."[91]

Two years later, Chen published "My patriotism" in *New Youth* and responded formally to this view and trend. Chen divided nations into two categories: those in which people's morality and strength are above a certain standard and those in which they are not, and concluded that the latter will "self-destroy and self-immolate, inviting powerful enemies and dictators as nails to magnets, with their countries always on the brink of destruction. Therefore their death is self-inflicted; their demise is self-propelled . . . Even though their death is brought about at the hands of powerful enemies or dictators, what causes their death is the behavior and nature of their people. In order to attain total salvation, a complete transformation of our people's character and behavior is needed." Thus, "my patriotism is not to sacrifice my body for my country, but to counsel the self-respecting citizen to safeguard the reputation of our country, to stop the source of national unrest, and to add to the substantial strength of our nation, my patriotic youth!" He then listed the virtues of "diligence," "frugality," "integrity," "cleanliness," "honesty" and "trust" as "the principal ways to national salvation," to counter the claims of "envy-nationalism" with "continuing holistic patriotism."[92]

Clearly the debate over civilization was also a political one. "Our Final Awakening" referred to the problem of assessing China and its political values—would China still preserve any of its political tradition and values if it took the West as the standard and political paradigm? Did the Chinese transformation require a complete change of cultural tradition (and a totalistic importation of Western progressive values) as a precursor? The heated debate between *Eastern Miscellany* and *New Youth* was not a conflict between those who approved of the theory of cultural reconciliation and those opposed it; rather, it was a controversy over the "nature of self-awareness."

The Hongxian Monarchy, the Crisis of the Polity and the Question of "New and Old Thinking"

The Republican Crisis, the Allocation of Power and National Tradition

Before delving deeper into the question of the relationship between "civilization self-awareness" and the political attitudes of early republican intellectuals, we must first discuss the severe fractionalization that occurred between various cliques of intellectuals on the question of the Hongxian monarchy. This debate, too, had deep connections with the cultural debate. Without an understanding of the logic of the above discussion of civilization and its relationship with early republican politics, our understanding of this political debate would be limited to a superficial account of a clash between "old and new thinking."

Before Yuan Shikai became emperor (on December 12, 1915), following the activities of the Peace Planning Society and the publication of Frank Johnson Goodnow's essays defending monarchy, a series of actions were undertaken to solve the so-called "question of national polity."

Once again, constitutional monarchy and republicanism became the most sensitive topics in the realm of Chinese politics. On December 11, 1915, a "General Referendum on the Solution of National Polity" took place, and the Hongxian monarchy formally came into being the very next day. As *Eastern Miscellany* was published at the beginning of each month (though occasionally it came out mid-month), there were no reports or commentaries on the monarchical restoration at the end of 1915. As early as October 1915, however, *Eastern Miscellany* published, in its column "Domestic and Foreign Times," a "Debate on the Peace Planning Society," which included Goodnow's "On Republicanism and Monarchism" and Yang Du's extensive essay advocating monarchism titled "Constitutional Monarchy and National Salvation (in Three Parts)," as well as Wang Fengying's "Letter to the Peace Planning Society", and Liang Qichao's skeptical article "Strange! On the so-called question of national polity." The events and details surrounding Yuan's ascendancy to the throne were recorded in the first issue of 1916, volume thirteen, and again in the monthly column "Major Events in China" which chronicled happenings of the eleventh to fifteenth days of the previous month.

Both issues observed strict objectivity and did not express an explicit opinion, but with a close reading, *Eastern Miscellany*'s strong concern about the event is quite evident. Politically speaking, *Eastern Miscellany* believed that the restoration incident was not a conflict between republicanism and monarchism, but rather a crisis in which the Chinese polity had been prevented from developing into an organic unity. As a result, even though *Eastern Miscellany* did not approve of monarchism, it affirmed the importance of the question of national unity and independence.[93]

In the early years of the Republic, Du portrayed the problems of "regionalism" and "foreign debt" as the Republic's Achilles' heels in his essay "The future of the Republic of China." In "Chronicles of the success of the revolution," written around the same time, he attributed the revolution's success to such causes as "the rallying of the provinces," "the collaboration of the navy," "the staging of the peace talks" and "the shifting of the borders," rather than to the uprising of the members of the Revolutionary Party.[94] In 1914, Du again wrote that "those who discuss current affairs heave a deep sigh and say: 'It's been several years since the Republic has been established, yet internal strife is so rampant, the financial situation completely bankrupt, and the international situation so perilous that if this continues, our nation will not be strong enough to survive.'" He sought, in this article, to increase the people's interest in the frailty of national identity, the powerlessness of the central government and the deficiency in the national treasury. His "continuism" condemned the complete rupture of republican and traditional politics and proposed a nationalistic continuity that transcended the difference in polity as a solution to the problem of national unity. In February 1915, he published "Discourse on self-rule," analyzing the post-republican engagement or rejection of regionalism and concluded that "the meaning of self-rule is that the people are given the right to rule themselves, but since the average educational experience of our people is still elementary, we must guide and check them."[95]

Judging from this perspective, the imminent danger was not the quagmire of a debate over the merits of democracy over authoritarianism, but the crisis of Chinese polity. The lead article of the March 1916 issue (the third of volume thirteen) was Jia Yi's "The fundamental problem of nation building." Whether from timing or topical content, it can be considered a response to the Hongxian monarchy, but the author declined to mention republican politics or the problem of imperial autocracy once. Instead he attributed "the fundamental problem of nation building" to the faulty distribution of power between central and local authorities. The author pointed out:

> The desire to build a nation in today's climate necessitates endorsing the principle of the division of powers. Firstly, one must realize that the concentration of power at the center and its sharing of power at the local level is a problem of distribution and not exclusion. Secondly, one must recognize that the central government and the self-rule organizations are complementary institutions and not ones to undermine one another. This is the only way to quell all sorts of meaningless debates and reach proper solutions in the future. This is indeed the fundamental problem of nation building.[96]

This theme was continued in issues seven and eight of the same year; by then the Hongxian monarchy had collapsed. *Eastern Miscellany* on the one hand clearly regarded the monarchist movement as an act against popular will and the mandate of heaven[97]; on the other it recognized that the central–local conflict had not been resolved. Consequently, "authoritarian politics will be stymied, and those favoring a sharing of power will certainly expand."[98]

Eastern Miscellany's prognosis was based on post-restoration conditions. After the 1911 Revolution the crises of provincial fragmentation, central government and diplomacy rose and fell, and the problem of the unification of authority was never solved. The collapse of the Qing dynasty resulted not from revolution, but from political disunity and the militarization of local powers. Du analyzed the situation thusly:

> When the revolutionary army rose, provinces simultaneously flew the flag of independence [in support], and each set up its own military government, electing its own governor. When the situation settled, a provisional government was established over them. The Nanjing Provisional government resembled a federal government.[99]

This situation differed from the Chinese traditional provincial system and resulted in the early republican political problem revolving constantly around the issue of centralizing or sharing power. After the monarchical restoration, the above conditions were instrumental in elevating the general crisis, but the crisis of regional fragmentation stood out. Shortly after Yuan ascended to the throne, Cai E, Dai Kan and Li Liejun led an insurrection in Yunnan declaring independence; Guizhou and Guangxi followed suit. After the debacle of monarchism, the wave of independence did not subside. First Guangdong declared independence, then Zhejiang, Shaanxi, Sichuan and Hunan followed in various modes. Other provinces flexed their muscles, and the situation immediately became chaotic. Corresponding to this was the crisis of the central government. When the military flag of "Protect the Nation" was first unfurled, the central government coerced Cao Kun, Zhang Jiyao and Li Changtai to retaliate. War broke out in Sichuan, in the western part of Hunan and on the border of Guizhou as the internal power struggle in the Beijing government intensified. Duan Qirui and Xu Shichang resigned in succession to protest the restoration. On June 15, 1916, the navy, controlled by the central government, openly opposed the monarchy; led by the powerful First Fleet, it openly elected Li Dingxin as general marshal, joined the "Protect the Nation" army and declared independence from the central government. These were the military and political factors that created the crisis of the central government and its military structure.

Accompanying the crisis over the Chinese polity, the intensification of the split in the central government and the fragmentation of the local powers, diplomatic pressure from various foreign powers surrounded the question of formal recognition, driven by their competition for gaining a foothold in China. Not only were border areas such as Manchuria, Mongolia and Tibet experiencing extreme instability, but the sovereignty of Shandong and other inland territories hung in the balance as well. The diplomatic crisis of the Republic of China directly connected the issues of territorial integrity and autonomous sovereignty.

Along this line of thinking, *Eastern Miscellany* explained the republican crisis as one of "cyclical politics" rather than the conflicting political values of republicanism and authoritarianism.[100] While the triggering of the wave of independence was directly related to the restoration of the monarchy, the trend toward regional factionalism was an ever-present and unresolved crisis since the 1911 Revolution. During this period *Eastern Miscellany* formulated an important paradigm for political thought on how to maintain a positive relationship between central authority, local division of power and social autonomy which not only contrasted sharply with its critique of "central authority" and "dictatorship" before the 1911 Revolution,[101] but also differed greatly from Du's advocacy of "government reductionism" after the 1911 Revolution.[102] In his "Centralization and decentralization of power," Du pointed out:

> The changing incidents in the past half year . . . are no different from federalist rule. Tracing the cause as to how the policy effects of a centralized government came about, one is because there is no coherent spirit in the implementation of the government's centralizing policy . . . two is because extreme centralization can never be achieved. If there were not a certain amount of decentralization of power, then centralization would consequently perish as well.[103]

He admitted that "the incidents within the past six months arose due to the monarchist movement, and bore no connection to the question of centralization and decentralization," but at the same time emphasized that "in our country's present condition, while extreme centralization is impossible, extreme decentralization must not happen. An overly decentralized state would appear weak to outside forces, and inter provincial conflicts would be bound to happen and sabotage the unity of the country. Especially the so-called local sharing of power today is not really the sharing of power with the localities but in effect letting a dictator rule each locality." As China faced a full-blown political crisis, his advice was:

> first to divide government administration into three parts: central rule, bureaucratic rule and self-rule . . . Military, foreign affairs and communication issues should directly accord to the center, affirming central control in order to maintain national unity. Finance, judicial affairs and police matters in the civil service should belong under bureaucratic control. Education and industry and other public welfare issues be relegated under self-rule. This would [prevent] local organizations from oppressing the people and instead work purely for the welfare of the people.[104]

The Distinction between "Statism" and "Politics-Centrism"

In focusing on the problems of nation building and the division of power between the center and localities as a response to the crisis of the Hongxian monarchy, *Eastern Miscellany* indicated more interest in the questions of national unity and independence than the political values of republicanism versus authoritarianism. Discussions in the periodical of the need for national unity and centralization of power did not mean, however, that it opposed authoritarianism from a democratic perspective, nor that it approved an aggressive expansion of national borders.[105] Du opposed big government but did not consider it a product of traditional authoritarianism; to the contrary, he viewed big government as a common contemporary phenomenon in countries around the world.

In a discussion of *Eastern Miscellany*'s approach to the question of governmental size, therefore, the dichotomies between tradition and modernity and between democracy and autocracy were irrelevant; the periodical's process of analysis can only be situated in the context of the crisis of modern politics itself.[106] This discourse was a turning point; it implied that *Eastern Miscellany* and its peers had begun to place the crisis of the Chinese political system within the framework of the modern political crisis, and not solely locate the problem of autocracy within the context of the authoritarian tradition. After the failure of the Hongxian monarchy, Du explicitly announced: "The claim that republican politics does not suit our national conditions was propagated by monarchists to prevent a reform of the national structure. Nowadays some journalists dare to parrot their argument and say that 'the political ideals of a constitutional democracy do not suit the current situation.'" As far back as the early days of the Republic, Du had been concerned with questions of "federalism," "decentralization or centralization of power" and "a modified republicanism"[107] but maintained a positive and optimistic view toward the revolution and constitutionalism. In his 1913 "Overview of Chinese politics," he summarized China's political trends as the revolutionary and the constitutional movements; the former "changes a monarchy to a democracy," and the latter "changes autocracy to a representative government . . . The democratic and constitutional Republic of China is shaped by the interaction of these two great political trends."[108] A few years later, however, he raised the question himself of whether "constitutional democracy" was suitable for China.

Explaining "politics-centrism" (*zhengzhi zhuyi*), Du wrote:

Democratic constitutionalism is the political ideal of our countrymen; even though I say that it is not suitable for the times, I do not suggest that the demolition of this ideal would suit the times better . . . In my opinion, instead of opposing this political ideal, we must come to its aid, and hope that this ideology would become reality quickly. Only when this ideology has been realized then can our people, in an effort to meet the exigencies of the time, contend with the great powers in the world of the twentieth century. Those who say that this political ideal does not suit our times are only warning our people and forcing them to examine conditions by which to promote this ideal. Our country must in a short time pass through this ideology in order to achieve *guojia zhuyi* [hereafter translated as "statism"] . . . Normally a nation progresses through certain stages. The various European nations progressed from democratic constitutionalism to statism, and our nation's future must not overlook this progression. If our nation today discarded this ideal, we would not be able to bring about statism. Living in the twentieth century, we must not acquiesce to engage with democratic constitutionalism, but to seek a completion of this stage of political idealism . . . If on the problem of internal politics, all of our countrymen were stymied by party politicians or evil bureaucrats, then looking to the future, how can we realize statism? This would pose a difficult situation for the twentieth century.[109]

"Politics-centrism," or democratic constitutionalism, centered on the government and emphasize the reform of the internal conditions of the nation. It scrutinized the boundary between the rights of the individual and those of the group, and aimed to expand the people's rights while curbing those of the state. "Statism" centered on the state, focusing on reforming and adapting the country to its external environment and emphasizing the duty of its citizens to defend national interests, thereby placing the state above the interests of the people. Unlike the modern ideology in which "politics" is relegated to the confines of the government, Du's concept of the "state" contained a certain natural property and was not a recommendation for state control over all political life. Du did not reject politics-centrism but hoped that it could be incorporated into the paradigm of statism. Following his analysis of the "current times," if the citizens overly favored "politics-centrism," then internal fissures could easily occur, which could lead to invasion by external enemies. *Eastern Miscellany* discussed on numerous occasions the losses sustained by the Republic over the questions of Manchuria, Mongolia and Tibet. From Du's point of view, aside from the aggression of the great powers, this resulted also from the "politics-centrism" of the early Republic.[110]

The heart of "politics-centrism" was party politics framed by parliamentary politics; his criticisms of "politics-centrism" necessarily targeted party politics. Following the 1911 Revolution, commentaries abounded over questions of constitutionalism and political parties. Du pointed out that "every country must have political parties to ground the constitution" and suggested that political parties assume "investigating political affairs, researching policies, and guiding the citizens as their mission."[111]

Parliamentary politics sank into chaos, however, after the founding of the Republic. During the Hongxian monarchy, most of the anti-Yuan movements were organized by party activists, as evidenced by the fact that local fragmentation and the crisis of the central authority were largely tied to the question of political parties. This departed from Du's assessment that "political parties cannot base their existence on geographical areas" but must "come together based on ideology and not sentiment."[112] Even as the nation's fate hung in the balance, political parties nevertheless competed out of self-interest and often relied on the help of external forces, further contributing to the disunity of the country. In 1912, *Eastern Miscellany* published Xuan Lan's article which compared "the Young China Party and the Young Turk Party," pointing out that neither the Chinese nor the Turkish revolution was "a revolution by all the people, but a chance victory of a minority of politicians . . . The words of the Guangdong progressives were none other than those of the Young Thessalonian Party. If the rulers were corrupt, sending the nation to the brink of collapse, then foreign capital would greatly gain in power. Everyone was after wealth and fame, but the upright citizen remained powerless. Those honest, brave, deeply worried and genuinely loving patriots were ironically dismissed by the office-seeking scholars and the arrogant and violent soldiers. Thus China and Turkey have suffered the same fate."[113]

The Young Turks (Jöntürkler), that is, the Ottoman Committee of Union and Progress, changed its name to the Committee of Union and Progress in 1913. The party's aim was to overthrow Abdul Hamid II's authoritarian regime and to restore the Constitution of 1876; because the coup failed, however, many members were exiled. This group of exiles divided into several factions. The faction headed by Murat Bey was influenced by pan-Islamic ideology and sought compromise with the sultan by way of moderate reforms. The faction led by Ahmed Riza continued the struggle against the sultan's authoritarian rule, demanding the introduction of popular and fair elections by secret ballot, power to the parliament, and judiciary independence. The liberal faction led by Sabahheddin Bey not only wanted the ethnic groups to exercise self-rule, but also advocated that European powers involve themselves in the internal affairs of Turkey.

In April 1909, the Young Turks Party abolished the monarchy, propagated Ottomanism, suppressed ethnic movements and adopted a pro-German stance. The Turco-Italian War broke out from 1911 to 1912, and the First Balkan War erupted in 1912 when Bulgaria, Greece,

Serbia and Montenegro simultaneously launched a war against Turkey. On November 2, 1914, goaded by Germany, Turkey declared war against Britain, France and Russia, becoming engulfed in the First World War.

In January 1917, Du published "Foreign affairs exposed," analyzing in detail China's diplomatic crisis and the imminent threat of partition. He again used the Young Turks as an example of the relationship between political parties and fragmentation of the state. Du warned,

> If our nation's political parties do not observe the current situation and emulate the behavior of the Young Turks Party (which caused the fragmentation of the Balkans), then our nation's prospect of partition is imminent.[114]

In 1918, a year and a half after Du published the above comments, Turkey lost the war and surrendered. On October 30, Turkey was forced to sign the Armistice of Mudros, and the reign of the Young Turks Party ended. The party dissolved itself on November 4.

Du published the above opinion at a time when he had been forced into a debate with Chen Duxiu, but a comparison of their opinions on political parties reveals many similarities. In "Our final awakening," Chen blamed China's political crisis on the Chinese apathy toward their country and toward political participation: "The ordinary citizens and merchants do not consider it their duty to participate in politics; the transformation of national politics is entrusted to the government and the political parties."[115]

Upon further inspection, however, divergence and difference in emphasis are also apparent. Chen hoped for a form of politics including all people, defining the "final awakening" as having two levels: "political awakening" and "moral awakening." He incorporated "morality" into the definition of "politics." In other words, morality was the ultimate meaning of politics, and mass participation and freedom of speech were the necessary prerequisite of this moral politics (or the political manifestation of morality). In 1916 when Chen responded to Wang Shuqian's query about his critique of party politics, Chen distinguished the "opinions of the parties" from the "general will of the people," emphasizing that the latter was the true foundation for constitutional politics. "To conduct political affairs by the popular will is the essence of constitutional politics. Flaunt this essence and governing would turn oppressive, the party into a lawless entity."[116] In his view of the political structure, Chen also recommended that the national assembly "be vigilant on behalf of the people against the illegal activities of the executive branch," pointing out that the national assembly rightfully exercised its democratic power in investigating government borrowing, the pact between Russia and Outer Mongolia, the assassination of Song Jiaoren and other incidents.[117]

Departing from this view, Du was concerned about the relationship between party politics and the stability of the country. In his opinion, the goal of party organization was to "maintain the political balance, aiding the development of the country"; but Chinese political parties could very likely repeat the travail of the Young Turks. "[They] abused the [political] genre, contested against each other, and this competition without knowledge nothing but a waste of time. This was seen at the political level, and if we examine the social aspect, the disparity between old and new morality resulted in the divergence in theory and practice. As neither side would countenance the other, conflict arose constantly."[118]

There was a close link between the issue of political parties and that of freedom of speech in the context of parliamentary politics. At the same time practicing freedom of speech in itself created a new crisis: "Freedom of speech and freedom of publication, which were used by others to advance civilization, became contentious subjects when we attempted to emulate them."[119] Because freedom of speech was unable to convey the general will of the people, and the discussions generated in the context of party politics were mired in disputes driven by special interests, Du's and Chen's views were not always opposed to one another. In "The Reason for the demise of the power of speech," Du argued that the modern condition for public discourse was worse than in the traditional period. The present discourse not only could not adequately describe the vicissitudes of political events or the gains and losses in political affairs, it could not even achieve its self-appointed duty of management and supervision of ordinary social issues.

The root of the problem stemmed from the fact that in one respect modern discourse aimed to cultivate public discussion, in another it was

controlled by vested interests, political factions and monetary relationships, and thus by its very nature could not bring about social
consensus.[120] This view was in accordance with his later argument
during the debate on Eastern and Western civilizations that modern
Chinese politics exhibited only "differentiation" and lacked "integration." Before Yuan Shikai's restoration of the monarchy, his criticism
of party politics concentrated on its chaotic condition in China, but in
the "debate of Eastern and Western civilizations," his political criticism
gradually pointed to the modern Western political model itself.
Accordingly China's political crisis was not one of traditional politics,
but a crisis resulting from blindly imitating the modern Western political model.[121]

From a superficial angle, Du seemed to criticize both monarchism
and republicanism without exhibiting a clear political bias. However,
the monarchy had already failed by this time (1917). He also cited the
national fragmentation caused by the Young Turks Party as evidence,
thus quietly but clearly directing his sharp attack toward "party
members," "party factions" and even the entire system of republican
politics. As Du put it:

> In this movement the monarchists and the supporters of republicanism
> did not appear to have any open international associations, but they
> inevitably involved foreigners participating in a private capacity. For
> example, foreign advisors working for Yuan Shikai and foreigners exert-
> ing their efforts for the popular parties appeared to be at odds with one
> another. From now on politicians and party members must be vigilant to
> be free of factional views when considering foreign relations. One
> cannot recruit external forces into political disputes.[122]

Du's critique of party politics supplemented and deepened his reflection
of "politics-centrism" and "constitutional democracy." In the climate
of political opinion where monarchism and republicanism stood opposite each other, the fact that his posture was later interpreted by Chen as
being supportive of "restoration" was not surprising. Du's comparison
of "politics-centrism" to "statism" already featured a transition from
"political issues" to "cultural issues," a precedent for the unfolding of
political debates in the May Fourth era through discussions on civilization and culture.

Two Concepts of the State: Civilizational State and Nation State

Through the distinction between state and politics, Du hinted at the differences in types of states. In his view, those countries founded upon "politics-centrism" comprised a distinctive civilizational model. Due to the pressure of "the times," China needed to absorb the important elements of "politics-centrism," but concern itself even more with the continuity of the state itself. In other words, a nation must be founded upon its indigenous civilization and history—not on some exogenous factor. This is a concept of nation with civilization at its core; its political definition does not rest on its political structure but on the disparity and opposition between civilizational states.

In another article, Du argued, "Politics is an institution for administering affairs but not for generating energy. For politics to function effectively, the people must be energetic and businesses prosperous."[123] This view on a superficial level imposed a restriction on the political domain but in reality situated "politics" on the solid foundation of everyday life. We can find similar veins of reasoning in his earlier work. For example, at the end of his article "The shortcomings of modern civilization" published in March 1913, Du wrote, "When the foundation for the state had just been laid, constant unrest occurred; there was not enough strength to solve internal issues, let alone deploy our civilizational force to counter the great powers. At the same time, we have not yet arrived at a point where we could come into contact with the world through our civilization." And what one must work on today is "to develop material strength and augment our spiritual impact in order to compete on a civilizational level, all in an urgent and not laggardly pace."[124] Here, the main actor in the competition between civilizations was the state, but the competing countries belonged to different civilizations.

Therefore as distinct from the competition among the European nation-states, the competition between China and the West was one between civilizational nations. This theory also indirectly demonstrated that the nation-state was not the universal form of statehood, but a product of a particular civilization. According to Du's observation, "politics" must be founded on a unique national civilization and its way of life. China need not duplicate the political culture of European countries. As a result, at the same time that he advocated "statism," Du also harshly criticized the militaristic orientation of modern nationalism.[125] He declared:

> We did not have so-called "associations" (*tuanti*) in our society. City, township, and village are geographical names with province, prefecture, county as further administrative divisions; they do not contain concepts related to their individual characters. The term "state" is a relic of the feudal times, referring to the fiefdom of the lords. Above the states there was "all under heaven" (*tianxia*), which is far from the definition of state in modern times. There were no others besides the king, and certainly no equivalent relationships, and therefore it is natural that it disregarded human character. Our nation never entertained the concept of an ethnic nation (*minzu*), either.[126]

Following this argument, the Chinese state was different from a nationalistic polity; China's local regions would not form into individual entities in the manner of the European nations. Within in this description of a non nationalistic form of state lay an abhorrence for fragmentation, implying that this unique state theory encompassed a cultural orientation that would overcome the crisis of fragmentation. If the disparity between nations is one between cultures, then *Eastern Miscellany*'s analysis of the issue of monarchism and the crisis of republicanism should veer from a political to a civilizational or cultural attitude.[127] Under the premise of the distinction between China and the West, Du pointed out two different value orientations from two different types of statehood.

Within these parameters, the oppositions between imperialism and pacifism and between nationalism and internationalism were only two sets of paradigms[128] founded on the basis of Western politics. Du sought to explore the disparity of civilizations outside of these oppositions. The logic of this analysis was identical to his treatment of the question of political structure—that is, republicanism and authoritarianism represented polar opposites in traditional European politics; they also represented the internal contradiction of European political culture; the true disparity in their value was as the disparity in national polities established on the basis of two different types of civilization. This was the inherent meaning of Du's so-called "war of ideas." His rather nebulous concepts of state and statism make sense only in the context of his unique understanding of the question of state.

The "War of Ideas" and the Binary of "Eastern and Western Civilizations"

Eastern Miscellany's suggestion of framing the problems in terms of nation building and centralization versus decentralization did not mean that it was avoiding the contradiction of political values; rather it sought to generate a new definition of "politics." Simply conceptualizing China's political problems as conflicts between republicanism and constitutional monarchism, it posited, already fell into a simplistic culturally and politically specific framework — it mistook modern Western statehood as a universal, trans-civilizational political structure. Here, the question of the intrinsic value that of the difference in the old versus new relationship and Eastern versus Western civilizations. Qian Zhixiu asked in "The lethargic citizens," "What is the source of our nation's ailment? Some suggested it hinged on the racial question; but after waging a revolutionary war [to overthrow the Manchus] to save the country things remain the same. Some say it was autocratic rule that terrorized the people; yet the sickness is still the same after applying the remedy of republicanism . . . I can sum up our nation's ailment in one word: lethargy. The only way to cure this is to apply a spiritual remedy. Morality and religion are the most appropriate medicine, while knowledge and politics are supplemental remedies."[129]

From this perspective, *Eastern Miscellany* raised the question of the relationship between "new and old thinking." Prior to this, in February 1916, the second issue of volume thirteen had featured a lead article by Du's student Yuan Sheng (Huang Yuanyong) titled "Conflict between new and old thinking." The author clearly interpreted the "conflict between old and new" as a "conflict in thinking":

Since the influx of Western culture, the conflict between the old and the new has never been as serious as now . . . Our people need to know that the root of the difference between old and new does not rest in military technology or in the political or judicial systems and so on. As the source of water cannot be found in the drops or that of the plant in the green leaves, the source does not reside there. The source is in their thought.[130]

One can detect from Yuan's tone that he was clearly a strong proponent of "new thought."

Two months later Du's response emphasized a reconciliation of the old and the new, East and West, refusing to choose one over the other. For Du, even though the struggle in the thought of Chinese citizens stemmed from their contact with Western ideas, it could not be simply viewed as a clash between Eastern and Western thought. He wrote, "The so-called new thinkers among our people cannot break away from their ingrained Eastern way of thinking; it is just that they have absorbed a few Western thoughts. As to the so-called old thinkers, they cannot remain entirely faithful to their ingrained Eastern way of thinking and boycott Western ideologies. Whether it is old or new, it is only a matter of degree. Although the reasons for the difference in degrees are complex, overall it comes down to a disparity in new knowledge, or a difference in sentiment." In addition to these inherent reasons, he also added "desire and will" as external factors that distinguished the new and old factions. "This journalist believes that if one day our nation is annihilated, the reason for its fall will not be its reforms nor its conservative stance, but the two factors of desire and will."[131]

This is the origin of the "theory of the reconciliation of the old and the new." Half a year later, Du no longer considered the question of old and new as a "matter of degree," but reconfigured the relationship between the "old and new" and "East and West" as a disparity between civilizations. In this argument, the basic theme of reconciliation did not change, but the conflict in value between the Eastern and Western civilizations was foregrounded. The article "Tranquil civilization and active civilization" is symbolic of this transition:

> In my personal opinion, the difference between our civilization and that of the West is a one of nature and not of degree. Our civilization would be well suited to amend the failings of Western civilization, and enrich the paucity of Western civilization.[132]

In contrast to the author's earlier opinion that "the inadequacy of our present civilization is an inescapable reality,"[133] the tone of this article was significantly different—a change not in judging China's current state of affairs, but in its basic evaluation of the crisis of the European war from a civilizational standpoint.

Du believed that the difference between the Eastern and Western civilizations resulted from two differences in the social conditions of the East and West. First, Western society had relied on ethnic nation as the unit on which to form the nation-state, whereas the degree of assimilation of the various so-called ethnic nations of Chinese people was great. Whether in times of division (such as the North and South Dynasties, the Five Dynasties, and the Liao/Jin periods) or during times of minority rule (such as the Yuan and Qing dynasties), "it was always a battle of survival for one surname and one clan, and could never be considered a popular national war." Second, ocean trade was well developed in Western societies, which led to a situation of fierce economic competition, while the Chinese inland economy was based on agriculture, which brought about stability and less competition.

These two differences in social formation allowed two binaries to manifest: "tranquil civilization and active civilization" and "natural existence and competitive existence." Du used corresponding but drastically opposed binaries to describe the nature of these civilizations: man-made versus natural, extroverted versus introverted, group competition versus individualistic nature, winning through competition versus moral cultivation, and bellicosity as a chronic state of being versus pacifism as a norm. From his point of view, civilizational clashes did not necessarily have to arise because of their differences; frequent exchanges, mutual interaction, learning from each other and "embracing reconciliation" were the real ways to resolve conflict.[134]

This judgment on the disparity between civilizations could not but have deep implications for political and societal considerations. *Eastern Miscellany*'s analysis of political structure and its study of the cause of war had an inherent connection—both pointed to the reflection on "the question of civilization" and "the issue of the old and new thinking." From an editorial perspective, *Eastern Miscellany* strove to provide a global perspective on the political and social problems of China and attempted to find solutions. In that sense, the two issues—international war and domestic politics—were linked together in various ways. First, on the two very distinctive questions of war and Chinese polity, *Eastern Miscellany* emphasized in both cases the function of "thought": both the essence of the war and the heart of the polity's conflict as deriving from thought. This allowed the analysis of war and the political debate to shift into the discourse on the clash of civilizations and debate on thought. Second, even though the European war and Chinese political discord emanated from dissimilar historical causes, both belonged to the same times and were bound by the same logic. As a result, the methods of overcoming the crisis of war and resolving political conflict were both related to the "question of thought." The March 1915 issue of *Eastern Miscellany* (the third of volume twelve) led with Du's article "On the war of ideas." The author argued that "the cause of war can be divided by the process of human evolution into three stages. In the beginning the fight was over gains or losses, later over interests, and lastly over right or wrong. The struggle over gains and losses is a physical war, which over interests is both a physical war and one of ideas, and the war over right and wrong is a war of ideas." He thus concluded,

This is the era of a war of ideas. The spread of the concept of individual rights in the eighteenth century resulted in American Independence and the French Revolution . . . With the proliferation of nationalistic thought of the nineteenth century, there was the Italian unification, the fragmentation of the Balkans, as well as an explosion of countless ethnic wars in various places. This surge of ideas traveled from the Pacific and Indian Oceans to East Asia, reached our country and resulted in the 1911 Revolution. Our nation's war of ideas has its root in this [phenomenon].

The term "war of ideas" considered all forms of war, conflict and confrontation to comprise a struggle between ideas. Following this logic, all political questions since the late Qing dynasty had originated in the transformation of ideas around the world.

The 1911 Revolution was therefore a reaction to ultra conservative thought after Wuxu [the 1898 Hundred Days' Reform]; the recent restoration of the monarchy is a reaction to radical reformist ideas since the 1911 Revolution. The earth's existence is due to the interaction of the centrifugal and centripetal forces; the establishment of society resulted from the reconciliation of selfish and altruistic impulses. Thus if one does not understand the logic of reconciliation but instead wishes to seize an opportune moment to radically advocate his own views, he will meet with opposition and bring about swift disaster.[135]

From this perspective of universal association, both the reflection on warfare (such as using "continuism" to study the nation's problems) and the discussion on political structure (such as the critique of "politics-centrism" in the "Discourse on the unsuitability of democratic constitutionalism for our times") indicate a focus on the nation and its civilizational values. The reflections on the European war and domestic wars did not simplistically lead to a negation of "war" but redirected "war" toward the intellectual sphere, using ideas and culture to reframe the politics that had been suppressed by war and violence. As a result, the spheres of "culture," "civilization" and "thought" gradually ascended to the top as focal points for reflection and discussion.

The Theory of Reconciliation and the Old (New) Civilization of the Twentieth Century

The Demise of the Nineteenth-Century Political Model

To study the issue of politics within the paradigm of civilization also meant to develop the issues of politics, economics, military affairs, administrative structure and technology into questions of "culture," "civilization" and "thought." As such, reflections on war and examinations of the republican crisis shifted into ruminations about the old versus new and Eastern civilization versus Western. As discussed above, this formula was derived from observations on the European war and the social crisis and implied a holistic judgment on the political and economic systems of the nineteenth century: that is, on the political and economic models represented by nineteenth-century Europe, and the inherent general crisis that these values were developing.

Any arrangement which failed to confront this systematic crisis would be unsuitable as a model or measure for China's future reform. As Du wrote, "the social organization rooted in modern civilization will perish, and similarly the political organization nurtured by this structure will also expire . . . The end of the Great War signifies the demise of the old civilization and the birth of a new civilization." He laid out the distinction between the "two types of civilization":

> The old civilization is the present civilization, which is grounded in the struggle for power; but the new civilization will be a future one rooted

in justice and fairness. But while this is the case in Europe, in our country we have the demise of the new and the renaissance of the old civilization. This is because today our nation considers the struggle for power as a new civilization, while [the concepts of] justice and humanity [are considered] the old civilization. The nearly two decades of turmoil in our country are marked by a struggle for power, fueled by the blessings of this new civilization, which shared identical roots with the European turmoil on the international stage. Europe competes for national interests and produces global war; while we compete for personal gain, resulting in civil wars. Even though the scope of the conflict differs, the cause and effect relationship is the same . . . Therefore our civil war is really a miniature version of the European world war.[136]

If both the European war and the republican crisis were the crises of modern civilization itself, then it was important to consider how to evaluate modern civilization and its political quality. By raising the "question of old and new," Du and a few colleagues sought to examine the decline of the new concepts, new values and new politics of the nineteenth century in an effort to redefine a "new civilization" for the future.

The new politics, or the "modern civilization of the West," starting with the Hundred Days' Reforms, was a political culture based on a democratic state and a capitalist economy centered on a material civilization. They composed a social-political system centered on individual rights and interests, which was in turn supported by the state. The relationship between state and politics was rooted in the question of authority.

To quote Weber, "What do we understand by politics? The concept is extremely broad and comprises any kind of *independent* leadership in action. One speaks of the currency policy of the banks, of the discounting policy of the Reichsbank, of the strike policy of a trade union; one may speak of the educational policy of a municipality or a township, of the policy of the president of a voluntary association, and, finally, even of the policy of a prudent wife who seeks to guide her husband. Tonight, our reflections are, of course, not based on such a broad concept. We wish to understand by politics only the leadership, or the influencing of the leadership, of a *political* association, hence today of a *state*."[137] When we discuss the concept of politics today, we take for granted the elements of state politics (political parties, the military, parliament, diplomacy and so forth), forgetting completely that the special relationship between politics and the state is only a characteristic of nineteenth-century politics, when the political entity of the nation-state appeared. The European war was indeed one of the nineteenth-century state and its political culture; its precipitating factors, such as authoritarian politics, secret diplomacy, the arms race and economic exploitation were by-products of the modern state and its political culture. Du acknowledged the distinction between the democratic politics of Great Britain, the United States and France and the monarchical politics of Germany, Austria and Russia but did not consider the latter group to be in the realm of traditional states.[138] In "A consideration of statism" published at the end of the war, Du cited German nationalist practice of being autocratic on the domestic front and aggressive on the international front as an example, and argued, "Such a cruel and vicious statism cannot be tolerated by humanity."[139] Here, the criticism of the German state was not limited to Germany but could be applied as criticism of a particular model of the nation-state and its political culture.

As indicated above, Du's revision of his early position on nationalism effectively stemmed from his distinction between the two types of nation-states. In his earlier and later essays, he defined the nation-state as a modern political formation that differed from the traditional political configuration. As a result, his critique of the nation-state was not aimed at the traditional political formation but represented an observation on the political configuration of the modern nation-state—a polity that encompassed parliamentary rule, multiple parties and the military.

In July and September 1917, *Eastern Miscellany* featured two articles by Du, "The world situation in the future" and "The thesis that true republicanism cannot be achieved by force," and conducted a thorough examination of two key issues in the question of Chinese politics, namely the problems of national polity and political parties. In the first article Du posed a rhetorical question: "Even though it is a natural outcome of democracy that political parties are self-serving and military men pugnacious, should democracy not be promulgated and autocratic monarchy not abolished?"[140] In the second article he suggested that "there are no more than two factors needed to establish true democracy: one is for the nation to enjoy thriving agricultural production, industry and commerce, and the other is to make education universal."[141] These opinions converged in Du's thoughts on the future polity, when nation-states would disappear and super-nations or alliances of super-nations will appear. Within this political superstructure, the two political forces of traditional nation-states—the political parties and the militarists—would deteriorate. From the perspective of the future, the democratic polity is not an "immutable law of nature." Du wrote:

> Those who align with political parties should not believe themselves to be the true representatives of the popular will when they gain office by means of demagoguery or enticement; they should not hold dear the dream of joining the cabinet, as if doing so would last for eternity. Those who side with militarists should not act wantonly when backed by force; democracy survives because of the goodwill of these men, but do not assume this will be an unchanging principle. I sincerely hope that our unenlightened and uninformed citizens will pay heed to the great trends of the future, and be prepared to install a scientific laborer as the master of the twentieth century.[142]

Here he mentioned "the master of the twentieth century," a "scientific laborer" for the future polity, which differed radically from the main component (such as the political party) of democratic politics.

The "scientific laborer" was a new political subject; its appearance heralded a change in the solid linkage of politics and the state formed in the nineteenth century. In the context of the wars between states and between classes, the power struggles between the political structure and the military and the struggles between interests produced by the market, new political subjects such as the political party, the military as a political actor, and the laboring class came into being. It was the appearance of the last of these, the "master of the future," that would usher in a new politics that transcended the paradigm of the state. Even with regard to the question of war and peace, class struggle and the labor movement hold more sway in political decisions than the governments of numerous states. Starting from the beginning of Du's tenure as editor, *Eastern Miscellany* always maintained a thematic interest in studying the "political problems of the twentieth century."

For example, in April 1911, Xu Jiaqing published "The political problems of the twentieth century" (translated from an article published in the first issue of volume two of *New Japan*, originally titled "On the world not at peace") and listed as the major themes of the new century "the liberation of the human race, the awakening of individuality, the freedom movements of Asia and Africa, the rebellious movements of labor, the political movement of socialist parties, the women's liberation movement and the suffrage movement."[143] In March 1915, in the third issue of volume twelve of *Eastern Miscellany*, Peng Jinyi outlined "three great problems of the twentieth century": "The twentieth century has inherited many problems from the nineteenth century, but chief among them are three great questions that must be resolved in the twentieth century. First is the problem of gender equality—women ought to occupy the same political and social status as men. Second is the question of labor, that is, the attitude of the capitalists toward the laborers. Third is the question of colonialism, which is the problem of nation versus nation. A commonality runs through all three issues, and that is the question of the strong against the weak."[144] These wide-ranging social problems, not issues of national polity and political parties, would form the core of politics in the future.

This reorientation was closely related to Du's and *Eastern Miscellany*'s longtime concern with "social maladies" and the issue of equality. In 1913, Du described Chinese "social maladies" as rooted in the distinction of "producers" and "nonproducers," and found a greater proportion of "nonproducers" in his investigation. He also attempted to investigate the principles of production and allocation in Chinese society based on criteria of political economy, such as land, capital and labor[145]; his query into "equality" related to issues of livelihood, gender equality and political rights, among other issues. Therefore, at the same time when *Eastern Miscellany* delved deeply into the questions of war, international relations, national polity and political parties, it also carved out a large space to explore issues of marriage, family, language, individuality, class, labor, land, population, migration, education and other social problems (such as "class struggle," "gender" and so forth).[146] When Du followed this thread of discussion to examine the "new politics" and "new civilization" of the twentieth century, his political conceptualization surpassed the nineteenth-century theory of state that foregrounded government, political parties and the state economy. In short, in the analysis of the European war crisis, an opportunity to liberate political thought from the paradigm of the state was born.

The Crisis of the Economic System of the Nineteenth Century

Eastern Miscellany's critique of the nineteenth-century polity was always linked to its analysis of the relationships between land, capital and labor. This provided a new orientation for its political thinking toward socialism, which had at its core the critique of capitalism centered on the struggle of interests.[147] For Du, this critique also originated in his analysis of the relationship between world war and class struggle in Europe. In "The state of our people's awakening after the Great War," he argued that capitalism and its system of social allocation bred intense class struggle, with war the political manifestation of this struggle, those who sincerely sought peace were not the political leaders but "the lower class of those countries." From the perspective of war between states, Britain, the United States, France and Italy were the victors; but from the angle of class warfare, Russia's, Germany's and Austria's "socialist parties actually triumphed over their monarchs, bureaucrats, warlords, and created new nations." In this sense, the Paris Peace Conference "could possibly be defined as a peace conference of a class war." The Russian Revolution and the "radicals," the German Revolution and the Socialists, the nationalist liberation movements in the disintegration of the Austro-Hungarian Empire, the waves of social democratic movements in Belgium, the Netherlands, Spain and other countries all exhibited a directional force from lower to higher and shaped the climate for the peace negotiation.[148]

Because of the distinction between interstate war and interclass war, the seed for a transnational paradigmatic form of socialist politics was planted. Du wrote:

> The patriots in our country should seize the moment to persuade our countrymen to carry out socialism politically and spiritually so as to prevent future calamities, as well as take heed of the great trends in world reforms—to know the truth, to understand their mission and to familiarize themselves with the opportunities and dangers."[149]

Here, the term "socialism" was intended to express limits on capitalism with its free competition, and the phrase "to prevent future calamities" warned against Bolshevik-style radical revolution. As mentioned above, Du clearly saw the "scientific laborer" as the "master of the twentieth century" and attempted to draw a distinction between the politics of the nineteenth and twentieth centuries.[150] Around the end of the war, he specifically studied the methods of solving of European labor disputes for China's future needs,[151] and traced the concept of the "theory of labor" to its roots in Chinese tradition.[152]

During the years 1917 and 1918, Du and *Eastern Miscellany* conducted an investigative study of the outbreak of the Russian and German revolutions and their social basis. Not only did they fully agree with the socialists' condemnation of capitalism and its method of production, but they also acknowledged "radicalism" as a reaction to "capitalist brutality," the "harshness of authoritarianism," the "suffering of a hard life," the "debasement of intelligence and morality" and other "deficiencies of modern society." These analyses share more similarities than differences with those of Li Dazhao in "Victory of the proletariat," Cai Yuanpei in "Laborers are sacred" and Tao Lugong in "The political situation after the European war."[153]

Indeed, *Eastern Miscellany*'s viewpoint may have been closer to that of the European socialists than it admitted. Du's core aim was to cure the ills of capitalism by "implementing social policies," "establishing democracy," "encouraging industry," "universalizing education" and other socialist solutions. *Eastern Miscellany* diverged from *New Youth* in the details of its solutions (contrast with Li Dazhao's views in "The Victory of Bolshevism"). In "Sequel to the chronicle of Russia's latest news," Du argued that while the French Revolution had earned the sympathy of the middle class, the Russian Revolution was a radical revolt from the lower class. In his view, because the Russian monarchy had the characteristics of a theocracy, overthrowing the system necessarily led to the demise of religion. The result of the demise of religion was a lack of support for morality and spirituality, which would inevitably bring about social turmoil.[154] This explanation of Russian theocracy was somewhat similar to Kang Youwei's interpretation of Confucianism. In "How to prepare for the future of the world," Du wrote:

> Socialism points out the fundamental errors of the present-day economic system that gave rise to unequal distribution of the fruits of production and to the great disparity in wealth; the radicals thus call for the abolition of the special interests of the capitalists, and to relegate all fruits of production to the proletariat. This manner of equalizing

wealth, or communism, shocks those who learn of it, and my generation is not willing to implement it. However, the broken parts of the
world economic system that this theory points out can no longer be
hidden . . . In my opinion, in the near future in the world . . . communism
can be applied in countries without equal distribution of wealth; and
the ideal of free competition, a legacy of the eighteenth and nineteenth
centuries, will greatly diminish in stature when the right to survive
creates a backlash.[155]

Along these lines, *Eastern Miscellany* attempted to differentiate socialism, theoretical communism (and anarchism), and democracy from
"radicalism" (or Bolshevism). In June 1919, *Eastern Miscellany* created
its "Strategy to prevent radical thinking" as a special topic to discuss
ways to avoid "radicalism";[156] its basic position was very clear.

Eastern Miscellany's stance on the Russian Revolution and especially
toward "radicalism" was very different from that of *New Youth*'s later
views, but at this point in time *New Youth* had not yet wholeheartedly
endorsed Marxism and the Russian Revolution; the main points of
contention between the two publications did not center on the question
of Bolshevism and "radicalism." Both *New Youth* and *Eastern Miscellany*
chose for discussion the core questions of Eastern and Western civilization and old and new thinking; an all-encompassing debate in the form
of a cultural discourse evolved precisely due to this shared premise.

Thus it is worth noting how Du, Chen Duxiu and others situated
political analysis within the framework of cultural analysis, as in, for
example, Du's essay on "The reasons for the failure of China's political
revolution and the lack of transformation of China's Society." In this
article, Du situated political and social revolutions in the context of their
separate social conditions and their separate cultural traditions. In his
view, political revolution and social revolution could only exist within
specific historical circumstances and cultural traditions; their success or
failure could not be attributed to accidental human factors for we must
take into account the relationship between the form of the revolution
and its corresponding civilization.[157]

In studying the Russian October Revolution, Du attempted to
describe the rise of the revolutionary core from historical forces and
pointed out that the proletariat comprised two different groups, the
"labor class" and the "middle class." In traditional societies, the "middle

class" was born out of the opposition between classes such as the aristocracy, the military and the religious order. They served as bureaucrats, educators, free professionals and other specialists, and truly formed the "bedrock of the social organization." However, under capitalist conditions, the economic position of a portion of the new middle class sank to a "proletarianized" level and became a distinct social stratum apart from the propertied "middle class." Revolution or "radicalism" was initially triggered by this particular class.[158] Because the Russian bourgeoisie was not developed, the intellectual class that split from the aristocratic class directly merged with the proletariat, skipped over the stage of political revolution and produced an unprecedented social revolution. In Germany, the political revolution had yet to succeed when the aristocracy and the bourgeoisie united against the proletariat. World War I began as a result of Germany's intentional provocation because, when faced with the rise of the proletariat, the aristocracy and the bourgeoisie attempted to expand their own power by waging an external war; in the end, however, the proletariat rejected militarism and ushered in a social revolution.[159]

In short, it was through a socialist analysis of the nineteenth-century economy and its attendant class issues that the possibility of founding politics on the bases of society and civilization was born.

The Dialectic of "Old and New Civilizations"

In evaluating the eighteenth- and nineteenth-century Western political models, *Eastern Miscellany* and *New Youth* shared many premises. I have already discussed Chen's pronouncement that "the political system in existence since the eighteenth-century is already bankrupt."[160] His plea to "stand on the foundation of society and forge new a politics" was a call to reform society by transcending the stage of political revolution. He did not plan for the state or political parties to serve as the foundation of the "new politics." According to this new political formulation, politics was no longer confined to the state, nor political problems to polity and the problem of political parties. The distinct demarcation between the domains of politics, economics and other social spheres was eliminated. This view was also the basic stance of *Eastern Miscellany*. In this sense, although Du and Chen differed drastically in their outlooks on republican and traditional values, their critical analyses of the capitalist economy and political system both pointed toward a new way of life, completely different from eighteenth- and nineteenth-century European capitalist civilization.

Paralleling the expansion of the parameters of politics from the polity and party politics to the social realm was a shift in emphasis from the objective to the subjective sphere. Politics not only emanated from institutional foundations such as political structure, but also from the subjective conditions that framed this foundation. The New Culture Movement situated culture and not politics at the heart of the movement and, as such, did not differ greatly from Du's view. Du attributed "the reasons for political disturbances" to "amoral individuals," the "impotence of the citizen," and the "paucity of the economy," the first two factors of which dealt with a subjective state. More specifically, both the New Culture Movement and the way of thinking represented by Du placed both culture and morality at the heart of political analysis, even as their opposing stances in the spheres of culture and morality also reflected a profound political divergence. Du wrote, "The recent political unrest emerges from a psychological condition, which is a state of anxiety and unease." Even though bureaucrats, people's parties, politicians and soldiers differed in their status and diverged in their opinions, the strife and infighting did not effect any concrete change. The key factors lay in their depressed and lethargic state of mind as well as their decrepit moral character.[161] Accordingly Du declared, "Rather than instill socialism on the political state, it is far better to instill it in the mind of the people."[162] Thus, the new politics was a form not of state politics, but of politics for the mind.

The debates in the May Fourth period raged over the the topics of "Eastern and Western civilizations" and "old and new thinking"; the debates were enabled by the fact that the various sides shared some common premises. In this debate, through the process of thesis, antithesis and synthesis, divergent thinking and hypotheses were developed and gave birth to theoretically related new politics. *Eastern Miscellany* and *New Youth* differed widely in their assessment of "radicalism" and the Russian revolution, yet the debate focused not on their respective political disagreement on the Russian and German revolutions and republican politics but instead on "the discourse on reconciliation of the old and the new."

In the spring of 1917, Du published "The reconciliation of eastern and western civilizations after the war." He began by quoting Tolstoy:

"In our time a great revolution is taking place in the life of humanity . . . the vocation of the Eastern nations, China, India, Persia, Turkey, Russia, and perhaps Japan . . . consists in indicating that true way towards freedom." This indicated Du's own cultural prognosis on the crisis of the West against the backdrop of war. Du pointed out that following the war, morality based on Western aggressiveness, imperialism and materialism must develop in a reverse direction, and that the socialist current created by the Western capitalist economic crisis would dictate the form of the future state. "Our China, which represents Eastern society, must possess self-awareness and self-confidence when the trend of the world reverses itself."[163]

At the end of the year, *Eastern Miscellany* published Zhang Shizhao's essay "The latest trend of thought in Europe and my awakening," in which he delineated his view of the meaning of "self-awareness and self-confidence." He wrote, "In the past the change in Europe's intellectual trend benefited from its cultural Renaissance; and even today its thinking still echoes a return to antiquity. In the future when our country renews itself, we must simultaneously carry out the task of creating new knowledge and reevaluating the classics, for the two are closely intertwined."[164] As such, "return to antiquity" became a new endeavor, while the "new thought" from after the cultural renaissance in turn became considered old.

The tenor of *Eastern Miscellany* as a whole was dominated by the dialectic of old versus new, and this preoccupation was not limited to the question of the Eastern and Western civilizations. In February 1918, Du published "Mediating Contradictions" and noted the contradictions in the European political domain, in which "populism" (equal rights for all the people and so forth) was juxtaposed against "dictatorship in the economic sphere" (monopoly as well as centralized economic models), and "statism" juxtaposed against "socialism." Du believed that one must derive a "multiplicity of enlightenment" from these contradictory juxtapositions. First, there needed to be more than one ideology to administer affairs in the world, and several ideals could coexist and supplement each other (such as political freedom and economic control). Second, it might be possible to reconcile two seemingly opposing ideologies if they overlapped or shared certain similarities (such as "socialism" and "statism"). Third, an ideology was a vision of what should be and not a natural condition; the neat order of theory did not clearly demarcate reality, and therefore opposition and reconciliation took place in "real conditions."[165]

As it was closely identified with a theory of juxtaposition, Zhang Dongsun invoked Hegelian philosophy as a paradigm, arguing that "any theory must have a positive and a negative side," and that "both of these theories must each claim some truth without distortion," which led to the "need to reconcile." Therefore he attempted to reconcile various theories, "theories of majority rule and minority rule," "theories of selective representation and freedom of expression," "egalitarianism and class-based representation theories," "monist and pluralist theories," "nonindividuality and individuality theories," "simultaneous advancement and selective advancement theories," "individualism and collectivism theories," "populist and statist theories" and "utilitarian and rationalist theories"; this was his reconciliation-driven "politics of the able-minded."[166] As a result, the issue of reconciliation was not just a method to interpret the formula of Eastern and Western and old–new civilizations, but also a universal tool.

In "The compromise between old and new thinking," Du proposed a way to interpret the question of "old and new" by delineating "current conditions" and events as the narrative framework, for while "old and new" always existed at particular points, they shifted according to the situation, and thus "old and new" could not be determined simply by a linear chronology. Secondly, ideas of "old and new" came about from events and the processes by which they occurred, and must be marked by events as their central locus. Based on these two considerations, "the so-called 'old and new' of the 1898 period" and "the so-called 'old and new' of the modern period post–European war" could not be treated as one, nor should one negate the other. The 1898 period considered "emulating Western civilization as being new, and insisted on regarding Chinese tradition as old"; but war changed conditions throughout the entire world, and "modern Western civilization [i.e., the 'new' of the 1898 period] no longer suited the current times, and it would soon lose its effectiveness."[167]

Du thus argued that China's wars and the political foundation that produced them arose from emulation of nineteenth-century European civilization; while it seemed to be an orientation favoring the "new," it was, in fact, adhering to the "old" (pre-War European civilization). Similarly, European "people's politics" and the Chinese philosophy of "benevolent rule," European pacifism and China's "great unity" concept, European socialism and the Confucian "great peace" ideal corresponded seamlessly; while each concept appeared to revert to antiquity, in reality it represented a renewed effort.[168] After the war, because "China and Western nations experienced similar circumstances, the creation of future civilization could not be regarded as the need of Westerners alone"; therefore "China's previous civilization" could possibly contribute to "future civilization."[169] In this sense, the relationship between "old" and "new" was reversed when war became the pivotal marker, as Chinese traditional "old civilization" became "new," and the "new politics" since 1898 became "old"; the requirements of the new era became a return to antiquity." An easily derived conclusion was that the new civilization would emerge from the reconciliation of Chinese tradition and new twentieth-century European civilization.

In his first manifesto challenging *Eastern Miscellany*, Chen cited three articles, namely "A critique of Chinese and Western civilizations" translated by Ping Yi from the Japanese magazine *Light of East Asia* that appeared in *Eastern Miscellany* (volume fifteen number six),[170] Qian Zhixiu's "Utilitarianism and scholarship"[171] and Cang Fu's [Du Yaquan's] "The confused mind of modern man," which appeared in the fourth issue of the same volume. Du's essay was a classic example of presenting the Chinese political crisis in the framework of civilizational discourse, and Chen's critique of this article was comprehensive and trenchant.

But how did Du's theory of reconciliation of "old and new" become the key trigger for the "debate between Eastern and Western civilizations"? The most critical point is that the premise of the article attributed China's crisis to the "mind of the modern man" and not to tradition. Based on this premise, Du listed four factors as symptoms of the modern Chinese crisis, namely "the loss of national integrity," "bankruptcy of the spiritual realm," "strongman politics" and "pragmatism in the education world." These four factors were interrelated and mutually reinforcing. Among them "loss of national integrity" was the root. Explaining, Du argued that "modern thinking develops but loses its unity. From the perspective of differentiation we could call this progress, but from the perspective of integration, this is without doubt regress." This subtly described how parliamentary politics, multiparty competition and freedom of speech were either hampered by sectional interests or produced fighting for the sake of fighting; they gathered together people's opinions but could not form a consensus of public opinion. This is the crisis of modern democratic politics.

"Bankruptcy of the spiritual realm" referred to modern man's obsession with "material life, oblivious to other needs, and devoid of any idealism," while the few so-called "men with ideals were no more than falsely couching their tactics for competing for power and extravagance. Modern "idealism" was evidently just a manifestation of material interests; "idealism" itself lacked a transcendent character and became a manipulative tool for opportunists, incapable of forging a public consensus. Due to the decline of righteousness and the public will, the "'might is right' style of politics," or "autocracy," resulted. Chinese "Qin-style imperial rule," European "pan-Germanism" and the strongman politics of the republican era were in reality products of a lawless and discordant time. Corresponding to the disparate factors above was "pragmatism in the educational realm," in which a pragmatic approach to education abandoned the classic tradition and thus spiritual life and the value of life were emphasized. Instead it "buried" education in "material life . . . Dedicating education to pragmatism, or an idealism where living exists only for the sake of living, was nothing but an idealism with no ideals."[172]

Practically every intellectual in these various schools recognized the above-mentioned phenomena at the time. The difference was that Du attributed this situation to the "confused mind of modern man," while Chen considered it a relapse of an old Chinese malady. According to Du's diagnosis, the cause of China's illness was too much emphasis on "differentiation" and too little on "integration," favoring "materialism" and rejecting "spirituality," emphasizing "pragmatism" and eliding "quality"; the strongman politics in the political realm were a product of this modern disease. Importing Western civilization would not cure this illness, because Western civilization itself "is mired in confusion and dissonance, and is urgently looking for a remedy." Western concepts were a blend of the Greek and Hebrew traditions and lacked an inherent uniformity. Therefore, "the solution would be to integrate our existing civilization, to clarify what is systematic and to correct what is wrong." In short, Du argued that what was needed was to skillfully reorganize what was pertinent in Chinese civilization, selectively absorb Western civilization, "and if in the future we can integrate Western thinking and reassess world civilization, then not only would we be saved, but the salvation of the whole world would be found."[173] In other words, all the "isms" that had been imported into China hastened China's disintegration and the discordance of the Chinese spirit, and all the paths to salvation lay in the "integration" of Chinese civilization.

If we place what Du regarded to be the two central issues of civilization, "integration" and "differentiation," into his analysis of the European war and the republican crisis, we can readily see their close relationship with the political judgments he made on several levels, on such as issues of centralization and decentralization, overarching unity and division, traditional polity and republicanism, political criticism and freedom of speech. The difference lies in the fact that these binaries were basically concrete, while the categories: "integration" and "differentiation" are more abstract and universal. Du used this basic premise to encompass the different orientations of Chinese and Western civilizations; his political intention in employing old-new and East/West binaries as markers to formulate the theory of the reconciliation of civilizations was very clear.

Chen fired off seven questions to contest this objective: Did Chinese civilization flourish before or after Confucian unification? Could the unity of Chinese civilization be defined only by Confucianism or did it encompass multiple schools of philosophy? Which of the two was better, a unified Europe of the ancient era or the competitive West of today? Was the Chinese spiritual realm bankrupt before the infusion of Western learning? Under the conditions of a republic, would observing the ruler-subject loyalty and the three bonds and five relationships be a "subversion of republicanism"? Did this author, who lamented that "there is no strong leader in China today," rejoice during the Hongxian monarchy? And finally, was ancient spiritual life truly faithful to the three bonds and five relationships, and could the materialistic Western civilization also possess spiritual civilization?[174] These questions were very pointed, and, except for the slightly contrived sixth question, all hit their mark.

Amid the universal crisis of the European war, the Russian Revolution and modern capitalism, the "debate between Eastern and Western civilizations" was in the end a grand debate on how to assess the modern crisis and the future path of China. Regardless of how it unfolded, the debate would ultimately be decided by the subject who forged this path. In "China's new life," Du argued:

> There are only two ways to find China's new life: 1) generate a new power to eliminate the old power; 2) reform the old power to create new power. Other countries in the world such as France and the United States received a new life by way of the former process, while Japan and Germany obtained a new lease on life from the latter process. Generating new power is extremely difficult . . . but it is even more difficult to eliminate the old power . . . thus an easier, more profitable and efficient way would be to reconcile old and new powers in order to forge a new power.

Eastern Miscellany was unparalleled in its coverage of the world situation and China's predicament but ironically it could not provide an answer as to who would "reconcile old and new powers in order to forge a new power." If politicians, party members, bureaucrats and academics were all lost in "confusion," could they be expected to attain Buddhahood through self-cultivation?[175] If the tolling of the bell of "self-awareness" did not resonate in their minds, who would be able to stir them?

I believe that the divergence between *New Youth* and *Eastern Miscellany* cannot be completely explained by the concepts of East versus West and old versus new. Both periodicals critically assessed the "old civilization" of the eighteenth and nineteenth centuries (from their political model to their economic formation) and both embraced the "new civilization" (socialism) of the twentieth century, but they differed in their political orientation. With its foregrounding of "youth" from the beginning, *Youth* magazine clearly advocated for the creativity of the new generation to lead the way in political and social transformation. In place of the old historical consciousness of *Eastern Miscellany*, which had already run its course, *Youth* substituted a type of "youthful philosophy." The framework of "reconciling civilizations" posited Eastern and Western civilizations and old and new ideologies as objective constructs. Du carefully outlined the mechanics of the process but had no suggestions for who would carry out the selection and reconciliation, leaving behind a circular methodology without a subject.

Meanwhile the New Culture Movement engaged a "movement" to redefine "culture," and used "culture" to create a "movement." It called forth a subject in motion, and a politics for this subject in motion. Its passionate critique of tradition and its call for a new political subject were equally important. Du believed that new politics could only be born from existing history and civilization, while *New Youth* maintained that new politics could only emerge from a historical rupture. At the moment when Du quietly receded from the stage of *Eastern Miscellany*, the clamor of the May Fourth student movement still reverberated all over China, and a new form of politics was ready to take the stage. This new form of politics emerged from the rejection of politics and the residue of the "war of ideas." Culture and morality were at the heart of the new politics. This was modern China's first "transformation of culture and politics," and its echoes resonated throughout the "short twentieth century."

3

From People's War to the War of International Alliance (1949–53): The War to Resist U.S. Aggression and Aid Korea from the Perspective of Twentieth-Century Chinese History[1]

At the sixty-year anniversary of the Korean War[2] armistice, the division of the Korean Peninsula and the separation of Taiwan from mainland China both persist in this post–Cold War era of so-called globalization. This state of separation also manifests itself in historical memory: South Korea, North Korea, the United States, Japan, mainland China and Taiwan each have different memories and historical interpretations of the war. If we compare the War Memorial of Korea in Seoul and the Fatherland Liberation War Victorious Museum in Pyongyang, while at the same time referring to the narrative of the Korean War in mainland China and the almost deliberate consigning of the Korean War to oblivion in the United States, we perceive very different interpretations of this event. The war is called the "Fatherland Liberation War" by North Korea, the "6.25 War" (for June 25, the day the war broke out) or "*Hanzhan*" (Korean War) by South Korea, and the "Korean War" by the United States. China entered the war on October 8, 1950, after U.S. forces had not only landed at Inchon but also advanced toward the Yalu River, and therefore called it the "War to Resist U.S. Aggression and Aid Korea" (*kang Mei yuan Chao zhanzheng*).

The politics of naming implicates the politics of memory. Chinese army units confronted the UN Command forces composed of combat soldiers from sixteen countries as well as South Korea, and led by the United States. Compared with the Vietnam War, memories of the Korean War in the United States remain vague, almost approaching a sort of conscious oblivion. According to recent research, Japan, too, secretly participated in the war[3]: "Between October 2 and December 12, 1950, 46 Japanese minesweepers, one large 'guinea pig' vessel used for activating pressure mines, and 1,200 former naval personnel were employed in operations at Korean ports—Wonsan, Kunsan, Inchon, Haiju, and Chinampo. Japanese forces swept 327 kilometers of channels and anchorages extending 607 square miles."[4] Aside from logistical support, thirty of the forty-seven tank landing ships used in the Inchon landing were manned by Japanese crews.[5] In July 2013, the South Korean government declined a proposal by Japan to partic-ipate in activities in Seoul commemorating the armistice. The Korean Armistice Agreement was signed on July 27, 1953, by North Korea, China and the UN Command represented by the United States. Months earlier, on April 12, the South Korean president Syngman Rhee had opposed peace talks and claimed he would lead South Korean military forces to march north on their own; he also passed a resolution on April 21 that the Republic of Korea (ROK) would move north and unify the country. Rhee did not sign the armistice. Another voice opposing the peace talks and advocating for escalation of the war was Chiang Kai-shek, whose regime survived in Taiwan under the aegis of the United States. These two details are rarely mentioned these days, while it is rather routine to criticize Mao Zedong for cross-ing the 38th parallel.

The Korean War has been one of the most active fields of historical research in China during the past twenty years. The main approach of this scholarship has been to situate the War to Resist U.S. Aggression and Aid Korea within the framework of historical studies of the Cold War under supposedly non-ideological terms, aligning the Korean War and in particular the history of China's intervention in the war with scholarly research based on Soviet, U.S. and Chinese archives as well as memoirs of those directly involved, all in accordance with the new norms of contemporary social sciences and historical studies. While these studies come to diverse conclusions, we can perceive an overtone of nationalism in their research methodology; Korean War studies have clearly shifted away from such antagonistic categories as capitalism and socialism, imperialism and internationalism, toward discussions of the historical significance of this war from the stand-point of relations between nations and national interests. Writers who support the War to Resist U.S. Aggression and Aid Korea emphasize that it was a war to establish New China (the People's Republic) as a new state (*liguo zhanzheng*), while those critical of the war argue that it caused not only tremendous casualties but accelerated and consolidated the formation of the Cold War structure of Sino-Soviet alliance and Sino-U.S. confrontation resulting in the loss for mainland China of the possibility of reclaiming Taiwan. But while the Cold War order was structured by many different interests, within which nations and states played an important role, this does not mean that all of the hot and cold wars of this period should be measured by the yardstick of national or state interests.

This chapter examines current mainland Chinese research on the Korean War and then situates and evaluates the War to Resist U.S. Aggression and Aid Korea in the context of the preceding revolutions and wars of twentieth-century China. This context gives us an "internal perspective" which can provide insight into the formation and implementation of the political decisions related to this momentous event. The entanglement, juxtaposition and confrontation of the dynamics revealed by this perspective as well as other perspectives constituted the forces that gave rise to the politics of this period. When we attempt to situate political decisions within their historical circumstances, we cannot (contrary to the view of some social scientists who regard themselves as occupying an objective vantage point) exclude from discussion the principles, values and confrontational politics that shaped the actions of people in that period. As the structure of internal division, separation and confrontation still persists in Northeast Asia today, it is imperative that we search for a political energy that can transcend it. It is with this motive that we cannot consider the war only in the context of national interests but must explore its course within the historical context in which political decisions were shaped. By doing so, we can determine what the revolution and wars of twentieth-century China offer us today.

The Historical Circumstances of the Korean War: "To the Advantage of China, Korea, the East and the World"

"Resist U.S. Agression and Aid Korea; Protect Our Homes and Defend the Country" and the Significance of New China

Declassified archives and memoirs show that when the Korean War broke out neither China nor the United States was fully prepared. This fact does not mean, however, that the outbreak of the war was accidental. The People's Republic of China was established in October 1949, and in September 1950, less than a year later, China gave clear indication that it was willing to join the war.[6] At a time when China was still recovering from an extended period of warfare and when countless pressing domestic issues were awaiting attention, the dominant opinion within the Chinese Communist Party (CCP) was against joining the war. In 1949, it was considered more important to first mop up the remnant forces of the Guomindang (Chinese Nationalist Party, henceforward GMD), to transform the functions of army and party organs at all levels, to shift the focus of work from the countryside to urban areas, to regularize the People's Liberation Army (PLA), to promote education, to solve the problems of the minority nationalities and border areas and of course to rebuild the country that had been devastated by a series of wars. At the second meeting of the first Chinese People's Political Consultative Conference (CPPCC) in June 1950, the urgent need to carry out land reform on a national scale was stressed repeatedly.[7] Mao Zedong warned the Party: "Don't hit out in all directions."[8] When the Korean War broke out, the main force of the PLA was moving toward Xinjiang and Tibet and fighting with the GMD on the southeast coastline. In short, New China was not prepared to join the war.

But this is not to say that the outbreak of the Korean War had nothing to do with China. With regard to China's relations with Korea, during the period of Japanese colonial rule the resistance on the Korean peninsula was from very early on tightly connected with the Chinese People's Liberation Army. In May 1949, Mao Zedong agreed to transfer to North Korea three Korean Divisions that were part of the Fourth Field Army. Two of them arrived in North Korea in July 1949 and another reorganized division arrived with an additional regiment in March and April of 1950.[9] This was an extension of the relationship between the Chinese Revolution and neighboring areas and essentially a response by Chinese revolutionaries to the North–South confrontation on the Korean Peninsula. From the perspective of the United States strategy in Asia, the Korean War was from the beginning connected with the issue of the Taiwan Strait. Two days after the Korean War broke out, Truman brought up Taiwan, Vietnam and the Philippines during his statement on the plan to enlarge the war. Truman also directly targeted China: "the occupation of Formosa by Communist forces would be a direct threat to the security of the Pacific area and to United States forces performing their lawful and necessary functions in that area. Accordingly I have ordered the 7th Fleet to prevent any attack on Formosa."[10]

At the beginning of October 1950, Mao decided to enter the war. This decision was based not on who had started the war but on his judgment of how the war was progressing and impacting the structure of political forces on the global scale. He sent a telegram to Zhou Enlai, who was on a visit to the Soviet Union, stating that a proactive policy of joining the war would be "to the advantage of China, Korea, the East and the world."[11] The slogan "Resist U.S. Aggression, Aid Korea; Protect Our Home and Defend the Country" accurately summarized how joining the war would benefit China and Korea.

After landing in Inchon, U.S. forces rapidly advanced north, approaching China's border and threatening its Northeast. North Korea was in imminent danger of military collapse. China's dispatch of soldiers provided clear support for the North Koreans. Then Director of the CIA Walter Smith sent a memorandum to President Truman presenting two probable reasons why China had crossed into Korea: to guard the northeast border from UN forces and to protect the Shuifeng Hydropower Station and other hydroelectric facilities on the Yalu River.[12] On November 10, 1950, France raised a proposal at the UN calling for the withdrawal of Chinese forces from Korea with a guarantee that Chinese borders would not be violated. This proposal was supported by six countries, including the United States and the United Kingdom, but was vetoed by the Soviet Union. These facts provide fodder for recent historical narratives arguing that China, having misapprehended the situation, entered the war because of this Soviet veto. If the United States did not plan to invade China, what meaning could there be to the slogan "Protect Our Homes and Defend the Country"?

Two explanations can be offered here. First, neither a few telegrams between the U.S. president and other government branches, nor resolutions passed at a UN that had been manipulated if not completely dominated by the United States, can give insight into all of the complex processes at play leading up to the war. Historically speaking, neither the Manchurian Incident nor the Marco Polo Bridge Incident engineered by Japan in 1931 and 1937 were staged at the direct order of the emperor or the cabinet of Japan; rather, they resulted from the decisions of military commanders at the front (and today there are those who continue to defend Japanese wartime policy on this basis). Bruce Cumings has pointed out that U.S. intervention in the Korean War and U.S. diplomatic policy making was often generated by a "decision matrix" and not directed by any individual.[13] Obviously one or two telegrams or declassified documents cannot definitively determine whether the United States would have pressed forward to the Yalu River or attacked China. It is impossible to predict the sudden changes in military conditions in Korea and on the Sino Korean border that could have resulted if no effective response had been carried out when MacArthur ordered his units north. In fact, before France raised its proposal at the UN, the U.S. Air Force on November 8 began bombing the bridges on the Yalu River. During the bombing, U.S. aircraft "violated Chinese borders and bombed Chinese towns and villages at the border."[14] Even earlier, starting from August 27, 1950, U.S. aircraft crossed the Sino-Korean border numerous times and "strafed and bombed Chinese cities, towns and villages, killed and wounded Chinese peaceful inhabitants, and damaged Chinese properties."[15] The U.S. Navy also stopped a Chinese merchant ship on the open sea. The incursions and attacks by American aircraft persisted even after the Chinese government protested to the United States and appealed to the UN.[16]

Second, China's position was not merely that it should not be attacked by the United States, but that the U.S. forces should not have crossed the 38th parallel. On October 3, 1950, Zhou Enlai summoned the Indian ambassador to China, Kavalam Panikkar, and requested that he inform the United States and the United Kingdom that if the American army should cross the 38th parallel, China would send forces to Korea. But apparently the United States did not realize that China was firmly committed to this position. On October 7, the United States bypassed the Security Council, in which the Soviet Union had veto power; it used the General Assembly instead to pass a resolution to occupy North Korea and unify Korea under its leadership. The next day, American troops crossed the 38th parallel. Mao Zedong emphasized that if China did not send forces to Korea, the circumstances would immediately become difficult for Northeast China: The entire military force in the Northeast would become tied to the border area and China would lose control of the supply of electricity in southern Manchuria. Underlying this judgment was the determination that New China should absolutely not be cowed by foreign military threats.

While the military and political bottom line for China was not to allow the U.S. Army to cross the 38th parallel, the aim was not simply to protect the Shuifeng Hydropower Station and other Yalu River facilities. In a sense, China's position had something in common with the U.S. strategy in Korea: In truth, Mao Zedong did not regard the 38th parallel as an impassable demarcation line, and stated after the first two military campaigns of the Chinese army forces in Korea that "the 38th parallel must be crossed."[17] On December 13, 1950, the United States and the United Kingdom requested that Chinese troops stop at the 38th parallel. On December 7, a day after the People's Volunteer Army (PVA) retook Pyongyang, Indian Ambassador Panikkar presented a memorandum to Zhang Hanfu, China's vice minister of foreign affairs, describing a joint proposal by thirteen Asian and African countries to hold an armistice at the 38th parallel.[18] Zhou Enlai retorted by asking why these thirteen countries had not spoken up when the U.S. forces crossed the 38th parallel, and why they did not openly request all foreign forces to withdraw from Korea or condemn the invasion of Korea and China by the United States.[19] On the next day, when the UN passed a resolution requesting that both sides cease military actions, Truman proclaimed a state of national emergency in the United States. China and the United States were already engaged in a war that had not been openly declared, and both began nationwide mobilizations by the end of 1950.

Hence there were two motivations behind Mao's decision to cross the 38th parallel. First was to shake the determination of the United States and the United Kingdom. After China's Fourth Campaign (from January 25 to April 21, 1951), American forces broke through the 38th parallel again and were planning to land behind Chinese troops. Militarily speaking, if Mao had not decided to cross the 38th parallel, it would have been much more difficult to shake the morale of the UN Command forces and the American forces in particular: They would have been allowed a brief respite before launching another offensive, and the Chinese forces would have lost the opportunity to rest and reorganize afforded by defeating the enemy. Second, when the UN forces had been defeated and were withdrawing, the United States manipulated the UN into passing a resolution requesting that both sides stop at the 38th parallel. Mao Zedong regarded the UN of that time as little more than an "international machine" under the control of the United States and acting on its behalf during the war; thus, in his opinion, China was not obliged to accept any UN resolutions or strictures. In this sense, crossing the 38th parallel was not only a refusal to acknowledge the boundary set by American hegemony but a military response to its political offensive. The U.S. Army's defeat in this campaign proved decisive for MacArthur: When he subsequently proposed in April 1951 to bomb Chinese territory and arm GMD forces to bring them into the Korean War, he was quickly removed from his post by President Truman, who feared that MacArthur's proposal might result in a full-scale war with China. Truman's decision was deeply influenced by the recent U.S. defeat in Korea.

China was an Asian country freed from a fate of servitude only after a prolonged, arduous and eventually triumphant revolution. It was not a powerful country in the conventional sense, but it symbolized the promise of a state completely different from those of the imperialist era, a stance different from all historical countries or dynasties, and a democratic socialist country where the people would rule. Mao explicitly linked the Korean War with the Chinese Revolution in the speech "The Korean War situation and our policy" given on September 5, 1950. He wrote that "the Chinese Revolution has a global quality—it was the first education given to the people of the world from the East. The second is the Korean War."[20]

On the anniversary of the Chinese army's entrance into Korea in October 1951, Mao spoke specifically about the Korean War in his opening remarks at the third meeting of the first Chinese People's Political Consultative Conference. He pointed out that, above all, the war was defensive—if the United States had not occupied Taiwan, invaded the Democratic People's Republic of Korea (DPRK) and attacked the northeast border of China, the Chinese people would not have engaged with American troops. Second, after this attack by American invaders, the Chinese people could not but raise the banner of resisting the invasion. This was thus an effort to strike back against an unjust war with a just war. Third, the Korean problem could be resolved peacefully, and as long as the American government was willing to address the issues on just and reasonable terms, the Korean armistice talks would succeed.[21]

Mao emphasized that if there had been no Taiwan problem and if the United States had not invaded Korea and threatened the Chinese border, China would not have joined the war. One historian has argued that if Chinese army forces had entered Korea before the Battle of Pusan became serious, the United States would have lost the opportunity to land at Inchon.[22] This argument is identical to MacArthur's in October 1950 when he conferred with Truman on Wake Island about whether China or the Soviet Union would send troops to Korea: China, he maintained, had missed its best opportunity to join the war and hence would not send troops. Militarily speaking, this judgment was valid to some degree. But this assessment of the progress of the war from a purely military perspective differed greatly from Mao's grasp of the conflict.

For perspective on this, we should consider the course the United States took during the war. At the beginning of the war, the United States used the North's intrusion into the South as justification for its own intervention, which it portrayed as a police action undertaken to enforce international law. Early on, this legitimizing framework limited the United States' military activities. For example, when the U.S. Senate was debating the issue, both senators and government spokesmen all agreed that the president's actions could be restricted to the south of the 38th parallel, such that U.S. forces could not cross this temporary demarcation line to pursue or attack North Korean forces or positions.[23] But with the Inchon landing this framework was set aside, and the U.S. ambassador to the United Nations, Warren Austin, declared that "the aggressor's forces should not be permitted to have refuge behind an imaginary line."[24]

One might say that with this act, the self-legitimization strategy used by the United States for its entrance onto the Korean Peninsula was doubly undermined. The charge that a Korean army moving from the north to the south of the peninsula to engage in an internal war of national unification constituted "aggression" was itself already a tenuous claim. Acheson had at the beginning of the war rejected unification as a U.S. war aim, apparently implying that the intervention was similar to a state's domestic law enforcement aimed at stopping a crime and restoring the "status quo ante." Crossing the 38th parallel not only shattered the United States' own framework of "limited war," but "now it [became] the American goal . . . to unify Korea by force of arms and create a new (democratic) government. And that required not limited attacks within the borders of North Korea, but the conquest of the entire country."[25] If the United States interpreted the North's move south as "aggression," then how could it explain setting aside its own aim of restoring the "status quo ante" through its actions during the war?

From the moment United States forces crossed the 38th parallel, the United States' Korean War had already made "regime change" its ultimate aim. From the perspective of its own original promises and the permission it obtained through its manipulation of the United Nations, the war then lost whatever sense of justness it could originally claim. Although the United States' action of breaking its own promise of "limited war" again obtained authorization from the United Nations, this did not give the war any more legitimacy, but only demonstrated again that the United Nations was an institution subject to unilateral manipulation. In contrast to this, after the U.S. military crossed the 38th parallel, China's entry into the war not only had justification as opposition to aggression, but it also had justification within international law. Mao Zedong was not, contrary to the way he is portrayed by some historians, completely ignorant of international law. In fact, the opposite was true. During the War of Resistance against Japan, he had already begun an intense study of Western theories of war and international law, and he was able to make unique use of them. Mao's flexible diplomatic struggles at the beginning, during and after the end of the war clearly demonstrate the political understanding of war he shared with Zhou Enlai and other leaders, as well as their adept use of their knowledge of war and international law. The Five Principles of Peaceful Coexistence raised at the end of 1953 were based on the foundation of this knowledge and understanding and demonstrated that Chinese leaders were more able than U.S. leaders to use the tenets of international law to establish just principles for war and diplomacy.

The consolidation of New China contained in itself an opportunity to break through the Cold War framework. First, while the birth of the

Soviet Union after the October Revolution was not able to prevent the three imperialist nations of Germany, Italy and Japan from hatching an ambition to dominate the world, Mao believed that China confronted a completely different situation: "the founding of the Soviet Union, the founding of the People's Republic of China, the founding of the People's Democracies, the consolidation and unity of the two great countries of China and the Soviet Union on the basis of the Treaty of Friendship, Mutual Assistance and Alliance, the consolidation and unity of the entire camp for peace and democracy, and the profound sympathy that the broad masses of peaceful people of all countries in the world hold for this great camp have proclaimed once and for all the end of the era of imperialist hegemony over the world."[26] Second, in the middle of the twentieth century a new global configuration was emerging—one that had never before appeared in world history—and the success of the Chinese Revolution helped catalyze the anticolonial process unfolding throughout Asia.

The goal of this process was to establish peace by fighting imperialism, and war was one of the means of doing so. In Mao's words, "War is transformed into peace."[27] This strategy was developed during the wars leading to the Chinese Revolution. Before the War of Resistance against Japan broke out on a full scale, Mao had pointed out that there was only one way to extinguish war—"to oppose war with war, to oppose counter-revolutionary war with revolutionary war, to oppose national counter-revolutionary war with national revolutionary war, and to oppose counter-revolutionary class war with revolutionary class war."[28] The Korean War fought against a war of invasion with a war against invasion. The political demarcation between just war and unjust war lay exactly here. For Mao, New China itself was the factor allowing for the consolidation of that "great domestic and international unity"[29] that differentiated the War to Resist U.S. Aggression and Aid Korea from all previous wars that had taken place during the process of the Chinese Revolution. Victory in the War to Resist U.S. Aggression and Aid Korea would provide ample testimony as to the significance of Mao's proclamation of the founding of New China at Tiananmen Gate on October 1, 1949.

The Korean War and the Relationship
between China and the Soviet Union

During the past decade, research on the Korean War in mainland China has undergone a shift, increasingly abandoning the perspective of internationalism and adopting a more simplistic nationalist framework. A related tendency has been a shift in focus from the confrontation between China and the United States to greater scrutiny of Sino-Soviet relations. Representative arguments include:

Stalin and Kim Il-sung conspired behind Mao Zedong's back to plan the war, and tricked China into joining the conflict.[30]

The Soviet Union allowed the DPRK to launch the war for unification because it had lost confidence in its ability to keep Northeast China under its own control, and China sent troops to Korea to prevent the Soviet Union from using the Americans as an excuse to send more soldiers to keep control of Northeast China;[31] others argue that the Soviet Union supported the DPRK's military offensive in an effort to prevent Mao from becoming Asia's Tito.[32]

The Soviet Union suffered a major strategic loss from the war: It not only lost control of its interests in Northeast China, but it also provided technical support for the establishment of 156 industries in China, laying the foundation for New China's own independent industrialization.[33]

The Korean War hastened the signing of the Sino-Soviet Treaty and ruined an opportunity to improve Sino-U.S. relations.[34]

To analyze these arguments, one would naturally ask to what extent China's relationship with the Soviet Union influenced its decision to enter the war. Mao argued that China's entrance into the conflict was not only beneficial to China and Korea, but also to "the East" and to "the world." These two categories cannot be understood from within the framework of national and state interests. "The East" referred to the Eastern Camp in the Cold War division of the East versus West conflict, specifically the socialist camp with the Soviet Union as its center; the Sino-Soviet Alliance was one of the core components of this category of "the East." "The world" referred to the oppressed nations of the world that were attempting to liberate themselves from imperialist domination. From the founding of New China to the War to Resist U.S. Aggression and Aid Korea and after, the core of Chinese foreign policy was its alliance with the Soviet Union and Eastern European countries. This was not a new policy, but a continuation of alliances that had already been consolidated during the process of the Chinese Revolution.

In June 1950, Mao touched on this issue in his closing remarks at the second meeting of the first CPPCC. He remarked that China should have an ambitious goal: After the people of China were ready and when conditions were ripe, China could unhurriedly and appropriately enter a new era of socialism. He proposed that in order to accomplish this great goal, China and the Soviet Union, all people's democracies and all peaceful democratic powers of the world should unite, while domestically the united front of all nations, classes, democratic parties, people's organizations and all patriotic people who embraced democracy should be consolidated. That is to say, although the Korean War facilitated their military cooperation, China and the Soviet Union did not become allies because of the war. The alliance between these two countries and other socialist countries was the outcome of an important set of events. From the time of its founding, and especially after the defeat of the Great Revolution (1925–7), the Chinese Communist Party's relationship with international communist movement and the Soviet Union was well known to all—there was no need to wait until the Korean War for such an alliance to appear. The American preference for and support of the GMD during the Chinese Civil War only further solidified the alliance of New China with the Soviet Union.

Mao opposed the military interference of the United States and its henchmen in the Korean Peninsula and remained loyal to the socialist camp.[35] His discussion of the war focused on two aspects. The argument that the War to Resist U.S. Aggression and Aid Korea was beneficial to China and Korea was directed at convincing the people of China, and particularly the national bourgeoisie, to support the effort. The idea that the war would benefit the East and the world was product of Mao's assessment of the world order as a whole, and of the relatively new appearance within that order of two camps, the East and the West, with China belonging to the former.

Five months before the Korean War broke out, in January 1950, the Soviet Union announced its boycott of the United Nations Security Council (UNSC) to protest the failure of its proposal to allow the People's Republic of China a seat in the United Nations. It was thus absent from the Security Council deliberations on the Korean War on June 25 and after. Some scholars have interpreted this absence as a ploy by the Soviet Union, such that without its veto power on the UNSC, the UN would adopt a U.S.-directed resolution organizing a UN army to enter the Korean Civil War.[36] This interpretation seems to be supported by Andrei Gromyko's memoir, which states that Stalin refused to let Soviet representatives participate in the UNSC and deploy the Soviet Union's veto power. It is not entirely unreasonable to suspect that a scheme was in place; at the beginning of 1950 Stalin and Kim Il-sung met in secret and did not inform Mao Zedong, who was in Moscow at the time of their meeting.

But if the Soviet Union supported the unification war launched by the North, why did it intentionally let the UN Command forces enter the Korean War legally? Russian scholars have made public an archival document (a telegram sent by Stalin to Klement Gottwald, president of Czechoslovakia) giving a relatively convincing piece of evidence concerning Stalin's objectives. In this telegram, Stalin explained four aims of the Soviet boycott:

> First, to show the solidarity and union of the Soviet Union and New China; second, to highlight the absurdity and stupidity of American policy since it only recognizes the clownish GMD as the representative of China in the UNSC and refuses to let the true representative of China enter the UNSC; third, to render illegal whatever resolutions are passed in the UNSC with two major countries absent; fourth, to give the U.S. a free hand and use its majority vote in the UNSC to make more mistakes so that its true colors will be revealed to the public.[37]

The fourth point referred to the Korean War. Stalin's letter also recounted,

> After we withdrew from the UNSC, the U.S. has been mired in its military intervention in Korea, damaging its military prestige and moral authority. Now few honest persons will not suspect that the U.S. is acting as an aggressor and invader in Korea. Militarily it is not as powerful as it

claims to be. In addition, obviously the attention of the U.S. is diverted from Europe to the Far East. Does this not give us an advantage from the perspective of the global balance of power? It surely does.[37]

Further developments more or less confirmed Stalin's prediction. After the UNSC resolutions were passed, Truman ordered American troops in the Far East to give complete support to the Syngman Rhee regime. He also sent the Seventh Fleet to patrol the Taiwan Strait in order to prevent any possible attack by the PRC. From Stalin's perspective, the attention of the United States had indeed shifted from Europe to the Far East, but from America's perspective, its intervention in Far Eastern affairs and its struggle with the USSR over spheres of power in this area had begun long before 1950. The absence of the USSR from the UNSC does not seem to have been a decisive factor in American intervention in Korea.

Because of the Soviet Union's special role within the Eastern Camp, the question of how to distinguish what elements of its behavior constituted the self-interested actions of a hegemon and what constituted its political leadership within the Cold War political order remains an issue requiring further analysis. From the Stalin to the Brezhnev periods, the Soviet Union took up the great responsibility of internationalism; yet at the same time there also existed different degrees, different forms and even different essential types of hegemonism in its behavior. In the Sino-Soviet relationship, the two parties first cooperated, then split and finally openly debated with each other; the two countries politically cooperated, clashed and were eventually involved in military confrontation. The course of this relationship was exceedingly complex, and it requires concrete investigation along different threads. After World War II, the Soviet Union had a prominent presence in Northeast China, which it had helped liberate from the Japanese, and it jointly administered several aspects of the region with China from 1945. Various voices in the West, and especially in the United States, repeatedly declared that the USSR would eventually annex the region (which it still referred to as Manchuria); the U.S. Department of State repeatedly made this claim from late 1949 to 1950 before the Korean War broke out. Such claims are similar to those reports in British newspapers that Mao was placed under house arrest during his visit to Moscow. Should such claims be taken as "facts" in historical research? Rather than accord these claims the status of discoveries of twenty-first-century historians, it would be better to regard them as the inventions of U.S. Secretary of State Dean Acheson and strategic contrivances of the American government produced to estrange China from the Soviet Union and further its own hegemony. After New China was established, China and the Soviet Union held a series of talks over the interests of the Soviet Union in Northeast China, including the Chinese Eastern Railway and the port of Lüshun (or Port Arthur). The Korean War accelerated the process of China taking full administrative control of the region; this does not mean, however, that without the Korean War, the Northeast would have been annexed by the USSR. To illustrate this point I will provide two points of refutation here—two familiar instances well known due to lucid observations by Mao.

On January 20, 1950, Hu Qiaomu, Director of the Central People's Government News Office, issued an interview to refute precisely this allegation. On the same day, the Xinhua News Agency published a commentary drafted by Mao Zedong—"Our Answer to Acheson's Fabrications"—that criticized the long speech given by Acheson before the National Press Club on January 12, 1950. Mao singled out two of Acheson's claims in particular. On the relationship of the United States with Asian countries, Acheson had remarked,

> Our interests have been parallel to the interests of the people of Asia . . . [Americans' belief that it would not be in their interest for China to be controlled by a foreign power] was not contrary to the interests of the people of China. There was not conflict but parallelism in that interest . . . And so from the time of the announcement of the open door policy through the 9-power treaty to the very latest resolution of the General Assembly of the United Nations, we have stated that principle and we believe it.[39]

Second, on the presence of the Soviet Union in China, Acheson claimed that

> the Soviet Union is detaching the northern provinces of China from China and is attaching them to the Soviet Union. This process is complete in outer Mongolia. It is nearly complete in Manchuria, and I am sure that in inner Mongolia and in Sinkiang there are very happy reports coming from Soviet agents to Moscow. This is what is going on. It is the

detachment of these whole areas, vast areas—populated by Chinese—
the detachment of these areas from China and their attachment to the
Soviet Union . . . I should like to suggest at any rate that this fact that the
Soviet Union is taking the four northern provinces of China is the single
most significant, most important fact, in the relation of any foreign power
with Asia . . . What does this mean for us? It means something very,
very significant.[40]

Mao retorted that the basic policy of the United States was to infiltrate
China by all possible means and turn it into an American colony. His
supporting evidence included not only American support for the GMD
regime during the Chinese Civil War from 1945 to 1949 but also the
American intervention in the Taiwan Strait. On January 14, two days?
after Acheson gave his speech, ITAR-TASS reported that Angus
Ward—former American consul in Shenyang, who had been arrested,
tried and deported by China—had spoken with officials from the State
Department upon his return to the United States. When he met with
journalists after the conversation, Ward stated that the Soviet Union
managed the railway in the Northeast jointly with China according to
treaty rights, but he "had not seen any evidence of Soviet control over
Manchuria" and "had not observed any indications of Soviet efforts to
incorporate Manchuria." When he was asked if Manchurian communists were under the control of Beijing, Ward reported that "all
Communist governments exercise highly centralised control and as far
as he knew, 'Manchuria is part of Communist China.'"[41] Mao
commented sarcastically, "People can see for themselves what has transpired over in the Western Hemisphere. One person says the Soviet
Union has annexed Manchuria. Another person says he never saw such
a thing. Both of these persons are none other than well-known officials
of the U.S. State Department."[42]

 Although the Soviet Union hoped to maintain some influence in
Northeast China for a relatively long period, the presumption that China
would lose the Northeast area as a result is entirely groundless. The
Sino-Soviet relationship was one of the most significant relationships
between great powers after World War II, but it differed from all previous relationships between great powers. This was a relationship between
New China and the Soviet Union, a relationship within the newly emergent socialist camp. This is not to say this no longer counted as a

relationship between countries, but rather to emphasize the fact that the international politics of this era were characterized by connotations and qualities that differed from both earlier and later periods. Relations between socialist countries contained an internationalist element: The Sino-Soviet relationship was not only a relationship between China and the Soviet Union, but a relationship within the Eastern Camp as well. Generally speaking, the Sino-Soviet split manifested its first signs at the Twentieth Congress of the Communist Party of the Soviet Union and became known to the world as the debates moved out into the open. According to declassified CIA archives, American intelligence services still maintained even during Sino-Soviet debate that the alliance between China and the USSR had not truly fallen apart. All things considered, this judgment by the United States was rooted in its experience and understanding gained during the Korean War that the relationship between states in the socialist camp was not simply one between sovereign states in general but instead focused on interparty relations, with ideology and values playing significant roles.

One of the preconditions for China's entrance into the war was the support of the Soviet Union; this was not, however, the ultimate determinant. In his telegram to Zhou Enlai on October 13, 1950, Mao Zedong stated that "the third and the fourth issues" were not certain. The third issue referred to the telegram sent to the Chinese Communist Party and signed jointly by Stalin and Zhou, which promised that the Soviet Union would provide the necessary armaments such as aircraft, artillery and tanks. Mao's question was whether such armaments would be rented or bought from the Soviet Union. He hoped renting instead of purchase would be possible, as New China had just been established and it urgently needed funds for economic, cultural, military and political projects. If available funds that were already in short supply had to be spent on the purchase of armaments, it could lead to the slowing down of economic recovery and to opposition from the national bourgeoisie and petty bourgeoisie; "the unity of the majority of the country" would dissolve as a result.[43] The significance of "preserving the unity of the majority of the country" was also illustrated by a telegram from Mao to the Tianjin Municipal Federation of Industry and Commerce on December 2, 1950.[44] The federation had organized a march at the end of November and telegrammed Mao on November 30 to affirm its support for the patriotic war to "Resist U.S. Aggression, Aid Korea; Protect Our

Homes and Defend the Country." It is worth noting that by the start of the war, nationwide mobilization had already begun. Why did Mao telegram the Federation of Industry and Commerce instead of peasant, worker or student associations? The answer lay in his concern for national solidarity: If the war should drag on and become a great financial burden, China's national bourgeoisie might become discontented, and this could impact political and social stability.

The fourth issue in the telegram was a request that the Soviet Union send a volunteer air force to assist ground fighting by the PVA in Korea and to cover Northeast China.[45] Several hours after he sent the October 11 telegram to Mao and the CCP Central Committee, Zhou Enlai received a call from Vyacheslav Molotov that the Soviet Union was not yet prepared to send a volunteer air force to Korea. Though Mao then asked Zhou to extend his stay in the Soviet Union to seek more assured promises of support,[46] the determination of China to enter the war was certain even without backup from the Soviet Air Force. The day after he sent this telegram, Mao began the strategic deployment of the PVA to Korea.[47] On October 23, he wrote to PVA Commander Peng Dehuai and then commander of the "Northern Frontier Guards" Gao Gang that "all possible efforts should be made to achieve a secure and certain victory."[48]

The Establishment of the Cold War Order and the Opportunity to Dismantle It

Just after the Korean War broke out, Mao made a statement that the affairs of the nations of the world should be left to their peoples, and affairs of Asia to the Asian people. This principle, which would later characterize the theme of the Bandung Conference, formed the underlying basis for Mao's evaluation of the War to Resist U.S. Aggression and Aid Korea as a necessary and just war. Since the Cairo Conference in November 1943, the United States had been maneuvering to contain the USSR by allying with powers in Asia, including postwar Japan and China under GMD rule. As the Second World War was drawing to a close in Europe, the Allied leaders met at Yalta in February and Potsdam in July and August of 1945. The question of how to delineate their respective postwar spheres of power had become a real issue in the context of the competition for power between the United States and the USSR.

It should be remembered here that, although the nuclear attack on Japan in August 1945 was partly aimed at intimidating the Soviet Union, it impelled the Soviet Union to promptly declare war on Japan and to capture Manchuria, the north of Korea, Sakhalin Island and the Kuril Islands. The U.S. Army had already landed on the Korean Peninsula in the summer of 1945 and was the first to draw a military demarcation line. After the Iran crisis in 1946, Churchill declared that an "iron curtain" had descended across Europe; the Marshall Plan to rebuild Europe was not extended to the Soviet Union. It was largely to challenge the presence of the United States in the Balkans and the Middle East that the Soviet Union supported Kim Il-sung to attack the South. The establishment of NATO between April and August of 1949 was a serious provocation of the Soviet Union and the Eastern Camp. In August 1949, the Soviet Union detonated its first nuclear bomb and the structure of nuclear deterrence solidified.

Division of the Korean Peninsula was first raised during the Yalta Conference under the framework of international trusteeship. While Korea was not one of the defeated nations nor had it incited the war, the Korean people were not allowed to participate in these negotiations over their fate. Nor was China, as a close neighboring country of Korea, involved in this so-called "international decision." After Berlin was captured, the United States and the USSR focused their attention on the Far East. The war against Japan became one of the major issues at the Potsdam Conference, and it is from here that the occupation of Korea entered the war plans of the two countries. The trusteeship plan was soon set aside. When Stalin met a delegate sent by Truman in May 1945, he still insisted on a four-country trusteeship for Korea according to the Yalta Agreement. But after the Potsdam Conference and the USSR declared war on Japan and entered Korea, the United States proposed to divide Korea along the 38th parallel. This change just before New China was established was a momentous event for the Korean Peninsula.

The leaders of the CCP had decided before 1949 to ally with the USSR and join the Eastern Camp. Consequently, after New China was established, the United States shifted its main focus in Asia toward containing it. This new configuration of events and forces might have been the key factor in Stalin's reversal of his previous stance and support for the DPRK's plan to march south. Archival materials demonstrate that Stalin did not express to Mao support for the DPRK's plan to move south in January 1950; we can deduce that the establishment of New China and the signing of the Sino-Soviet Treaty of Friendship, Alliance and Mutual Assistance in February 1950 contributed to Stalin's decision to change his stance on this issue.

Thus, the Korean War was not the product of any event transpiring in 1950, but an extension of the processes described above. When Mao proposed that "the affairs of the nations of the world should be left to their peoples and affairs of Asia to the Asian people," he aimed to criticize the global order framed by the Yalta Conference, and in particular that framed by the Potsdam Conference, in which hegemonic states could dominate the fates of smaller countries and incorporate them into their own spheres of power.

After Soviet forces entered Korea and were approaching Seoul, the U.S. military, in order to prevent the Soviet Union from gaining control of the entire peninsula, decided that the 38th parallel north should be the demarcation line of where the United States and the USSR should each accept the surrender of Japanese troops. In an important sense, the Korean War shared a similar goal with Chinese Civil War, in that both were driven by (among other issues) the goal of national unification, and as such they cannot be equated with outside invasion.[49] As a civil war, any external intervention—especially that based on hegemonic strategic interests—lacks justification. After accepting Japan's surrender in the south of Korea in September 1945, U.S. forces flew Syngman Rhee, who had spent many years in the United States, back into Korea in a military aircraft on October 12, 1950. But they delayed the return of members of the Korean Provisional Government (KPG) (including its right-leaning president Kim Ku and left-leaning vice president Kim Kyusik, among others), who had been at loggerheads with Rhee, and who had been in exile in Chongqing and supported by the GMD government.[50] Kim Ku and his fellow KPG members flew from Chongqing to Shanghai on November 5 and spent more than ten days there before the U.S. military, after negotiations with the GMD, allowed them to return to the Korean Peninsula as private individuals.[51] Kim Ku was the central figure within the KPG, and, like Rhee, he opposed communism and favored the United States. The United States'. refusal to recognize the KPG may have been partly influenced by its unwillingness to allow the expansion of China's influence in Asia after World War II, motivated by a desire to maximize its own interests and become the sole dominant power in the area.[52]

The Moscow Conference convened by American, Soviet and British foreign ministers in December 1945 decided on a five-year international trusteeship overseen by the United States, the Soviet Union, China and Great Britain.[53] The announcement of this plan provoked a storm of protest by the Korean populace in the South. The American military claimed publicly and falsely that the trusteeship agreement had been initiated by the Soviet Union, hoping to turn the antitrusteeship movement against them.[54] At the same time, the Soviet Union withdrew the majority of its forces from the North, where a land reform movement was already under way. In 1946, after economic policies enacted by the American military caused severe inflation, the people of the South rose up, beginning with a general strike in September and proceeding to a mass uprising in October, during which "over 300,000 persons participated in this huge outbreak of popular resistance that produced over 300 dead, over 3,600 missing, over 26,000 injured and over 15,000 arrested."[55] One of the demands of the peasants was to "carry out a land reform similar to that of North Korea."[56] In October 1947, the United States proposed through the UN that elections be held simultaneously in the North and South to establish a unified government, but, as the North refused to recognize or participate in an election held under the particular conditions stipulated, the American proposal amounted to using the UN to legitimate an election for the South alone.

On February 10, 1948, Kim Ku, referred to as the father of the nation in the Republic of Korea, published an announcement entitled "A Tearful Appeal to Thirty Million Compatriots" to call for opposition to the establishment of a separate South Korea. In April, he proposed that the South and North negotiate to form a unified government, and he traveled to the North to hold talks with Kim Il-sung.[57] Kim Ku's opposition to the UN resolution was in vain, and his insistence on unification and contact with North Korea made the American military believe that Syngman Rhee was a better choice to lead the country. The election was held in May, with Rhee declaring himself the president of the Republic of Korea on August 15; this outcome was immediately approved by the UN. On September 9, only after South Korea had already carried out its own a separate election, Kim Il-sung was elected chairman of the Democratic People's Republic of Korea and was immediately recognized by the Eastern Camp. In the same year, all Soviet forces withdrew from Korea, and the majority of U.S. forces departed in June of the following year.

In June 26, 1949, when U.S. forces were leaving the peninsula, An Tuhui, a Korean army lieutenant, assassinated Kim Ku.[58] After both U.S. and USSR forces had departed, the hostility between the North and South appeared ready to erupt at any moment. As the North actively prepared for a war and the United States armed the South, skirmishes broke out frequently. Khrushchev wrote in his memoir that Kim Il-sung informed Stalin of his intention to launch a unification war and later drafted a war strategy to which Stalin gave his support.[59] Just before the war broke out, on June 18, 1950, John Foster Dulles suddenly visited the 38th parallel. This visit was regarded by the Eastern Camp as a signal that the United States was going to wage war in Korea; the United States declared it a mere coincidence.

Coincidence or not, it should be clear that the Korean War was an extension of World War II and the outcome of the balance and imbalance of the strategies of the U.S. and the USSR. The cause of war thus cannot be attributed to the actions of one side or another, but should be evaluated on the basis of how the strategies of both sides were developing: Who caused the division in the Korean Peninsula? Who disrupted the probable unification process? Who, motivated by self-interest, broke the strategic equilibrium after the Cold War opposition had been created? When the causes of the Korean War are considered carefully, these questions may be more significant than that of who fired the first bullet.

If Mao's assertion that the Korean War would be "beneficial to the East" was based materially and theoretically on the existence of the Sino-Soviet Alliance and the socialist camp, the idea that it would be "beneficial to the world" should be evaluated within the context of a broader historical process. In 1951, frustrated by its setbacks on the battlefield in Korea, the United States conceived a plan to rearm Japan, sign a separate agreement with Japan during the summer and conclude it at the Treaty of San Francisco in September. Both the United States and Japan have refused to disclose the details of Japan's participation in the Korean War. There are two possible reasons for this. First, the United Nations Charter contains so-called "enemy state clauses" that name the Axis countries as "enemy states." If Japan had openly entered the Korean War, it would have complicated the international political situation.[60] Second, the proposal by the United States to negotiate a separate peace, with Japan and allow it to enter the Korean War encountered objections from India, the Philippines, Burma, Indonesia and other countries, and ignited large-scale demonstrations. Concerned that its actions would violate Article 9 of the Japanese constitution renouncing war as a means to settle international disputes, the Yoshida government ordered that the participation of Japanese ships in the war be kept secret. On the eve of the treaty, the Japanese government was forced to publicly express misgivings about rearmament. Following the signing of the Treaty of San Francisco on September 8, 1951 (which the USSR and other countries refused to sign), the United States and Japan signed a Treaty of Mutual Cooperation and Security.

In 1953, when the war and negotiations in Korea were at a stalemate, Eisenhower attempted to force China to divert troops from Korea by exerting pressure from the southeast through intervening in the war in Southeast Asia. But the United States, having learned from China's warning that the 38th parallel should not be crossed, never sent land forces across the 17th parallel to launch attacks on targets in North Vietnam. This represented a long-term restriction put on the U.S. military by its defeat in the Korean War. A military situation had turned into a political one, and war had transformed into peace. But this peace was achieved through military success, not defeat or compromise. After the Korean War, Zhou Enlai put forward the Five Principles of Peaceful Coexistence during a meeting with an Indian delegation in Beijing. At the Geneva Conference in April 1954, China, the Soviet Union and North Korea proposed that all foreign forces leave the peninsula before a free all-Korea election was held. The United States supported the South Korean proposal that its government alone was legitimate and that an election should be held in North Korea according to South Korea's constitution—a position of course unacceptable to North Korea, China and the Soviet Union. International negotiations on the Korean issue were fruitless, but negotiations related to Indochina made progress.

The attenuation of the relations of the United States and the United Kingdom with their colonies, former colonies and some of their client states in the developing world accelerated during these negotiations, presaging the conditions Mao described in his theory of Three Worlds put forward in the seventies. A year later, in April 1955, at the Bandung

Conference promoting the national independence of Asian and African countries, participating countries not only raised issues of anticolonialism and national independence that facilitated economic, cultural and political cooperation between oppressed nations in Asia and Africa, they also put forward ten principles to build peaceful international relations that expanded and deepened the Five Principles proposed by Zhou in 1953.

That the Korean and Vietnam wars were closely associated with these political processes indicates that the military struggle against imperialist war was accompanied by a broad and complex political process entailing the weakening and decline of imperialist dominance. By the 1960s and 1970s, anticolonial and national liberation movements extended throughout Asia and Africa, and movements against war and in support of Third World national liberation surged in the United States and the Western world. While the UN acted as little more than a political machine to support the United States and its imperial allies in the 1950s, it still preserved its forms of operation as an international organization, so in a real sense, its exposure as a tool of the imperialists during the Korean War actually paved the way for a subsequent political struggle within the UN. If it had not been for the War to Resist U.S. Aggression and Aid Korea and all of its aftereffects, the formation of national liberation movements in Asia that peaked in the sixties would have encountered considerably more difficulties. If we connect the military struggle of the War to Resist U.S. Aggression and Aid Korea with the conflict that appeared among the Western nations during the Geneva Negotiations, the alliance that formed between China and Vietnam as well as other nations, the new spirit of national liberation expressed by the Bandung Conference, and the later military and political struggle associated with the Vietnam War, we have good cause to argue that the War to Resist U.S. Aggression and Aid Korea promoted the formation of a worldwide united front of oppressed nations and helped usher in a new era of national liberation. It is on this level that the establishment of New China, the solidarity of the people of the world, the birth of the Eastern Camp and the national liberation movements that arose within this context broke apart the historical order that had held dominance since the beginning of the modern era. The logic of anti-imperialist war thus connected the War to Resist U.S. Aggression and Aid Korea with the later anticolonial and anti-imperialist national liberation movements in Asia, Latin America and Africa. This situation could only have been enabled by the appearance of a new political subject.

Only when we begin from this historical process can we understand what Mao meant by "beneficial to the East and to the world," the implication of which has been intentionally concealed by many historians today. These historians replace in their arguments the entire Eastern Camp and the world with the Soviet Union, and substitute the interactions between the Eastern Camp and the national liberation movements of oppressed nations in the middle of the twentieth century with a simplistically delineated relationship between two states—China and the Soviet Union. Historical studies of this type erase the internationalist nature of the War to Resist U.S. Aggression and Aid Korea, or, to be more precise, erase the internationalism necessarily inherent in every national liberation movement aimed at resisting imperialist invasion and dominance. The preference of some Chinese historians for replacing "War to Resist U.S. Aggression and Aid Korea" with "*Hanzhan*" (one of the terms for the "Korean War" used in South Korea) follows a similar logic by altering the political connotations of the war. With respect to its being "beneficial to the world" and to the broad historical process discussed above, it could be further demonstrated that the short-term effect of China's entering the war was the consolidation of the Sino-Soviet alliance; in the long run, it also implied the disintegration of the Cold War structure of American hegemony.

Hence, the PVA's entrance into Korea had multiple purposes: to aid Korea, to defend Northeast China, to protest the UN's refusal to admit the PRC, and to reject the global order in which a hegemon could hold sway. All these implications were condensed in the slogan Mao put forward during the Central Government Conference on June 28, 1950: "People of the world unite and defeat American imperialism." In Europe, the year 1948 marked the establishment of the Cold War order. In Asia it was also a turning point, as the Korean Peninsula veered from potential unification of the divided North and South to a structure of North–South military confrontation. The United States allowed Japan to revive its military industry during the Korean War in order to guarantee its supply of armaments and other military materiel, and returned to the Japanese government 850 military enterprises that had originally been given up as war reparations. Japan used the Korean War to revive its economy, and it became the most important ally of the United States in East Asia during the Cold War. It was during this war that Okinawa was built into the largest United States military base in Asia. It is because of its conflict with China during the war that the United States strengthened Taiwan's military and tightened its blockade of the Taiwan Strait. The end of the war in 1953 and the division of the Korean Peninsula consolidated by the "armistice system" thus became a marker for the Cold War order in Asia. The Korean War took place at the crucial moment when this world order was coming into being. From a long-term perspective, the War to Resist U.S. Aggression and Aid Korea had a powerful influence on the consolidation of the Cold War order, but a series of events, including the establishment of New China as an important international actor, the results of the Geneva and Bandung conferences, and the development of the national liberation movements in Southeast Asia, also provided an opportunity to undermine it.

The Political Significance of the Transition from People's War to War of Internationalist Alliance

People's War as a Political Category

The war in Korea joined by the Chinese People's Volunteer Army was distinct from previous people's wars within China: one, because it was fought in a foreign country, and two, because it was a conventional war waged under the threat of nuclear attack. Could this war waged in a foreign country be "revolutionary," or could it only serve national interests? Could the principle of people's war still be meaningful under the threat of nuclear attack? What did the Korean War have to do with the people's war fought during the Chinese Revolution? This question is crucial to understanding the War to Resist U.S. Aggression and Aid Korea and its significance for the history of twentieth-century China.

We must first consider people's war from a theoretical perspective. People's war was not a purely military concept, but a profoundly political one. Within the particular conditions of the twentieth century, people's war was a process that created a new political subject with its own political structure and forms of self-expression. People's war fundamentally changed the nature of party representation in modern politics: The birth of "the people" (*renmin*) as a new political subject, with the peasants as its essential component and the alliance between the peasants and the working class as its foundation, facilitated the generation or transformation of all forms of politics (for example, border area governments, the Party, peasant associations, labor unions and so on). When the CCP was established, it was composed of what Henk Sneevliet (known in China as Maring, 1883–1942) called petty bourgeois intellectuals who were even less connected with the peasants and the working classes than the GMD. In 1925–6, as the GMD adopted the policy of allying with the Soviet Union and the CCP, the two parties cooperated to promote peasant and workers' movements. The Peasant Movement Training Institute in Guangzhou led by Mao was a product of the peasant movement.

The political innovations of the GMD during the period of the Northern Expedition focused on two goals: to build a politicized army for a party free of influence by the old warlords, and to carry out peasant and workers' movements in cooperation with the CCP that could support the Northern Expedition. The concepts of a politicized army for the party and of resisting armed counterrevolution with armed revolution were initially inventions not of the CCP but of the GMD still under the influence of the Comintern during its revolutionary period. After 1927, however, the GMD abandoned social movements, and with the unification of the party and the state, the political nature of its army declined. The transformation of the CCP would not have been possible without the people's war developed after it was betrayed by the GMD and its activity in the cities brutally suppressed beginning in April 1927.

In terms of its members, social basis, modes of operation, and the implications of its revolutionary politics, the Communist Party born in 1921 and composed of a handful of intellectuals with no substantial connection to the working class or the peasants was a world apart from that which had emerged by the Jiangxi Soviet period (1931–4). The urban uprisings and workers' struggles led by Qu Qiubai, Li Lisan and Wang Ming not long after Chiang Kai-shek's all-out attack on the CCP and its activists in 1927 also differed from the strategy of the "countryside encircling the cities" later developed during the people's war.[61] The Party's unification with the army, with the "red political power" of the soviet governments it established, with the peasant masses through the agrarian revolution, as well as the change in the Party's relationship with other parties, social classes and their political representatives, all accomplished in or through the people's war, remind us that the people's war created a type of political party that differed from all political parties in the past. It created a class subject different from all working-class parties of the past, a class subject structured by a membership composed mainly of peasants. I call what had emerged a "super party" (*chaoji zhengdang*), which included supra-party (*chao zhengdang*) elements.

People's war also produced a unique form of war. The joining of the two armies that had participated in the Nanchang and Autumn Harvest uprisings and creation of the Jiangxi Soviet Revolutionary Base Area in 1928 were milestones marking the beginning of people's war. Within the base area, land reform and military struggle enabled party politics to transform into a mass movement. The pivotal issue of the Jinggangshan era therefore became land reform and government building under the conditions of revolutionary war. The union between the Party and the army, as well as between the Party, the peasant movement and land reform through the army, the administration of economic life by the Party and by the rural soviet governments under the guidance of the Party, and the cultural and ideological movement launched by the Party during its work among the people, together not only changed the substance and the central task of revolution, but this complex overlapping and intertwining between Party, army, government and peasant movement also created a completely new revolutionary political subject.

This was the political foundation of people's war. These political processes that unfolded in the midst of war gave people's war characteristics that distinguished it from other forms of war. Mao argued that the army and the people were the foundation of victory. This proposition embodied the general principles of people's war: 1) War could only be carried out by mobilizing and relying on the masses; 2) in addition to a strong regular army, there must be local military forces and militias; and 3) the category of "the army and the people" implied a political process closely connected to military struggle centered on land reform and the construction of political power.

Third, one of the crucial achievements of the people's war was the establishment of "red political power," the main form of which was the independent governments or soviets in the border regions between provinces. While the Party attempted to take what it could from foreign and Chinese historical experiences, this form of government differed from the general idea of a bourgeois state: through continuous political and military mobilization, it was the political form of a class that had acquired self-consciousness.

In his well-known article "Why Is It That Red Political Power Can Exist in China?" Mao pointed out that China was neither an imperialist country nor one ruled directly by imperialism; it was an internally unbalanced country ruled by imperialism indirectly.[62] Under these conditions, warlords associated with and depended on different imperialist powers, and hence the country became divided. It was also this very situation that weakened class domination and produced the external condition for the survival of a red regime in China. The domestic mobilization initiated during the Great Revolution (1924–7)—though it failed in its goals—survived as a movement. Frustrated by the Great Revolution, the CCP was forced to search for a totally new path: It attempted to establish an independent red soviet government under conditions of war, and created a new politics of people's war by uniting the Party, the army, the government and mass politics. This was the internal condition for the red regime to survive. During the War of Resistance against Japan, the CCP and its governments flourished, and military struggle, the mass line and the united front became the guarantee of success. During the Chinese Civil War, the anti-Japanese guerrilla war transformed into large-scale mobile war, which, together with positional war, became the major form of armed conflict.

Fourth, during the people's war, the CCP and the base area governments attended to not only simple military issues but also the organization of daily life. The mass line was created by the Party and the government with several principles in mind. First, serving the needs of the largest number of people would be the starting point and ultimate goal of the Party's work. Second, the border area governments sought to organize the lives of the people—only if the government solved the people's problems, improved their lives and won their trust could it mobilize the broad masses to join the Red Army, support the revolutionary war and defeat the Encirclement Campaigns launched by the GMD. Thus people's war not only was an effective military tactic to defeat the enemy, it dealt, out of necessity, with issues that constituted the crucial aspects of people's lives, including land ownership, labor issues, daily necessities, gender equality, education, trade and even monetary and financial issues. The mutual permeation and transformation of the military and daily life became a core component of people's war. Mao reminded CCP members repeatedly that they must stay with the people, mobilize them, care for them, sincerely work for their interests, and solve problems they encountered in production and daily life, such as housing, rice and salt, clothing and childbirth, in order to win the support of those who would risk their lives on the battlefield.[63]

The mass line was the basic strategy of people's war. It was a Party policy as well as a way to reconstruct the Party: Without the Party organization, it would not have been possible to define the masses; if the Party did not mix with and learn from the masses, the organization would become a cumbersome structure riding on the backs of and dominating the people. In the vast unindustrialized countryside, this peasant-based party acquired its political expression through its movements and campaigns. In this sense, it was the Party and its mass line under the conditions of people's war that created the self-expression of a class and, thus, a class in the political sense. No party in the past could create a proletarian class primarily composed of peasants. This task could only be accomplished by a party that reconstructed itself through people's war. Unlike such political phenomena as parties, party politics, the soviet governments, which had ultimately originated in nineteenth-century Europe and twentieth-century Russia, people's war was an innovation particular to the Chinese Revolution. Without an understanding of people's war, one cannot comprehend the uniqueness of the Chinese Revolution or grasp the deep differences between party construction in this revolution and previous party politics up to this time. Finally, without an understanding of people's war, one cannot understand the historical implications of of such distinctive political categories produced in twentieth-century China as the mass line and the united front.

A War of National Defense and a War for Internationalism

The War to Resist U.S. Aggression and Aid Korea was an extension of people's war, but it differed significantly from the previous form. If we situate it in the sequence of people's wars in twentieth-century China—the Revolutionary War during the Red Army era (1928–36), the War of Resistance against Japan (1937–45) and the War of Liberation (1946–9)—we can discern some of its particular characteristics. First, this was the first war to be fought in a foreign country after the establishment of New China. While the Revolutionary War fought to establish "red" soviet governments in "white" controlled districts and the War of Resistance against Japan fought to build and maintain base areas in the rear areas or behind enemy lines, the War to Resist U.S. Aggression and Aid Korea was premised on the fact that New China had already been established. The mode of war thus transformed from traditional people's war to a war of national defense. The shift in focus toward ensuring that the sovereignty and territory of the PRC could not be harmed marked the turning point from people's war to a war of national defense. The War to Resist U.S. Aggression and Aid Korea was a situation in which China's army of national defense in the form of the People's Volunteer Army fought against the UN Command forces led by the U.S. in a deadly war in a foreign country, aiming not to establish base areas outside of China or politicize social classes through people's war, but to defend New China. The People's Liberation Army of China reached a new stage in this war, becoming a revolutionary, regularized and modernized national defense army. In the past it had been a revolutionary army helping to initiate and spread the peasants' agrarian revolution, and an organ of violence to confront armed counterrevolution with armed revolution. Now it became a regular army whose prime task was to defend the country.

Second, during this war both the military and the construction of China's national defense infrastructure became deeply connected to China's overall process of industrialization. The first Five Year Plan centered on urban industrialization achieved fruition in the midst of heightened mobilization during the war. The slogan "Protect Our Homes and Defend the Country" inspired political enthusiasm throughout the entire society and produced an unprecedented degree of social mobilization; this became the main momentum for postwar recovery. The Sino-Soviet alliance also brought large-scale Soviet aid to China during the war and greatly helped build the foundation for China's industrialization.[64] Furthermore, the Korean War was also a crucial factor that catalyzed the process for China to become a nuclear power.

Third, the requirements of national defense furnished a political bottom line for the war: The U.S. troops could not be allowed to threaten China, and North Korea could not be defeated—therefore the armies of China and North Korea would not retreat from the 38th parallel. In October 1952, the U.S. military adjourned peace negotiations and launched the Shangganling Campaign (the Battle of Triangle Hill) six days later. This offensive-defensive battle was in its essence political for both sides: The new American commander Mark Wayne Clark hoped to help the Democrats in the coming election, while the Chinese army held to the political principle that a retreat from the 38th parallel was unacceptable. As the war was waged in a foreign country, the War to Resist U.S. Aggression and Aid Korea relied on the homeland at its rear and focused on mobile offense and defense. The PVA fought shoulder to shoulder with the Korean People's Army and endeavored to obtain the support of the Korean people, occasionally adopting harassment and guerrilla strategies, but its basic form of combat was mobile warfare and positional warfare.

Though it differed from people's war, the War to Resist U.S. Aggression and Aid Korea inherited some of its characteristics. First, although it took place outside of China, the war was premised on a degree of national mobilization unprecedented in China's military history. In twentieth-century China, only one other war was able to mobilize the entire nation: the War of Resistance against Japan, during which time the GMD took the lead in the main battlefield and within the political structure, while the CCP facilitated a mobilization of comprehensive resistance upon the formation of a united front against the Japanese invasion. Mobilization could occur in the War to Resist U.S. Aggression and Aid Korea because, after a prolonged series of revolutions and wars, China had achieved unification outside of Taiwan, and this built the foundation for a general and thorough political, economic, cultural and military mobilization. Mao's initial hesitation and final resolution from 1950 to 1953 was related to the question of whether this war would be supported by the whole people of China.

Under the conditions of war in a foreign country, the relationship between the army and the people changed drastically; while it was difficult to reproduce the "fish-and-water" relationship between the army and the people in the base areas achieved during the people's war, the PVA attempted to rebuild this relationship after crossing the border. On October 8, in the document "Order to the Chinese People's Volunteers" signed by Mao, it was specifically mandated that after the PVA entered Korea, it "must show fraternal feelings and respect for the Korean people, the Korean People's Army, the Korean Democratic Government, the Korean Workers' Party and the other democratic parties of Korea as well as for Comrade Kim Il-sung, the leader of the Korean people, and strictly observe military and political discipline. This is a most important political basis for ensuring the fulfillment of your military task."[65] This order shows the CCP's clear recognition of the particular challenges inherent to fighting in a foreign country as well as the PVA's intent to flexibly apply the experience of people's war gained during the Chinese Revolution to the task of fighting in a foreign environment.

While the domestic precondition of the War to Resist U.S. Aggression and Aid Korea was the establishment of New China, internationally it was premised on the existence of the Eastern Camp and international solidarity between the people's democracies. This was a war different from the earlier people's war; it was an extension of the practice of people's war under the conditions of a multinational war. Under conditions of war, the people's democracies (including the Soviet Union) formed a united front with the national liberation movements in Asia, Africa and Latin America. When we explore the significance to the East and the world of China's entering the war, the profoundly political nature of the war manifested itself exactly in its close connection to the problem of the continuation of revolution under a new world order. As the politics of "Resist U.S. Aggression and Aid Korea; Protect Our Homes and Defend the Country" took place amid the confrontation between two great camps, the political nature of the war transcended the significance of typical wars between countries. Ignoring this political context and interpreting the war instead as a war between nations or states results in an incomplete historical understanding. This war had a dual quality: It was a national war and also an internationalist war that resisted imperialism. As it extended the logic of people's war, including military struggle, the mass line and the united front to an international scale, the War to Resist U.S. Aggression and Aid Korea was a continuation of China's twentieth-century revolutionary wars.

The core question regarding war waged outside the borders of one's own country centers on the nature of the war: Is it rooted in internationalist principles and fought to lend aid to another, or is it rooted in the purely nationalist desire to further the interests of one's own state? We must be careful not to repudiate all nationalist wars without distinction, however, for we should still consider the political connotations and contexts of these wars: There is a distinction between the nationalism of

the oppressed nations and that of the oppressor nations, between imperialist war and war for national liberation, between the nationalism of
the old world and the anti-imperialist and anticolonial nationalism of
New China and other nations. For China, the wars to aid Korea and to
aid Vietnam resisted both imperialism and colonialism and were therefore internationalist. China's so-called "Self-Defensive Counterattack
on Vietnam" in 1979, however, did not have this quality. It is in this
sense that this "counterattack" was not part of China's "short twentieth
century," but rather took place at a time when the curtain had already
lowered on the revolutionary century.

The First War under a Nuclear Threat: Do People or Material Decide the Outcome of War?

The Korean War was the first large-scale war in human history to occur
after the appearance of nuclear weapons. In 1945, after the American
nuclear bombing of Hiroshima and Nagasaki, George Orwell was the
first person to use the term "cold war." What did he mean by "cold
war"? This was his term for the condition of the world and the relations
between states after the appearance of nuclear weapons and the threat
of nuclear war. Under the strategic balance of nuclear deterrence, war
took the form of the Cold War. In the Korean War, China was engaged
in a militarily unbalanced war with an imperialist superpower that was
the first to possess nuclear strike capability. Before World War II, no one
knew that the United States was developing and might be able to produce
nuclear weapons. When China entered the Korean War and started
fighting with a dominant country that possessed nuclear weapons, how
could it not consider the possibility of a nuclear war? Could this sort of
war, extremely unbalanced in terms of armaments, change the possibilities for people's war?

The United States twice made concrete plans to use nuclear weapons
during the Korean War. These two plans were linked to the idea of
rearming Japan and allowing Taiwan to enter the war. Since 1945, the
United States had consistently considered the possibility of using
nuclear weapons. After American forces had suffered a severe military
debacle in late 1950, MacArthur sent a telegram to Chiang Kai-shek
requesting that he send Squadron 52 to Korea, to which Chiang
responded promptly and with enthusiasm. Earlier on, MacArthur had

drafted a list of targets to be attacked with atomic bombs, which included not only Chinese forces in Korea but also sites in China. On December 30, he suggested to the Department of the Army that the following measures be adopted: 1) Blockade the coast of China; 2) destroy logistical industrial facilities in China; 3) secure the support of GMD troops from Taiwan; and 4) remove existing restrictions on the GMD and possibly allow a counterattack on China.[66] Public opinion around the world was shocked when Truman stated in a press conference on November 30 that all necessary measures, including the atomic bomb, would be used to stop the spread of communism in Korea.[67] After Eisenhower assumed the presidency in 1953, he revisited Truman's plans, reopening the nuclear attack plan and urging Chiang Kai-shek to attack mainland China.[68]

Though Mao understood the power of atomic weapons, he was not overly awed by them. Just after the United States deployed atomic bombs against Japan in 1945, Mao discussed the issue of nuclear weapons in "The Situation and Our Policy after the Victory in the War of Resistance against Japan." He argued that atomic bombs alone, absent people's war, could not have ended the war. "The theory that 'weapons decide everything,' the purely military viewpoint" represented a "bureaucratic style of work divorced from the masses, individualist thinking, and the like"—degenerations in thinking resulting from nuclear intimidation. Those who believed that "the atom bomb is all-powerful" were "more backward than [Lord] Mountbatten," who had conceded that atomic bombs did not end the war.[69] In August 1946, Mao raised what would become the famous image of the "paper tiger" in an interview with American journalist Anna Louise Strong.[70] While he was well aware that atomic bombs were massively destructive, Mao believed that people were the ultimate deciding factor in war. That "the atomic bomb is a paper tiger" was not a positivistic statement, but a statement of political resolve. If nuclear intimidation could prevent China from confronting the United States on the battlefield in Korea, this invalidated the claim that China's history of being bullied had ended forever, and that the establishment of people's democracies such as China and the Soviet Union had ended forever the world order dominated by imperialists who could do as they pleased. If China had not effectively resisted U.S. aggression, the historical significance of the establishment of the PRC would have been completely different, and the world order that took shape due to the appearance of the Eastern Camp would have changed. Mao's assertion indicated a political bottom line.

That people rather than weapons decide the outcome of war was one of the key propositions that distinguished people's war from imperialist war. Why did the United States set aside the proposals to use nuclear weapons soon after they were broached and eventually concede that it could not achieve complete military victory, thus opening up the possibility for peace talks? We can delve deeper into archival sources for detailed explanations, but it is undeniable that these developments represented a vindication of Mao's military judgments rooted in his analysis of the global political and military situation, as well as the victory of the logic of people's war—that people and not material determines the outcome of war—over the Cold War logic of nuclear intimidation. The basic principle of people's war was to rely on the power of the people to defeat the enemy, mobilizing them in their daily lives while maintaining flexible strategies and a strong fighting will. Emphasizing the power of the people did not imply a negation of the importance of armaments. At the beginning of the war, Mao requested support in the form of air power, weaponry and technology from the Soviet Union, and he placed great emphasis on modernizing the PLA. In 1950 Mao called on the army to improve education among the soldiers, and the regularization of the army accelerated. But none of these undertakings altered his view that people's war was based on people and not weapons, nor did they change his judgment of the course of the war or its political nature.

The War to Resist U.S. Aggression and Aid Korea was the first war fought by the army of New China in a foreign country, the first large-scale war under a nuclear threat and the first war of national defense after New China was established. Could war fought under these three unique conditions be a people's war? The fact that troops were dispatched to Korea indicates that Mao believed that nuclear weapons did not alter the logic of people's war, that the determining factor of war was not material but human. Armament was an important but not the deciding factor in war, whose outcome would be decided by objective conditions such as the military, political, economic and natural environment, and by subjective conditions such as abilities, willpower, strategy and tactics.

Mao insisted in "Problems of Strategy in China's Revolutionary War" that a military strategist could not create victory beyond given material conditions, but could strive for victory within their limits.[71] Here is the issue of subjective initiative in war. Mao argued that conscious subjective initiative was a human characteristic powerfully revealed in war, making the outcome of a war, although dependent on the political and economic status of the two sides, the nature of the war and the amount of international aid among other factors, impossible to determine.[72] The politics of subjective initiative characterized the revolutionary politics of China. When the War to Resist U.S. Aggression and Aid Korea geared the mass line of the revolutionary era toward comprehensive social mobilization in New China, the subjective initiative of politics became apparent. Mao was relieved that the national capitalists in Tianjin supported the war: If even national capitalists were mobilized, the people of China as a whole had been sufficiently mobilized and the logic of people's war and the united front had come together under a thoroughly different kind of war. Through international alliance and war in a foreign country, New China was able to apply the logic of the united front developed in its domestic revolution to international war. After the Kaesong Negotiations broke down in 1951, the U.S. military used its superior air power to launch the so-called "Operation Strangle" targeting crucial PVA supply lines. Yet, on the basis of popular support within New China and the comprehensive mobilization of the Chinese army, the PVA formed supply routes that could not be cut by intensive bombing.

War is an extension of politics, and people's war the highest form of politics. The War to Resist U.S. Aggression and Aid Korea was not simply a war of technology but a war of politics. People's war is characterized by its highly political nature. Mao pointed out in "Problems of Strategy in China's Revolutionary War," written in 1936, that war was the highest form of mutual struggle "between classes, nations, states, or political groups."[73] If one does not comprehend war and "understand the actual circumstances of war, its nature and its relations to other things, you will not know the laws of war, or know how to direct war, or be able to win victory."[74] That military struggle had to coordinate with such political processes as the mass line, the united front and the construction of base areas indicated the political nature of the war. Since war has a political quality and the decisive element of war is people, just war and unjust war can be distinguished. There is no justice in imperialist wars that aim to carve up the world, while wars against imperialist domination are just. The

War of Resistance against Japan was different from the War to Resist U.S. Aggression and Aid Korea, but they both resisted attempts by imperialists to carve up and dominate the world. Defeating armed counterrevolution with armed revolution was a characteristic of the Chinese Revolution, and opposing imperialist war with an international war of resistance was one of the political means (or military means of a political nature) of defending peace when New China was newly established.

The War to Resist U.S. Aggression and Aid Korea was a just war that differed from such domestic people's wars as the Revolutionary War and the War of Liberation. A just war is characterized by an aim toward peace and a move beyond common pacifism. During the Korean War Mao again emphasized the dialectics of war and peace that he had explored in "On Protracted War," and pointed out that the strategic balance produced by nuclear deterrence would not lead to peace. The concept of just war is closely associated with the demand to terminate the logic of imperialist war. Revolutionary war and just war ultimately aim at permanent peace, but as war, the goal of peace must be related to effective strength that can defeat the enemy.

After World War II, the United States possessed not only nuclear weapons but strong naval and air forces armed with the most advanced weapons and soldiers trained during the war in Europe and Asia. In the Korean War, U.S. forces included such elite units as the First Marine Division and the First Cavalry Division and held absolute air and naval supremacy. Shockingly, however, American forces could neither prevail in situations in which heavy armament was too unwieldy and guerrilla war was at an advantage nor during mobile and positional warfare in which large units of infantry were advantageous. If its defeats on the battlefield happened only at the beginning of the war it might be argued that U.S. forces had been caught unprepared. Yet even during the middle and the end of the war, the American military only managed to launch limited counterattacks when the PVA was experiencing logistical hardships and still failed to achieve victory. It was in military defeat that American military commanders found respect for the courage and tactics of the Chinese army: China was no longer the old China and the Chinese army no longer what it had been. After World War II, U.S. understanding of China was completely reshaped by its defeat in the Korean War—the arrogance and superciliousness in scholarly attitudes had to be adjusted and balanced by discretion. For the United States, the

Korean War and the Vietnam War were both military and political defeats. Though America's political defeat during the Vietnam War is easier to see, the foundation of this defeat was related to America's defeat in the Korean War.

War and peace transform into each other. The dialectical relationship between war and peace is mainly determined by the political nature of the war in question, which also manifests itself in how the relationship between ourselves and our enemies is established and transforms. War is premised on the clear distinction between the self and the enemy, and aims at eliminating the enemy and protecting the self. But war is a form of politics, and the political relationship between the enemy and the self changes along with changing historical conditions. Enmity on the battlefield could transform into a nonhostile relationship under other conditions. The contradictions between the enemy and the self can transform into nonantagonistic contradictions and into a relationship that embraces both struggle and solidarity. Such a transformation of the contradiction between the enemy and the self is not its negation—we cannot use the outcome after the transformation to evaluate the struggles before the transformation. In the War of Resistance against Japan, when the contradiction between nations rose to be the principal contradiction, the contradictions between the working and the peasant classes and the national bourgeoisie and landed classes gradually became secondary contradictions: The broad united front was constructed as a result of this change. This logic of contradictions and of their transformation also existed in domestic and international relations during the War to Resist U.S. Aggression and Aid Korea. War is a form of politics, and it can build a path for the development of a new politics. Without an understanding of contradictions and their transformation, we cannot understand how a new politics was able to unfold.

Not a Conclusion: The Armistice System and War under Depoliticization

Sixty years after the end of hostilities, the armistice system remains on the peninsula. North Korea is isolated and the logic of nuclear deterrence has produced the nuclearization of the peninsula. We must never forget that the nuclear problem on the Korean Peninsula began when the

United States intervened in Korea. America's "pivot to Asia" policy (when has the United States ever left Asia?) has intensified tensions on the Korean Peninsula and aggravated the conflicts between China and Japan, Korea and Japan and China and Southeast Asian countries. As far as the severity of such conflicts is concerned, this situation may be no more dangerous than that of the past. But the justness and unjustness of wars have lost their clear demarcation, the Bandung spirit that promoted solidarity among Third World countries has ossified into a historical relic and liberation and resistance movements that challenged hegemonic dominance have long dissolved. Structures of dominance and oppression can be seen everywhere, but dynamics that might alter such structures are difficult to discern. Whence can a new politics be born? When will the question of justice be raised? Where can we find a new internationalism that transcends the Cold War order? It is these questions that stimulated me to situate the Korean War in the context of the historical processes of the twentieth century.

In "On Protracted War," Mao argued that war is the highest form of politics. The political category of people's war profoundly demonstrates this proposition. With the close of the twentieth century, however, this theory seems to require revision: Under contemporary conditions, war is not so much the highest form of politics as the outcome of the failure or disappearance of politics. The presence of imperialism indicates that this proposition remains valid, but war can no longer ignite revolution. Depoliticized forms of war abound in our generation. They neither demonstrate the agency and decisive role of people nor do they distinguish between justice and injustice. It is thus difficult for these wars to spark movements capable of producing the mutual inspiration and powerful support that developed in the 1960s between the antiwar movement in the West and the national liberation movements of other regions. This is precisely why we should revisit the War to Resist U.S. Aggression and Aid Korea: Even though the nuclear threat was very real, the War to Resist U.S. Aggression and Aid Korea and the Vietnam War did not remain subject to Cold War dynamics as Orwell envisaged, but unfolded as political processes that fought for peace in the form of "hot wars." Compared with earlier people's wars, technology played an unprecedented role in the Korean War, but the outcome of the war still depended on the determination, aims, military strategy and resourcefulness of the commanders and the morale, ideals and technical and tactical abilities of combatants. But as this process unfolded, the "role of people" was not only expressed in battlefield struggles, but also in the rise of national liberation movements, in antiwar movements in the United States and throughout the West and in the rich history of diplomatic struggles in and outside the UN. It is precisely this broad historical process that forced the United States into a corner, leading to the failure of this dominant country on the battlegrounds of both warfare and politics.

Why revisit this issue today? After the Vietnam War, imperialists set off a series of wars of invasion, such as the Falkland Islands War, the wars in Yugoslavia, two Iraqi wars, the wars in Afghanistan and Libya and the continuing Syrian War. Yet these wars have not generated resistance movements or social revolutions similar to the people's wars of the twentieth century. Apparently the essence of contemporary war has changed: Without advanced weaponry one cannot win a war. While the large countries compete to protect their own interests, the sort of deep and broad political process that was generated by uniting military struggle with the mass line, the united front and cultural politics no longer exists. Does this mean that the basic principles of people's war and the political quality of war have disappeared? Answers to this question vary widely. My answer is that the adoption of new weapons did not change the nature of war. It is rather that political conditions have changed, and as a result the logic of people's war has lost its primacy. The role of people in war not only manifests in the contrast between people and weaponry but in the distinction between the political and the nonpolitical. In short, the element of people in a war resides in its political nature.

In the field of military affairs, the negation of people's war and of the decisive role of people, together with the worship of military technology, form the theoretical background for depoliticization. As I discussed in "Depoliticized Politics," the process of depoliticization extends far beyond the categories of war and military affairs; complex phenomena such as "the statification of party, the corporatization of government, the partification of media, and the mediatization of politicians" are symptoms of this process. There are some who are attempting to challenge this current configuration by drawing on the historical legacy of the twentieth century. In the fields of politics and theory, revisiting the mass line represents one such attempt. In today's context that differs so completely from that of the twentieth century, what would it mean to return to the mass line, the product of people's war? The emergence of the masses, a political subject in formation, signified the birth of a new form of politics. Revisiting the concept of the mass line does not so much hark back to a particular period in the past, but rather aims at exploring possibilities for the future. This inevitably leads to the following questions: What political force and what sort of political subjects do we need to create? What political future should we point to?

The above discussion moves beyond the context of the Korean War but is crucial for an understanding of contemporary debates on this war. I would like to restate a proposition here: The War to Resist U.S. Aggression and Aid Korea and the ensuing War to Resist America and Aid Vietnam were both extensions and the ends of people's war of the twentieth century. Our search for peace today operates within a post–people's war and depoliticized contemporary context. In this new historical moment, what will allow us to deter imperialist war, to break through the division of the Korean Peninsula and between China and Taiwan, and to ease international tension in East Asia? People's war was a political category and a process that generated political energy. While many celebrate the disintegration of the Soviet Union and the Eastern Camp, it is this very process that has enabled the wars in Iraq and Libya—the arrival of an era in which U.S. supremacy has nothing to fear. Many show disdain for the political innovations of twentieth-century China, but can China today generate any political process that can lead to a truly new and different future as it did in 1949? The answer to this question is far from clear. Today there is no people's war and no just war; as a result war can no longer signify the extension of politics but only its end.

It is in this sense that the twentieth century has ended and repoliticization has become the task for the new era.

4

The Crisis of Representation
and Post-Party Politics[1]

The Global Decline of Representation in Politics

The decline of representation in contemporary politics is the result of an unprecedented, multilayered political crisis. First of all, its core aspect, a crisis of party politics, is a breakdown of representation, a discursive failure of established political values in actual political processes and consequently a crisis of legitimacy. Party politics took its modern shape in nineteenth-century Europe. In China, it was the most important political innovation of the twentieth century. The party politics of the 1911 Revolution period, especially between 1911 and 1915, attempted to emulate the multiparty parliamentary system developed within the framework of European constitutional politics. Faced with the challenges of secessionism, monarchical restoration and the crisis of the republic, the revolutionaries and many political elites began to shift away from their original political objectives.

There were three prerequisites for the formation of China's unique form of modern party politics. First, after the establishment of the Republic of China, regional secessionism, military separatism, and partisanship interlocked with one another and led to the formation of a new national politics crucial in early republican-period political thinking. Second, during World War I, many political parties in the West participated in nationalist war mobilization and supplied a political impetus for the war. Consequently, reflection on traditional modes of party politics peaked among European intellectuals after World War I.

The reconstruction of Chinese party politics occurred in this intellectual atmosphere. Lastly, when the Russian Revolution erupted during World War I, some Chinese revolutionaries believed that Bolshevism as a political model could overcome the limits of bourgeois party politics.[2]

In other words, the party system that became the political nucleus of that revolutionary century was born out of a crisis and failure of party politics. In contrast to the parties in crisis, this new model of political party influenced by the Russian Revolution and the Comintern bore the dual features of a super-political party (*chaoji zhengdang*) and a supra-party (*chao zhengdang*). The term "super-political party" indicates that while both of the two competing parties, the Guomindang (GMD) and the Chinese Communist Party (CCP), were obliged to adopt some of the elements or forms of party politics and claim to be political parties, neither of them intended to participate in competitive party politics within the structure of a parliamentary system. Instead, both aimed to become the hegemonic party or "leading party." "Supra-party" is meant to indicate that both parties' representational politics were different from those in a multi- or dual-party parliamentary system, and were much closer to Gramsci's so-called "modern prince," which aimed to represent the future.

In the case of the CCP, the role of the Party was to be the vanguard of the proletariat. The theory and praxis of people's war that was developed in the late 1920s and expanded during the War of Resistance against Japan (1937–45) and the Civil War (1945–9) generated a new form of party politics. It consolidated military struggle, land revolution, the building of revolutionary base areas and the construction of a revolutionary constitutional state into an unprecedented practice, the core of which was a set of political strategies, namely, military struggle, the mass line and the united front. With its class politics based on the proletariat, the alliance between the workers and the peasants and the united front for national liberation, the CCP eventually defeated the GMD, which had deviated from the peasant movement and mass politics toward state politics.

In both the multiparty system in the West and the system of multi-party cooperation under one-party rule in China, the degree to which political parties represent their constituents has become increasingly obscure. In the case of China, the Party's politics and ability to represent the people have changed drastically as categories such as the proletariat, the alliance between the workers and peasants and the united front have lost their clarity. After the PRC was established, the Communist Party searched for a new path for its own renovation after the period of people's war. The failure of the Cultural Revolution signified the end of this search, as well as the beginning of the full integration of the Party into the framework of the state.

In my view, the decline or breakdown of representation is the consequence of depoliticization, the most severe symptom of which is the statification of the Party: The Party has submitted itself increasingly to the logic of the state, depriving itself of its essence, which should be a form of political organization and political movement, as both its function and form of organization have been assimilated to the state apparatus. This process implies the end of the "mass line" that engendered the political dynamism of the CCP.

Two interrelated forms of the statification of the party can be identified: first, the bureaucratization of the Party in the early days before economic reform, which became one of the pivotal triggers for the launch of the Cultural Revolution; second, the marriage of the Party and capital in the process of the corporatization of government during market reform. For the Party, the breakdown of representation manifests itself most intensely in the incongruity between its abandonment of the category of class and claim to represent everyone, while at the same time increasingly distancing itself from the people, especially those from the lower social strata. There are of course policies protective of workers and peasants, yet it is difficult to detect any organic connection between the politics of workers and peasants and the politics of the Party.

The detachment of the political system from the social form occurs not only in socialist or post-socialist countries, but in European and American parliamentary party systems and in political systems based on them as well. In China, the relationship between the Party and its class base has become ever more vague, just as in Western political parties the distinction between left and right has also blurred. In the contemporary world, the breakdown of representation has intensified enough to suggest the complete disappearance of the type of party politics that flourished in the nineteenth and the twentieth centuries, or its persistence only in confined areas. Party politics is transforming or has already transformed into a state-party politics—that is, it has become part of the structure of state power. Unlike in the nineteenth and early twentieth centuries, it is difficult to find in contemporary party politics political movements with a clear agenda. The growing scale of political parties and their monopoly of state power are normally interpreted as the expansion of party politics.

However, it is the logic of the state that has come to control parties, not political parties that have come to control the state. The boundary between party and state is vanishing, the outcome of their assimilation the dissolution of political representation itself, which in turn renders power relations in the political sphere no longer capable of balancing or reducing inequality in the socioeconomic sphere, providing, instead, institutional support for such inequality. Under the conditions of the breakdown of representation, the political rhetoric of politicians degrades into a performance aimed at attaining power, while the role of technocratic bureaucrats has increased dramatically. In the Western multiparty or dual-party structure, the main function of political parties is to mobilize voters for elections every four or five years, amounting to little more than a state apparatus for the rotation of leaders.

The superpolitical party in China originally possessed an intensely political nature sustained by rigorous organization, a straightforward value orientation and mass movements carried out through the vigorous interaction of theory and political practice. Under the contemporary mode of political parties, however, Party organization has come to resemble an administrative organization, and the Party has become a component of the management apparatus, its mobilization and supervisory functions increasingly identical to state mechanisms as its bureaucratic system intensifies and its political nature diminishes. The crisis of representation in party politics is not only a crisis for the ruling party, but for the other parties as well—in China today, the question of who or what the democratic parties represent has also become more elusive than ever before.

The waning degree to which public institutions that mediate between state and society (parliament in the West, and the National People's Congress and the Chinese People's Political Consultative Conference in China) represent the people echoes the aforementioned process. In parliamentary democracy, seats in parliament are usually determined by political parties. There are theoretical debates regarding whether parliament functions as part of the state or as an institution that includes certain domains of the public. But with the statification of political parties, the connection between parliament and society is gradually being severed. During my visit to India, I noted that grassroots social movements prospered there. Even the most active types of social movement, however, could not play a parallel role in the area of public policy making because political parties monopolized parliamentary power.

In theory, the method of apportioning representatives used by China's National People's Congress seems far removed from those of party-centered parliamentary systems, but in practice, the actual application of China's system required support from a people-centered politics. Once such a politics is lost, both the process for producing delegates and the role of the People's Congress in political life in general is undermined. The ratio of representatives from different segments of society in the People's Congress has been criticized in the past—it has been pointed out that the number of worker and peasant representatives is quite small and far out of proportion to their contributions to Chinese society. This problem with the system of representation and its connection to power relations within society is an expression of the crisis of representative politics and a consequence of depoliticization.

The second aspect of the decline of representation refers to the fact that certain important domains within the public sphere, such as the media, are also losing their "public" aspects. The large-scale expansion of the media has entailed the contraction of the public sphere, as freedom for the media industry has replaced freedom of speech for the citizens. The media not only form unprecedented alliances with capital and power, but, in some cases, have even attempted to take up functions previously held by political organizations such as political parties. In Italy, Silvio Berlusconi's media group enabled Berlusconi, a suspected criminal, to be repeatedly elected prime minister. The media, especially large media groups—regardless of whether they are private or state-owned—must be considered not as independent conduits for citizen and public opinion, but as agglomerations of interests draped in public garb. The permeation of media influence in political and other public spaces cannot be considered part of the process of democratization; to a large extent this permeation represents the colonization of these spheres.

In China, though the media may appear to be controlled by politics, the political sphere has, in fact, been gradually colonized by the media. Political figures pander to the public with platitudes, increasingly adopting rhetoric shaped by the logic of the Eastern and Western media. Since the 1990s the Chinese media have been corporatized and concentrated into large media groups, the result of new political and economic strategies of the Party aimed at adapting to marketization and globalization. But with the statification of the Party, the corporatization of the government, and the "partification" of the media (acting as a party in itself), the relationship between the media and the Party has turned into a contest between two entangled interests that, in their mutual jockeying for influence and power, appeal respectively to ideals of democracy and liberty or to stability, rule of law and consideration of "the overall situation." The confrontation between the editorial department of *Southern Weekend* (*Nanfang zhoumo*) and the Guangdong Provincial Party Committee in the early spring of 2013, for example, was not a struggle between public opinion and the state but an entanglement that arose as both sides struggled for control over public sentiment—a confrontation emerging from within the current power structure. The two sides had different discourses but their political interests were very similar.

Censorship of the news has been a long-standing problem, and real reforms are needed in the realm of open public discourse. But within the current political configuration, reforms concerning freedom of the press will likely amount to an illusion concealing a struggle for power behind the scenes. Today, the methods used to squelch public opinion have changed, as the media, too, often serve as a mechanism to suppress popular sentiment. In the political competition between the "partified" media and the traditional party that spawned this media force, the former possesses more political energy and style, and the latter resembles a hapless power apparatus that has lost its ideological function, no longer a political organization in the classical sense. In fact, the two entities are organically linked, each maneuvering for their own gain in order to replace and obscure free speech and political debate among the citizenry.

The third aspect of the decline of representation is the crisis of law. Under depoliticization, legal procedures are often manipulated by interest groups. This manipulation appears not only in general legal procedures, but in the process of legislation as well. Instead of simply asserting proceduralist opinions, therefore, it is an urgent and necessary matter for the legal reforms of our day to reconsider the relationship between law and politics.

The problems in the three aforementioned areas constitute the essence of today's political transformation. I therefore raise the following question: As party politics has degenerated into state-party politics, is a post-party politics possible? While modern political parties are still widespread around the world, the specter of a post-political-party politics I raise here refers not to politics after the disappearance of political parties, but to the fact that political parties today have already assumed "post-political" characteristics. Nineteenth-century political parties were established on the foundation of political movements. In twentieth-century China, party politics, especially Communist Party politics, were reshaped by people's war and its political aftermath. A "post-political party" is a party that still acts as a leading political entity but that in reality no longer represents its constituents as did parties in the nineteenth and twentieth centuries and has parted from its original logic. Accompanying this development is the formalization of politics: Major political institutions are still based on the principle that party politics represent the people, but precisely because of this, the breakdown of representation has become the chief malady of today's political crisis.

The concept of "post-party politics" is directed at the question of how and in what sense representation can be reconstructed. In the practice of politics and within the politics of twentieth-century China, elements of post-party politics were already active, but only as the practice of a super-political party—namely, as people's war, the mass line and the united front. All these practices of representation attempted to move beyond conventional relations of representation. Although present-day party politics in China evolved from such super-party politics, today we have the product of the degeneration of this super-party politics into a state-party system. In order to overcome the crisis of representation, we must first explore the question of in what sense we can reconstruct representation, and then search for new paths for post-party politics.

Today, representation cannot be reconstructed simply by repeating old slogans or practices. We have to find out what went wrong with representational politics and how changes in the social structure caused its dislocation from the political system. From this perspective, exploring post-party politics requires two points of entry. We must reexamine the principles of representative politics in twentieth-century China while also exploring the conditions of possibility for post-party politics.

Rethinking the Principles of Representative Politics in Twentieth-Century China

The question of representation and the subsidiary question of a system of representation have been the core issues for modern political systems. In the nineteenth and twentieth centuries, representative politics was defined by such categories as party and class, both inside and outside the framework of state politics. After the decline of monarchical systems, representative politics became connected with problems of democracy. The political principles of representative politics in China differ from those in the West, where they center on multiparty parliamentary systems and universal suffrage. This is an issue that is easily misunderstood and glossed over. We should be clear on the issue of the form of democracy: Western democracy based on general elections is not the only model of democracy, nor is democracy a merely formal practice. Democracy must be predicated on political momentum. Once this momentum is lost, no form of democracy can survive.

To analyze the principles of Chinese representative politics, we could start with the constitution of the PRC. Few scholars of constitutional government have broached the subject of the Chinese constitution in discussions about the meaning of constitutionalism. Article One states that "the People's Republic of China is a socialist state under the people's democratic dictatorship led by the working class and based on the alliance of workers and peasants." Article Two asserts that "all power in the People's Republic of China belongs to the people." These two articles illustrate the principles of representative politics during the socialist period, which were constituted by several fundamental political categories. These political categories cannot be reduced to commonsensical terms: They cannot be verified by simple a priori principles or treated as general empirical facts. They emerged in twentieth-century China in the political praxis of revolution.

For example, what does "the working class is the leading class" mean? In the first half of the twentieth century, the Chinese working class was weak. The Chinese Revolution, judged by the composition of its participants, was mainly a peasant revolution. How could the working class become the leading class when, in empirical terms, the question of whether the bourgeoisie even constituted a class is still open to debate? For most of the twentieth century, the working class only made up a small fraction of the Chinese population, but it generated class revolution and class politics. Now China has the largest working class in the world, but there is no class politics of a commensurate magnitude.

Class and class politics are related concepts, but they need to be treated separately. Modern Chinese class politics certainly had its objective reality and material basis, but this objective basis could only be grasped from within a type of purview connected to universality. Without theoretical analysis, there could have been no political mobilization, no people's war from the 1920s to the late 1940s, no practice of class politics in which the peasants were represented by the working class, no efforts by Third World countries to industrialize through a socialist approach and no movement to create a working class subjectivity—the objective existence of the working class cannot in itself spontaneously produce working-class politics. Without the formation of a working-class political organization, and without a movement fighting for the working class and its liberation, there could be no working-class politics.

That the working class was the leading class was a political assessment rather than a positivist one. It arose out of a political and economic analysis of the state of China and of other oppressed nations in the context of global capitalist development, and emerged only in the context of the people's war and the movement to build a socialist state. In this sense, we can say that working-class politics emerged from a theoretical analysis of the internal contradictions and unevenness of capitalism (manifested in the socialist movements of the so-called "backward areas"). Here "class" is a category of political economic analysis, not of general positivistic analysis. It chiefly originates from an analysis of the process of capitalist production and its expansion. As capitalism and imperialism expanded, all the non-Western areas, including China, were woven into the structure of the global capitalist division of labor. Industrial capitalism centered on the West subordinated all other social classes and social domains. Consequently, in every society, struggles against local conditions of inequality as well as struggles against local rulers all aimed to abolish class exploitation.

Capitalist class exploitation is the final stage of class exploitation. This is why, although China in the early twentieth century did not have a large working class, it witnessed a rapid growth of working-class politics within large-scale political and military struggles begun by peasants, students and urban dwellers. The genesis and reality of working-class politics cannot be refuted by citing the small number of working-class participants. In other words, class politics refers to movements against the contradictions created by the logic of capitalism and the class inequality it produces. Hence the political concept of class or the concept of the leading class cannot be equated with class in the sense of social stratification or occupational division. The essence of leadership is located in the fact that it embodies the momentum—which has different manifestations in different historical periods—to change this capitalist logic.

Two crucial social conditions were necessary for the working class to become the leading class representing the people's general interests. First, China was an agricultural society, with peasants composing 90 percent of its population. Hence the ability of the working class to represent society had to connect with the problems of the peasants and include them in its movement. This was the basis for the establishment of the political category of "the people." Second, the working class was not merely an appendage of capitalist production, but also a political identity constructed as the opponent of the capitalist class; it reflected the general interests and the future of the people.

The existence of the working class as an appendage of capitalist production—namely, a reified form of labor—is not equivalent to the existence of class politics. Class politics, manifested as a general force liberated from the capitalist logic of production, originated from an analysis of the global capitalist division of labor, of the dynamic of its internal contradictions and of its political practice in many areas, including those lacking industrialization. As the character of national oppression under capitalism differed from oppression in the precapitalist period, class politics also represented the interests of the oppressed nations, and the liberation of the working class included within it the goal of national liberation. The concept of "leadership" signified political momentum for a comprehensive social movement. Although in different periods it has been represented by particular dominant political forces, "leadership" is not a rationalization or justification for an authoritarian or bureaucratic political system. The logic of this modern political transformation was generated not by established social structures but through a theoretical analysis of capitalist development. This theoretical analysis and its political praxis directly shaped a new political subjectivity. It is for this reason that, even when the structure of social classes changes, political momentum that emerges in response to inequality can still remain vigorous by means of diversified political participation, theoretical debate and social experimentation.

Today, however, the political logic of the twentieth century has receded. Most intellectuals interpret China's current social stratification and its politics from a positivist perspective: Right-wing and even some left-wing intellectuals believe that because the working class in twentieth-century China occupied a very limited space in social life compared with the peasants and other social classes, and because the capitalist class was immature, the nature of China's modern revolution could not be socialist and the working class could never truly become the leading class. This positivist view undermines the foundational principles of the Chinese Revolution and modern Chinese politics. The increasing popularity of this positivist view forms the backdrop for the receding of historical analysis based on the particular elements of twentieth-century politics. Intellectuals adopting this approach share the view that "class" is a an essentialist structural concept, and in doing so abrogate the political nature of the class concept manifest in a political economic analysis of capitalism.

With the abrogation of the political sense of the class concept, following a positivistic logic the concept slips toward a structural concept of "stratum," such that even when the concept of class is used, its connotations barely differ from the notion of stratification in contemporary sociology. The concept of social stratification is centered on an analysis focused on the state in which social strata are seen as objective structures without any internal political capacity. The twentieth-century concept of class was by contrast political. Its connection with the state, such as the concept of the workers' state or the socialist state, was expressed through the vanguard party and its class allies. Without the background of people's war and the campaign for the construction of a socialist state, there would have been no class politics in practice.

Taking class as a structural concept referring to social stratum, one could establish a corresponding structural system of representation; for example, a proportional system of representation could be established in the Party or in the National People's Congress. But although the twentieth-century concept of class contained the idea of social stratification as one of its important elements, and because its politics thus implied a sense of proportional representation, the concept was also fundamentally political and intimately bound up with the concepts of political representation and political leadership. The "mass line" policy was the expression of this sense of political representation and leadership. This is why the social science of today can explain neither the current crisis of representation nor why representative politics took the form it did in the twentieth century. Under the conditions of depoliticization, the morass caused by the breakdown of representation cannot be resolved by the nonetheless necessary and positive steps taken to increase seats for certain classes, whether workers or peasants, in the Party or the People's Congress. The need to reconstruct representation and the necessity of repoliticization both arise from the same problem. This implies a need to analyze anew the internal contradictions and imbalances within contemporary capitalism in order to uncover and change their driving force and logic.

The Mass Line and the Conditions for Post-Political-Party Politics

At the time when class politics was forming in China in the early twentieth century, it already contained elements of supra-representative politics, in that the political parties that played the central role in politics at that time had features of supra-political or super-political parties. The distinction between "supra-representation" and "representation" can be explained by comparing them to the logic of "rites and music" (*liyi*) as opposed to the logic of "statutory measures" (*zhidu*) within the classical Confucian tradition. As broad social and spiritual influence as well as the ability to facilitate the creation and maintenance of a certain order was attributed to the correct "rites and music," so too did the various processes entailed in "supra-representation" facilitate people's participation in the formation of a new order. The concept of "supra-representation" is meant to emphasize this type of political process. The results of this process were eventually consolidated into a representative system, but the process was not the same as establishing a representative system.

After World War I, prolonged debates on parliamentary politics broke out among different political schools and even among communists from different countries. A key issue in the debates was the redefinition of the political party. In the struggle between the GMD and the CCP and in the war against the Japanese invasion, the practices developed in armed struggle, the mass line, the united front and party construction became political assets for the CCP. The mass line, summarized as "all for the masses; all relies on the masses; from the masses and to the masses," was the guideline by which this supra- or super-political party politics was consolidated. First applied to the construction of the base areas and later to the governing of the whole country, the mass line was a political praxis that inherited or borrowed from some forms and principles of the Western representational system that originated in the nineteenth and twentieth centuries, such as the election of representatives and the narrative of representation. This was true not only of the CCP but of all the other democratic parties as well. But it remains clear that this particular political praxis contained supra- or super-political-party elements that embodied the endeavor to establish organic and political connections between the political party and society.

In the political heritage of twentieth-century China, the supra-representation of Chinese representative politics was characterized by two essential features: the importance of culture and theory, and the sustaining of the political dynamics of the Party through the practice of the mass line.

Using Theoretical Debate to Provide Space for "Self-Revolution"

A recurrent phenomenon in modern Chinese history is that cultural movements have established the foundation for new politics, and that political parties in turn have attempted to discipline cultural movements. The emergence of political representation and political subjectivity has been closely linked with cultural movements and theoretical struggles, to which historical research has often been subordinated. I do not have enough space here to thoroughly discuss these cultural movements and what we could learn from them. Instead, I will focus on one point: that political dynamism always comes from the interaction between culture and politics. This dynamism will be lost if the political party overly interferes with or disciplines cultural movements, thereby destroying the interaction between politics and culture.

Today, culture has been categorized as an independent sphere opposed to politics and economy. It is no longer a space for the continuous creation of new political subjectivity. The term "culture industry" encapsulates the position of culture in an economic society. In "On Contradiction," Mao Zedong wrote that in backward countries theory normally occupies the primary position. It is impossible to establish a new politics without theoretical development. But founding a theory does not mean drawing up plans behind closed doors. The relation between theory and its praxis determines the results of theoretical struggle: Is it a relation between theory removed from reality and its dogmatic politics, or between theory that comes from and develops with praxis and its application? To emphasize the importance of praxis is not to deny the importance of debates on ideas, theories and political lines (*luxian*), but to oppose the kind of dogmatism that could produce a separation between the policy orientation of the political party and the demands of society.

The Chinese state system is characterized by a union between the Party and the government. This generates energy as well as crisis. Simply praising or criticizing this union will not resolve any problems. We should rather try to understand why this system could under certain conditions generate political energy and in other circumstances weaken the political energy of the Party to an unprecedented degree, forcing it to prostrate itself before the logic of power and capital. In other words, it is not productive to simplistically denounce the union of the political party and the state in general. Instead, we should analyze its various forms and connotations.

The structure of Chinese party politics was closely associated with Chinese revolutionaries' exploration of the socialist path. State ownership that aimed at resolving the contradictions inherent in capitalist private ownership provided a historical prerequisite for the direct union of the state and capital in the early days of the reforms. That the state was in control of a large amount of capital had the benefit of freeing it from manipulation by a single capitalist or oligarch and allowing it to maintain strong regulatory capacity. But in circumstances of depoliticization, political energy is mainly manifested through state power, especially administrative power over political power. With the weakening of political power, state power gradually surrenders to the control of interest networks centered around capital. Accordingly, like privately owned capital, state-owned capital faces the same problems of corruption, monopoly and, as a result, inefficiency.

Hence, the crucial problem is not the privatization of state-owned property but freeing state-owned property in China from interest networks centered on capital. The dissolution of subjective initiative due to the alliance between power and capital is a consequence of depoliticization. Since the positive and negative elements of the system are entangled with each other, we will inevitably face a political crisis if there is no continuous "self-revolution" to create new political energy.

During the Chinese Revolution and the subsequent socialist period, theoretical debates within the Party were one of the methods by which political energy was generated and the direction of development adjusted. The elevation of practical problems to the level of theoretical discussions and debates on the political line generated a new political momentum; it was also key to demonstrating that the best way to correct mistakes was through debate based on praxis and implementing institutional adjustments accordingly. Even during that time, such debates were not confined to the intra-party sphere, but were enriched by the mass line and the reciprocal relations between theory and praxis. Since the economic reforms such theoretical debates have ineluctably extended to the social sphere.

There are several prerequisites for post-political-party politics, namely, citizens' freedom of speech, space for debate in the political sphere, citizen's political participation supported by modern technology, and the reinstallation of laborers at the center of Chinese political life. The healthy development of political debates and citizens' political participation will not be achieved without reforming the political sphere, the essence of which is to set ourselves free from the logic of media capital, as it conglomerates and functions in the role of a party, in order to create a space of true tolerance and freedom. Only on this basis can there be positive interaction between social debate and public policy adjustments. Today, the forces suppressing citizens' freedom of speech come not only from the traditional political sphere but from media power that has been corporatized and partified as well.

Expanding the public sphere and opposing a media monopoly do not contradict each other.

Theoretical debates cannot be treated as abstract discussions removed from political practice; they represent rather the recapitulation of practice, evaluation of the outcome of practice and new practices examining previous theories and practice. The experience of the Chinese Revolution was based on praxis; it corrected its mistakes through theoretical debates and political struggle and consequently created premises for new strategies and new practice. In "On Practice," Mao argued that the Chinese Revolution had no preexisting model and that the nation was always learning and exploring. Throughout the twentieth century, whenever theoretical debates and the struggle over the political line were relatively active, the political realm was also more lively and innovations in the political structure more dynamic. The current practice of decentralizing power and allowing profits to stay with the state-owned enterprises (*fang quan rang li*) has increased the importance of local experiments. Theoretical orientations should be diverse. The dynamic of reform in China largely derives from different local experiments and their competition, as well as from the constructive dialectical interaction between central and local governments; this is referred to as "initiative from two sources" (*liangge jijixing*).

Struggles over the political line in the Chinese Revolution created new political paths and were closely associated with theoretical debates. The process of reform has also witnessed such line struggles. Theoretical and political struggles have the ability to correct mistakes during revolutionary politics. To emphasize the rectifying ability of theoretical and political struggles does not preclude criticisms of the violence and despotism that sometimes appeared in the process of struggle. The cruelty and brutality that appeared during certain line struggles have taught us a heavy lesson—that the CCP must resolve problems on the basis of democracy and law. Still, we should not regard theoretical debate and line struggle as merely signifying power competition and political repression because of the existence of violence in these struggles. Political repression marks the end of theoretical debate, of line struggle and of the practice of competition within the party.

Today, the suppression of intellectual debate implemented by political and media power also marks the end of politics. A large amount of writing claiming to recount and reflect on the violence of the revolution- ary period actually focuses on discrediting necessary theoretical debate and line struggle, leading to the dysfunction of the self-rectifying mech- anism of the Party and to the self-enclosure of the political sphere. This type of research is a product of the politics of depoliticization. An urgently relevant question is this: Why did some theoretical debates, especially those that concerned the political line, turn violent? Consideration of this issue cannot avoid the process of the statification of the Party through which the necessary boundary between the Party and the state disappeared and the Party no longer maintained a relatively independent theoretical space. In addition, this issue cannot be under- stood without considering the partification of the media, by which media power tries to become a sort of political agent for the state, capital or both and begins to colonize the public sphere. Criticism and self-criti- cism used to be key elements of political life in China but were eliminated after Deng Xiaoping promoted the dictum of "don't debate" (*bu zheng- lun*) in the 1980s. Without debates, struggles and tests, how can the practice of criticism and self-criticism continue? How can political inno- vation be achieved?

The Mass Line and the Political Vigor of Social Organization

In today's conditions, with party politics closely bound up with struc- tures of power, the possibility that political parties will transform themselves and formulate a new politics is extremely low. The level of bureaucratization in state and party structures is unprecedentedly high in the current system of statized party politics. The power of political parties alone cannot diminish bureaucracy. The mass line could not only serve as a channel for a party to maintain its political vigor but also acquire a new dimension—that is, meaningful interaction with the masses promotes political openness and can greatly increase political participation.

The mass line policy was first put forward by the Central Committee of the Communist Party of China in 1929 in a letter to the Fourth Route Army. However, "all for the masses; all relies on the masses; from the masses and to the masses" was not just a political and military strategy, but a description of an organic revolutionary politics as well. Like "the people" (*renmin*), "the masses" (*qunzhong*) is also a political category containing a new political subjectivity produced by uniting the Party and the common people (*dazhong*), especially the peasants. The mass line policy reveals the underlying affinity between the politics of the Party and the politics of the larger society. This is a unique element in Chinese politics. The Party was said to be the political representative of the masses, but in fact it embodied the process of shaping the masses into a political subject, and a mechanism by which the masses could represent themselves in the people's war and the campaign for the construction of their own state. It would be difficult to find precedents for this development in nineteenth- and twentieth-century Europen party politics or its extensions in other regions.

The mass line, "from the masses and to the masses," as well as the cultural politics of "for whom" (*weile shei*) and "how to serve" (*zenme wei*), are all questions about the relationship of the Party with the masses and society. Since the crux of modern politics is the state, political movements cannot operate by themselves, detached from political power. The problem of a representative system emerged when the Party and the state became affiliated, which is to say, the political system required a certain type of representation for its construction. In the Jiangxi Soviet and the other base areas in the war against the Japanese invasion, political regime construction, occurred under people's war. The issue of a representative system arose during this process of regime construction but the representative system of this period was closely associated with the praxis of supra-representation—"from the people and to the people." After 1949, as people's war ended, the formalization of the state system required the formalization of the representative system as well; consequently, the relationship between the Party and the masses gradually transformed from one of supra-representation to a representative system rooted in the state system. A system of representation can function in the form of general elections, local elections, elections within political parties, recommendation, rotation or election by lot. The merits or disadvantages of these forms are relative—they should be determined by analyzing concrete circumstances, that is, as long as active politics of the people and for the people exist.

When discussing the problems of the system of representation, however, we often neglect the element of supra-representation in the politics of representation. The mass line policy contains such an element. The concept of "the masses" in the mass line points to a political process, and contains the connotation of a political subjectivity about to germinate and take shape. "The masses" constitute political energy in formation. Their relationship with the political party also changes in this process, as duality gradually integrates into a relative unity. In other words, this relationship often transcends representation. The two sides mold each other in the struggle to accomplish their purposes so that the mass line becomes the process of creating a new political subjectivity. In this process, the masses become a political category and the political party part of mass politics; the two define each other and intermingle. Hence, formulating the correct response to a changing era and to the different composition of the masses in new social conditions becomes a major agenda for political organizations seeking to to reconstruct political representation. Without this process, political representation, regardless of its form of application, will face the danger of becoming empty, as a consequence of the political system's detaching from public life. This aspect of supra-representation in representative politics should not be neglected when discussing the problem of representative systems.

As class politics has declined, party politics has shifted to post-political-party politics. Contemporary China is undergoing a historical process of class restructuring and the suppression of class politics. This contrasts sharply with the class politics of the twentieth century, which were extremely active despite the relatively small size of the working class. What are the political connotations of the "mass line policy" under post-party politics? In the Chinese Revolution, and especially in the people's war, the mass line could be roughly described as a political process through which a mature and highly disciplined political party, according to its clear political orientation and mission, mobilized the masses and recruited members active among the masses. It did so to strengthen and reform itself while fully guaranteeing the freedom and legal rights of broader mass organizations and mass movements and respecting their independence.

For instance, after the War of Resistance against Japan broke out, the CCP Central Committee issued the "Policy on mass movements" on October 16, 1937. It emphasized the need to "establish organizations that truly belong to the masses, including labor unions, peasants' unions, student unions, merchants' unions, and other organizations for youth, for women and for children, based on the political, economic and cultural needs of the masses" and that "it is necessary to organize as many workers and hired farm hands as possible into labor unions and as many peasants as possible into peasants' unions." These mass organizations practiced "extensive democracy" within themselves and participated in government work as autonomous groups while promoting the economic and political interests and cultural activities of the masses.

In today's state-party system (*guodang tizhi*), we can use the mass line policy concept but should not and cannot recreate the previous form of politics. One of the results of the statification of the Party is that the relationship between the Party, as the end point of a political movement, and the masses gradually transformed into one between the state and society. Nowadays a meticulously organized and highly disciplined political party with a clear agenda, that is, a political party in the twentieth-century sense, no longer exists, and the politics of the masses created by the mass line policy have also vanished: Politics have degenerated into the category of management, a politics of depoliticization. The statification of the Party signals the end of the era of the mass line. In a context completely different from that of the twentieth century, what does it mean to broach the topic of the mass line again? Should we talk about the masses in the relationship between the state and the citizens, or in the relationship between the political party and classes? The birth of the masses, as an emergent political subject, proclaimed the birth of a new political form. Under globalization and marketization, what does the mass line—a product of people's war—signify? What political power could any reference to the mass line today hope to bring forth? What political subject could it seek to cultivate? And what future could the mass line actually point to?

The mass line is not simply rhetoric, and as a political project its meaning is not self-evident. To revisit this issue is not a call to return to a particular historical period but to pursue a possible yet uncertain future. To rely on the masses does not simply mean having social supervision or participation but a certain form of social organization. When we say there is no class politics in the twentieth-century sense today, it does not mean there are neither active class movements nor citizen politics. Among contemporary social organizations, nongovernmental organizations get more media attention, whereas the working class and peasant movements are seldom covered. These two groups engage in political, social, ecological and cultural issues in different ways. Currently, many social organizations and social movements have political potential, but they might not all lead to more positive politics. Under the conditions of financial capitalism, even social movements are penetrated by the capitalist system. Therefore, whether we discuss civil society or analyze class politics in the contemporary world, we cannot avoid examining new forms of contemporary capitalism.

Financial capitalism is a global problem. Just as the accumulation of capital and its internal contradictions have reached an unprecedented level, so too the gap between fictitious economy and real economy has become extraordinary. This distorted process of accumulation continues to disrupt social relations. Compared with Western countries, China has a larger real economy and a larger labor population active in the real economy. The economic regulatory capability of its state is also stronger than in many developed countries. Financial capital, highly mobile and transnational, has escaped from the traditional restrictions of industry, guild and even the state. What significance do these new developments have for the political dilemma we are discussing in this article? How are the state, political parties, class and social organizations changing? These are problems remaining to be discussed. What we can be sure about is that we must redefine and reanalyze a series of fundamental concepts that constitute the modern state system and power structure, including sovereignty, citizen, class and labor. In the Chinese context, our understanding of these issues is directly linked with the issue of political practice.

For example, in the Chinese context, reconstructing representation is one of the methods of overcoming the crisis of representation. The question is what type of representation should be adopted. Is it necessary to reemphasize the importance of the working class or the alliance of workers and peasants? In the era of financial capitalism, Western countries have experienced and are still experiencing deindustrialization. Many intellectuals have noted the radical shrinking or even disappearance of the working class as a revolutionary class and have begun to challenge theoretically the idea of class and class politics. The other side of this social process, however, is industrialization and the formation of a working class on a grand scale in China and in many other non-Western countries. Under globalization, this structure of class formation is not stable. An important phenomenon in contemporary China is the restructuring of class society. Here it is inevitable that the concept of class will be reused. But the expansion and reorganization of the working class and the decline of working-class politics happened almost simultaneously. The newly emerging working-class politics have not been able to reach the depth and scale of those that preceded them. We can immediately identify its two predominant features: First, it is detached from party politics; second, the new working class is unstable due to the mobility of the contemporary system of production. This instability renders the new working class different from its equivalent in the era of socialist industrialization and in the early stage of their formation.

We can roughly identify four types of workers' struggles. First, there are strikes and attempts at self-organization (unionization) in order to protect workers' own personal rights and interests. The workers' strike at the Guangzhou Honda factory in 2010 is an example of typical working-class politics. Second, there are attempts to shorten the contract period. Workers refuse to work in a factory or for a company for a long time. Instead, they stay in one position for a year or two before taking another job. From a classic perspective of class politics, this tactic jeopardizes the solidarity of workers. But to demand a higher salary from the state and capitalists, it is a highly effective action. Third, in addition to traditional forms of organization such as unions, new forms of organization have appeared. The so-called "foreman system" (*linggong zhi*), formerly seen as a way of enabling double exploitation, has become a new organizational form for workers' struggle. It protects some of the interests of workers through informal contracts. There are also associations for people coming from the same province, town or village and for ethnic minorities, all of which have the same function organizing workers on a relatively small scale. Lastly, rights protection (*weiquan*) movements focus on the protection of legal rights of individuals. In addition to these four types, rural reconstruction (*xiangcun jianshe*) provides an alternative form of support for the labor movement. Discussions on these issues are myriad but are mainly conducted within the framework of social stratification, barely exploring the political potential of these forms of organizations or their overlap with and differences from traditional class politics.

*　　*　　*

If the breakdown of representation is manifest in the decoupling of the political form from the social form, what kind of political form can organically connect with a social form? Classes and class politics exist in China today. Reconstructing representation requires directly confronting and addressing the recent redivision of Chinese society into social classes. But as the statification of the Party intensifies, instead of reconstructing it as the political party of a particular class, a better approach would probably involve formulating a more independent social politics (including political organizations in a broader sense, such as workers' unions, peasant associations, and other social organizations) and shifting to an active labor politics that focuses on reforming the relations within the production system. This may be a path to a "post-party" politics. In truth, urban versus rural conflict and its repercussions, regional imbalances and their reverberations, class relationships and their transformation, as well as the ecological damage caused by contemporary modes of production and consumption, are the most intense manifestations of the contradictions in modern capitalism. Therefore, rural reconstruction, environmental protection, transformation of the development model, protection of ethnic equality and cultural diversity and improving the social status of the working class should all become the impetus for a contemporary politics of equality.

Why raise the issue of post-party politics? The answer lies in the understanding that two conflicting proposals for contemporary political reform share the same premise of returning to party politics. For the right wing, the basic political model is the classic multiparty system based on the parliamentary politics framework. For the left wing, it is important to recuperate or reconstruct the Party's political representation and consequently to raise a series of questions concerning class and its political forms. China's reality reveals that the latter poses the more urgent question. But it is sure that contemporary political reform will not necessarily return to the political model of the nineteenth or twentieth century but rely on the new political and economic reality. Reconstructing representation through the mass line policy, theoretical debates and organization reconstruction is an inescapable political process, but its purpose is unlikely to be a return to the old political party model.

Today, although the organization called the "political party" still exists, its political connotation has changed significantly. In the early twentieth century, this change was undertaken deliberately, and was accomplished by establishing a super-political party to overcome the crisis of multiparty politics. In the late twentieth century, however, the change was more passive as it was completed in the shift from a partified state to a statized party. Under today's conditions, understanding how social power can engage in political processes on a larger scale and in a more direct fashion becomes a necessary project in the exploration of a new political framework. This is also the precondition for a party to practice the mass line. Therefore the process of rebuilding political representation cannot simply rely on traditional party politics. It must include the practice of post-party politics, for which current technological developments also provide possibilities. So-called post-party politics does not negate the function of political organizations, but rather can highlight how they can be open, unfinished and nonbureaucratic. The mass line and mass politics are sources of political vigor and can be the foundation for resisting right-wing populism.

Creating a New Universalism

Today social structures are changing drastically. Considering their course of development and reconstruction should be everyone's concern. A new political agency needs to be established based on the interests of the majority of the Chinese, which in the past demonstrated its political implications and social significance through the category of "the people." Since the concept of "the people" is generally shifting toward the meaning of "population," its political connotation has dissipated to such a degree that we can no longer find any political term for the general interest aside from the concept of "citizen." The disdain for the concept of "the people" is an ideological reflection of the fragmentation of society. In modern Chinese history, "the people" was a disputed concept constantly appropriated by different political powers, but it was not always empty. In the period when mass politics and the mass line were active, it was a vibrant political category. Its rich connotations have been drained as a result of depoliticization, as mass politics and the mass line have been replaced by bureaucratic state politics.

I revisit the concept of "the people" here not to oppose it to the more popular concept of citizen, but on the contrary, I argue that it is essential to reestablish a political connection between these two categories. The politics of the citizenry should not be a politics centered on the individual as the main subject, for it should also embrace the politics of the masses and society and thus the politics of the people. In ethnic minority areas, it should include the politics of ethnic equality as well. In the twentieth century, progressive parties that proposed a political role for the proletarian class were not prompted by the interests of the working class or workers' groups alone. They believed that the mission of the proletariat had a universal significance that surpassed the limits of its own interests. It would necessarily become the people's politics, and the politics for every citizen. In the system of state power, people's politics express the politics of true equality. The politics of equality is neither the policies of providing relief for the poor nor meeting the national target of eliminating the poverty. It includes reflections on the premises and motivations of politics. I discuss the various connotations of the politics of equality in Chapters 6 and 7.

Current research on social stratification can quickly identify the interests of particular social classes but fails to identify a general interest. This is a problem that positivist methodology cannot resolve. Whether or not our politics in the future can develop in a positive direction is determined by whether or not the latent power that represents the future can be discovered within social transformations. This latent power is universal, and what is dormant now will become manifest in the future. To discuss a "reconstruction of representation" is to unearth the universality of this suppressed potential. This discussion is essentially a battle for the future. For any type of political system, only when it can create universality, namely when it can represent universal interests, will it be truly representative of society. Hence the process of reconstructing representation is the process of creating universality. I have no interest in the widely celebrated official slogan of "great cultural development and prosperity." My inquiry is more motivated by the problem of the relationship between culture and politics. Can we, as was done in the twentieth century, redefine the boundaries of politics by developing cultural practices which could not only help us contend with the structural transformation currently taking place, but also help us grasp its possible trajectory? And can we, from the experience of China's development as well as that of the world, unearth a new universality that can represent the future? This is a question that must be raised. This is also a challenge we must overcome.

The twentieth century was in a sense a prophecy, one that was soon trapped in crisis after its articulation. But it was also a suppressed potential. Reexamining the cultural and political legacy of the twentieth century does not imply a simple return to the practices of the past. Rather, the goal must be to discover its untapped power containing universality and potential for the future. This suppressed potential reminds us that returning to the old politics of the nineteenth century is not our destination. Our attention should be drawn to all of those aspects of the historical legacy of the twentieth century, including elements of the socialist state and its constitution, which may provide inspiration for the construction of a post-party politics of the future.

5

Two Kinds of New Poor and Their Future

The Decline and Reconfiguration of Class
Politics and the Politics of the New Poor

This is an old topic for a new era. In China, this topic can be traced at least as far back as the end of the First World War. On November 16, 1918, five days after the proclamation of the end of the "European war," Cai Yuanpei, the president of Beijing University, gave a speech congratulating the Allied nations for their victory. During the speech, he used the slogan "Laborers Are Sacred," and explained:

> When I say laborers, I mean not only metal workers, carpenters and so on. All those who use their own labor to accomplish work for others, regardless of whether it is manual or mental labor, are laborers. Every farmer is an agricultural worker; commerce does the work of transfer; employees at schools, authors and inventors are educational laborers— we are all laborers! We must ourselves recognize the value of laborers! Laborers are sacred![1]

The idea that "laborers are sacred" quickly spread among intellectuals, and by 1919 it had replaced "Mr. Science and Mr. Democracy" as the most prominent slogan of the day.[2] In 1920, the sixth issue of volume seven of *New Youth* was named its "Labor Day Memorial Issue," with "Laborers Are Sacred" in Cai Yuanpei's calligraphy adorning the cover. The slogan connected workers and the sacred for the first time. It not only addressed the question of the dignity of laborers, but it also combined "laboring with strength" (manual labor) and "laboring with the mind" (mental labor) to introduce a new concept of "laborer" (*laogong*). This development initiated a continuing exploration of the question of laborers and their dignity in twentieth-century China. The richness, complexity and tragic nature of this exploration far exceeded Cai Yuanpei's expectations. Our rejection or reaffirmation of this slogan has implications for our evaluation of twentieth-century history, as well as the ways we judge our own individual relationships to this history.

The twentieth century has already become history. Even as China takes up its unprecedented role as factory for the world, what has been called the "postindustrial society" of the West has now reached the "end of the era of production," according to Baudrillard, who writes,

> in the past, labour was used to designate the reality of a social production and a social objective of accumulating wealth. Even capital and surplus-value exploited it—precisely where it retained a use-value for the expanded reproduction of capital and its final destruction . . . Today this is no longer the case since labour is no longer productive but has become reproductive of the *assignation to labour* which is the general habit of a society which no longer knows whether or not it wishes to produce . . . It remains, however, more necessary than ever to reproduce labour as a social ritual [*affectation*], as a reflex, as morality, as consensus, as regulation, as the reality principle. The reality principle *of the code*, that is: an immense *ritual of the signs of labour* extends over society in general — since it *reproduces* itself, it matters little whether or not it *produces.*[3]

When Baudrillard published this piece, many Marxists regarded his claim about the increasing disappearance of productive labor as an interpretation of phenomena confined to post-industrial European society, holding that on a global scale the capitalist division of labor still persists—that is, that labor in the peripheral areas is still productive, and these laborers are exploited within the unequal global system.

Here we can examine another phenomenon associated with capitalism that acts as the supplement to productive labor—"nonproductive labor." For example, during an economic crisis, investment aimed at stimulating production is undertaken specifically for the purpose of reproduction, this often taking the form of the overproduction of commodities. But in contrast to twentieth-century economic crises, the current crisis is long term. In the process of China's current large-scale industrialization, "productive" production has constantly been in search of laborers. But under the influence of the economic crisis, overproduction and demand for this type of "reproductive labor" have become constant as well. In 2008, in order to alleviate pressure from the fiscal crisis, the Chinese government spent 4 trillion yuan as stimulus investment, causing even more overproduction. In a real sense, this too can be understood as production aimed at preserving reproduction.

In 2010, the tragedy of thirteen workers in succession committing suicide by jumping to their deaths occurred at the Foxconn factory complex in Dongguan, Guangzhou. But just as a discussion of the value of workers' lives and their dignity began to gain popular attention, the head of Foxconn declared that one million workers would be replaced, in the future, by machines. The government, the media and the entire society immediately shifted their attention to the problem of future unemployment. The question of the dignity of workers was quickly replaced by a discussion of the problem of maintaining and reproducing the workers as a group. In Henan, a province densely packed with labor power, multinational companies recently migrated from the coastal areas are suddenly facing a labor shortage. In response, the provincial government has agreed to give large-scale companies, including the Foxconn complex at Zhengzhou, a subsidy of 200 yuan per worker every month. While this may not signify the end of production, it does without doubt constitute a new phenomenon produced for the "reproduction of labor." With regard to the issue of the "sacredness of workers," "reproductive labor" has made the situation ever more dismal.

The concepts that structured the politics of dignity within twentieth-century China, such as class, the political party of a class and the associated political categories were long ago or are currently being replaced by the concepts of modernization centering on "development." The theory of the "end of history" seeks to finish the "history" organized by those categories. After the great changes of 1989–91, politics relating to the Chinese Revolution and the workers' state have even been regarded as standing in opposition to the politics of dignity. Is any purpose served by bringing up these old topics? To regard China today as a "post-class society" does not imply that the phenomenon of class has disappeared, and it certainly does not refer to the classless state of communism spoken of by Marx. Rather, it aims to distinguish the class phenomena of contemporary society from the class politics of the nineteenth and twentieth centuries. After the decline of class politics, "class" does not necessarily invoke the political connotations of the nineteenth- and twentieth-century class revolutions, and the concept of the "new poor" is not equivalent to the proletarian class of the last century. Within this context, the politics of dignity are not the same as the politics of egalitarianism born in opposition to the European system of aristocracy and its concept of honor. This being the case, within exactly what historical context does our discussion take place, and what action does it call for?

If class and working class are regarded by contemporary people as antiquated concepts, then what of the fate of dignity, an even more antiquated concept? For those familiar with European philosophy, the concept of dignity is the foundation of modern egalitarianism and universalism and worth frequent review for renewed discussion. From constitutional rights to cultural pluralism, from individual rights to collective identity, a concept of dignity continually reappears in new forms, contrasting with a concept of honor based on a traditional hierarchical system. In the private realm, dignity was connected with a new understanding of personal identity. According to Lionel Trilling, Charles Taylor and others, this type of individualized identity can be related to either the concepts of authenticity and inwardness or the rational subject.[4] The former can be traced to a narrative first developed by Rousseau in his synthesis of other ideas (though it appears more clearly in Herder in his account of the self-identification of nations). The latter comes from the discussion of dignity by Kant grounded in the concept of reason—that is, we are worthy of respect because we are rational subjects who can direct our lives in accordance with the principle of reason. In the public realm, the concept of dignity is most clearly expressed in the politics of equality and recognition: Such differences of identity as nation, ethnic group, gender and class must all be subordinated to the equal rights and dignity of citizens.[5]

Contemporary debates relating to a universalist concept of dignity and the politics of equal recognition center on two issues. The first is the narrative of pluralism emerging from gender, ethnic and cultural studies. This takes the politics of difference or the politics of recognition as its focus and approaches the problem of the recognition of difference from the standpoint of egalitarianism. From here it initiates a theoretical debate on such issues as difference and equality, the production of difference and homogenization. The second issue has provoked a long-standing but increasingly acute debate: In contrast to the classical liberal perspective that views equality only in terms of the rights of citizens and the right to vote in elections, socialism and socialist democracy hold that equality must be expanded into the economic realm, because inequality within modern economies has already produced new hierarchical and hereditary systems which invalidate the politics of dignity. These two public debates on dignity have in fact caused an internal crisis within the politics of universalist equality. The politics of difference seeks to bring differences in gender, race and cultural background into the politics of equal recognition, thus endangering the universalist nature of these politics. And the demand for economic equality brings collectivities with a common goal and their distribution mechanisms into the politics of equal recognition, which conflicts with a view of rights centered purely on the individual.

In the nineteenth and twentieth centuries, we witnessed the opposition and competition between the liberal democratic model and the socialist movement and its attempts to establish workers' states. We can consider this opposition and competition as internal to the universalist politics of dignity and the political struggle for equal recognition. The category of class and the politics associated with it also arose with the decline of the traditional concept of honor. What they attempted to solve was the reappearance of a hierarchical system within modern society, and they were therefore internally connected with the modern concept of dignity. Class, gender, nation and other concepts became the main political categories through which to conceptualize dignity on the foundation of a universalist politics of equal recognition. After 1989, cultural pluralism in the form of the politics of difference replaced the twentieth-century narrative of class to become the main rhetorical challenger to liberalism and its concepts of public recognition and equal respect. In the era of the financial crisis, however, the conflict between the so-called "1 percent" and the "99 percent" has returned the issue of economic inequality to the fore. The categories of the poor and the new poor have revived public aspirations to overturn capitalism. Research on social division and social stratification has seen partial efforts to "bring class back in." I say "partial" not only because class is only one of the concepts that this type of research has begun to use, but also because within practical politics, and even within the practical politics of equality, the concept of class has lost its power. The civil society yearned for by the liberals, the multitude raised by the radical left, and the "new poor" raised by some new Marxists are in fact all substitutes for the traditional concept of class.

I will discuss the questions of difference and equality in later chapters in this volume. The present chapter discusses two types of "new poor" within two interrelated contexts—the globalization of capitalism and the defeat of the workers' state. I attempt an inquiry into the crisis and possible future of the politics of equality, as well as the question of whether the problems of class and dignity are still linked.

The New Poor and the Birth of the New Workers

Polarization between the rich and poor, between urban and rural areas, and between regions are normal conditions in the age of capitalism. Under these normal conditions, there is no question as to who is poor: Relative to capitalists, workers are poor; relative to city dwellers, peasants are poor; relative to developed regions or the First World, underdeveloped areas or the Third World is poor. Marx explained the relationship between class exploitation and poverty as inherent to the relationship between labor and capital in his analysis of the capitalist mode of production. Theodore Schultz in *The Economics of Being Poor* centered his analysis of the poor on rural people. His concept of human capital was aimed at addressing the problem of rural development in the context of industrialization, but in fact it used the standpoint of development to ultimately negate the question of class. Dependency theory argues that capitalism continuously reproduces relationships between the metropole and the periphery, such that the Third World becomes a region dependent on the First, incapable of its own sovereign development and remaining mired in lasting poverty. This argument has been the theoretical conclusion of the application of class analysis to global relations since Lenin. Bankrupt and nearly bankrupt farmers, workers in the process of proletarianization and the masses of poor and hungry spread throughout the villages and urban slums of the Third World provide footnotes to this notion of the poor.

After the Cold War, a change has occurred in this idea of the poor. The most important factors propelling this change are those taking place under the direction of financial globalization: the new processes of industrialization and the development of information technology influencing the entire world, and the collapse of workers' states and the concurrent and related development of a new international division of labor. In the first decade of the twenty-first century, newly rising economies produced outstanding achievements in manufacturing:

> China has been behind most of the changes. In 2000, China was responsible for 7 per cent of world manufacturing output. By 2005 this had risen to 9.8 per cent. Over the six years to 2011, China's share doubled again to 19.8 per cent. That put China above the US in terms of share of factory production. It was a historic change: 2011 was the first year for more than a century in which the US was anything other than the world's top dog in factory output.[6]

As the new industrial revolution taking place under the conditions of economic globalization has changed the relationships between and positions of the advanced and developing countries, it has also created a new model of the poor. According to *The Blue Book of Social Administration— Report on the Innovation of China's Social Administration*, China's Gini coefficient in 1980 was 0.275, while by 2010 it had reached 0.438.[7] The largest portion of the new poor is made up of the so-called migrant workers—that is, those on whom urban and coastal industries and services now rely. This "floating population" has departed from agricultural production, yet to a certain extent preserves links to the land that was apportioned to them in the rural areas. This differentiates them from traditional farmers or rural people who have lost their land, such as hired agricultural laborers, transients or the type of poor now living in slums in Latin America or South Asia.

At the beginning of the reform period, rural reform was aimed at reducing the urban–rural gap. Since the initiation of the urban reforms of the mid-1980s, however, this gap has continuously increased. By the end of the 1990s, the "three rural crises" (*sannong weiji*)—that "rural peoples' lives are really bitter, the countryside is really poor and agriculture is in crisis"—came to occupy the center of public discussion, and the relationship between poverty and the status of the rural areas in the context of urbanization and industrial reform became increasingly apparent. The bankruptcy of the rural areas, the impoverishment of rural people and the crisis of agriculture created a limitless supply of labor for the ever-expanding "factory of the world." Discussion of the "three rural issues" opening up after 1999 and the subsequent attempts at new rural reconstruction pushed forth by the government were directed at this situation. The elimination of the agricultural tax and the expansion of the medical insurance system in the countryside produced significant achievements and partially improved conditions in rural areas.

But the "three rural crises" were not fundamentally solved: The vast rural areas still face the predicament of young people leaving, the old staying behind to till the land and the countryside emptying out. According to residential statistics, 240 million people in China had by 2008 migrated from the rural areas to the cities to look for work, over 60 percent of whom made up a new generation of "rural migrants" who had never participated in agricultural production and had no plans to return to the countryside. With the implementation of the new land transfer policy, this group of workers is transitioning from rural migrant workers with definite land rights into urban workers whose lives are in the cities and who cannot return to the countryside, but who also are barred from enjoying equal status with urban residents. They are also distinct from the classical proletariat—they are not farmers who were forced into the cities and the system of industrial production after losing their land. They are inheritors of land relations established in the socialist period, entering a new market society. The vast majority of them own a piece of land, and thus they are not "proletarians" (*wuchanzhe*: literally, people without property). After entering the cities this status did not change, but even under the conditions of the economic crisis, the many who returned to the countryside and neighboring rural areas did not necessarily return to agricultural production.

Huang Zongzhi has shown in his new research that the traditional categories of "worker" and "farmer" are not adequate to describe the reality of contemporary Chinese society. Labor regulations established on the basis of these old categories are out of sync with the realities of laboring people, and to a large extent have become regulations which protect a minority of privileged blue-collar workers, white-collar workers, public functionaries and employees of medium- and large-scale enterprises. He further argues that today the vast majority of laboring people in China are neither industrial workers in the traditional sense nor farmers in the traditional sense, but half-worker half-farmers, people with rural residence permits who are both workers and farmers. Most of them exist outside of the protections of the labor laws. They are thought to provide temporary "labor services," thus falling under the rubric of "labor service relations" rather than "labor relations." Their living conditions fall far short of those of the actual middle class. Statistics show that the "formal economy," in which workers (including those of the middle class) enjoy the protection of labor laws, accounts for 16.8 percent of employed people, and the "informal economy," which employs the half-worker half-farmer laboring people without the protection of labor laws, accounts for 83.2 percent.[8]

This group of new workers is the product of shifts in the relations between classes and the growing opposition and polarization between the cities and the rural areas during China's transformation into capitalism's world factory. According to calculations in the 2013 *Migrant Workers Monitor Survey Report* issued by the National Bureau of Statistics of China, 27.5 per cent of migrant workers are employed in the manufacturing sector, 20 per cent in construction, and the remaining portion in the service sector.[9] Because the construction industry to a large extent relies on outside contractors and subcontractors, only a small minority of construction workers sign labor contracts, and the vast majority have no means of enjoying the protections of labor contract law. According to the "Plan for paying attention to the new generation of migrant workers," a large-scale research survey investigating the recruitment and employment of construction workers throughout the country and led by teachers and students from Qinghua University, Beijing University and Hong Kong Polytechnic University, in 2011, 75.6 percent of migrant workers in the construction industry had not signed labor contracts, and of those who had signed contracts, 63.6 per cent had not been given copies.[10]

In reality, such contracts exist in name only. In 2013, 82.6 percent of migrant workers in the construction industry had not signed contracts. In the cities of Chengdu, Wuhan and Zhengzhou, where the number of new construction sites has increased rapidly, the percentage of workers who had not signed labor contracts in 2013 reached 85.5 percent, 87.9 percent and 93.2 percent.[11] While the situation is dire within the construction industry, it is even more difficult for workers in the service industry to obtain the protection of labor laws. In fact, to this day only migrant workers in the manufacturing industry have been able to express a meaningful degree of dissent and protest.

Shining light upon and integrally linked with the situation of new workers described above is the decline of the socialist-era working class. In the reform period, this group's status quickly slid from that of an urban class with a relatively high degree of social influence into urban poor or unemployed. The profound nature of this transformation is little understood by most people today. Perhaps it will take another generation before we can fully understand its historical implications. The new workers far exceed China's twentieth-century working class in number and scale, yet as a group they have almost no position within the realm of politics or culture. Even the question of whether they make up a "class" or a "stratum" is still debated by scholars.

A separate group, different from both the traditional working class and the new workers, is far more active within the realm of politics and culture: those who can be called the "new poor." This group, too, is the product of the industrialization, urbanization and spread of information technology brought about by globalization, but unlike the rural migrant workers, they are victims of a consumer society lacking in "internal demand." They have often received higher education, work in various fields and live on the outskirts of the large cities. Their income, though similar to that of blue-collar workers, is insufficient to meet the consumptive demands stimulated by consumer culture. Aside from their material poverty, scholars often describe this group as "spiritually impoverished" and having "lost their social values" (even though those using these concepts have spiritual lives no more rich than those they describe). This type of poverty cannot be eliminated by an improvement in the economy. These are the new poor of consumer society, who, as described by Zygmunt Bauman in *Work, Consumerism and the New Poor*, are consumers without the ability to consume.[12] If the classical idea of the poor is that they are produced by capitalist processes, then the "new poor" are by-products of consumer society and consumer culture. At the same time, they are products of a capitalist economy's move from manufacturing toward finance capital, from a real economy to a virtual economy. The new workers and the new poor together constitute the two sides of contemporary China's concept of "poor people."

But discussing the new poor only from the standpoint of consumption risks overlooking the political capacity of this group. Due to the fact that the new poor often have relatively advanced cultural, educational and technological backgrounds, their understanding of the world is closely connected with developments within consumer society. In the realm of politics, it is not difficult to see their likeness in the protest movements of Egypt and Tunisia, the Occupy Wall Street movement in the United States, the various other "Occupy" movements that drew inspiration from it as well as the street demonstrations in Moscow. In contrast to the new poor born of the process of de-industrialization in Europe and the United States, China's new poor sprout from the transition from a socialist to a post-socialist system. Their fate is intimately bound up with the change in the status of labor from being the central source of values to the means through which the value of capital is increased. But, similar to the situation in Europe and the United States, this group actively participates in new forms of media and displays a much stronger consciousness regarding political participation and ability to mobilize its members than the new workers. From the microblogging platform Weibo to every other form of Internet media, the "new poor" are exceedingly active, and whatever topics they discuss reach all levels of society.

But until today, the mobilizing ability and political demands of this group have had little to do with the newly ascendant working class or the fate of rural migrant workers. This is a stratum that lacks a long-term social goal. Its typical members are those who have extricated themselves from poverty, are active in consumer media and frequently reference global political and cultural discourses. But regardless of the particular rhetoric, these global political discourses use every means available to promote the idea that "history has ended." The political potential of the "new poor" has yet to be explored: They are discontented and restless, but they cannot put forth a new political imagination. Their inability to satisfy their material desires disillusions them, yet they constantly reproduce a logic of action that exactly fits with consumer society. They care about social reform and promote all manner of differing and sometimes mutually contradictory values such as democracy and freedom, equality and pluralism and nationalism and globalization, but they have given very little consideration to the connections between their own fate and that of the other stratum of new poor.

*   *   *

Why, when discussing the new workers, must we raise the role and fate of the new poor? I offer this as an explanation: Whether in traditional agricultural society or after the appearance of industrial society, the power behind great political and social changes has not come solely from the productive laborers—traditional peasants or productive workers in the modern era—but rather has been produced by the mutual interpenetration and stimulation of the "lower strata" of two or more social realms. Modern class politics in fact arose at the boundaries between classes where they overlapped; or, one might say, it was the product of crossing the boundaries between classes. After the 1911 Revolution, the commentator Du Yaquan claimed that, in spite of the fact that the revolution had been deeply influenced by political revolutions in Europe, "most of" the Chinese bourgeoisie

> did not understand what a constitutional republic was, and at the beginning had not necessarily even heard of such a thing. The revolution's promoters were part of the surplus of the intellectual class, and those who joined were an army composed of the surplus from the laboring class. In fact it differed little from overthrowing the emperor in the past. It took European revolutionaries as models, but the name "Republic of China" amounted to little more than a few ephemeral articles in the constitution. After the revolution, though it was claimed that an aristocratic politics could not be established, in fact the officials and military men who took power were for the most part vagabond [*youmin*] leaders transformed into new aristocrats. I cannot refrain from speaking of the lack of achievements of this political revolution.[13]

This analysis was rooted in observations concerning peasant rebellions in traditional China—that is, that peasant uprisings were often the products of collaboration between "vagabonds" coming out of the peasant class and the fallen from the ranks of the scholar-gentry. Following this logic, Du suggested that the path to transform China and realize positive political and social change should begin with eliminating the troublesome excess strata produced by these two classes as well as their cultures. In fact, this counterrevolutionary conclusion has many points in common with the view of the 1911 Revolution given in Lu Xun's "The True Story of Ah Q." It differs, however, in that the former promoted civilizational remedies as a solution to China's political problems, while the latter implied that political revolution could not be avoided.

If we compare this analysis of vagabonds with Marx's description of the formation of vagabondage and the proletariat, we can perceive two distinct yet related groups that come together to form the proletariat in the process of industrialization. In *The Communist Manifesto*, Marx states that "entire sections of the ruling classes are, by the advance of industry, precipitated into the proletariat, or are at least threatened in their conditions of existence. These also supply the proletariat with fresh elements of enlightenment and progress."[14] Groups that have lost their social position exist in every era, but only in the era of industrial capitalism did there exist the phenomenon of the vagabonds as a group becoming proletarians. In fact, even before *The Communist Manifesto* was published, Marx in *The German Ideology* had already given a clear account of the emergence of the proletariat:

> The entire proletariat consists of ruined bourgeois and ruined proletarians, of a collection of *ragamuffins* [*Lumpen*], who have existed in every epoch and whose existence *on a mass scale* after the decline of the Middle Ages preceded the mass formation of the ordinary proletariat, as Saint Max can ascertain by a perusal of English and French legislation and literature. Our Saint has exactly the same notion of the proletariat as the "good comfortable burghers" and, particularly, the "loyal officials." He is consistent also in identifying the proletariat with pauperism, whereas pauperism is the position only of the ruined proletariat, the lowest level to which the proletarian sinks who has become incapable of resisting the pressure of the bourgeoisie, and it is only the proletarian whose whole energy has been sapped who becomes a pauper.[15]

Thus, to Marx, the proletariat included vagabonds, but vagabonds were impoverished proletarians who had lost the power to resist. Class revolution arises from internal contradictions within the system of production, not merely from the phenomenon of impoverishment. Conservative commentators have attributed modern revolutions to the phenomenon of vagabondage, and in doing so have attempted to find ways to circumvent revolution and find a path to reform.

However, the international division of labor and national oppression that arose during the age of imperialism caused members of every stratum within the oppressed nations—aside from the comprador stratum—to constantly face the prospect of bankruptcy. This new vulnerability and precariousness were initially understood by many in terms of the imminent danger of national enslavement or extinction. But over the next several generations, many activists made the transition from national salvation to class politics, or sought national salvation through class politics.

Yet the fact of imperialism made class mobilization within the modern Chinese revolution different from Marx's description of the interaction between classes during the European revolutions, and also different from the intersection of classes during the peasant rebellions of traditional China. Under the conditions of imperialism and colonialism, not only those from the ruling strata who had become newly destitute, but many from of the upper strata and the elite as well transcended the boundaries of class identity as determined by their property rights and social position and joined the tide of class and national liberation. Many pioneers of the 1911 Revolution era—such as Sun Yat-sen, Zhang Taiyan, Xu Xilin, Qiu Jin, Zou Rong and Cai Yuanpei—did not come from the lower ranks of society. Such figures of the May Fourth era as Chen Duxiu and Li Dazhao, as well as later revolutionary leaders such as Mao Zedong, Zhou Enlai and Deng Xiaoping, were likewise not from working-class or poor peasant families. The advent of the December 9th Movement in 1935 spurred a great number of progressive students to devote themselves to the cause of national salvation, many of them hastening to Yan'an to take up the banner of the Communist Party amid the extremely arduous conditions of revolution and war. It would be difficult to categorize these several generations of revolutionaries as "bankrupted members of the bourgeoisie." On the contrary, at the time that they joined the revolutionary movement, they themselves or their families belonged to the middle or upper classes or the educated elite.

The new workers and the new poor of contemporary China have characteristics different from the vagabonds of traditional agrarian society or the proletarians of the era of industrialization. The new workers still maintain a connection to the countryside through the land system, due to the historical legacy of the workers' state. They are participants in the urban economy yet retain specific rights to land in the villages. As to the new poor, they are not the products of the collapse of the traditional system, but rather a group with a certain level of education, dreams of advancement and unfulfilled consumer desires. Their concern for individual rights and related political reforms does not fundamentally conflict with the system of values of the newly emergent socioeconomic system. Even as new forms of media flourish and the division between classes widens, it is difficult for the new workers and the new poor to achieve genuine social unity and political cooperation. Thus there seems to be little prospect of their social unity and cooperation producing a new politics.

Also clear is the degree to which contemporary Chinese intellectuals have been constrained by the forces of professionalization and social stratification. This situation contrasts sharply with the mutual interaction and cooperation between members of different social classes achieved during the general social mobilization of the twentieth century, which produced a social subject completely different from any of the old society—the aforementioned and formerly extremely active, but today utterly crushed, working class.

An Indeterminate Subject: Migrant Workers, the Working Class or New Workers?

As discussed above, the new workers compose a group that many have become accustomed to calling the "rural migrant workers" (*nongmin gong*: literally, peasant-workers). Regardless of the fact that the new workers differ widely in their occupations, geographical locations and wages, they constitute an objective social group—that is, the group of *dagongzhe* (informally employed wage laborers working in the private sector) working and living in the cities but possessing rural household registration.[16] This group is the product of the reform and opening-up process initiated by the state. It is the product of the new policies, laws, standards of ethics, urban–rural relations and social model created in the process of China's development into the world's factory. This group resides, works and lives in the cities but looks to the rural areas as "home"—the site not only of their hometowns, parents and children, but also of a portion of property given to them by the land policy left over from socialism.

But the concept of "rural migrant worker" must be reevaluated. First, the mass media, government documents and some scholars use "rural migrant worker" to define newcomers from the standpoint of urban identity, particularly that of urban consumers. But with the passing of time the membership structure of the group has changed—for the new *dagongzhe*, the home in the village has become more and more a symbol of something to which they cannot return, while the cities have become their real homes. Hanging on the wall of the Culture and Art Museum of Migrant Workers in Beijing is a chart titled "Informal Labor *(dagong)*—Thirty Years—The History of Migration." The chart clearly outlines the historical formation of the group. From 1978 to 1988, rural migrants entered the cities under controlled conditions; due to an earlier concern about rural people "blindly flowing" from the villages to the cities, rural migrants during this period were referred to as the "blind flow." By 1988 their number had grown to 20 million. The period from 1989 to 2002 can be called the "rural migrant worker" stage, during which their numbers reached 120 million. In this period, the government no longer limited the movement of the population, but prejudicial policies toward outsiders were commonplace in the cities— migrants were given only temporary residence permits and constantly threatened with deportation to their home counties. From 2003 until today is the era of "*Dagongzhe* Becoming New Workers and New Urban Residents."[17] By this time their number has reached 240 million or more. During this period, the policy of returning people to their home counties has been repealed and the Labor Contract Law has been enacted. Today *dagongzhe* squeeze into tiny rooms in the cities; trading their labor and sweat for wages which they often send to build houses in "villages to which they cannot return."

Observations of new changes in this group indicate that we should reject the term "rural migrant workers"—that the idea that the rural migrant workers will eventually return to their villages is likely illusory. The system of collective ownership of land ensures that, with rural residence permits, those taking up informal work outside of their native places at least in theory own specific parcels of land; they could, therefore, return to the villages when urban–rural income disparity decreases or when an economic downturn occurs. But this prospect has become increasingly uncertain with the implementation of the land transfer policy (allowing for the first time the contractual transfer of land in the countryside) and movement toward the outright privatization of land. Migrants work, reside and live their lives in the cities, but the village "home" in their hearts (or at least its symbol) cannot support their actual existence or provide their children with a future. Held at both the periphery of the cities and the periphery of the villages, migrants are "lost between the cities and the countryside"; from the perspective of the basic reality of production, labor and existence, calling them rural migrant workers is not as accurate as calling them new workers.

The basic fact is that they should receive the exact same treatment as urban residents. The reality is that, in contrast with the first generation of migrants born in the 1970s, the second generation of migrants born in the 1980s has no history of supporting itself by farming. The third generation of migrants, born in the 1990s, was born and has grown up in the cities; the majority of these migrants have never engaged in farming at all. Because they have never lived in the villages or engaged in agricultural production, many local governments have stopped giving them any land allocation; they no longer own any land. Replacing the concept of "rural migrant workers" with "*dagongzhe*" is not pedantry but the manifestation of an accurate understanding of this enormous social group. While contemporary Chinese debates on the land system generally center on private versus collective property rights as well as commercial versus agricultural use of land, we must raise an additional question: Will China's transformation treat urbanization and rural construction as equally important, or will it focus on urbanization above all else? The answer to this question will have tremendous implications for the fate of the new workers. In this sense, they are an indeterminate subject.

If the new workers have come to constitute a stable group rooted in a specific system of production, why not refer to them as the "working class" rather than the "new workers" or the "group of new workers"? We live in a class society in which the discourse of class has almost disappeared. In the vast majority of research on the new workers, we see descriptions of social stratification, but not analysis of class differentiation. In avoiding use of the concept of the "new working class," I am not following this model of "de-classing" social science. On the contrary, the concept of the "new workers" was produced in the process of rethinking the question of class. From the perspective of the changing mode of production, the new workers make up that group of "newly arising industrial workers" brought into being by the processes of industrialization and urbanization taking place under the conditions of China's reform and opening-up. Because they have left the villages and the land, they are gradually becoming wage laborers separated from the means of production (land). Even though a portion of them own definite parcels of land, the group completely relies on production, or increasing capital by selling their labor in order to survive; they are not a group that relies on the profits from any type of capital to obtain their means of livelihood. Yet a large part of the group has difficulty obtaining the protection of labor regulations, and their fortunes and survival depend on the market's demand for labor. From this description, they strongly resemble the classical proletariat, though certain aspects distinguish them.

Looking through the published research on the Chinese working class, we can quickly find the following definition: "The working class is the product of China's industrialization in the modern era. China's working class was produced and developed along with the modern industries established by foreign capital, early Chinese bureaucratic capital and national capital." The earliest industrial workers "were produced by foreign capital's enterprises operated in China."[18] Following this definition, we can say that the group of new workers is the product of China turning itself into the "world's factory," and it was produced and developed along with the wave of manufacturing and service industries following the entrance of transnational capital, the transformation of China's state-owned enterprises and the rise of private capital. While the vast majority of workers in the period of China's early industrialization were bankrupted farmers, the industrial workers of China today come from the vast countryside in an era in which the disparity between the rural and urban areas grows by the day. As an objectively existing social group, in terms of their role as a product of the process of industrialization and economic development, the new workers and the working class of the twentieth century are extremely similar.

From the perspective of politics, we can see in their intermittent discontent and protests the beginnings of an increasingly active collective consciousness. The new workers have not yet formed into a class in the political sense, however. In China's twentieth-century revolution, class consciousness and class politics were extremely active, and they permeated various aspects of parties, the state and social organizations. This lays bare the multifaceted nature of the concept of class—it is objective and subjective, structural as well as political. In the reform era, the construction of the "world's factory" not only calls forth capital, but also calls forth labor as a commodity. Another expression of marketization and the new phase of industrialization is the restructuring of class relations. But precisely during this large-scale restructuring, the discourse of class has disappeared from China and many other formerly socialist states. The concept of a "post-class society" does not point to the disappearance of the phenomenon of class or class stratification, but rather the weakening of class politics. For contemporary Chinese social research, the perspective of class is crucial to understanding the political, economic and social condition of Chinese workers. The following assessment rings true:

> In the period before the reforms, the combination of Marxist discourse and the experience of capitalist productive relations produced elements of a strong and sophisticated class consciousness among China's workers. The urgent necessity to "bring class back in" to transition studies not only holds for China, but for other pre-capitalist countries as well, and not just for analyzing the working class, but also the capitalist class.[19]

However, research into the process of "bringing class back in" makes clear that in the context of actual worker resistance, aside from a small number of cases, efforts to appeal to class consciousness to call forth a new type of politics have not met with success. Here my use of the term "worker resistance," rather than the previously ubiquitous concept of class struggle, implies an assessment of the political character of the labor movement as it currently stands. For example, to what extent does prominent movement centered on preserving legal rights (*weiquan*) amount to "class struggle," and to what extent does it amount to no more than a struggle to preserve the interests of urban residents? While class struggle is a movement that transforms society and the system of production, the *weiquan* movement is a struggle that uses the legal framework of this system to defend individual rights. Consequently, it fights for incremental improvement within the transitional system rather than overturning it entirely. Aside from this, attempts to preserve legal rights have been ineffective or largely ineffective for those workers who have not received the protection of labor laws.

Thus, within the process of "bringing class back in" there is a need to analyze anew the concept of class itself, otherwise we will not be able to comprehend the weakening or disappearance of class politics. First, in the process of production and life, the new workers have gradually developed a certain simple collective consciousness; both in terms of its depth and its prevalence, however, it differs greatly from the "class consciousness" of the twentieth century. We have no way of judging whether this simple collective consciousness will, as the classical theorists suggested, rise from a condition of "in itself" to "for itself"—that is, rise from the condition of being a stratum controlled by the division of labor to a political force or political class that has its own social goals and can make efforts to realize these goals. Marx states in *Capital*,

> Being independent of each other, the labourers are isolated persons, who enter into relations with the same capital, but not with one another. This co-operation begins only with the labour process, but they have then ceased to belong to themselves. On entering that process, they become incorporated with capital.[20]

Laborers who have become incorporated into capital are only a form of capital; this in itself does not and cannot produce any kind of self-consciousness.

Thus the objective existence of the workers as a group does not mean that a working class in a political sense already exists. In his study on the formation of the English working class, Thompson distinguished his view from an overly rigid, dogmatic view of class:

> By class I understand an historical phenomenon, unifying a number of disparate and seemingly unconnected events, both in the raw material of experience and in consciousness . . . I do not see class as a "structure," nor even as a "category," but as something which in fact happens (and can be shown to have happened) in human relationships . . . I am convinced that we cannot understand class unless we see it as a social and cultural formation, arising from processes which can only be studied as they work themselves out over a considerable historical period.[21]

But in the large coastal industries in the present period, with the assembly-line model of production, the model of housing segregated from urban society, the condition of existence in which one merely moves back and forth between the dormitory and the workshop, "human relationships" have been reduced to a minimum. In factories like Foxconn's, even relations between the workers have disintegrated. Only in venues outside of the factory grounds is there some limited space for socialization. Every worker as an isolated worker forms individual relations with the same capital. Under these conditions, it is more difficult in this period than in any other for class culture to develop.

Here it is useful to compare the circumstances facing the new workers with those of workers in the state-owned enterprises of the previous era. Not only in terms of material well-being and moral symbolism, but also with regard to their legal status and political position, the situations of the new workers and the old working class are poles apart. One of the clearest differences between the new and old workers is that of their remuneration and treatment. Despite the fact that the new workers and the old working class are both workers, workers at the state-owned and collective enterprises of the past had positions and salaries that were centrally mandated and protected, while new workers do not. Within many fields, new workers do not even receive the protection of contract law. The difference between new workers and old workers is in part rooted in the difference in status between the city and the countryside from the socialist era—that is, new workers do not receive the benefits of urban residence enjoyed by workers in the state-owned enterprises of the past. Here I emphasize workers in the "state-owned enterprises of the past" in order to draw attention to the fact that the difference in status between these workers is not a product of the type of entity that owns the factory, but a result of a transformation in the social system. Within the contemporary context, the status of workers is not fundamentally determined by whether an enterprise is state-owned or privately owned. Under the conditions of the market, the recruitment of workers by state-owned enterprises differs little from that by private enterprises and multinational corporations. Regardless of whether the new workers are employed by state-owned, privately owned or multinational corporations, their status and position are completely different from those of the working class in the socialist period.

Thus the difference in the remuneration of old and new workers only touches on one aspect of the issue. Yet even this aspect is a result of the change in the social system. The life and work of the old working class was tied to the work unit, which was a society in microcosm. The space in which the new workers exist today is by contrast a productive facility that exists solely to increase the value of and to reproduce capital. Within the work unit, people did not form relations with each other merely as producers; they formed persisting political, cultural, economic and familial ties and would engage in all manner of diverse activities. During the past twenty years, the work unit system of the socialist period has been subject to an increasing amount of criticism, the chief of which is that it gradually turned into an instrument of political control such that it no longer acted as a space for community social life. This criticism fails to acknowledge that the perfection of the work unit system into an instrument of control was inextricably linked with its increasing transformation into a space solely focused on production. The decline and disappearance of participation in decisions about production was one sign that the "people's democracy" promoted by the Chinese Revolution was being undermined. This was a prelude to the transition from a socialist system of production to a "market society" system of production.

In addition, aside from the reduction in human relationships among the workers due to changes in the production process and living conditions, we rarely discover political cooperation between the new workers and any other social stratum. The production and development of twentieth-century working-class culture was not the spontaneous product of the working class alone. Rather, it was the result of a complicated historical process brought about by the entrance and engagement in politics of many outside elements. The early political representatives of the working class did not emerge from among the workers themselves, but rather were intellectuals who cast their lot with the proletariat, "betraying their own class" to take up politics. Aside from those who directly entered the party that presented itself as the vanguard of the proletariat, countless intellectuals, artists, cultural figures, lawyers and others joined with the workers' movement, and together they contributed to the formation of a highly politicized working-class culture. Contrast this with the "new poor of consumer society": Unlike the intellectuals who joined ranks with the proletariat in the past, it is unclear with whom the new poor identify; furthermore, their political demands vary. Their capacity for political mobilization greatly exceeds that of the new workers, but their consumerist political language—including their anti-state discourse—connects insufficiently with the workers' experience.

Thus, on the one hand, though the new workers have vast numbers and are largely responsible for China's position as "factory of the world," they are unable to match the ability of the new poor to utilize the media for social mobilization. On the other hand, because of the lack of mutual interaction between classes and relative indifference among the "educated stratum" within the new poor toward politics, the question of the "fate of their class" never rises to the status of a political issue. The kind of political movement characterized by the "class treason" of revolutionary intellectuals joining with the proletariat in the twentieth century (the political process by which they betrayed their own class to throw in with the liberation of the proletariat) is almost completely absent among the new poor and other social strata. Enveloped by the pervasive culture of consumerism, many new workers share the same dreams as the new poor; in the dreams of the new poor, however, and even in their political demands, there is almost no sign of the "new workers." We can find nothing like the "class treason" that appeared in twentieth-century political culture, and in these circumstances it is difficult to imagine the rise of a revolutionary movement or one intended to recreate society toward a universalist goal. All of this reveals the political ruptures between social groups within the new social system, and the chasm between the new workers and the new poor—these are two connected yet mutually alienated strata produced by the same process. Within the public realm, a small number of researchers committed to studying worker issues do frequently make policy suggestions and appeals to protect their rights, but in most situations, these appeals and suggestions invariably take "nonpolitical" forms—that is, technical solutions.

The transformation of the working class would not only involve material and legal processes, but also moral and political processes. In contrast to the lively state of the "new poor" within the new media, the new workers are almost entirely without a voice in the political realm. This is not only due to differences in the culture, education and technological backgrounds of the two groups, it is also a product of the political process entailed in the restructuring of class relations. The absence of the new workers from the realm of politics is a sign of the defeat of the workers' state that appeared during the twentieth century.

From the perspective of politics, the defeat of the workers' state and the transformation of the working class's political party—I have also referred to this as the political party of the working class's "breakdown of representation"—are two sides of the same process. The complete hollowing out of the constitutional principle that the working class is the leading class within the state is the necessary outcome of this process. In the National People's Congress, the National People's Political Consultative Conference and the representative institutions of the Chinese Communist Party at every level, one can find scarcely any sign of the new workers (or of course the farmers), nor can one hear their collective voice. The new workers and capital are conjoined twins, and they can only be represented by capital. The monopolization of China's basic political structure by capital and power is not at all a coincidence. The fall of the workers' state and the legal and political changes produced by China's adaptation to market economics are inextricably intertwined.

Decreasing Employment Time, Protecting Legal Rights and Political Justice

Under these new historical conditions, it is claimed by some that the interests of workers can no longer be defended through the constitution or politics, but must instead be protected through delineating their legal rights. Until today, however, the *weiquan* efforts to protect legal rights have not altered the silence of the new workers within the political realm. Writing, music and other forms of new art coming from the new workers (on display at the Culture and Art Museum of Migrant Workers, among other places) are providing the workers with some measure of cultural support, but there is still nothing resembling the active participation in politics that characterized the workers of the twentieth century. Here I analyze the three major forms of struggle undertaken by the workers' movement today in order to reveal the nature of the depoliticization characterizing it as well as the possibility of repoliticization.

The first form of struggle is reducing the duration of employment. The new workers eagerly seek higher wages, their own houses and social insurance, the ability to keep their families together and treatment equal to that enjoyed by urban residents. To contend with their employers, they rely not only on such traditional methods as protests and strikes, but also on the method of "firing the boss." According to sociologist Lü Tu's survey research, the main reason workers change jobs is not that they have been fired by their employers, but rather because they find their conditions and protections poor and their work boring, and they seek better treatment or to improve their own technical skills.[22] There is also a minority of workers who leave because their factories are producing counterfeit or inferior goods. Workers can use "labor shortages" to their advantage as a "weapon of the weak" with which to contend with enterprises and local governments, and this has helped alter the relations between labor and capital. Reducing the duration of their employment has both benefits and drawbacks from the perspective of organizing potential. On the one hand, such methods of passive resistance undertaken by individual workers can hasten the formation of self-consciousness by workers as a group. On the other hand, the high turnover rate this produces makes it more difficult for workers to form ties with each other. Furthermore, adopting the practice of "leaving early" violates preexisting agreements with employers, leaving workers without the protection of the Labor Contract Law. Factory owners can then "legally" employ exploitative measures, such as withholding back wages.

There are two forms of struggle available to workers seeking to reduce the economic losses incurred when they walk off the job. The first is to pursue legal help to win back part of their losses. This usually means relying on the "foreman system" (*linggong zhi*)—that is, using a labor contractor who can mediate between workers and owners. This system was used in Europe during the early stage of capitalism. It ensures that the owners' demand for labor will be met and provides a representative to the workers. While this arrangement can reduce some of the workers' economic losses, the contractors in fact subject workers to yet another layer of exploitation and make it more difficult for workers' economic struggles to move in the direction of class struggle. The reduction of employment duration destabilizes the relationships between workers, and in truth, this is not a voluntary choice of the workers, but a result of the new forms of production and circulation that have emerged in China under the conditions of globalization.

The second form of struggle is attempting to safeguard their rights (*weiquan*) through the legal system. The commodification of labor did not naturally arise from the development of the capitalist market in itself—without corresponding participation of the state in the development of the market economy (including the establishment of laws, the appearance of new policies and various other government activities), it would be impossible to understand the development of wage labor.[23] Because today there is no longer any goal or even idea of establishing a new socialist state, the struggle over wage labor takes place within a market versus state framework using the *weiquan* strategy of attempting to protect workers' legal rights. Li Jingjun makes a point of emphasizing the relationship between the establishment of new laws and the condition of the workers in the reform period, explaining,

> aside from serving the needs of the economic reforms (protecting private property, contracts, operating licenses), the new regulations also govern the interests of different social groups, institutionalize the regulation of social conflicts, and as a by-product expand the parameters of citizens' legal rights. The Labor Union Law, the Labor Law and the Law to Protect the Rights of Women passed in the 1990s have had a great impact on the working class. Aside from these, a series of other management regulations and social policies that touch on every aspect of workers' lives were also promulgated, including the arbitration of labor disputes, social insurance, the minimum living standard, and unemployment insurance . . . Today class struggle not only exists between capitalists (both foreign and Chinese) and rural migrant workers in privately owned enterprises, but also between managers and older workers in state-owned enterprises that have undergone management reform. Labor conflicts have greatly increased under the market economy, but they are no longer handled by individual leaders from the enterprises' local Party organizations. Instead they rely on an external generalized (legal) system. Although the capacity of the state to enforce its laws is still far from ideal, it has at least begun to bring class conflict into a new expanded legal realm in which the rights of workers can be legally established and they can be provided with new avenues for legal appeals to make use of in their struggles.[24]

Aside from the laws mentioned above, conflicts between labor and capital are now unfolding around particular articles within the Labor Contract Law and Property Law. Struggles to protect legal rights—an important aspect of the working-class movement in the nineteenth and twentieth centuries—have had a positive effect on the development of self-consciousness among the new workers. However, safeguarding legal rights can hardly give full protection to the workers. First, as the earlier quotation from Huang Zongzhi explains, the vast majority of the working population works without contracts; their rights and interests cannot be implemented by preserving their legal rights. Furthermore, efforts to protect legal rights are chiefly concentrated on protecting the rights of individuals. It is true that struggles centering on legal justice can under certain conditions change into broader struggles concerning political justice—the 2003 case of Sun Zhigang, for example, precipitated a struggle to end the detention system and the division between urban and rural household registration.[25] In other words, there is an intersection between legal justice and political justice, and they overlap in many areas. But in most disputes between labor and capital, efforts to protect legal rights do not touch on the question of whether or not the current state of society is just. Thus, even though efforts to protect legal rights can expand the interests of the working class, the defeat of the workers' state precludes these efforts from addressing the loss of rights by workers.

If we compare the new workers and their struggles with those of the old workers, we see that the social standing of the latter was the product of a political process—that is, the old working class fought to link its fate to that of the new social system. It did not limit its struggle to maintaining individual rights or protecting the interests of the class as a whole. In my research on the strike and legal struggle that erupted during the restructuring of a state-owned textile factory in Yangzhou, I discovered that, although the efforts of these older workers were originally motivated by self-interest, their struggle appealed to a set of common, general values. For example, was the working class the master of the factory? What does it mean for state property to belong to the entire people?

Although the workers' lawsuit was categorized as a civil case, it unfolded more like a political debate centering on the constitution.[26] Article One of the Constitution of the People's Republic of China declares that "the People's Republic of China is a socialist state under the people's democratic dictatorship led by the working class and based on the alliance of workers and peasants"; Article Two of the constitution declares that "all power in the People's Republic of China belongs to the people."[27] To understand the leadership of the working class, we must at the same time understand the constitutional principle that "all powers belong to the people"—that is, the role of the working class is intimately connected with a type of general interest. It does not represent the interest of a minority or the working class itself. In the socialist period, the position of the working class was intimately connected with this constitutional right and, more specifically, the political process which generated this constitutional right. Without an understanding of the political processes of the twentieth century and the political culture they produced, it is impossible to understand the emergence of this political principle. The old workers in Yangzhou attempted to use a legal struggle to reaffirm the constitutional position of the working class, seeking to oppose the local government's effort to assert its claim to ownership of the factory and invite in outside investors. The factory was public property, and the working class should, according to the articles of the constitution, be counted among its owners with all the decision-making rights granted to owners concerning its use. In the struggles of the new workers to protect their rights, we rarely see such attempts to use legal rights to open up political struggle.

What makes the situation even more complex is that while efforts to protect legal rights arise from disputes between labor and capital, workers' struggles often involve protests against the state, and workers' conflicts are frequently intertwined with other types of social conflicts.[28] When economic questions are elevated to the political realm, protest movements are often directed at local governments. To some, this appears to demonstrate that these new contradictions and conflicts are nothing more than the ill effects of the "socialist system," rather than a process engendered by the defeat of the workers' state and the globalization of capitalism. (In some narratives and media accounts, all of these protests are interpreted as reactions to an "authoritarian government" which routinely violates human rights.) According to the logic of this ideology, the conflicts between the workers and the state could be solved by consolidating the market order. But without a reappraisal of the state's role in standardizing, managing, regulating and shaping the relations between labor and capital, it is impossible to correctly grasp the relationship between preserving legal rights and the political process. In the nineteenth and twentieth centuries, capital always relied on every manner of state power, and this is particularly true with respect to states with colonial operations and highly bureaucratic systems. The contradiction between labor and capital was most clearly expressed in the direct confrontation between labor and capital, but when the workers' movement realized that the state was a "committee for managing the common affairs of the whole bourgeoisie," the struggle against the factory owners changed from an economic struggle to a political struggle.

With the shift toward a market society, what was formerly a workers' state began to play the role of dual representative of both labor and capital. The leadership of the state produced significant trends, among them, an army of free labor formed as rural people poured into the cities after the relaxation of the residence permit system and changes in urban–rural relations, the policy to attract outside investment, the shaping and limiting of workers' organizations and the standardization of the financial system. The increasingly close alliance between capital and power has made the state's representation of the rights and interests of labor increasingly hollow, but its formal role as the representative of labor has not undergone a fundamental change. With the tremendous transformation of the workers' state, the state that claimed to represent the interests of the workers has developed a rupture with the working class; as a consequence, opposition between capital and labor often takes the form of a contradiction between labor and the state. However, unlike the class struggles of the nineteenth and twentieth centuries, the direct conflict between the workers and the state is not developing toward the formation of a workers' state, but toward the formation of a nineteenth- or early twentieth-century economic system—that is, utterly abandoning its character as a workers' state, and instituting legal rights based on the right to own property.

Within the realm of legal rights, there is one area, concerning collective rights, that can provide a political space between individual interests and the interests of the workers: the sphere of influence of labor unions. In the first half of the nineteenth century, before working-class political parties appeared, unions led workers to strike. They organized the workers and helped them protect their interests in their struggles with capitalists. The development of guilds, professional associations and unions was the major form in which the workers' movement first appeared, and the union movement today is still the major organizational form of the workers' movement in Europe. From nineteenth-century through early twentieth-century European society, labor unions were the basis on which working-class parties were formed. Put another way, working-class parties were outgrowths of unions. The working class movement was not the creation of political parties; on the contrary, class-based parties were born from the working class on the foundation of the workers' movement.[29] In China and many other agricultural societies that have undergone revolutions in the modern era, however, labor and peasant unions were tools with which political parties organized laborers and promoted class movements. Within the workers' state, the union mediates between the masses on one hand and the party and state on the other, its function being to "bring conviction to the masses," or to play the role of what Lenin called the "'reservoir' of state power."[30]

However, with the transformation of the workers' state and the "statification of the Party" during the reform era, the labor union has changed from an instrument aimed at "bringing conviction to the masses" to strive toward socialism or communism to one that "brings conviction to the masses" to transition toward a market society. Because the unions are conjoined with the state, with the restructuring of the state-owned enterprises the unions have almost completely lost the function of protecting the interests of the workers and have instead become organs that assist local governments and capitalists in the restructuring of enterprises and deprive the workers of their rights. Because of this, workers need to "reorganize the unions." Reorganizing does not merely imply changing their membership and especially leadership through elections, but also changing the role of the unions: With the loss of the workers' state and the statification of the Party, unions no longer mediate between the workers' state and the masses as "persuading instruments," nor are they the workers' state's "reservoir." Unions should constitute a self-empowering network that protects the rights and interests of the workers, promotes their unity and develops a new egalitarian politics.

Today capital permeates the state as never before. In the process of the restructuring of state-owned enterprises, the creation of capital within China seems to resemble the account of the nineteenth-century anarchist Bakunin: the "state has created capital . . . The capitalist has his capital only by the grace of the state."[31] But this is merely the appearance. In reality both the state and capital have been restructured under the conditions of globalization. Capital's creation in China through the "grace of the state" is only another expression of the "retreat of the state." We would have no way of understanding the behavior of either "transitional" or neoliberal states without an analysis of the underlying forces driving marketization. The problem facing workers today thus on some level repeats a nineteenth-century debate within the workers' movement: Should the target of workers' struggles be the state or capital, and should the workers' movement change from an economic struggle to a political struggle? During the nineteenth century, anarchists argued that revolution should first and foremost do away with the state as a political organization, thus declaring the state as the target of the workers' movement. Communists argued, on the contrary, that capital was the source of the workers' predicament, and that "class antagonism between capitalists and wage workers . . . has arisen through the development of society."[32] Bourgeois theorists and liberals, for their part, made great efforts to divert the workers' movement from economic struggles toward independent struggles divorced from politics that could be addressed by various legal reforms.

Within the contemporary context, the three choices described above have all failed. First, the political goal of the nineteenth-century communist movement—that the working class propel the transition to socialism by taking control of the state—has, with the defeat of the workers' states, already vanished. Workers' struggles against capital can no longer take revolution aimed at seizing state power as their goal. Labor unions can no longer, as Lenin and others hoped, act as "political organs" for the transition toward a seizure of political power.[33] Second, within the highly financialized global capitalist system of today, focusing on the state as the target of struggle overlooks the relationship between the condition of the new workers and capitalism's systems of production and circulation. The high frequency with which workers change employers mirrors the extraordinarily high degree of capital mobility, the general crisis of the rural areas is linked with the new relation between the cities and the countryside emerging under economically driven urbanization, and the dehumanization of the new workers linked with a mode of production that makes increasing productivity to achieve high profits its only goal.

The state and its policies are no more than political institutions that have adapted to this enormous transformation. On the one hand, the new workers face low wages, few protections and thorough dehumanization in the production process. On the other hand, the new workers still endure the burden of an unequal social identity and the emotional trauma caused by the disintegration and transformation of their homes in the vast Chinese countryside. This predicament cannot be solved through a mere redistribution process—rather, the worsening relations between the cities and the countryside brought about by the process of urbanization must be transformed. Moreover, the growing dominance of finance and capital over production affects other areas outside of the direct relations between labor and capital, such as the relations between the cities and the rural areas, the educational system, inequality between regions, interstate relations and the relations between development and environmental protection. Therefore, demanding only that the "market system" be perfected while following the advice of the liberals in refusing to alter the basic relations of production or the development model while confining the struggles of the workers to the sphere of legal rights cannot possibly change the current situation of the workers on a fundamental level. Under the present conditions, not even labor unions of the nineteenth-century model could meet the demands of today's challenges on their own.

The questions of today are more similar to those of the nineteenth-century than those of the twentieth-century labor movement. The workers must reorganize themselves to construct a political force, but they will not be able to use the framework of the workers' state to realize their own "leadership" function. This is not to say that the socialist tradition no longer has any meaning. On the contrary, the workers' political demands require that they reaffirm the basic principles of the workers' state in order to mobilize themselves. Within the new context, attempting to pursue political justice while at the same time avoiding the question of the workers' collective economic struggle, as does the *weiquan* movement to protect legal rights, is an empty, unrealistic dream. If we cannot expand the search for legal justice into an effort to fundamentally change this model of development—that is, if we cannot seriously discuss the relationship between legal justice and political justice—then we cannot fundamentally change the predicament of the workers.

But reaffirming and defending the rights and interests outlined in the constitution of the socialist state may be an effective path toward linking legal justice and political justice. Compared with nine-teenth-century Europe or China in the early twentieth century, the political realm of today has already undergone a profound change: The ability of existing political processes to drive the formation of classes has already vanished. The revolutionary institution that drove class politics, that is, the working-class political party, has already trans-formed into a part of a state structure that takes as its key mission the development and management of the economy. Precisely because this political force is absent, today—even as China is now generating a group of workers larger than any other in the world—the concept of class has lost efficacy in the political realm.

"Repoliticizing" is thus a necessary choice, but how and on what foun-dation? The liberal category of the "end of history" and the radicals' "empire" and "multitude," in spite of clearly opposing each other on the dividing line of left versus right, share in their negation of class as a possible foundation for a new politics. Thus the question of today is different from that of the past: In this age of flourishing new social move-ments, can a new politics be built on the category of class? Here the real challenge is not that of simply replacing the struggle for legal justice with one for political justice or dogmatically reaffirming the leading position of the working class, nor of finding a way to link legal justice and politi-cal justice, but of redefining the concept of political justice.

For this process to begin, the new workers can only look to and evalu-ate their own life experiences and their relations with others to discover new motivations and hopes. Within the broader struggles of workers, we can hear the voice of this group's desires and demands in the silent strug-gle of the Foxconn workers, in the strike at the Yue Yuen shoe factory and in every minor and miniscule effort of the new workers to improve their material and cultural fate. But how can this group elevate its desires and demands to the level of a political force and lend impetus to a general politics of dignity? How can the efforts of this group transcend its boundaries to become a part of the general politics of the Chinese masses? In what sense must Chinese society, in its struggle for equality, defend and extend the socialist constitution and its system of rights?

The Defeat of the Workers' State and the
Breakdown of Representation

These questions must begin with an interrogation of the defeat of the workers' states formed in the twentieth century. The emancipation of labor and the equality and freedom of workers achieved by the twentieth-century labor movement were consolidated in the workers' state and its constitution. The principles of the workers' state constitution were the product of a political process that took the interests of the working class as the general interest or the core of the general interest. The point of raising the principles of the constitution in the current context is to ask the following: With the defeat of the workers' state, is it necessary to reaffirm the position of labor within social life, as well as the political process that took the working class and its interests as the general interest?

In order to answer this question, we must ask how the working class first attained its position within the constitution of the socialist state and then subsequently lost it. During the transformation of the Party from a class-based party into a "total representative"—that is, the shift toward the statification of the Party—the relationship between class and party changed, and then the relationship between class and the state began to waver. Today the old working class has not only lost its representative in the political realm, but its cohesion as a group has been destroyed as well by the process of restructuring the state-owned enterprises. And while the new workers cherish the liberation they have gained through the freedom of movement, they have no power to produce their own political representatives in the systems of production or life. They are not unlike Marx's description of the French peasantry in the mid-nineteenth century:

> They are consequently incapable of enforcing their class interests in their own name . . . They cannot represent themselves, they must be represented. Their representative must at the same time appear as their master, as an authority over them, as an unlimited governmental power that protects them against the other classes and sends them rain and sunshine from above.[34]

Under these conditions of "being represented," the new workers are not even clear as to the identity of their opponents, much less the relationship between their own interests and a "general interest."

This change in the position of the working class was the product of three interrelated political processes. The first was the transformation of the workers' state. The heart of this change was the enormous transformation of the working-class political party and the disintegration of its corresponding principles of political justice. I call this process the "breakdown of representation," or the disjuncture between the political form and the social form. The collective expression of political justice in the workers' state was located in the principles of its constitution. These principles were expressed clearly in several key concepts appearing in the first and second articles of the Constitution of the People's Republic of China quoted above: The working class is the leading class, the alliance between the workers and the peasants is the political foundation, the people's democratic dictatorship is the form of organization of state power, the people are established as the source of power and the Party of the workers is the political representative of this system. Political party, class, class alliance, the people and the state form derived from this made clear the relations of political representation in modern China.

The reason why I say the "relations" of political representation and not representation in general is that if there had not been an accompanying political process, there would be no organic relationship between these categories, and there would exist no question of representation. The precondition for understanding the breakdown of representation is an analysis of the crisis, stagnation and breakdown of this political process, and the resulting dissolution of relations of representation on the level of the system. For example, within such representative institutions of the workers' state as the People's Congress, the portion of representatives made up by workers and their peasant political allies has greatly declined. This is a symptom of the breakdown of representation rather than the cause. Without a continuous political process, an increase in the number of worker or peasant representatives within the People's Congress would be of little use in restoring the workers' state.

Let us begin by analyzing the concept of class within the principles of the constitution. Regardless of whether one is explaining the formation of the workers' state or analyzing its defeat, one must address the issue of how the relationship between the general interest and political representation taking class as its basis was constructed. Because these broader issues are at play, the concept of class cannot be defined solely from the perspective of property rights; a full understanding requires that it be linked with the categories of leadership and the politics of representation. The questions of leadership and representation are arise from an analysis of the internal contradictions and unevenness of capitalism. Marx wrote:

> Now as for myself, I do not claim to have discovered either the existence of classes in modern society or the struggle between them. Long before me, bourgeois historians had described the historical development of this struggle between the classes, as had bourgeois economists their economic anatomy. My own contribution was 1. to show that the *existence of classes* is merely bound up with *certain historical phases in the development of production;* 2. that the class struggle necessarily leads to the *dictatorship of the proletariat*; 3. that this dictatorship itself constitutes no more than a transition to the *abolition of all classes* and to a *classless society.*[35]

The "dictatorship of the proletariat" that leads the transition to a classless society referred to here is the working-class state. The concept of the proletariat in the "proletarian state" refers not only to the class produced by capitalist production, but also to a universal class. In this sense, the working class within the workers' state is a political concept. Because the working-class state is a society that has expropriated the expropriators, it is a community of the laboring people. Even former emperors, capitalists, war criminals and others become part of this community of laboring people. The concept of the "people's democratic dictatorship" in the Constitution of the People's Republic of China is a transitional historical category. It preserves the distinctions between classes taken from the division of labor and at the same time emphasizes the particular quality of the working class as the universal class. The issues of representation and leadership are inherent within this type of state as a transitional form.

In his investigation of the exploitative nature of capitalist production, Marx discovered that this mode of production divided society into two great classes; thus the politics of the capitalist period cannot escape from a politics of opposition between classes. But the existence and polarization of classes do not in themselves necessarily lead to a revolutionary politics—without a dynamic political force that could link the existence of classes with a revolutionary political movement aiming at the abolition of classes, a revolutionary politics of representation cannot emerge. We must examine this from two different angles: Why in early twentieth-century China, when the working class was small and weak, did proletarian class politics sweep the entire region? And why has China today, the "world's factory" with almost 300 million workers, been unable to generate a working-class politics of the sort produced in the nineteenth and twentieth centuries?

Although class politics depends on the working class as an objectively existing social stratum, it presupposes an orientation toward political struggle rooted in a broad theoretical analysis. This kind of class politics can only be produced by a class looking beyond its own interest and becoming representative of the general interest. That is, only when the abolition of classes and class divisions becomes the conscious mission of a class can this type of class politics be born. Based on his analysis of the process of capitalist production and its contradictions, Marx identified the working class as this type of class in the political sense—the struggles of this class pointed in the direction of a future in which class would be eliminated, which meant that it represented the general interests of the people and the ultimate liberation of humankind.

Precisely because of this, neither the role of the working class within the revolutionary process nor the unique role of the workers' state could be reduced to or derived from the actual condition and proportion of the working class within society as a whole. From a theoretical perspective, if this political sense of the concept of class is abolished, the concept of class would, following the logic of empiricism, slip toward the concept of social stratum, such that the working-class movement would be seen as no more than a movement with unions as its principal organizational form aiming to protect the interests of its own class. Taking its place within the empiricist framework constructed by such concepts of social strata, middle class, rural migrant workers and so forth, the often emphasized concept of "social stratification" from the very beginning elides the politics of class.

The fall of the workers' state is not only expressed in the decline of the political representation of the working class, but also in the disintegration of its political basis—the worker-peasant alliance. The Chinese Revolution took place in a predominantly peasant society, a country in which the working class was relatively small and the bourgeoisie had not fully formed. Describing the modern Chinese revolution as a bourgeois revolution without a bourgeoisie or a socialist revolution without a proletariat is not without some factual basis. But from the political perspective, the question of whether China had a mature bourgeoisie or a proletariat cannot be used to directly negate the historical existence of a bourgeois or socialist revolution.

In fact, the relationship between revolutionary politics and the actual numerical population of a particular class has never been a direct one; this is not a phenomenon unique to China. In the mid-nineteenth century, Marx argued that all of Germany's problems would be decided by whether there could be a repeat of the peasant wars to support a proletarian revolution. Lenin explained, "In Europe, in 1871, the proletariat did not constitute the majority of the people in any country on the Continent. A 'people's' revolution, one actually sweeping the majority into its stream, could be such only if it embraced both the proletariat and the peasants. These two classes then constituted the 'people.'"[36] Because the working class did not make up the majority of the population, it could only push forward a "people's revolution," and only then could it realize the general interest or "future" embodied in its class mission. This general interest or future has two sides: The first is that the proletariat directly embodies the general interest of the people, and the second is that it implies the elimination of class and the opposition between classes, and thereby envisions a future in which the proletariat itself is eliminated.

The politics of representation within the workers' state had two concerns: the alliance between the workers and the peasants and people's democracy.[37] The theoretical status and implications of these two concepts was inextricably related to the concept of the capitalist periphery. Societies on the periphery of the developed capitalist states, such as China and Russia, faced a fundamental problem: At the moment when socialist thought and socialist movements began to emerge, these regions were still primarily agricultural and peasant-based societies. At the end of the nineteenth century, the Russian Narodniks contrasted the land-owning peasants of their own society with Western European capitalism, saying that Russia was still a "peasant semi-subsistence economy." Chinese thinkers such as Liang Shuming and his followers also believed that rural reconstruction was at the heart of China's problems.

In emphasizing the significance of China's chronic agrarian crises, the socialists shared many concerns with the Narodniks and advocates of rural reconstruction. But the difference was this: Socialists believed that within the global system of uneven capitalist development, the economic form driven by the production of commodities was subordinate to the logic of capital. The subordination of agriculture to industry, the subordination of the countryside to the cities and the division of the peasants into farmers who provided food for the cities and migrants to the cities became universal phenomena in the nineteenth century. It is these very subordinate relations that provided the basis for a socialist movement that included the peasant question as an organic aspect of global opposition to capitalist rule. Yet the working class, and not the peasantry, became the representative of the people, because liberation of the working class in the end pointed toward the heart of the capitalist system itself.

The working class could not achieve a revolutionary victory by itself. It had to win the support of "the people" by means of a political process through which it gained the ability to represent other classes. The question of the leadership of the Chinese Revolution was intimately related to the transformation of agriculture and the mobilization of the peasants throughout the twentieth century. The authority of China's revolutionary party was even more closely linked to the peasant movement than it was to the workers' movement. As described above, the working class's leading role cannot be understood outside of the foundational category of the alliance between the workers and the peasants. But class politics unfolds within situations in which one class takes the lead. It cannot be reduced to an objective measurement of the various proportions of the class structure as a whole. The alliance between the workers and the peasants was a political alliance achieved through a particular organizational form. From this it became the center of the politics of representation. The political party of the working class was no longer simply the vanguard of the working class; it was the political representative of the worker–peasant alliance. The politics of representation was directly expressed in the leading position of the working class in the workers' state, as well as in the leading position of the worker-peasant alliance with respect to the peasant class.

Related to this, the category of "the people" was also rooted in the concept of class. In addition to the workers and peasants, "the people" also included the petty bourgeoisie and the national bourgeoisie. As with the concept of class, if there had been no political movement to distinguish relations between potential friends and enemies in the age of capitalism, then the concept of "the people" would not have been tenable. The working class is not merely an appendage produced by capitalism, but a political identity constructed in opposition to the bourgeoisie and its political representatives. The politics of representation were expressed on the one hand in the leadership of the working class in the realms of politics and culture, and on the other hand in their power to realize the general interests of the people.

The concept of leadership explains that the alliance between the workers and the peasants (or the people) was not an overlapping of different classes, but rather a new political subject born out of struggle. The goal of the worker-peasant alliance was to win over the peasants from the influence of the bourgeoisie and organize them into a revolutionary force.[38] Representation and leadership overlap, for representation is also a concept of struggle. People's democracy was one form of a system of political representation that preserved the worker–peasant alliance while at the same time preserving the leadership function of the working class.[39] Because of this, relations of representation imply a clear relation of opposition and unity—that is, representation and leadership have to express a general interest and not the interest of a single class or interest group. But this general interest can only be realized through class politics. The defeat of the workers' state and the breakdown of representation are expressed and necessarily occur on two levels: the rupture between the leadership and its erstwhile class basis, and the unraveling of political representation from the general interest.

In the Chinese Revolution, the connection described above between the politics of representation and class politics could not be separated from the problems of national liberation and state sovereignty. This made the politics of representation with class at its center take on an even more complicated appearance. In the developed capitalist countries of Western Europe, the national question had already been solved, and political struggle usually took the form of alliances and struggles between classes. But in the colonized or semicolonized states, national oppression was the main obstacle to the proletarian movement, so the task of allying with other classes to achieve national liberation and establish a unified state became the task of the proletariat. In the words of Mao Zedong, the trends of this era were that "states want independence," "nations want liberation" and "the people want revolution." Because revolution was given the tasks of establishing the new nation and new state, revolutionary politics centered on class liberation developed a connection with centralized, often unitary state systems. Under conditions of the breakup of states and national crisis, centralized systems, as opposed to decentralized and federal systems, were seen as beneficial and necessary. According to Lenin,

> The great centralised state is a tremendous historical step forward from medieval disunity to the future socialist unity of the whole world, and only *via* such a state (*inseparably* connected with capitalism), can there be any road to socialism.[40]

Because of this, the politics of representation developed a historical connection with centralized authority in multiethnic states. One of the political consequences of the breakdown of representation has been the spread of ethnic identity politics in multiethnic countries, and this kind of identity politics has been accompanied by a suspicion of the unified state. From this political perspective, the contemporary crisis in China's ethnic minority autonomous regions is a result of the breakdown of representation.

Aside from the requirement within the workers' state to reconstruct ethnic relations on the basis of class, representation within the workers' state also included an internationalist content:

> That the emancipation of labour is neither a local nor a national, but a social problem, embracing all countries in which modern society exists, and depending for its solution on the concurrence, practical and theoretical, of the most advanced countries.[41]

As the political organization of the working class, the working-class political party can be traced to the founding of the International Workingmen's Association in the nineteenth century. Its original goal was to unite the spontaneously arising working-class movements and put them on a common track. But with the growth of national liberation movements in the 1930s, the nationalization of these political organizations became increasingly clear. The communist parties were no longer

purely the representatives of the working class and its universal interest—they also attempted to become the representatives of the national
liberation movements. The formation of communist organizations and
states and their development toward becoming the representatives of
whole nations had a great influence within the communist movement
throughout the entire twentieth century. After 1949, the Chinese
Communist Party was no longer only the political representative of the
working class or the alliance between the workers and the peasants; it was
also the representative of state sovereignty. This also implied that the
representative of a class at the same time became the representative of
the country, and from this point the roles of the Party as a political movement and as the state authority mutually permeated each other. When the
Party and the state were unified, internal struggles within the Party were
closely linked with internal jockeying for power within the state.

The fully national and international aspects of representation arose
from the logic of capitalist development. The alliance between socialist
countries, the Non-Aligned Movement in the Third World and the
international effort to "export revolution" (that is, using military, political and ideological methods to build relations and cooperation with
classes in other countries) all gave the politics of representation an international aspect. The international face of this kind of politics of
representation contained two distinct levels. The first was class politics
reaching across national borders. To use Marx's words:

> Even under the most favourable political conditions all serious success
> of the proletariat depends upon an organisation that unites and concen-
> trates its forces; and even its national organisation is still exposed to split
> on the disorganisation of the working classes in other countries, which
> one and all compete in the market of the world, acting and reacting the
> one upon the other. Nothing but an international bond of the working
> classes can ever ensure their definitive triumph.[42]

The other level was the extension of the national liberation movements,
that is, the formation of alliances between sovereign nation-states. The
alliance between these nation-states differed from the allied relations
between socialist states. Their alliance was not the class alliance that
Marx spoke of, but rather an international united front formed under the

conditions of an unequal international division of labor. Its political logic was similar to that of a class alliance within a single nation. Because of this, this internationalist alliance was necessarily connected with a struggle for leadership over political representation.

Political justice in a workers' state was a universalist justice with the concept of class at its center. It included the leading role of the working class, the political foundation of the alliance between the workers and the peasants, the nation-state as the general representative, and an internationalism focused on the oppressed classes and the oppressed nations. Within this framework, the problem of the dignity of the working class was the problem of the liberation of classes and the universal liberation of humanity. Pushing forward this "liberation movement" was the working-class political party—it pushed forward and created the workers' movement, the peasant movement, the alliance between the workers and the peasants, the united front and the international class alliance. Because of this, the political transformation signaled by the transformation of the Party into an apparatus of state power not only indicated a change in the economic form, but also a process of depoliticization. It implied the defeat of the workers' state and the disintegration of the vision of political justice centered on the working class. With today's new reorganization of classes, the constitution's determination of the leading role of the working class has become completely farcical. With the three-sided crisis of the rural areas and the polarization between the cities and the countryside, solidarity between the workers and the farmers has completely evaporated. With the polarization between regions, economic and social disparity directly produces ethnic conflict. Within international politics, the logic of the market has replaced international unity. This is what implied by the "breakdown of representation," or the coming apart of the political form and the social form.

In our discussion of the fate of contemporary Chinese workers, what aspects of the political legacy of the twentieth century are worth our consideration? What aspects of its failure force us to explore a new concept of political justice? To address these questions, we must turn to an analysis of the "breakdown of representation" and the creation of a new politics of equality.

6

Three Concepts of Equality

The Decline of Representation

The Disjuncture between Political System and Social Form

Over the past thirty years there have been endless discussions about democracy and its numerous interpretations. The "end of history" thesis formulated in 1989 treated liberal democracy as the final form of politics and a sign of the arrival of universal history. This discourse was premised on the perceived failure of both mass democracy and the socialist movements, and assumed that popular democracy led invariably to political authoritarianism. The October Revolution in 1917 confronted the capitalist world with its own antithesis. Under the conditions of the Cold War, the conflict between these two systems led to the ideological dichotomy of "capitalism" and "socialism." One consequence of the creation of this dichotomy was that the end of the Cold War gave the capitalist side a discursive monopoly over "democracy," rendering other conceptions of democracy hostile to it.

But, as the British historian Eric Hobsbawm noted, this dualism is an arbitrary construct only relevant to a specific location and period.[1] The "end of history" construct cannot make sense of the very different systems that have prevailed in China, the former Soviet Union and other socialist countries, nor can it effectively explain the wide variation of paths and models between the United States, Japan, Great Britain, Germany, Brazil, Korea, India and Northern Europe. It is even less capable of explaining the ways in which these competing systems adapted and changed by observing their rivals and drawing appropriate conclusions, imitating and copying those features of the opposing system that seemed most useful.

What is missing in the normative version of democracy (and human rights) constructed within the ideological constraints of the Cold War and post–Cold War periods is the social dimension. That is, democracy and human rights are understood solely as existing in opposition to "authoritarianism"; they are no longer regarded as the revolutionary goals of a "democratic society." In reality, the principal effect attained by this method—identifying friends and enemies and relegating the latter's system to the category of "authoritarianism"—has been ideological self-legitimization in the mass media. It has not contributed to discussion of the crisis of democracy.

After the collapse of the Socialist Bloc, the War on Terror, religious conflicts, ecological devastation, "high-risk society" and financial crisis all exposed the deep contradictions within the global capitalist system. Western-style democracy seems ever hollower, while newer democracies wrestle with their own internal conflicts and Third World countries struggle to find the right road to democracy. All of these phenomena are linked to the crises mentioned above, and discussions of modern democracy cannot afford to overlook them. One could argue that the crisis of democracy did not truly begin until socialism collapsed, but it would be more accurate to say that the crisis of socialism concealed the crisis of democracy. Still, why have both of these twentieth-century socioeconomic systems fallen into crisis? What factors account for the changes in the social character of democracy? Synthesizing numerous discussions of the crisis of democracy, I would suggest the following points.

First, socialism has lost its legitimacy. After the Cold War ended, superpower confrontation and class revolutions posed fewer dangers. With the victory of one social system, intersystemic competition disappeared. Socialism's claims to rationality and legitimacy were erased by the democracy versus authoritarianism dualism, making it difficult to envision any possible alternative outside of the system of electoral politics. The heritage of socialism has almost entirely lost its legitimacy in the face of this dualism. As a result of these trends, it is hard to see any alternative to electoral politics. Such shifts in macrolevel conditions have weakened the capacity of an exterior impetus to push Western democracies' self-renewal.[2]

Second, the role of the working class in the fight against global injustice has been undercut. Globalization, including the shift of production to new sites all over the globe, has been accompanied by deindustrialization in the former industrial countries, and as a result the working class there has been seriously weakened. The working class has been a key factor in the quest for social equality, and its dwindling influence means that it is now less able to force the state to make compromises and play a balancing role in domestic politics. (In comparing Germany with the United States, we have to inquire why German social democracy has fared so much better than its American counterpart. One possible answer is that the emergence of finance capitalism in Germany did not lead to the decline of large-scale manufacturing.) When the Cold War ended, class conflict was succeeded by new social movements quite distinct from the class-based ones they replaced. The rise of these newer social movements implied, to some extent, the end of class politics, though not of classes themselves.

The displacement of manufacturing industries out of Western countries has also driven industrialization on a grand scale elsewhere, notably in China, where the working class is rapidly expanding. China at the end of the twentieth century welcomed the era of a "re-formed working class." The relocation of manufacturing industries also signifies a spatial relocation of class relations and class conflict, but this has occurred during a period of the decline and transition of the socialist system and the decline and transformation of nineteenth- and twentieth-century class politics. The characteristic political expression of this transformation has been the "neutralization" of the proletarian political party. As a consequence, the working class is no longer represented in the political sphere, and public policy is thus inevitably inclined to favor the interests of capital. Under these conditions, experienced by both socialist and social-democratic systems, political forms have been decoupled from the social forms.

Third, with the rapid development of financial capitalism, finance capital has thrown off the constraints of industrial capitalism, and with a speculative character far surpassing that of previous eras, has refused any social responsibility. Finance capitalism is borne along by global investment flows. Political democracy, a system that operates within the confines of the nation-state and is based on the rights of citizens, has had a hard time coping with this novel global challenge. That means that a contradiction now exists between globalization and forms of political democracy within the nation-state. This contradiction is manifested in at least two ways: (a) If we cannot proffer or elaborate a new concept of the rights of citizens, we cannot pursue a new politics of equality; and (b) the new supranational institutions and schemes of regional cooperation that have arisen with globalization have not produced any genuinely democratic mechanisms. To be sure, theorists of liberalism and social democracy have had many debates on global justice, but this discussion has not given rise to any effective political practice. With the decline of dependency theory, the leftist camp has also failed to produce any persuasive, integrated political program for global justice and fairness.

Fourth, coterminous with finance capital's penetration into all sectors, the high-tech industry is parting ways with traditional industry, and conflicts between their respective interest groups are on the rise. The social compromises and compensatory measures that emerged in the period of traditional industry have lost traction under these altered circumstances, and social democracy is facing a political reorganization.[3] This political reorganization is related both to the specific social structure arising out of changes in economic relations as well as the mode of social mobilization brought about by the new scale of urbanization and spread of information technology. These two processes are interconnected but are not equivalent to one another. To take just one example, a research group devoted to "Political Development in East Asia," headed by Professor Fang Ning, reports that Thaksin Shinawatra in Thailand represents high-tech industries. His interest groups have come into conflict with those supported by the monopolies in the dominant older industries. In response, he has turned to the rural population for support. Thailand's political instability in recent years is largely due to the consequent polarization between city and countryside and the social conflicts rooted in it. In other cases (the resistance movements in the Arab world and in Great Britain, for example), the class character of the social mobilizations and their demands has been less clear. The demands of these social movements are quite varied, yet for the moment we see them as constituting a composite politics of equality. Even though we live in an age when class relationships are being reorganized, the revolution in electronic communication technology prevents us from interpreting the character of social mobilizations simply from the vantage point of class politics.

Fifth, oligarchical structures are on the rise in the void left by state transitions away from socialist programs. The de-linking of the democratic system from its associated social forms is characteristic of many countries in transformation. Under the influence of neoliberalism, the weakening of public ownership and social welfare under socialism has gone hand in hand with privatization, market orientation and globalization. This twofold process has broken the linkage between political democratization and forms of social democratization. As state property is privatized in the post-socialist era, it has become commonplace for political elites to form coalitions with the representatives of capital. In this way, a small ruling group in society enters into an alliance with the democratic (or nondemocratic) political system, causing a catastrophic decline in equality and the fracturing of society. If democratization is supposed to mean that the previous system of distribution and the heritage of equality under socialism are to be rejected entirely, then a two- or multiparty system would inevitably become the political framework for new oligarchical relationships. A multiparty system of democracy would then become tightly interwoven with the distribution of property according to oligarchical principles. In processes of transition to democracy, numerous parties typically form, but the ones that make it into parliament are usually those that represent the interests of monopolies formed in the redistribution process. As states in transition move from a one-party to a multiparty system, the media gains more freedom. (The expansion of the media does not mean that citizens have more freedom to express their opinions—in fact, the opposite seems to be the case. This requires further study).

Political democratization is linked to the total repudiation of historical achievements of socialism; equality, therefore, whether as a social form or as the primary social value under socialism, has likewise been rejected. Under these circumstances political democratization legitimates unequal distribution and new forms of monopoly. Since the democratic system, especially that of government by majority party, largely depends on capital and the media, monopoly groups—whether private or state-run—can easily parlay their economic power into political and media power.[4] The outcome is unequivocal: Not only are ordinary citizens excluded from political democratization, their right to appeal to the values of socialism to resist the monopolistic structure has also been taken away. Political democratization thus became accompanied by oligarchy and an ever-widening gap between rich and poor. In this way, what began as a process intended to liberate society transformed into a system of exclusion and oligarchy. That is the main reason why the "color revolutions" changed their colors so quickly.

The gulf between rich and poor, the contrast between city and countryside, the uneven development of regions and—last but not least—the ecological crisis all ultimately hinge on relations between labor and capital under current conditions of production. But the causes underlying these phenomena are extraordinarily complex: Questions of people's livelihood, as well as democracy, involve not just the political system, but also social forms. When there is a disjunction between political and social forms, all contemporary sociopolitical systems— the socialist system, social democracy and liberal democracy—face similar challenges. In view of this disjunction, I believe that as China explores transformations in its political form under these new conditions, it needs to draw on the egalitarian legacy of its revolutionary and socialist history. This would allow it to overcome the crisis of legitimacy that has arisen due to the incongruity of political and social forms. If one were to jettison socialism along with its entire heritage, then the unequal distribution of wealth would simply proceed apace. But if it were not possible to place this egalitarian legacy firmly within the process of political reorganization, then this legacy would do nothing to solve the legitimacy crisis.

A market society is not capable of self-generating equilibrium. To the contrary, without rational regulation and institutional safeguards, and without social struggles for equality and justice, the incongruity between political and social forms will become normative. This is not some "theory of the left"; it is simply the history of capitalism. Many Third World countries lack the social legacy of egalitarianism. Many South Asian and Latin American nations have not even instituted land reform. In the absence of this egalitarian legacy, democracy cannot develop in a balanced way, and this contributes to the emergence of new social conflicts. That is why intellectuals and social movements in many Third World countries hold China's socialist historical legacy in great esteem (even as many intellectuals in China have tossed it aside like a worn-out shoe) demonstrating the degree of importance held by the debate over land reform and public ownership in China. Inequality in China is occasioned principally by the lack of any effective definition of the public interest. The harm done to the interests of workers, peasants and many urban dwellers is coterminous with the damage done to public property rights. When the citizen masses are excluded from democratization, there can be no genuine democracy. Without substantive equality, without egalitarian relations between citizens, civil rights in political democracy becomes a purely formal concept.

These are all external factors touching on the contemporary crisis of democracy. With regard to the crisis of realizing democracy in the present age, I think that the notion of a "breakdown of representation" is most useful for elucidating what has occurred. In the wake of social and economic transformations, supposedly representative political systems have all at once lapsed into serious crises. Political, economic and cultural elites and their interests have disassociated themselves from the masses, thus forming the social basis for the breakdown of representation. Parties, media and the legal system, despite assurances that they stand for the general good, do not adequately represent social interests and public opinion. This is the direct expression of the breakdown of representation. It points to three kinds of crises in democratic politics: the crisis of party government (wherein the party becomes coterminous with the state), the crisis of the public sphere/media (an expanded media sphere uncoupled from public space) and the crisis of the legal system (wherein proceduralism is manipulated by interest groups). In the simplest terms, we have reached a limit wherein parties have been turned into instruments of the state, the state acts like a business corporation, the media have been reduced to political parties, politics has been media-tized and the justice system is hollow. Hence, in discussing the "breakdown of representation," we must pose the following questions:

First: Given the transformation of party politics into state-party politics, are we entering an era of post-party political democracy? "Post-party politics" harks back to certain political models of the nineteenth and twentieth centuries. Under current conditions, even though these political entities continue to be called political parties, they have different characteristics from those that prevailed in the nineteenth and twentieth centuries.

Second: How is the "public sphere" to be reconstructed, and how can one set up a new political system on legitimate foundations? A prerequisite for the reconstruction of the public sphere is the interpenetration of media and political power, whereby the media mobilizes public opinion in order to influence politics. To raise the question of the political system is not to deny the importance of forms and procedures, but to search for a political culture that will enable these forms and procedures to work.

Third: What forces are in a position to create the ideal foundations and moral culture for a new politics of equality? If the crisis of democracy can be understood as a breakdown of representation, and if the state continues to dominate the political sphere for a long time, is a "democratic post-democratic politics" possible, and if so, how can it be achieved?

Let me summarize the arguments laid out above. In the aftermath of the Cold War, democratic political systems have not undergone any significant formal changes, yet democracy at the social level is in crisis everywhere. In China, which still maintains a socialist system, while the system and form of government have also not undergone fundamental change, society has been so powerfully transformed that there is constant discussion about just what kind of society it is. While most commentators (in frequently polemical exchanges) trace the divergences between China and those democracies to differences in their political systems, I am of the opinion that, at its core, the current political crisis stems from the separation of the political system from the social form. The crisis in political legitimacy is a consequence of the breakdown of representation within the political system—that is, the separation of the political and the social. Before turning to the features that mark the breakdown of representation, let us first analyze how this separation and breakdown came about in the two social systems.

Let Us Ask Again: Equality of What?

Equality of Opportunity and Distributive Justice

Let us begin with the difficulties that beset social democracy. The French political scientist Pierre Rosanvallon has recently analyzed the current crisis of democracy on two distinct levels: those of political democracy and those of democratic forms of social organization. Understood as a political system, democracy embraces such concepts as the franchise, protections of individual rights, freedom of expression and pluralism, whereas the core meaning of democracy at the level of society is equality, embodied in social security, the availability of public goods to all of society, redistribution and so forth. Together, these two levels constitute what we mean by social democracy.[5] Rosanvallon holds that these two aspects of democracy overlapped in the era of the French and American revolutions. The notion of equality at that time concerned the character of social relationships, that is, whether they were equal or stratified. In the revolutionary period the politics of equality found direct expression in the abolition of hereditary privilege and fixed estates. In this way, a model of democratic society came into being that emphasized the nexus between citizen and state. At this historical juncture there was no need to define equality more precisely in terms of opportunity, results or distribution.

But in the nineteenth and twentieth centuries, democratic political systems and forms of social organization continually transformed. On the one hand, there were elections, freedom of the press and legally protected property rights, all of which composed a system of constitutional democracy. On the other hand, society became markedly polarized as the gap between rich and poor widened, monopolies formed in many sectors of the economy and class conflicts—accompanied by violent social clashes—intensified. This new hierarchy in society did not merely produce great class struggles and revolutions; it was also one of the roots of conflict between nation states. Ever since the latter part of the nineteenth century, but especially since the two world wars, fear of revolutions, anxiety about war and Cold War competition between the two social systems have fundamentally shaped conceptions of the path toward social compromise, class harmony and democratic practice. Social theory began to reflect on notions of foundational individualism and the system of social rights associated with it. The gravamen of these new reflections was an effort to theorize anew the relationships between rights and duties, welfare and responsibility, and self-reliance and solidarity. Today, when we talk about social democracy, discussion is generally limited to topics such as taxation, social insurance, labor unions, minimum wages and collective bargaining. Social democracy absorbed many of the accomplishments of the socialist movement and, through their institutionalization, transformed them into a democratic form of social organization. We could call this a form of capitalism beyond capitalism.

The most influential contemporary theories of democracy (those of John Rawls and Jürgen Habermas) have attempted to design both an egalitarian order in which diverse human beings can live peacefully together and the appropriate means to achieve consensus on it in order to overcome systems of conflict-based democracy (such as mass democracy), as they perceive them. This would be achieved, they argue, through a fundamental system (comprising a constitution, law and so forth) wherein, through a process of dialogue and communication, consensus could be formed and reproduced. This would satisfy rational demands (the defense of rights and liberty) and legitimize democracy (popular sovereignty). Yet the distribution of the wealth of society is closely connected to social conflicts, and struggles for equality aimed at redistribution of wealth have an unavoidably antagonistic character. In this respect the problem of equality is ultimately a political one. Chantal Mouffe has pointed out that the political philosophy of order and consensus overlooks matters such as emotion, conflict, politics and identity politics, which play a crucial role in questions of equality and justice. This political philosophy also offers little guidance for answering the questions raised earlier in this essay.[6]

If we consider notions of equality or theories of justice within the rubric of contemporary politics of equality, we may gain a better understanding of the question of the separation of the political system from the social form. Since the crisis of democratic forms of societal organization concerns equality, I would like to consider three versions of equality here. Of course, inquiries into the meaning of equality in ethics and philosophy are extremely complex, a point well documented by thinkers such as John Rawls, Amartya Sen and others, who have introduced distinctions such as utilitarian equality, total utility equality and Rawlsian equality.[7] To be sure, we cannot afford to ignore these debates, but I would like to discuss these notions and theories in a more accessible and integrative way.

The first category of equality is *equality of opportunity* (similar to utilitarian equality); the second is equality in redistribution or *equality of outcome* (similar to total utility equality, closely associated with the social contract). These two categories are the most familiar today. Equality is primarily defined politically and legally; the emphasis is on preventing discrimination. In the age of bourgeois revolutions the notion of equality was directed against the nobility and other systems of privilege, and involved both political and social rights. For Saint-Just (1767–94), a protagonist of the French Revolution, equality did not mean that everyone possessed an identical amount of power, but rather that every person had an equal portion of sovereignty.[8] It is precisely this radical, active notion that holds out the possibility of a version of political equality that breaks down distinctions of class, gender and ethnicity and that treats economic, social, legal and political issues of power as being within the purview of equality.

But, in the end, the intrusion of the logic of capital into every sphere of life transformed this radical notion of equality from the bourgeois revolutionary era into a notion of equality of opportunity wedded to market competition. The struggle over status difference was placed within a network of interests defined by economic criteria. According to the principles of equality of opportunity, "inequalities of income and other circumstances of life are natural conditions. The lower orders of society can improve their own economic and social situation by dint of their own efforts (industriousness, will-power, talent, and other legitimate means)." This is the "great principle" invoked by Abraham Lincoln, according to which the Union could long endure, and under which "all should have an equal chance."[9] In this context, the struggle for equality among classes, social strata, nationalities and ethnic groups is measured only according to the freedom of labor and its value under market conditions.

According to Marx, equality of opportunity rests on the logic of the exchange of commodities. Relations between human beings are expressed in the form of exchange relationships between commodities. Because the exchange of commodities presupposes the equality of their possessors, there is a historical link between equality and commodity relationships. "Each of the subjects is an exchanger [of commodities]; i.e., each has the same social relation towards the other as the other has towards him. As subjects of exchange, their relation is therefore that of *equality*."[10] Under market conditions, "the subjects in exchange exist for one another only through these equivalents, as of equal worth, and prove themselves to be such through the exchange of objectivity in which the one exists for the other."[11] "Equality and freedom are thus not only respected in exchange based on exchange values but, also, the exchange of exchange values is the productive, real basis of all *equality* and *freedom*. As pure ideas they are merely the idealized expressions of this basis; as developed in juridical, political, social relations, they are merely this basis to a higher power."[12] Since the exchange of commodities takes place on the assumption that labor is separate from the right of possession (according to Marx, "labor will create alien property and property will command alien labor"[13]), with the establishment of market society, the radical (progressive) content of the notion of equality transforms gradually into a form of legitimacy tied to exchange. According to the notion of equality of opportunity, equality is not a social ideal opposed to the logic of capital but is merely formal equality within capitalist society.

None of this implies that equality of opportunity has lost its attractiveness. When Marx first perceived the connection between equality and the exchange of commodities in bourgeois society, he focused most of his attention on the new forms of production and exchange. At that point he was less interested in the set of problems that he had already acutely analyzed in other contexts. He had already concluded that modern capitalist society, through the accumulation of wealth and the structure of money and power, unceasingly reconstituted the system of social classes as well as identity (especially inequality based on ethnicity, religion and gender, referring specifically to the transformation of ethnic, religion and gender relations into class relations). Therefore, the supposed autonomy of the human person was in fact dependent on material factors, and supposedly egalitarian human relationships were actually packed with unequal forms of exchange such as monopoly and racism.

It is no contradiction that the evolution of capitalism in the nineteenth and twentieth centuries was accompanied by (among other phenomena) the system of slavery, colonialism and ethnic and gender discrimination. The civil rights movement in the United States did not even achieve its major victories until the 1960s, and a variety of discriminatory practices persist in contemporary society. Gender discrimination in the labor market is an open secret. Social stratification according to gender and ethnicity has a long history but in capitalist society it has become an integral component of power and interest relationships, forming the objective content of relations of production and circulation in the modern age. That is why the whole notion of equality of opportunity, with its antidiscriminatory content, has retained a degree of emancipatory promise. The banner of equality of opportunity, however, proclaims discrimination to be a relic of traditional society, thus transforming the struggle for equality from one based on overcoming its internal crisis into a struggle for legitimacy and stabilization.

Distributive justice and equality are part of the heritage of the social-ist movement. They overlap with another notion, namely, the equality of condition. Under capitalism, especially in the industrial age, technol-ogy and capital made a mockery of so-called equality of opportunity. In consequence, the labor movement began to define equality of condition as one goal of collective bargaining: "Greater equality of condition was to be achieved primarily by government programs aimed at raising wages by reducing the supply of labor . . . and by supporting union efforts to raise wages and improve working conditions."[14] Beyond this, the redistribution of social wealth via taxes has been an important component of equality of condition.

"Distributive justice," as understood by John Rawls, has surely been the most influential contribution to the equality debate. Within the framework of justice, actual conditions of inequality were clearly exposed. Rawls evaluated the theory of justice based on the dominant position of utilitarianism (Hume, Bentham, Smith, Mill) from the tradi-tion of social contract theory (Locke, Rousseau, Kant). In Rawls's view, this theory of justice is based on principles of a society composed of individuals who pursue maximal satisfaction of the individual will and the greatest possible expansion of their individual wealth. A utilitarian theory of justice obscures the distinction between demands for freedom and power and between individual will and the increase of social wealth, and thus is incapable of determining the primary principles of justice. It views the principles that regulate social groups as expansions of the principles of individual choice and neglects the importance of general consent. It presupposes that increases in quality and quantity lead directly to legitimacy. Since it does not understand that real principles of justice must be presumed a priori, it has no means of drawing conclu-sions from actual outcomes. Since it takes satisfaction of the individual will as its motivating force, it is incapable of considering the qualitative differences between wills, and the discrimination toward, oppression of or harm to others that results from these differences.

Rawls assumes that there is an original position, a bit like the state of nature depicted by Locke and Rousseau (forming conditions for an incipient social contract). He argues that a "veil of ignorance" must initially be postulated in order for us to think rationally about our obligations and rights. This is the basis for justice as fairness and other principles linked to it. By means of a series of complex theoretical hypotheses, Rawls defines justice as the equal distribution of all social value, fundamental goods that "are to be distributed equally unless an unequal distribution of any, or all, of these values is to everyone's advantage."[15]

Here there are two important principles of justice: the first postulating the liberty and equality of each person and the second, the difference principle of distributive justice. According to the latter, social and economic inequality can only be justified on rational grounds if it can be expected to serve the interests of everyone in a society and if positions and offices are open and accessible to all members of society. As far as the first principle is concerned, constitutional democracy cannot guarantee the fair value of political liberty. Unequal distribution of wealth and property exists alongside political liberty, so that inequality in the socioeconomic system vitiates political equality.

As for the second principle, Rawls draws a sharp distinction between justice and efficiency, refusing to allow the former to be subsumed by the latter but emphasizing the compatibility between distributive justice and the search for utility. In order to achieve distributive justice, he institutes the "difference principle," which holds that differences of income or social position are to be permitted only if they serve the interests of the least advantaged members of society, and that when benefit accrues to the smallest group, then this benefit must accrue to all of society. In order to put the difference principle into practice, it is essential to compensate for inequalities due to talent and so forth. Furthermore, mutual aid, friendship among citizens and solidarity must be attained by means of social communication. To bring about justice as fairness, institutions will be needed that administer, regulate and distribute social goods. The market and the state are posited as the basic mechanisms for solving the problems of poverty and civil rights.

Rawls attempts to combine the principles of equality and liberty with equality of opportunity and the difference principle in order to restore the radical character of equality.[16] But in the real world of capitalism, equality of opportunity and equality of outcome are often in conflict. The former puts a high value on equality of starting point but in fact is only creating the prerequisites for competitive market relations and has no interest in analyzing how unequal social conditions limit equality of opportunity. Nor does this address the fact that competition, even assuming equality of opportunity, produces monopolies and inequalities (from the Marxist viewpoint the production and reproduction of surplus value) and thus reproduces unequal competitive conditions. When this occurs, opportunities at the starting line become unequal. At the time of the French and American revolutions, equality of opportunity and of starting point were regarded as the appropriate societal forms of equality, but subsequent capitalist developments have shown them to be ideas that served as a pretext for social inequality.

Equality of outcome must be viewed in the context of capitalism's process of production and distribution. It seeks to hold in check as far as possible those inequalities that result from the process of production and the functioning of the system (what Marxism views as exploitation) including those in the market. Social democracy does not rule out private property and the market. Indeed, they are taken for granted as the prerequisites that allow for redistribution via the fiscal system, thus alleviating or regulating class conflicts. This is the way in which the "social market economy" emerges in the context of social democracy. It is also the reason why social democracy has placed such a high value on distributive justice since World War II. Equality as distributive justice concerns not only the resources available for equality of outcome, but also its very meaning. To achieve equality using redistribution as the core mechanism, one must confront a daunting task: namely, how to prevent private property from getting transformed into monopoly capital, a process that would ultimately bring about the collapse of the welfare system. Unfortunately, equality understood as distributive justice has fallen into a deep crisis in the wake of the development of neoliberalism in the 1970s and the end of the Cold War. This crisis is much deeper than it was when Rawls published his *Theory of Justice* in 1971.

Amartya Sen's Equality of Capabilities

In his essay titled "Equality of What?" Amartya Sen begins by analyzing the relationship between human beings and things. Following Rawls he formulates a new concept: namely, the equality of basic capabilities. This notion designates the extent to which people are capable of fulfilling their basic needs and includes such capabilities as that of obtaining necessary nourishment, clothing and living space as well as the capacity to participate in the life of society.

There is nothing altogether new about analyzing equality under the rubric of capability. In Marx we read: "The right of children and juvenile persons must be vindicated. They are unable to act for themselves. It is, therefore, the duty of society to act on their behalf . . . There exists no other method of doing so, than through general laws, enforced by the power of the state."[17] From this vantage point, education must be guaranteed as a universal right. What is new in Sen's approach is his effort, via the notion of capabilities, to redirect his discussion of justice away from preoccupations with the distribution of income, resources and the like. Instead, he wishes to focus attention on the potential capabilities of individuals to achieve what they strive for or to get certain things accomplished. His discussion of capabilities is really about freedom, especially the freedom to make choices. Sen criticizes Rawls's theory of justice for its excessively materialistic tendencies. As he sees it, the theory of distributive justice concentrates too much on the material aspect of interests, thereby failing to understand rightly the relationships between human beings and things. If poverty or other factors prevent a person from getting an education or acquiring skills and status, then that person will not be able to get ahead in a competitive environment; worse still, she or he will not even be able to take part in the life of society.

From Sen's point of view, neither equality of usefulness, nor equality of goods, nor some combination thereof, can account for the importance of equality of capability. To be sure, where distribution of the material sphere is concerned, one may classify this according to those social foundations of rights, liberties, opportunities, income, wealth and dignity. In this sort of classification the material sphere lies at the heart of the matter, yet there is no attention to the relationship between human life and the material sphere. The notions of usefulness or utility manage to forge that link with human life but fail to consider the capabilities of human beings, focusing instead only on their mental dispositions.[18]

Thus, equality of opportunity remains an empty concept as long as there is no equality of capabilities. Without the protection of an adequate system of social guarantees (including redistribution), equality of opportunity only serves to legitimate inequality. But without equality of basic capabilities, even the redistribution of the material prerequisites of life will not be able to ensure equality in practice. Equality of capabilities presupposes the equal political and social status of all members of society. It is not determined solely by the autonomy of individual human beings, but also by the protective function of society. Hence, we must distinguish at least three levels of equality: equality of opportunity, distributive justice and the equality of capabilities.

Distributive justice as understood by Sen, particularly in the concept of capability, diverges somewhat from the theory of justice developed by modern social contract theory.[19] In his view, social contract theory focuses on a just social order, especially the ways in which "just institutions" might be established. Sen tries to find the common ground in the theories of a variety of philosophers, from Adam Smith, Marie-Jean-Antoine-Nicolas de Caritat and Mary Wollstonecraft to Karl Marx and John Stuart Mill. Despite their great disagreements, all of these theorists, he alleges, are interested above all in comparing diverse ways or forms of human life. A variety of factors are seen to influence these ways of life, notably the system of human action and the interaction between human beings and other factors. Sen is not looking for a single contract that would include all human beings and determine their relations; rather, he uses concrete case studies (for example, the abolition of slavery) to determine what sort of consensus might arise on the basis of public reasoning. He does not concern himself with the "institutions of justice," but rather with the way people actually live in their daily practices.

In this manner Sen has shifted the problematic of justice from institutions to human beings and from a contract to the process by which it is put into effect in the real world. Whereas justice in the social contract is restricted to only those people living in sovereign states, Sen takes everyone in the world into consideration. For him, justice is a question not of contracts but of reasoned arguments. To summarize: In investigating justice, Sen shifts attention from institutions to the triumph over inequalities that arise in everyday life. His starting point in this endeavor is not so much formal rights as it is the degree of freedom available to a person in the real world.

This emphasis on the substance of liberty, rather than formal power, can be illustrated in a consideration of China, India and other Third World countries. Sen has compared the development of China with that of India. On the one hand, he points to the advantages of India's democratic system (tragedies such as the Great Leap Forward, partly the result of blocked information channels, have not occurred in India). On the other hand, he takes note of India's backwardness vis-à-vis China in respect to education, the struggle against poverty, health care and mortality rates. India was a British colony, and after independence it opted for a democratic system complete with a parliament, multiparty system, voting rights and freedom of the press. Yet India has always remained a highly unequal society. The caste system has seen to it that only a small minority of people are able to involve themselves in politics. Even from the perspective of the French revolutionary era, when the democratic system meshed almost perfectly with corresponding forms of social organization, in India the divergence of the political system from the form of social organization is especially noticeable. English is the language of the civil service there, but only about 10 percent of the country's population can speak it. Nevertheless, the language plays a crucial role in determining one's opportunities in the political realm as well as in India's dynamic economy. Since India has never had land reform (except in Kerala and a few other places), many peasants are forced to eke out an existence by leasing farms from big landholders. Because they have no land of their own, they end up living below the poverty line. All this suggests that equality of capabilities is sorely lacking in India, and that claims about equality of opportunity there are little more than empty phrases.

In India (and throughout South Asia), there are stark inequalities in the ownership of land (which explains why the preconditions for reforms in China differ so much from those in India). Because the political system is so thoroughly decoupled from the form of social organization, the functions of the multiparty system, voting rights and press freedom have been limited in crucial ways. This does not mean that political democracy is unimportant. India's democratic system provides not only a basis for progress but also a potential political identity to a society marked by complex ethnic differentiation. Highlighting India's democratic deficits does not mean denying the necessity of political reform there but suggests that the formal notion of democracy alone does not allow us to gauge how successful India has been in achieving social equality. Rather than search for the perfect formal democracy, we must ask how a nation might overcome the separation between the political system and the form of social organization. We may further inquire whether a society may be called "democratic" on the strength of its democratic procedures alone. Many Third World countries have followed the model of Western political democracy and yet have failed to institute a democratic society. Hierarchy, dictatorship and monopoly are coterminous with the democratic system. All this means that the issue of democracy cannot be discussed in a one-dimensional way.

Sen puts public reasoning at the center of his notion of justice, just as he moves capabilities to the center of his discussion of equality. In so doing he opens up a new set of possibilities. First, the question of justice now hinges on the degree of freedom that a person may access in everyday life rather than on formal rights and law. That step enables us to go beyond an inventory of democratic practices in Europe and North America, and to include the experiences of other countries in considering participation in governance. In the case of China, we can investigate such phenomena as the "mass line" and other forms of participation in that country's modern history, as well as intellectual debates carried on within China's Confucian tradition and forms of village autonomy. Second, when one departs from the social contract framework, it becomes possible to expand discussions of justice and equality beyond the threshold of sovereign states. The field of global justice can now focus on a variety of activities, concepts and organizations that transcend national boundaries.[20]

Nevertheless, even the capabilities approach has its blind spots. The heart of the problem can be summarized in this way: When Sen uses "equality of capability" to disrupt the "materialist" tendency of distributive justice, he does not analyze the commodification (in the Marxist sense) inherent in "things." Thus, human capability can only be defined as the capacity to gain corresponding objects, so that human capability becomes equivalent to commodified labor. In his book *Development as Freedom*, Sen refers to two aspects of the development process. First, labor has been liberated from the maze of restrictions that have long prevented it from participating in the free labor market. Second, this process does not exclude use of social support, public administration or government intervention. We may regard this framework as the guarantee of "equal capabilities" offered by the political system.[21] If one explores the link between the two themes of "development as freedom" and "equality of capabilities," it becomes clear that the latter presupposes freedom of contract on the part of labor. However, the notion of free labor power limits human beings to the value relationship between worker and capitalist; it does not express the full range of humanity and human capabilities. But if "development as freedom" is intended to express equality of capabilities, then the author must redefine "freedom" or risk providing merely a one-sided depiction of capabilities.

We must therefore rethink the notion of an equality of capabilities, broadening it in two ways. The freedom to enter into labor contracts should not be granted inside nation-states alone; it must also be extended to the field of global relations. Furthermore, the dynamic of the expansion of the capitalist market is based on the simultaneous freedom and unfreedom of labor power, and we must research the relationship between social development and this condition of freedom and unfreedom. We also need to reflect on the meaning of the tendency for relations of trade and exchange, propelled by the expansion of markets, to penetrate every sphere of life. This tendency will culminate in the reification both of human beings and of things themselves, as the latter are thus completely subordinated to the logic of commodities. In this logic, peasants themselves, as well as the land, forests and water around them, are constituted as semifree commodities; the modes and meaning of life of villages and other social groups (local communities and national minorities) are devalued, and the social organizations and capacity for self-renewal at the village level are broken apart. Under these conditions, everything related to this way of life becomes thoroughly functionalized and constituted by value, and "things" become commodities. These trends suggest the following observations: First, the sphere of village labor power and its guarantees is key to understanding the relationship between the market system and the freedom of labor contracts. Second, a labor force that is able to move freely does not flow aimlessly, but implies a broad structural arrangement. This arrangement should have as its precondition the elimination of all structures of inequality (not only the *hukou* [residence permit system]).

The freedom to enter into labor contracts is a problem not only in China, as the example of migrants there suggests. It is one of the most important criteria for determining whether today's global markets really operate freely. If development is limited to ensuring the freedom of labor contracts without considering other social conditions, it can lead to social disintegration. For this reason we need to forge a solid link between the free labor contract (which serves to undermine hereditary hierarchies) and other values such as systematic social equality, respect for cultural pluralism, and development itself. Furthermore, rural problems can no longer be dealt with in isolation from urban ones; otherwise, the freedom of labor contracts will automatically give rise to a new form of alienated labor. The free movement of the labor force, public administration and government intervention are the necessary conditions for sustaining the market system. So how can we limit the destruction of nature, traditions, customs, rituals and other forms of life and values as the development process continues?

These are all crucial themes in development studies. They represent necessary steps in the efforts to extricate the value of "freedom" from various forms of compulsion (especially those tied to economic relationships) by embedding it in a wider context. From a more radical perspective, the freedom of the labor contract (the exchange relation appears in the form of a labor contract entered into by a private person) based on the exploitation of the surplus value created by a private person has replaced political dependency or compulsion in determining status. This historical development does not mean we can stop thinking about the full implications of contract-making in a market economy. Let us never forget that in China's coastal regions, laborers have been enslaved on the basis of signed contracts. What does the notion of equal capabilities imply for justice in education? Popular education is oriented to the market in the sense that it offers students specialized training for certain careers; even the educational system must meet the needs of the industrial and information society. That is why one cannot define the relationship between equality and capabilities without asking how equality of capabilities meshes with the all-sided development of the human person, or how justice in education can be combined with political and economic equality in the social process. If we derive our understanding of "freedom of capabilities" exclusively from the framework suggested by "development as freedom," we will not be able to find the road to liberation amid the fetters of capital.

The Situation of Working People

The equality of capabilities approach is a corrective to equality of distribution, which is commonly identified as a socialist characteristic. Are there elements of equality of opportunity and of capabilities in socialist practice? In the broadest sense, the aim of socialism has never been to redistribute wealth but instead to liberate labor power (that is, freedom). However, its real historical development has in fact also featured "a program for ongoing struggle over distribution": "Marx's heavy emphasis on productive processes should not conceal from us the simple truth that the struggle for control of the means of production is a distributive struggle."[22] The Marxian theory of transformation of the mode of production is closely tied to the politics of conflicts over equality.

This is precisely what is missing in Rawls and Sen (or they have attempted to avoid it). One cannot truly fathom the concept of "distributive justice" without a sense of the real struggles over equality in society. And that fact helps clarify the differences between two forms of social organization. From the point of view of distribution, the division, exchange and circulation of capital and land are fundamental economic relationships. Socialist systems endeavor to introduce common property ("people's property"), thereby converting workers into owners, in order to overcome the conflict between capital and labor and the separation between labor and property rights. Socialist production aims to satisfy needs rather than generate profits. This mode of distribution requires not only the institution of a system of distribution, but a complete reorganization of the mode of production. Marx had speculated whether the production of exchange values, "whose universality produces not only the alienation of the individual from himself and from others, but also the universality and the comprehensiveness of his relations and capacities," could create the conditions for "an association, in which the free development of each is the condition for the free development of all."[23]

In the practice of socialist countries, efforts to abolish the separation between labor and rights of ownership were always closely linked to broader issues of industrialization and forms of division of labor. Attempts at achieving equality, especially through reforming the ownership system, run up against a host of complex problems. In the course of industrializing the process of economic reproduction, how does one keep in check the excesses of the profit motive (developmentalism, or the theory of the primacy of productive forces)? And, as a practical matter, how can one prevent common property from becoming subject to state monopoly, which would again give rise to hierarchy, complete with new monopolies and new forms of exploitation? The socialist movement tries to overcome the "three great differences": those between workers and peasants, city and country, physical and intellectual labor. But the pressures of industrialization give rise to a conflict between the urban and rural populations, which, in China, led to the *hukou* or residence permit system in which citizens were registered in a certain locality and legally forbidden from living anywhere else without official permission. The antagonism between city and country has been a leitmotif of modern capitalist economies. But socialist practice, determined to move ahead with industrialization, ended up reproducing that separation between city and country in a different form, indicating that China's model of development in its socialist phase overlapped with capitalism. The separation of city and country stymies equality of opportunity, since distributive equality occurs principally within systems that are sealed off from one another. For example, while relative equality prevailed within rural society, the factory and gender relations, socialist industrialization and its dependence on state institutions inevitably lead to bureaucracy, privileges and monopolies of all kinds, generating differences in social position as well as the tenacious vested interests that accompany them.

It is not surprising, therefore, that the history of socialism records numerous movements against nascent inequality. In the 1960s these assumed a political character directed against the state and the Party, as mass mobilizations challenged bureaucracy in the former and monopolization of power by the latter. In the 1980s these movements shifted their focus from politics to economic reform. The notion of equality of opportunity was introduced in order to stimulate the struggle for equality. Market-oriented reforms rooted out many of the entrenched interest-positions that had been created by industrialization. In this atmosphere, the Marxist humanists' use of the concept of alienation to explain the social status differentiation that emerged during the socialist period was closely related to this new reform era view of equality. These two very different historical movements have in common a politics of equality, despite their radically different perceptions of equality.[24]

However, if we gauge the encouragement of competitive mechanisms by their impact on distributive justice, the outcome is clear: This putative "liberation" looks like a new form of repression. The effort to bridge the gap between urban and rural sectors led to a renewed dependence of the countryside on the city. In the wake of the urban reforms of the 1980s, the gap between the two widened once again in the absence of any effective rural policy and price regulation for agricultural products, which has in turn contributed to the current crisis in rural areas. Even in European models of social democracy, distributive justice is closely linked to equality of outcome. Fiscal and redistribution policies and social security all give systemic expression to the goal of distributive justice. More saliently, socialism produces entirely unexpected consequences when equality of opportunity in a competitive economy is allowed to negate the egalitarian achievements of the socialist period. When that happens, distributive justice is of course denied, but so too is equality of capabilities, which depends ultimately on the social position of working people—that is, whether they are dependent employees or the masters of their own destinies in society.

The notion of collectively owned property assumes that every human being is capable of satisfying his or her own needs. Socialism instituted a variety of educational measures, from compulsory school attendance to night school for peasants, all of which offered the average working person—and people from diverse socioeconomic backgrounds—the opportunity to get an education and thus to develop their own capabilities. In those days there were still quite a few university students who came from worker or peasant families. In addition, equality of capabilities shows up not just in education and technical skills, but also in enhanced initiative and autonomy. Even if one judges by the classical criteria of social democracy, China's socialist history laid the foundation not only for its reform-era achievements, but for a democratic form of social organization as well. To point to these accomplishments is not to negate the human tragedies involved, nor the high price paid to attain them. On the contrary, to reaffirm that working people should be dominant in society means that one is aiming to overcome alienation in the capitalist process of production (including capitalism disguised as socialism).

The debacle of socialism and social democracy is evident not only in the problem of distribution and the growing gulf between rich and poor; it is also implicit in the position of workers in the process of production and in social life in general. It is hard to disentangle democratic social forms from the economic structure in which they are imbedded. So, without democratizing these economic structures, even social democracy—let alone a socialist democracy—will not be possible. Therefore, besides achieving distributive justice through the fiscal system, the next crucial move must be to democratize the internal structure of business enterprises by giving working people some share in managing them.

We should recall the arguments of two formerly influential books that have fallen out of favor in the neoliberal era. In *Capitalism Against Capitalism*, Michel Albert takes a look at the "social market economy" that was expressed by the Rhine model.[25] Advocates of the social market economy regard the market as the best means to fuel an economic boom, but they then insist on a fair distribution of its benefits among different social strata. "From this perspective the joint management of large enterprises must be included among the progressive aspects of the Rhenish model. Co-determination was instituted in Germany. In accord with this scheme the firm's board of supervisors gives representatives of stockholders and employees each half of the seats on the board." In the long run this system provides not only greater social security and more just distribution at the level of the enterprise, it also operates more efficiently. The other book in question is Ronald Dore's *Stock Market Capitalism: Welfare Capitalism: Japan and Germany versus the Anglo-Saxons*. Dore concentrates on the model of the Japanese firm, emphasizing that the efficiency of a company cannot simply be measured by the size of the profits that the owners of capital rake in. One must also consider the gains attained by consumers, the local community, the state and the firm's employees (including both managers and workers). The managers of these firms are motivated not only by external stimuli from financial markets, but even more strongly by the reactions of consumer markets. Internal controls also come into play here.[26] Dore emphasizes certain organizational forms in Japanese industry, such as lifetime employment, the "capillary" management system within vertically integrated industry, the large size of boards of directors in large companies (sometimes including as many as fifty members), the structure of company unions and corresponding accounting practices.

The basic ideas in both books were presaged by the preface to Japanese industrialist Otsuka Banjo's 1947 publication, "Experiments in democratizing business enterprises: Propositions for revising capitalism." Its key idea was this: "Simply put, the democratization of the economy aims to include in the management of a firm all those, without exception, who have any direct or indirect role in its operations, and to reflect their wishes in management. In other words, industry in a country is supposed to function on the basis of the consensus and the creativity of all the participants in it. And that is only possible when the participants are mutually responsible and cooperative. In this sense economic democracy can only be realized if the position of the workers is enhanced."[27]

All the experiments with social democracy and intrafirm democracy that have been tried since the Second World War have emphasized joint administration and control on the part of owners, managers and workers. They came about due to the twofold fear addressed earlier in this essay: conservatives' worries about revolution and democrats' and liberals' apprehensions about communism and nationalism. Economic democracy, then, consists roughly of two elements: democracy within the business enterprise and distributive justice under the control of the state. In today's financial crisis, Wall Street is dominated by financial speculation. The owners and managers of major financial corporations divide up the profits earned through speculation, while the consequences of speculation must be borne by society and the state. This indicates the drastic degree to which the neoliberal socioeconomic model operates counter to democracy.

As far as the process of industrialization is concerned, China's socialist practice has primarily been evident in the system of common property and in worker participation in management. The Angang Constitution is characteristic in this regard.[28] In socialist enterprises, the workers' position was closely bound up with the *danwei* or work unit system, which originated in publicly owned enterprises. In theory, *danwei* did not designate the place where production takes place, but instead indicated a form of social organization in which production, life, politics, culture and other vital spheres were combined. It presupposed the dominant position of the party of the working class within the state, which thus became a workers' state. The central idea behind *danwei* was to overcome the abstractness of capitalist production and put labor at the center of a new social process. In other words, the *danwei* was nothing but a realization of new social relations under conditions of industrialization and abstract production. Under these circumstances the equality of capabilities was expressed directly through the subjective political and economic position of the working class. These capabilities were not limited to participation in production and competition; rather they were expressed as sociopolitical capabilities in a range of contexts. In this respect they could not be defined exclusively as an economic phenomenon.

When the *danwei* is treated as nothing more than a production site and the people involved in it are classified merely as workers (and not as political, cultural and social persons), it degenerates again into a form of organization dominated by production. If, in the post–Cold War era, the *danwei* is rejected out of hand as a model based on state control, then all *danwei*, whether in factories, business enterprises, schools or even the state itself would thereby be converted into institutions of production or circulation, the aim of which is only to generate increases in profit. Thus, their original social logic would be subordinated to a one-sided process of production.[29] It is worth discussing how state-owned capital in the system of distribution can become a mechanism for advancing social equality. It is not, fundamentally, a matter of the opposition between state and private property. Rather, the real question is whether genuine public ownership can be brought into being, and the state's monopoly can be prevented from hollowing out public property—a situation in which, according to a vague comment by Marx, public ownership and private ownership become the same. Using tax revenues and social dividends to make large state-owned enterprises genuinely popular (owned by all people) enterprises and creating new forms of labor relations, allowing workers to become owners and to participate in enterprise management, would be fruitful direction for exploration. But if state-owned enterprises develop in a different direction, say toward oligarchy, speculation-fueled management or a new bureaucracy, the demise of economic democracy would result. Capitalism has seen important changes in its form, but its basic contradictions, based on the private ownership of means of production and of public wealth, have not changed. To resolve this, the accumulated experience of the history of socialism concerns not only questions of ownership relations, but of its efforts to achieve new forms of integration of production into the social network.

In practice, the system of public ownership has not resolved the problem of state-capital monopoly. Genuine collective property (owned by the entire society) has not been fully achieved; hence, control over social property is continually subject to the logic of control. But experience shows that mutual relations between managers and workers, and the political energy borne of this interaction, is the basic means of overcoming monopoly or the formation of a "new class" of bureaucrats. This is also the primary condition for thwarting the transformation of common property into a monopoly of local government or interest groups. When a few years ago I participated in a study of the privatization of textile factory, the workers asked whether the factory was in public hands or if it belonged to the local government. They also posed more theoretical questions, such as whether they themselves were owners of state-run firms. At root, these are questions about democracy itself. The workers were not merely asking for wage increases or compensation for their change in status; they were raising the question of ownership from the perspective of political power—that is, of labor relations. Where private or international capital is concerned, the right to work is at the core of democracy. So, when workers in contemporary China ask such questions in the course of their struggles, we should not assume that they are doing so for solely economic reasons. Their inquiries concern workplace democracy: Are workers enterprise owners or not? Does the enterprise provide the proper framework and conditions for bringing about democratic management and shared responsibilities? Can they share—in whatever organizational form—in the management of the firm? Can one move beyond the traditional relationship between employers and employees toward a new model of production if one, let us say, offers shares of stock in the company to the workers?

By the same token, the ownership and transfer of property in land are not exclusively economic matters; they go to the heart of a democratic form of social organization. Under market conditions, how can property relationships be arranged so as to meet the needs of the market without jeopardizing the collective or social ownership of land? These are some of the big challenges that face both state-owned enterprises and the collective ownership of land.

A great quantity of research on Chinese rural questions has focused on democratic elections at the grass roots. The use and manipulation of democratic procedures by the wealthier strata—oligarchical politics at the village level—have largely escaped the attention of investigators.[30] We need to renew the study of the various forms of agricultural cooperatives and collectives that emerged in the course of the twentieth century. This is a prerequisite for integrating politics with economics and creating the conditions for peasant political subjectivity. And these are among the most pressing issues that urbanization and market-oriented policies have put on the current agenda. In order to adapt to economic development, some localities in China have considered novel schemes of organization such as the so-called "association for the comprehensive development of the new agriculture." Researchers describe the "agricultural association" as follows: It makes investments using both government subsidies and private or public funds and is run by a professional team. What distinguishes it from run-of-the-mill enterprises is that the management structure rests upon the active participation of village residents and a freely elected, autonomous board of directors. This scheme results in cooperation between management and society. China has a long tradition of small-scale agriculture that is being powerfully challenged by urbanization and modernization. Will it be possible to find a form of social organization capable of integrating a wide array of agricultural operations, such that models based on family, local community and associations can be concurrently developed? Here one must avoid interpreting a complex practice touching on a variety of production schemes in terms of narrow economic or efficiency criteria. Instead, it is crucial to embed economic measures in the wider context of society, culture, tradition and politics. The diversity of production schemes and participatory management practices acts as a counterweight against capitalist production, which severs the economy from various social networks.

The relationship between city and country is a crucial problem in the process of modernization. For Marx, the antithesis of city and country was a basic characteristic of capitalism. A key question is, thus, how equality between the city and country can be achieved through preservation and innovation. Let us caution that equality between city and country should not be understood merely in terms of equality of income or distribution. Human beings must be in a position to choose independently their way of life, and we should refuse to consider any of them as abstract labor power. Only through a supersession of capitalism can the antithesis of country and city be transcended. At the beginning of the twentieth century, the great thinker Kang Youwei conceived of a model of civic autonomy based on the village, a kind of social autonomy founded upon a nonimaginary community. In the modern world, migrant laborers who have left their villages behind often join together in a variety of "invisible communities." They attempt to restore their social ties in the midst of a system of production that has grown increasingly abstract. Inquiry is necessary into what systemic innovations are needed such that these social ties are able to bring about real change in the social position of working people. From this point of view, civic autonomy as practiced in some villages need not remain confined to those villages. It is a form of practice of social renovation that is present in other spheres. If it is possible to combine these village practices with modern management, then we can also imagine creating a model of social production that transcends the logic of capitalism.

In brief: It is more appropriate to describe studies and experiments in this area under the rubric of democratic forms of social organization rather than in terms of economic democracy. The reason for this category shift is that democracy on the shop floor or in land ownership cannot be pigeonholed as "the economy." These matters touch more broadly on the social position of working people and suggest a less hierarchical relationship between city and country. In the history of capitalism, there is no necessary link between political democracy and democratic forms of social organization. Yet the vitiation of democratic forms of social organization leads automatically to a crisis of political democracy. When the political system as a whole (including practices such as voting rights and the multiparty system) is incongruent with these democratic forms of social organization, then—inevitably—a fractured society will result. China's democratic practice, having passed through revolution and socialism, will have to overcome class conflicts and create forms of politics and society different from the ones that legitimize the system of exploitation. And it must reject any model of production that allows labor to become completely abstract. Is it not the case that humanism can only be realized in practice once all relations of enslavement and vassalage have been overcome, and once organizational structures have been put into place that integrate economic, cultural and political relationships?

7

The Equality of all Things and Trans-Systemic Society

The Notion of an Equality of All Things

Besides the three main concepts of equality presented in the previous chapter, I propose to offer a fourth: the "equality of all things," a notion used here in the sense suggested by Zhang Taiyan (1869–1936). This concept has certain elements in common with notions such as equality in diversity, equality in difference and pluralism. Yet none of these ideas captures the full meaning of the equality of all things.

Michael Walzer describes equality within pluralism under the heading of "complex equality," as follows: This notion is about the concrete distribution of goods in everyday life, not about grand, abstract philosophical problems.[1] "Complex equality" enlarges the content of "distributive justice." For Walzer, "the idea of distributive justice has as much to do with being and doing as with having, as much to do with production as with consumption, as much to do with identity and status as with land, capital, or personal possessions. Different political arrangements enforce, and different ideologies justify, different distributions."[2] Walzer adds that the objects to be distributed include "different distributions of membership, power, honor, ritual authority, divine favor, kinship and love, knowledge, wealth, physical security, work and leisure, rewards and punishments, and a host of more narrowly and materially conceived elements—food, shelter, clothing, transportation, medical care, commodities of every sort, and all the odd things (painting, rare books, postage stamps) that human beings collect. And this multiplicity of goods is matched by a multiplicity of distributive procedures, agents, and criteria."[3]

In other words, the "complex equality" version of pluralism focuses on the multiplicity of distributive systems and their justifications, which in turn reflects the multiplicity of the items to be distributed. As far as the multiplicity of the "objects" is concerned, there is quite a bit of overlap between the "equality of all things" and "complex equality." But it is clear that "complex equality," with its theory of the multiplicity of objects, operates in an anthropocentric frame of reference. Hence, the "things" can only be defined in light of their usefulness. Finally, this usefulness corresponds to what utilitarian thinkers mean by "welfare" or "the satisfaction of needs" and "preferences." By contrast, the "equality of all things" depends on the "point of view of the thing" as anchored in classical Chinese thought. In this theory, things are dynamic subjects, so they cannot simply be interpreted from an anthropocentric point of view as mere means to satisfying human needs.

For Zhang Taiyan, the "equality of all things" covers all the phenomena in the universe, which—including humankind and all entities in nature—should be treated from the position of their subjective equality. But this position can only be developed through the operation of negation or emptiness ("doing away with sensory perception"). These observations compel us to go beyond the distribution of objects and their forms and confront a broader philosophical issue. In European thought the "equality of all things" thesis would be assigned to the fringes of pantheism: "Everything that exists constitutes a unity (in some sense) and this all-inclusive unity is divine."[4] Pantheism assumes that the equality of all phenomena in the universe dovetails with the presupposed unity of God with the universe: Everything is God and God is everything. It follows from these assumptions that (a) God cannot be both transcendent and human, and (b) the essence of God is contained in every particular thing. Yet the notion of an "equality of all things" has nothing to do with the idea of God. Its origins lie in the philosophy of Zhuangzi (369–286 BCE), a representative thinker of Taoism, and in Yog c ra Vijñ nav da idealism (the Mahayana Buddhist doctrine of "consciousness only"). Pantheism, holding that the universe and every single thing in it form a totality, must as a rule assume that all things have the same essential nature. Something may display its own finite properties but also reveal the infinite totality. By contrast, the thesis of an "equality of all things" does not presuppose any such universal essence. It should be understood as a kind of ethical principle according to which each thing in the universe, along with its special properties, ought to be respected.

To categorize "equality of all things" as a nonanthropocentric discourse is not to imply that as a system of thought it neglects human existence and its conditions. Rather, it is to say that this "material perspective" observes human existence within the framework of natural history, liberating the relationship between humankind and things from a unidirectional logic of control. In his annotations to Friedrich Paulsen's *A System of Ethics*, Mao Zedong noted that "humankind is a part of nature and is subjected to the laws of nature. Where there is life there must be death, just as entities in nature are subject to formation and decomposition."[5] "We humans, although ruled by natural law, are also part of nature. So while nature has the capacity to dictate human life, we also have the capacity to dictate what is nature. Human capabilities, although limited, cannot be said to have no influence on the natural."[6] Thus, "equality of things" is not meant to negate human initiative, but to place this initiative within natural history.

The essential point of this "material perspective," then, is to place this capacity and its limitations within the sphere of relations between "things." Humans are a part of nature and, like other parts of nature, are also "things." Humans are not, then, merely the sum of their social relations, but a condensation of natural relations. Human social activity and human influence on nature should thus be understood as within the sphere of nature. The "equality of things" notion suggests that the defining character of each thing consists of its equality. Therefore, equality is compatible with freedom.

A revolution in epistemology enabled the emergence of the "equality of all things" theory. Zhang Taiyan wrote, "When one talks about things, they are all equal. This is merely to adduce some common feeling. For there is nothing good and nothing bad. For things must be spoken of without language, denominated without names, and affectively experienced without affect. Apart from language and names, all emotions are equal. That is the very meaning of the equality of all things."[7] When we avoid "language, names and affect," we also avoid fantasy about the world and ourselves (that is, the entire system of mere appearance). And that is what is meant by the so-called revolution in epistemology. By virtue of that revolution/negation, the "equal things" constitute a horizon within which entities can be observed in their concrete particularity. In other words, the procedure of observing things "apart from language, names and affect" is a method of knowing all things in the universe as the unique entities that they are. But one only gets to this point by following the method or procedure of negation.

Since the uniqueness of things has been obscured by the system of representation, we can only restore that uniqueness by altering the practice of cognition peculiar to the system and practice of representation, thus transcending the unequal relationships generated by language, naming and affect. Thus, the notion of an "equality of all things" implicitly absorbs human beings into the category of "all things." It neither abolishes the difference between humans and things, nor that between the things; instead, it considers these differences as the prerequisites of equality. This perspective works on two levels. On one level the unequal relationship between humans and things is a mirror image of the situation that prevails among humans themselves. A hierarchical arrangement of the relationship between humans and things (the person produces, distributes or consumes the things, for example) entails positing relationships among human beings as unequal as well.

On another level we find that unequal relationships are in fact created by language, names and affect. Essentially, as soon as things have been stripped of their concrete particularity, their function becomes their substance (in the form of their serviceability for human ends). "Objectification is the practice of alienation . . . Under the sway of egoistic need, he can only affirm himself and produce objects in practice by subordinating his products and his own activity to the domination of an alien entity, and by attributing to them the significance of an alien entity, namely money."[8] For example, from an anthropocentric viewpoint, modern equality creates a situation in which humans are the subject and things the object. Consequently, the object world is woven into a hierarchy of values as measured by its functional potential.

If each thing possesses its own special character, then all things are equal. This is not to say that the politics of equality is a politics of nonaction (*wu wei*). To allow the things to emerge as what they really are does not entail political nonaction. Things exist historically in language, naming and affect. The practices of speech, naming and affect are not simply fantasies or imaginaries; they are qualitative and evaluative representations of modes of production and circulation, of the forms of social organization. This system of representation constitutes our reality. Thus, the "equality of all things" is not simply a confirmation of things and their order. Rather, it offers a vision for changing an unequal world through a negation of things woven into the order of language and naming. By denying the conventional reality constituted by language and label making, one simultaneously creates a horizon of change that undermines the claims to absoluteness implicit in the world of inequality. The specific order in which things occur also puts its stamp on the status, language and names that characterize their interrelationships. To break the power of language and naming means also to break the spell of the particular orders constituted by such language and designations. Things thus identified lose their particularity. "The equality of all things" is a universal concept of equality that begins from the perspective of the things. In marked contrast to the anthropocentric standpoint, which defines, designates, uses and exchanges things on the basis of their functional character and human serviceability, the "equality of all things" insists that we take the perspective of the thing itself as our starting point. That means that we will free the things from their enmeshment in the human system of naming and utilization and understand them in a new way—as what they are in themselves.

If the equality of humankind is discussed only in terms of the distribution of things, even supposing that such a distribution were carried out in a variety of different ways, it becomes impossible to demonstrate that it is ultimately the form of things qua possessions that is the true source of domination and inequality. Equality on the basis of commodity exchange does indeed express a relationship among human beings, but one in which they appear as things. As soon as the "thing" is liberated from the logic of exchange, the relationships between things, or of things to persons, or of humans to humans is no longer congruent with the logic of commodities.[9] Thus, the notion of a "thing" disavows the alienation of "things" by rejecting the denominative relationship between human beings and things. The "thing" cannot be measured by the degree of its functional value (serviceability, for example, a human being as labor power), and still less by its monetary value (exchange of commodities). This is the case in part because the supreme forms of serviceability and exchange posit a division or hierarchy among men in respect to their functional utility and the exchange principle.[10] For these reasons, the negation and critique of unequal systems of representation such as naming invariably form part of a material process of trans-formative change.

Before delving more deeply into the implications of the theory of the "equality of all things," we should contrast it with two other mutually inconsistent theories that have bearing on issues of equality. Rawls employs the "veil of ignorance," which conceals the historicity of human existence, as a key premise of his entire argument. By contrast, communitarianism refuses to restrict questions of distribution and justice to the material sphere alone, pointing out that they are always intimately bound up with values, worldviews and social affiliations. Its advocates insist that any discussion of justice must therefore include a historical dimension.

What questions arise if we compare these two hypotheses with the theory of an "equality of all things"? Communitarianism shares some features with Rawls's veil of ignorance. Both argue that existing conditions and social distinctions should not simply be assumed as premises in the argument, as those conditions are themselves unequal. For Rawls, the contract must be the original position, which is ex hypothesi behind the veil of ignorance. For Zhang Taiyan, reality is enshrouded in language, naming and affect. We can only begin to talk about equality once we have eliminated this overlay. But there are important differences as well. In contrast to Rawls and his rationalist hypotheses, Zhang Taiyan bases his entire line of reasoning on the logic of negation: the struggle to move beyond the realm of naming and appearances. In this sense and from the very outset, the "equality of all things" is neither a hypothetical ideal condition nor a procedure of argument. It is more like a political process. Since the order of things exists in the system of representation, the reconstructed epistemological system (the transformation of the "standpoint of the subject toward the object" into the "standpoint of the object toward the object") only comes to fruition through the path of negation.[11] Second, the "veil of ignorance" evokes a state of being that lacks differentiation and in fact treats this lack as the premise of equality. By contrast, in the case of the thesis of "equality of all things," once names and appearances have been transcended, the differences that remain furnish the very premises necessary for a discussion of equality (equality as difference).

But what differences remain once names and appearances have been overcome? It is only then that the world displays its infinite variety and uniqueness. This uniqueness rejects the form of difference resulting from the one-dimensional differentiation occasioned by the fetters of naming and appearances, which implies freedom. And it is this insight that enables us to define the differences between communitarianism and the "equality of all things" thesis. The differences are especially salient in the way they formulate their approaches to politics of identity and recognition. Identity politics mobilizes people on the basis of names and appearances (tribes, language, religion, gender), whereas the politics of recognition assumes identity politics within the system of recognition. Identity and recognition replace the uniqueness of the human being with singular attributes, which cannot reveal the infinite diversity of the cosmos and nature. This infinite diversity is embodied as uniqueness under particular temporal and spatial conditions. If one begins from the epistemological practice of uniqueness (difference) without erasing difference in the manner of rationalism, the boundary between the "equality of all things" and the "veil of ignorance" is clearly demarcated. This demarcation sets the notion of an "equality of all things" well outside the tradition of contract theory, since contracts can only be made between equal subjects of the same kind. In contrast to a homogeneity within species, the "equality of all things" presupposes their difference. But difference as the bearer of infinite diversity and uniqueness is not characterized by self-identity, which would be synonymous with one-dimensionality. Identity always connotes some kind of exclusion, and what is excluded in identity formation is not just the other, but also one's internal diversity. Recognition, which rests on identity, belongs to the world of naming and appearances.

At this point, the "equality as difference" inherent in the "equality of all things" theory diverges from communitarianism, despite their seeming similarity. This theoretical or philosophical difference is critical for the exposition that follows.

"Things" and Equality in Difference: Extending the Concept of an "Equality of all Things"

The "equality of all things" can be further developed on two levels. The first concerns areas that have been overlooked in treatments of the themes "complex equality" or "pluralistic equality." The idea here is to integrate the relationship between humankind and nature into the discussion in order to overcome the anthropocentrism inherent in these notions of equality. The theory of "complex equality" emphasizes a kind of social autonomy and its significance in issues of distribution. Its aim is to defend the equal autonomy of every subsystem in society from within the realm of possession. For example, "through unions, resist the power of capital; through teachers, maintain the independence of schools against their misuse by politics (in the narrow sense) or religion; through medical professionals, take care of patients who most urgently need their help; through social welfare systems, attempt to keep people above the poverty line and make sure that their fate is not decided by markets." "The state remains the final court of appeal to which the people can turn. When efforts in a specific sphere of life have proven fruitless, the state must in any case intervene. This is something that happens frequently."[12]

"Complex equality" and pluralism likewise evolve in "society" just as the notion of autonomy does. As far as the defense of autonomy in social subsystems goes, the "equality of all things" follows "complex equality" rather closely, except that it is extended from humankind to the things, thus providing a new angle of reflection on the nature of human autonomy. From which vantage point do autonomous persons define the prerequisites of their own autonomy? Is it possible that an identification related to the ego is itself only part of linguistically mediated phenomena (the world of language, naming and affect)? Since "things" are positioned by humankind through a system of differentiated names, the notion of an "equality of all things" must itself be "philosophical" or "reflexive," given the new emphasis on the active, dynamic character of things.

Philosophical reflection is necessary in order for us to overcome our predicament. Since the exploitation of nature is one component in the distribution of society's wealth, the domination of nature qua resource is a source of inequality and domination. No matter how human civilization develops, humanity's subjugation and exploitation of nature, as well as its mode of life, is a part of natural history. In this respect, reconstructing the relationship between humans and nature is a necessary, decisive step for the practice of equality.

This does not simply mean that human beings ought to respect nature in order to understand it; it implies rather that human beings and their relationship with nature must be understood as a subset of natural history. In light of all this, the "equality of all things" approach is not restricted to a critique of the structures in which production, circulation and exchange operate. In fact, there is a good deal of overlap between it and ecological theory. Ecological theory is not a form of naturalistic fetishism superseding anthropocentrism, but a mode of observation based on the placement of humans and human activity within natural history. The "things" are a totality. Nature, which is composed of things, has infinite multiplicity; hence, the thing also possesses a kind of multiplicity. Utilitarianism would object that human beings, on the basis of the idea of the greatest happiness, can arrive at the idea of preservation of nature by recognizing that the destruction of nature ultimately harms humans themselves. But in the capitalist structures of production and consumption, nature is fragmented into many components such as land, animals (wild and domesticated), plants, water, energy, wood and air, all of which have productive or consumptive effects. Without exception, imperialism, colonialism and international capitalism were all driven by the imperative of subduing, carving up and conquering nature. The twentieth-century struggle for natural resources gave rise to reflections on issues such as the ethical treatment of animals and ecology. The mass extinction of animal species has led to the animal rights movement, in politics and in scholarship.[13]

These unprecedented ecological crises and environmental disasters have stirred up numerous discussions and unleashed movements devoted to addressing them. As long as the antinuclear movement sparked by the Fukushima disaster relies for its arguments on utilitarianism, it will never come up with any true alternative, because it will have only rejected one destructive form in favor of another one. Not to recognize the uniqueness of the other (and the social claims rooted in it) is tantamount to ignoring the ethics of "things." The Scottish philosopher T. L. S. Sprigge distinguishes three positions that human beings may hold in respect to their responsibility toward the nonhuman world. First, they may consider the potential enhancement of human prosperity as the sole criterion for judging the truth of a morally relevant proposition or policy. Second, they may include the potential enhancement of animal prosperity in addition to human. Here, the inanimate world is excluded, because its members by definition do not share in life or life's intrinsic value. Third, humans may take a universalist attitude, asking what would be beneficial to the existence of all things, regardless of whether it benefits humankind or not.[14] Just as human rights depend on the idea of inherent human worth or value, so too do philosophical and ethical discussions consider "whether nature has intrinsic value." The question is whether "values" and the "rights" that follow from them can be the only measure of "things," including human beings. Values involve life, consciousness, serviceability or exchange. Rights have to do with either the legal system or the exercise of power. Values and rights cannot serve as the moral foundation for respecting nature, when animals, plants or inorganic nature is concerned. This has always been a difficult issue for ethics. In the case of the "equality of all things" theory, the notion of "differentiation as equality" occupies a central position. In light of that theory, relying on values and rights to explain the equality of "things" would commit the fallacy of "equalizing the heterogenous."

On a second level, difference acts as the prerequisite of equality. Equality does not aim to abolish differences, but understands difference as equality. Formal equality is the hallmark of modern egalitarianism, especially in light of its premise that all persons ought to be subject to the same legal system. Viewed through the lens of formal equality, diversity often appears to be synonymous with hierarchy. To the extent that equality is built upon the eradication of differences, diversity is ruled out. And even when difference is acknowledged, its historical origins are concealed. In other words, equality floats on the linguistically mediated surface of appearances or forms, beneath which a hierarchically based differentiation lurks. In this sense, there is always conflict and tension between equality and diversity.

Understanding difference as equality does not mean weaving difference into the fabric of names and appearances, for that would only subject difference to hierarchical relations. It also does not mean that equality is equivalent to the abolition of differences. In what sense, then, may one regard difference as a prerequisite of equality? The philosophy of the "equality of all things" interprets equality as the overcoming of differences within the realm of names and appearances. Understood thus, equality is also freedom. This means that the equality of diverse things is a product of the active subject. These differences are not determined and ordained by some higher order. Nor can they emerge from a single perspective. They are actively determined by each thing (including human beings and their community). "Overcoming names and appearances" requires of human beings that they judge not from their own vantage point as singular subjects, but from the "thing-perspective." That is, they should consider things from the viewpoint of things.

What is at stake here is a subjectivity that is present everywhere, a uniqueness that refuses to depend upon a single order of things. Things' relations with one another do not correspond to the humanly created structure of names and appearances and their relationships. The "equality of all things" rejects the modern theory of knowledge, because the latter construes the relationship between human beings and things or one person and another as that between the ego and its other, between a human being and an alien body. Zhang Taiyan says, "It is despicable to make sameness out of difference." That would be a kind of equality without differences. The way to the equality of diverse things can only be premised on the "equality of the different."[15] The pathway to the equality of the different is impossible without a complete abolition of the hierarchical differentiation (names and appearance) that the modern world (state and society) created in the first place.

Since equality in difference is linked to the overcoming of names and appearances which are embodied directly in state and society, it can be interpreted as an actively political notion—one that refuses to let itself be defined by appearances. Defining differences actively means refusing to treat them as essential. Therefore, differentiation is interpreted as an active process and as the origin of the political. According to Zhang Taiyan, things, as depicted by the "equality of all things" theory, presuppose their own uniqueness, which is in turn characterized by activity and creativity. This is not the uniqueness posited by essentialism, which in fact represents the antithesis of the version propounded by "equality of all things." The former treats names and appearances as the essence of things, which are measured by their functional quality, their value in exchange and use.

The second level of "the equality of all things," namely, difference as equality, affirms the equality of each individual, but it also has two other fields of extension. One of these relates to the interrelated character of ecological and cultural diversity. The crisis of equality in the modern world no longer comes into view solely in terms of socioeconomic inequalities, but also in the inequality that is caused by cultural and ecological transformation. As far as the social system is concerned, this crisis of equality is expressed in the partial or complete failure of socialism's "nationalities" policy promising the autonomy of national minorities. "Making differences equal" is a radical notion of equality, and not an inequality that emerges from an affirmation of society through the recognition of difference. The "equality of all things" expresses the equality between individuals, between cultures and between everything in the natural world from the standpoint of their multiple subjectivities. In practical terms it addresses persuasively the concrete prerequisites and conditions that must be satisfied for freedom to flourish. Communitarians think that the primary goods of a society include not only rights, wealth, freedom and opportunities, but also values, beliefs and a sense of belonging. Obviously, the latter goods are not fully captured in categories such as rights and distribution. This is so because rights and distributive patterns such as the ones highlighted by communitarianism represent a kind of particularism masquerading as universalism.[16] In a certain sense the debacle of cultural pluralist policies in contemporary European countries can be traced back to the rupture between culture and civil rights within nation-states. Different cultures hold different views and even different concepts of what should count as rights, property, freedom and opportunity. Not even distributive equality can satisfy the "need for recognition."

Equality in difference suggests a different image of society, a kind of practice that moves beyond appearances constituted by speech and naming and yet knows how to preserve differences. It respects diversity, in which equality is already contained or presupposed. The very meaning or content of equality in this sense is, then, respect for diversity. Both elements are combined in one systematic practice. The "equality of all things" is not identical to the ethical disposition of communitarianism, since the latter's approach to recognizing diversity leads directly into the "politics of identity." Second, the manner in which the "equality of all things" idea defines and demarcates the world is the opposite of the tendency in capital, or money, toward homogenization. It is also the opposite of the social model that takes as its dominant principle an economic growth-based ideology of developmentalism. Third, it is opposed to the order of appearances in which differences are regarded as hierarchical and one-sided. From the vantage point of the "equality of all things," identity politics—whether nationalistic or regionally based—is nothing but the negation of individual diversity. But that does not mean that the "equality of all things" philosophy dismisses the rationality of identity politics. It stresses that the uniqueness of "things" (including human beings and groups) is rooted precisely in their diversity and multiplicity.

The Crisis of Equality in Difference: The Case of National Minorities and Their Territories

The following analysis uses the example of China's "national minority autonomous regions," which combine traditional institutions with egalitarian ideology. The central idea here is that the practice and realization of equality take place within a concrete historical setting. Citizens are not abstractions. Their lives are shaped by concrete historical, moral and cultural conditions, and so their habits, customs and preferences inevitably differ. In this respect citizenship can be linked to autonomous collective organizations. At the same time, difference and diversity are subject to historical transformation; they are in no way immutable essences. But concepts of change, integration and communication should not have as their aims the eradication of differences or diversity.

The idea of a "region" connects nature (geography shaped by long-term influences, such as climate) to the lives of human beings, including their mobility. Stability, change, internal diversity and continuing permeability all shape the character of a region. The emergence of a region is the cumulative product of nature (the long-term formation of geographic, meteorological and other regional characteristics) and of human life and movement. Regional character is formed through the internalization of stability, change and diversity, as well as through persistent permeability. Thus, the formation of a region is a part of social history as well as natural history. The autonomy of a region, which must itself be diverse, cannot be defined exclusively from the viewpoint of anthropocentrism and superficial appearances. It also derives from an understanding of and respect for the natural factors that constitute regions. In the course of long-term historical change, grasslands, mountains, rivers, deserts and steppes as well as the geographically determined climate together supply the basic conditions of human life. Ways of life, customs, beliefs and social relationships evolve in accordance with these natural conditions. Nature is subject to change. Human life is a factor intrinsic to the ongoing transformation of nature. But we still must inquire about the extent and precise ways in which such trans-formations influence the ecology of the regions.[17]

The system of minority autonomous regions aimed to put equality-in-difference into practice. The practice of equality involves more than simply acknowledging ethnic identity or the politics of difference. It is derived from a kind of pluralistic whole, or organic pluralism, shaped through natural transformation. Autonomous regions are mixed spaces, in which cultures, customs, beliefs and diversity, all depending on local ecology, are to be respected. At the same time economic, political and cultural structures are created on the principle that regions should be equal to one another.

The crisis now affecting the national minority autonomous regions is a crisis of equality in difference. Minority regional autonomy is collaps-ing on two fronts. On the one hand we are witnessing a sharp decline of their autonomous character (difference) in the territories of national minorities—so much so that the whole notion of autonomy there has been reduced to the level of names and appearances. On the other hand, the concept of the minority region in the minority autonomous regions is being simplified to one of mere ethnicity. When this happens, equality in diversity loses its meaning. It is soon replaced by an exclusive and one-sided politics of identity. The politics of identity have reduced the multiplicity of human beings and groups almost entirely to a one-sided emphasis on ethnic origin or religion. Humanity is here condemned to one-sidedness in a different way—and in this case by pluralism itself.

Both attacks are occurring in a social system in which an economic-centered developmentalism is hegemonic. The social system, along with the plurality of values it implicitly contains, is controlled and dominated by economic reasoning. For its part, identity politics are a form of resis-tance, based on the construction of identity (language, naming and affect). This leads to one-sidedness in humans and in social groups. It follows that the crisis can only be solved by addressing both of these levels. On the first level, the task at hand is to absorb differences into the practice of equality (including the recognition of identity). On the second level, one must negate differences that emerge in the order of appearances (monolithic hierarchy and nationalism or the nationalist or ethnic politics opposed to them) in order to guarantee equality in diver-sity. If we interpret equality in this way, we are not talking about differences in the sense of national majorities or minorities or a "politics of status" (politics of appearances). Instead, differences are preserved through an abolition of names and appearances. In the last analysis, we must view the question of culture in its connection with the cultural creativity of each individual person (not the abstract individual, but the concrete human being embedded in his or her historical development, value system and sense of belonging).

Nowadays the notion of equality in diversity involves not only social equality, but ecological issues as well. It is a concept opposed completely to the egalitarianism fostered by market competition and developmentalism. And it is a notion of equality that combines several disparate elements: economics, politics, culture and equal membership in society. Not only does it reject the dominant position of business, it also opposes the one-sidedness of a pluralism rooted in cultural identities.

Using Xinjiang as an example, we can examine the challenges that confront the national minority autonomous regions. Xinjiang's population is a complicated mosaic. Almost every nationality in China is represented in it, with Uyghurs, Han Chinese, Kazakhs, Mongolians, Tibetans and Hui composing the largest share. The mere fact that national groups dwell and coexist with one another need not, in and of itself, give rise to conflict. Even if there are historically rooted differences and disagreements among national groups, this circumstance still does not mean that the former must inevitably lead to conflict. For example, the Hui people are ethnically closest to the Han Chinese, but religiously most akin to the Uyghurs. Other ethnic groups such as the Kazakhs, Kirgiz, Uzbeks, Tajiks and Russians are transborder ethnicities; each of these groups has its own country outside of China's borders. Naturally, the members of such ethnic groupings in China feel an affinity with the countries in which their kin dwell. But that does not mean that they do not identify with China. The Uyghurs have cultural ties to Turkey, Iran and the other countries of central Asia. Their affinity is not the same as national identity, but it does entail cultural, religious and historical contiguity. Only at certain times and in specific constellations of power do such ties engender conflicts. The point is simply this: Ethnic and religious differences alone do not cause conflict. The trigger for and social origin of cultural clashes is the reduction of multiple or pluralistic identities to a single, one-sided identity. Among the most important factors in this shift of identity is the "new class division between ethnic groups."

How can this phenomenon be explained? In the wake of the social transformations sparked by economic reform and market competition, new class divisions have arisen in every ethnic group. New wealthy and impoverished class formations have emerged within the Han, Uyghur, Kazakh and other groups, but these formations are the result of extremely complex interplay between the particular ethnic and class characteristics of the national minority autonomous regions. The most important pillars of Xinjiang's industrial economy include natural gas and petroleum, followed by nonferrous metals and coal and then real estate and construction. Oil and gas production is dominated by a state monopoly; in fact, the state has been investigating energy sources there since the 1950s. On the assumption that socialism is the appropriate form of organization for a state controlled by working people, state property was never understood to be the exclusive possession of any specific ethnic group. Therefore, egalitarian practice focused on two areas. First, territories of national minorities received compensation in the form of tax revenues and redistribution of wealth, sometimes from one region to another (originally they retained 2 to 3 percent of the profits from oil and natural gas; this share later rose to 5 percent). The state's development strategy not only affects the balance between the central government and the provinces, but also seeks to create parity among national minority autonomous regions and other regions. Second, one now has to ask which policies and laws might be enacted to protect ethnic equality within the territories.

During the socialist period, operating within the legal framework of autonomy for the autonomous regions, the state adopted affirmative action policies that extended from birth control and education to daily necessities and food security programs. Furthermore, there was a quota system in place for job placement, rather than a laissez-faire system of competition in a so-called "free choice" employment market. Big state-run enterprises had to reserve a certain percentage of jobs for candidates from among the national minorities. However, due to economic reforms enacted in recent decades, these state enterprises have had to fire many of their workers; members of national minorities who have lost their jobs have had more difficulty finding new jobs than the Han Chinese. The coal and nonferrous metal industries as well as those engaged in infrastructure building and real estate are not among the sectors in which the state has a complete monopoly. In fact, private firms are strongly represented in these sectors. To succeed in any of these industries, whether mining, infrastructure or real estate, one must have strong backing from the banks and government; all require immense capital investment, state-of-the-art technologies and well-trained workers. Generally speaking, industries in these sectors located in the autonomous regions and run by members of those minorities are less competitive than their counterparts in other areas of China. (In Xinjiang the Uyghurs tend to dominate industries such as the processing of cattle and sheep hides and the demolition work that precedes urban renewal.) In highly competitive industries, firms usually prefer to hire Han workers, who are assumed to be more educationally and technologically qualified. Even in companies run by national minorities, hiring practices tend to follow this logic.

Each of these ethnic groups has its own culture and way of life, but differences in educational attainment and technological training do not mean that there exists a hierarchy of culture. To the extent that hierarchies do form, they are constructed on the basis of particular relationships and specific perspectives, above all according to economic logic and the market principle. If one defines "capabilities" and equality solely in terms of this logic, one has already laid the foundations for inequality.[18] For Zhang Taiyan, the structure of names and appearances is the one-sided result of a particular historical conjuncture. That conjuncture—the dominance of economic paradigms in our age—is the reason, notwithstanding the economic benefits that have accrued to them, for the economic marginalization of national minorities in Xinjiang.

The crisis now afflicting national minorities in Xinjiang is closely connected to the crisis in distributive equality. But under market conditions, this crisis becomes linked to the crisis in the equality of capabilities. The crisis in distributive equality emerged, rather, within employer-employee relations and became the core of the ethnically marked crisis in equality of capabilities. If we fail to clarify the concept of equality of capabilities and continue to interpret it in light of one-sided standards—especially those of economic laws and market competition—then the demand for equality of capabilities acquires overtones of discrimination. Capabilities cannot be defined in terms of one-sided criteria. Rather, the very concept of equality must be closely allied with diversity and difference. Equality of capabilities does not mean that the members of a given ethnic group should have to abandon their own cultural traditions and the forms of life that sustain them. Equality of capabilities should be understood in a broader sense. Cultural traditions and their accompanying ways of life form a kind of penumbra around equality, establishing the preconditions for the creative process that generates culture in the first place. In other words, cultural traditions and the creative process that generates them must themselves become part of our criteria for judging what counts as equality. Where market conditions prevail, most members of minority groups cannot even reach the starting line of the competitive race. The discriminatory view judges this lack of competitiveness as proof of differences in capability. What is missing in this "meritocratic" judgment is recognition that such differences arise from social conditions, not just from individual merit or lack thereof.

Under these macroconditions, capabilities are evaluated in one-sided ways. Let us consider the example of the labor market. The proportion of minorities who can speak Chinese is much higher than the share of Han Chinese who speak a minority language. But this linguistic advantage affords few benefits given the macrobackground of the entire economy, with the Chinese language dominating the larger context in which market transactions are conducted. The Chinese language is also the key to mastering specific production techniques and skills, so it also becomes a precondition for market communication.

Many graduates of the University of Xinjiang (particularly minority graduates) cannot find a job. Their failure can be explained on two levels. The first of these involves the language of education. Bilingual education is a reasonable option in regions with a high proportion of minorities. But market pressures ensure that most instruction will be carried out in Chinese, which handicaps the teachers of minority background, whose Chinese-language level is generally lower, while offering advantages to the Han teachers. Aside from such market pressures, the entire educational system, especially the evaluation criteria used in colleges and universities, has itself become a problem. For example, the number of key journals of minority research, in which one must publish to get ahead in academia, has increasingly declined, creating intense competitive pressure. As a rule minority academics must learn Chinese due to hard necessity, whereas Han students and academics do not have to master any of the minority tongues. That is the reason why language education cannot be a one-way street. Multilingual education is the only path to true equality of capabilities.

On the second level, we encounter a crisis in multilingual education that is reflected in economic structures. In the aftermath of recent conflicts, a few universities have started to encourage young Han Chinese to major in one of the minority languages and have tried to expand the number of jobs for graduates. But in the absence of any multilingual macroeconomic structure that might sustain it, the scope and effectiveness of this effort is seriously limited. As explained above, differences in property holdings among ethnic groups were kept to a minimum due to the presupposition of collective property under social-ism. But now the question arises whether, under current economic conditions, minority-controlled firms can gain a greater market share. In Mao Zedong's day the class question was always at the heart of egali-tarian policies in the cultural field. In the case of language reform, the goal was to reduce the number of illiterate citizens in order to overcome class distinctions rooted in different levels of educational and cultural achievement. This policy sparked a language reform (however defi-cient) even in regions dominated by national minorities, which aimed at achieving greater equality but which was abandoned after the Cultural Revolution. Today we must rethink equality and diversity as we design cultural policies.

The "new class divisions between ethnic groups" has another facet as well: increasing differentiation between city and country. Population policy has actually favored national minorities. The Uyghurs, for exam-ple, have a population of 9.5 million today versus only around 3 million in 1949. But population growth among the national minorities has two significant side effects. First, conflicts over land have sharpened as the number of people competing for it has continued to increase. Second, urbanization, market orientation and greater mobility due to economic factors have all led to an expansion of the Han Chinese population. In fact, the crises now besetting agriculture, villages and peasants as well as burgeoning migration are microcosmic versions of the crisis faced by Chinese society as a whole: that of inequality between city and country and among regions. But why have these related crises in agriculture, villages, the peasantry and migration turned into a source of ethnic conflict in the autonomous regions? Roughly speaking, these problems play out on two levels. In Xinjiang, national minorities live mainly in the countryside, whereas the Han Chinese cluster in the cities. Even in southern Xinjiang, where minorities form the majority of the local population, the proportion of Han Chinese in the cities is increasing rapidly and steadily. Conflicts between city and country can easily transform into conflicts between ethnic groups. Furthermore, the movement of capital and labor exacerbates regional inequality and the relations of dependency that ensue. Because inequality between regions finds expression in the form of capital, social networks and capabilities enhanced mobility has led to unequal competition within the sphere of capital, between social networks and in the quality of the labor force.

People who have migrated to minority-dominated regions are clearly not responsible for this state of affairs. If we want to assign blame, then we must pin it on the particular conditions that have arisen within macroeconomic structures. Conflicts over land and the increased marginalization of villages force young farmers to move to the fringes of cities. And in minority regions these new urban migrants are usually minorities. That is the reason why the current model of development cannot guarantee equal developmental conditions to the culture of every ethnic group. These phenomena can be explained as the results of two distinct crises: one of equality in distribution, the other of equality of capabilities. But in the regions where national minorities predominate, both crises must be explained by reference to the categories of equality in difference.

Equality in difference includes distributive justice, equality of capability, and respect for cultural values and ways of life. From the perspective of redistribution, socialism attempts to alter the relationship between employees and employers in order to overcome divisions in society that have arisen due to industrialization. This effort naturally affects two aspects of that relationship: distribution and capabilities. Besides taxation, investments and other means used to promote equality between regions, the system of distribution in minority autonomous regions is most clearly exemplified by the system of subsidies and benefits given to minorities to enhance their opportunities. Both sets of policies served the same goal: namely, to build socialism. Under the system of collective or common property, property rights did not pit one ethnic group against another. By contrast, where market conditions prevail, the privatization process has strengthend the tendency for property to become stratified along ethnic lines, and the original set of minority policies has been reduced to a number of purely economic measures, including a system of job allocations.

But in a market economy, the effects of such measures are minimal. Since the common goal envisaged by socialism is no longer in vogue, subsidy policies designed to help minorities often give Han Chinese (mainly ordinary working people) the feeling that they are treated more poorly than other groups. This policy is also one dimension of the discrimination that different ethnic groups practice against one another. The idea of a "national minority region" is a holistic concept; it is impossible to speak of ethnicity without reference to region, or to focus on region while neglecting ethnicity. On the level of policy, while focusing on the difference between minority and other regions, one must at the same time pursue or gradually introduce a policy of equal treatment within the minority regions. But unless we make certain systemic reforms, such a policy of equal treatment can itself be viewed as the source of new inequalities.[19]

Freedom of values and of religion is closely tied to ways of life and modes of production. In China's minority regions, particularly in Tibet and in Xinjiang, there has been a remarkable growth of religious institutions as well as of population. The number of mosques per capita in Xinjiang is among the highest in the Islamic world. Yet the conflicts between ethnic groups do not really arise either from religion or different cultures and customs. Rather, they have been triggered by the "new class divisions between ethnic groups" and its underlying mode of production. In this sense, the ethnic question cannot be considered solely a religious question existing outside of the secular sphere, but must be confronted within the secular sphere. The distinctive character of ethnic life is not cultural, divorced from the dominant logic of contemporary society. Members of ethnic groups participate in politics, economic life and other practices of daily life, and religion is only one of these. To separate one form of identification from other life practices is precisely an expression of the "transformation of ethnic difference into class difference." Only when real individuals take their demands for autonomy beyond religious life and into labor and other relations is the creation of an equal society actually possible. In an equal society, people can be masters of their own source of livelihood and thus come into being as individuals. This genuine individual life is by nature one of e pluribus unum.

The erasure of difference and the transformation of cultural difference into unequal social relations are consequences of the dominant developmentalist logic of our time. From the viewpoint of the "equality of all things," not only must equality of capability be translated into the question of the diversity of capability and its equality, but a dynamic view of "things" must be constructed. Both must be combined in order to realize an equality of difference, for the reification of humans (homogenization and one-dimensionality) has possessive logic as its precondition. The abstraction of capitalist production can only be held in check when production is embedded in social and cultural networks. Only in this way can human beings attain freedom.

With deepening trends of marketization, urbanization and globalization, the modes of life in the autonomous regions have been violently altered. The "new class divisions between ethnic groups" finds expression in the conquest, transformation and destruction of nature, and in the mode of life based on consumption. As Marx wrote, "Any distribution whatever of the means of consumption is only a consequence of the distribution of the conditions of production themselves. The latter distribution, however, is a feature of the mode of production itself."[20] A new kind of inequality in society presupposes a specific mode of production. The notion of a "new class divisions between ethnic groups" likewise presupposes some change in the mode of production. In regions with complex ethnic, religious and demographic relationships, this process is given direct expression in the fact that the dominant mode of production and its needs are declared to be the sole criteria for evaluating different cultures. Therefore, from a normative perspective, minority autonomous regions should place equal emphasis on ecological and cultural diversity, and the "genuine individual," a unity in diversity, should be placed within natural history.

The foregoing analysis demonstrates that the "equality of all things" perspective, although forming strong support for the concept of diversity, differs from the common understanding of cultural pluralism and difference politics. As described above, the "equality of all things" negates the one-sidedness of "things." Promoting difference politics through ethnic identity can contribute to the alleviation of inequality, but it also often achieves the opposite result. Using a one-sided viewpoint to combat another one-sided force contributes neither to the protection of ecological and cultural diversity, nor to the achievement of equality.

Equality in Difference in a Transnational Context

Equality in difference also applies on the international level. Here, it is a matter of equality vis-à-vis the international community, which in turn manifests identity in difference beyond the borders of nation-states. With the expansion of capitalism throughout the globe, the dominant forms of inequality on which nineteenth-century writers focused, such as class relations, were transformed. The modern age's primary contradictions could be found between the imperialist metropole and the colonies, and between the developed centers of industry and the agricultural periphery. This is commonly referred to as the North–South question. With recent transformations in the global economy, despite the persistence of unequal North–South relations, new complex questions of South–South relations have arisen (such as relations between the new Asian economies and Africa or Latin America). Here I explore, with international inequality as the background, how domestic inequality can also embody an international dimension. This should be regarded as a political condition that must be faced if we are to establish equality among states and on the international level generally.

Modern democracy is based on civil rights and the assumption that there is a reciprocal relationship among democracy, equality and the nation-state. But this pattern of reciprocity is facing a set of challenges that I will summarize under three headings:

First: Democracy in the context of nation-states has never stopped Western "democratic states" from militarily attacking and colonizing other peoples and states. On the contrary, democracy often has been the motivating mechanism for colonization and military action. Ultimately, civil rights within nation-states (the core of modern notions of equality) do not offer a notion of equality that extends beyond their own borders.

Second: The reciprocal relations among democracy, equality and nation-states in the age of globalization often set the stage for the exploitation of the resources and labor of other countries and societies. So-called globalization is mainly a product of the international expansion of capital, production and consumption. Once it has permeated a nation, the model of development adopted by one society often has repercussions for other societies. All of the economic and social decisions reached by very large entities such as the United States, the

European Union, China, Japan, Russia, India and Brazil exert a major influence on other countries as well. Using democratic procedures to foment imperialist mobilization is commonplace. In the contemporary model of democracy, people outside a given political community have no right to participate in the making of important decisions within that political community, even though those decisions will ultimately affect them. In this sense the right of citizenship is exclusionary.

To take just one example, the world's largest energy consumer, the United States, refuses to accede to the Kyoto Protocol. It may be that American politicians are supported for this domestically, even though it spells disaster for the rest of the world. Also, when the United States or nations in the European Union launch invasions of other countries, they need only the consent of their own legislatures (which may be regarded as an outcome of civic participation). Yet it is the entire world that must bear the consequences of these invasions. Moreover, even international law and UN procedures have had only limited success in preventing or restraining such imperialistic wars. This same logic applies to other countries as well.

Third: Another challenge to the democratic triad is the demise of the cultural pluralism resulting from large-scale immigration. Waves of immigration have been set in motion by globalization, market orientation and inequality in the countries of origin as well as on a global scale. Migrants alter the demographic mix in many of the countries they seek to enter. The host societies (including different nations and different regions within a nation) accept them only as a labor force without granting any official recognition of their cultural or affective identities, in the hopes of protecting their own interests. Identity politics in immigration host societies reflect the abstract character of capitalist production. The demise of cultural pluralism has two aspects. The nation-state cannot integrate the migrants into a unitary relation of names and appearances. The migrants' efforts to retain their own culture, however, ultimately impede their socialization. Compromise between the nation-state and the politics of identity usually takes the form of an endeavor to reshape differences into renewed hierarchies within the structure of names and appearances.

The socialist internationalism of the nineteenth and twentieth centuries was a grand experiment designed to overcome the interlocking triad of democracy, equality and the nation-state (especially of imperialist nation-states). But the experience of globalization has dealt a cruel blow to internationalism. Its downfall has been caused, in part, by international models of production and consumption. But the disappearance of the socialist heritage in the international arena has also hastened its demise.

In analyzing practices in the European Union, theorists such as Étienne Balibar have tried to redefine the notions of citizen and civil rights. His notion of a democratic border regime proposes new programs for conducting bilateral, multilateral and international negotiations, ones that take into account the plight of migrants and the circulation of commodities as well. Taking this set of issues as his starting point, Balibar questions the formalism of law and morality. He argues that solutions proposed by moral reasoning depend on the category of representativeness, which has exclusionary effects and thus can offer no satisfactory answer to the questions posed by contemporary reality. The rise of globalization has made it inevitable that we devote some thought once again to mechanisms of transnational citizenship.[21] At this juncture, the nation-state is still at the heart of international politics. Under those circumstances, how can one articulate a framework within individual states that would still take account of global equality, giving it an expanded and richer meaning in international affairs? That is a matter for careful consideration. According to Balibar, Europe must develop a civic space alongside the political community, a mechanism for deliberation that is both more creative and more pluralistic than the traditional one.

In light of the arguments presented here we may envision several possibilities for China. Might it be possible to set up some kind of coordinating mechanism in the Chinese People's Political Consultative Conference that would expand national issues into international ones? Or would it be possible to establish a mechanism in the Chinese People's Congress for investigation and control, in order to build international equality into the design of the entire system? Could one combine such reforms and innovation of the domestic system with other regional mechanisms? Any such reform of the political system would have to be accompanied by supranational social movements—the political public sphere is not limited to the framework of the nation-state. At the same time, however, the political public sphere that extends beyond the borders of the nation-state must be given concrete expression within the system of the nation-state.

For the time being, we assume the centrality of the nation-state rather than the international community, since the struggle for the "equality of all things" will continue, for the foreseeable future, to be waged on that stage. The value-orientations of different countries— or in different stages of a country's history—have a great influence on equality in the supranational context. If we take the global theme of "China in Africa" as an example, we find that China's policy toward Africa has gone through two phases. The first was the phase of internationalism or "aid to Africa," as Mao Zedong called it. In the second or supranational era, the economy has occupied center stage. The People's Republic of China cultivated relations with Africa on the basis of its membership in the Third World and alleged common interest in opposing imperialism and colonialism. In 1955 China took part in the Bandung Conference. Even though Third World states were divided on the role of communist movements, the conference was able to endorse a position calling on participating countries to "seek commonality in differences." As is generally known, this conference launched the creation of the Non-Aligned Movement, which came to fruition in 1961, establishing the foundation for an alternative to the bipolar world order initiated by the Cold War. At the request of the governments of Tanzania and Zambia, China drafted plans for a railway project for both countries as a form of foreign aid. Preliminary studies began at the construction site in 1968, and the project was completed in 1976. During this time, China dispatched some 56,000 engineers, technicians and laborers to Africa, while giving both countries interest-free loans of 988 million yuan as well as machines and other materials. Even after this project was finished, China continued to offer both Tanzania and Zambia interest-free loans. Between 1976 and 1999, more than 3,000 Chinese engineers and technicians worked in these two African countries.

Since China's reform policies were implemented in the late 1970s, its commercial interests have been increasingly prominent. By 2008, China's bilateral trade with Africa amounted to $107 billion, exceeding the country's trade with France and second only to its trade with the United States. Trade with Africa includes energy, mining, manufacturing industries, infrastructure and agriculture. Now that it has become part of the global trading system, China's relations with Africa in regard to trade and economic policy overlap more and more with those between that continent and the West. China's role is becoming ever more complex. The Western media have criticized the business practices of certain Chinese firms, and the African response has varied. For example, in 2006 the firm NFCA (Nonferrous China Africa Mining Company, a subsidiary of China Nonferrous Metals Mining Company, Ltd.) did not pay wages on time to its workers in Zambia's Chambishi coal mine. This refusal to pay then triggered a strike. Indeed, for quite a few privately owned Chinese firms in Africa that lack the long-term perspective of the national enterprises, profits are paramount. However, in contrast to Western companies, which concentrate most investment in the natural resource sector, China, disregarding risks such as war or political upheaval, invests a good deal more money in infrastructure and manu-facturing industries, which are considered high-risk by Western countries. Many such investments are not expected to be profitable for another twenty to forty years. These investments are not simply selfless aid projects that are indifferent to outcomes, but the result of long-term calculation of expected profit. In this respect they differ from the aid projects of the 1960s and 1970s that China undertook under the banner of anticolonialism in Africa. But Africa's long-term development is assumed in the calculation of future economic benefit, and in this sense, there is a clear connection between the strategies of state-owned enter-prises and the experience of the socialist period. These factors are some of the reasons why China enjoys considerable support in Africa despite Western criticisms.

The forum on Chinese-African cooperation at the November 2006 Beijing Summit occasioned considerable surprise and speculation throughout the world. The "Beijing Declaration," adopted at the first forum, emphasized that China and Africa had agreed on a collective framework for dialogue based on equality, mutual usefulness and coop-eration. It is worth noting that this declaration established a basis for potential cooperation that went beyond equal exchanges of commodi-ties and international trade. It also acknowledged the enormous gulf between rich and poor and North and South, injustice and inequality in international relations, political inequality, debt and disease in Africa. The whole point of economic cooperation and trade, according to the declaration, is to overcome these unequal relationships and to revise the dominant logic and unfair competitive conditions within the global system. Of course, this will only be achieved if all countries involved therein develop internally the requisite legal framework and behavioral norms.[22]

As a result of globalization, the transnational mobility of human beings has reached an unprecedented level. In different ways the notion of an "equality of all things" has transcended the democratic framework that was constructed around civil rights. At the same time, this notion represents a deepening and widening of civil rights, since they themselves, along with the egalitarian values that undergird them, may now be interpreted in a broader context. The idea of the "equality of all things" is closely allied with the concept of autonomy, which is by no means simply the product of the modern state-system. We find different forms of autonomy in a variety of political traditions, indicating that we may be able to extract formative elements of the notion of the "equality of all things" from a much more extensive history. In a way similar to the "equality of all things," internationally oriented concepts of equality have likewise moved beyond the notion of the rights of citizens. Even the concept of a "citizen of the world" can scarcely capture the full meaning of this kind of equality. The equality of mobility, which transcends regional and national boundaries, touches on complicated societal relationships. In order to render the notion of an "equality of all things" more plausible in this context, it will be necessary to adduce such notions as "supra-social systems" and a "trans-systemic society." In this way we may open up the necessary space for reflecting on a new civic culture and a more tolerant idea of citizenship.

The notion of supra-social systems was first introduced by Marcel Mauss, who used the term to describe a civilization composed of "social phenomena shared by several societies." According to Mauss and Durkheim, civilization is a social paradigm originating from long-term relations from diverse origins developed through various forms of mediation.[23] It is the "transmission of collective representations and practices." This definition goes beyond the regionally based characterization of the relation between the material and mental aspects of civilization and finds expression not only in "material culture," "geography" and "economy," but in religion, ritual, symbols, laws and ethics as well. Its scope is thus worldly, but also cosmological, legal and ethical.

In this respect one could characterize the networks that have existed between China and neighboring countries, whether organized around tribute, diplomacy, trade, marriage, religion or language, as "supra-social systems." Japanese scholars refer to these networks as the "cultural sphere of Chinese characters," the "Confucian sphere of civilization" or even just "East-Asian civilization."[24]

The notion of "trans-systemic society" also emphasizes the "trans-systemic" character internal to a society. Under conditions of global capitalism, the prefix "trans" has been greatly overused. It refers to trends superseding traditional categories such as ethnic groups, nations and regions. But the idea of "trans-systemic society" is different. At the heart of this idea we find a series of dynamic forces such as culture, customs, politics and rituals, whereas economic relationships represent only one of the activities in the complex social ensemble alluded to above. However, if relations between states and the supranational or transregional activities engaged in by modern capitalism create an abstract power that tethers all cultural and political factors to economic life, then a "trans-systemic society" would mean the exact opposite of this. The notion is really meant to depict a sociocultural condition arising from interrelations woven by contact, and the dissemination and coexistence of diverse cultures, ethnic groups and regions. For example, families in ethnically mixed regions often take part in different social systems (familial, religious and linguistic). It could therefore be said that these "systems" are present in a society, village, family and even a single person.

Recent anthropological studies indicate that migrant laborers from different regions and ethnic groups arriving at new job locations are drawn to migrant communities populated by earlier migrants from their home regions. In this way, communities based on place of residence are replaced by ties of "cultural affinity" not obvious to the casual observer. This new form of association is thus sometimes called an "invisible community."[25] In this respect, neither the right of individual liberty nor the notion of equality offers a satisfactory response to the demand for full equality for communities in our highly mobile society. Historical narratives, particularly in the period of nationalism, often take a community, a religion or a language group as their subject matter. But when these ethnic, religious or linguistic identities are blended within one region, one village or one family, then narratives such as these will most likely lead to oversimplification, exaggeration and distortion of complex states of affairs. The concept of a "trans-systemic society" is able to integrate phenomena that are at once unique and universal, and can thus describe them in new ways.

This concept, however, does not merely depict a blend of several civilizational networks originating in different societies; it portrays a society that has arisen due to cultural dissemination, contacts, integration and coexistence—in short, a society of complex systems. A "trans-systemic society" is one in which equality of the internal elements must be presupposed. Yet it is of course distinguished by its "trans-systemic" character so must presuppose not only equality, but also difference and historicity. This trans-systemic nature is not limited to interactions among distinct communities but also applies to every individual and his or her social relationships. Differentiation is simply what characterizes every subject. The difference-bearing social subject is neither the source of hierarchy nor the basis for a politics of identity that seeks out differences only to level them down. The trans-systemic society is a point of view in which equality and difference are mutually presupposed. And it serves as the historical and anthropological prerequisite for "equality in difference."

Immanuel Kant says of the state that it is "a society of men whom no one other than the nation itself can command or dispose of."[26] In Kant's case the state is equivalent to the nation-state. The foregoing discussion suggests a variation on Kant's statement as follows: The state as a society of human beings is a trans-systemic political structure. We are entitled to call it a society of human beings only when its unity and its trans-systemic character coincide. This society of human beings is constituted by specific modes of interpenetration. We can only understand any singular "society of human beings" as a trans-systemic society; the meaning of "singular" can only be understood in the "trans-systemic sense." We should not interpret it as an anti system or as a totality. Here, "singular" is "multiple" and "multiple" is "singular." The state as a human society embraces not only material culture, geography, religions, rituals, political structures, ethics, cosmology and the world of the imagination; it should synthesize the multi systemic character of all of these phenomena.

In this sense a "trans-systemic society" is not a social description from the perspective of "national community," nor is it that of the pluralistic society, which, for example, stresses "pluralistic unity" (Fei Xiaotong).[27] The "trans-systemic" approach tones down the unitary element and instead plays up the dynamic relations between and among systems. Systems are mutually interactive and do not stand in isolation, which allows them to form the essence of social networks. The foundation of a trans-systemic society is in the world of the interactions that characterize daily life. But this society depends on innovative practices and political culture that are capable of re-embedding production and consumption into networks of culture, politics and the natural environment. Such a practice and political culture can thus integrate the most important factors into a constantly changing ensemble without infringing on their autonomy or dynamism.

From the perspective of regional relations or transregional relations, the notion of a "trans-systemic society" cannot be separated from that of a "trans-societal system." This is the case because the factors that constitute the trans-systemic character of one society is often conjoined with that of other societies. For example, Chinese characters, Confucianism, Buddhism and Islam are factors in Chinese society, but they are also filiations linking China to other societies. The cultural sphere of Chinese characters, networks of tribute and activities from which such incense rituals arise are all supranational and could be characterized as a "system of trans-societies." The modern world has already been transformed into such a system due to globalization, which has put international production, migration and other transborder phenomena on today's agenda. To be sure, this is an unequal system bound by the standards of internationalized production and consumption. It is also an abstract system that has erased elements of culture, ritual, custom, politics and other essential ingredients of human life. That is why, in a globalized world, the notion of a "trans-societal system" stands in opposition to Mauss's idea of "supra-social systems."

The concepts of trans-societal system and trans-systemic society suggest that the practices of equality must unfold both internationally and within each community. The political practice of equality is directed against two related dimensions of capitalist logic: the meaninglessness and abstractness of the life-world and the consequent legitimizing of unequal social relationships.

In light of the notions of an "equality of all things," a "trans-systemic society" and "trans-societal system," we can reflect critically on the concept of "equality." The notion of an "equality of all things" offers a radically different concept of equality and thus a new vision of social possibility, one that may enable us to overcome the alienation of human beings, of labor and of things.

Appendix

Contradiction, Systemic Crisis and Direction for Change

An Interview with Wang Hui

FOREIGN THEORETICAL TRENDS (hereafter, "Trends"): The current severe crisis in global capitalism is a historical turning point for China and the world. What changes do you think this will bring to the international order? Regarding China's options in the new world order, some think that, as the scale of China's manufacturing keeps growing, continuing on the current path can lead China into the club of developed capitalist states. Others think that, due to contradictions both inside China and globally, China cannot possibly squeeze itself into the club and might instead encounter a great crisis. Therefore, they think it best for China to adhere to the "Three Worlds" theory of the 1970s and promote the construction of a new world order. What kind of international strategy do you think China should adopt in the aftermath of the global financial crisis? What kinds of old and new theoretical resources should we combine so that we can find a new possibility and direction for China's relationship with the world?

WANG HUI: Your questions are centered on "China" rather than on different regions, classes and their relationships in China. There is a relationship between the two, but posing the question as you do assumes a possibility for China to pursue an autonomous development, or assumes that the question is how China might pursue an autonomous development. China's financial institutions and market institutions have encountered grave difficulties, which are forcing us to rethink the current development model. Rethinking this development model began some time ago, but it has not been fruitful. The problem does not lie at the intellectual level, but rather the entanglement of interests is such that there is no way to turn this rethinking into public policy. Some have proposed further globalization, marketization and privatization; others have proposed democratic socialism. In my view, the critical question today is whether there can be a reform in a socialist direction, and whether it is possible to move in this direction. If the issue is one of direction rather than a mere technical adjustment, then the question will emerge as to what kinds of experiences and practices can be mobilized for creating a new development model.

But this is not only a question for China. For example, many people criticize the Occupy Wall Street movement for lacking a concrete program, but this precisely demonstrates that this movement is attempting to address fundamental questions of direction rather than simply questions of tactics. The movement recognizes that the problems of today are systemic, not individual problems that can be solved by technical adjustments. The movement states that we are now the 99 percent struggling against the 1 percent. It has brought forth the question of the relation between ourselves and our adversaries, posited a united front and outlined a political strategy. This is surely not to say that the movement can quickly achieve results, because first, if a society has created a system in which it is 99 percent against 1 percent, changing the system would necessarily imply a revolution; second, even if one does consider revolution, after the transformations that took place at the end of the twentieth century, the conditions, forms and premises of revolution have all completely changed. Absent a long period of buildup and the emergence of a new situation, achieving fundamental change will be extremely difficult. With regard to the revolutions of the nineteenth and twentieth centuries, we now live in a post-revolutionary period. How should we analyze our situation and what actions should we take in light of the systemic crisis of the present? This is a real question with which many people are struggling. In spite of this, this is the first time since the end of the Cold War that the question has been raised in this form and on such a scale. Even if the movement is somewhat immature and preliminary, it's very much worth thinking through.

The transition in China's form of development is currently framed in terms of "upgrading and updating" and industrial transfer. From the Arab Spring to Occupy Wall Street, many people—from the standpoint of very different political aspirations—have predicted that a similar situation would occur and even encouraged one to occur in China. But, disappointingly for these people, this expected "revolution" has not yet appeared in China, while street revolution is already widespread in Euro-America. Why? It is not because social contradictions and conflicts do not exist in China or because there are no problems with China's mode of development. It is rather due to two reasons: First, the fact that China is vast and regions are unevenly developed has ironically acted as a buffer in the context of the financial crisis. Regional disparity, rural–urban disparity, disparity between the rich and poor and so forth have all provided room for adjustment in China. Second, China has actually been in a constant process of adjustment during the past ten years. This adjustment results from a range of social practices, including internal jockeying, social struggle, public discussion, policy changes, local experiments and so forth. Social experiments and debates about different modes of development still continue in Chinese society. This indicates that there is still the possibility of self-directed, autonomous reform. But because the situation is changing so quickly, if action in this direction is not taken immediately, this possibility may be fleeting and quickly disappear. But introducing something resembling a "color revolution" from the outside, it seems to me, can only induce turmoil and can hardly produce a positive result.

Resolute actions are necessary, but without a clear sociopolitical vision, the question of what direction macroadjustments should take will become increasingly pressing. The debates surrounding the "Chongqing model" and the "Guangdong model" have gone beyond these specific experiments and their technical details. Even debates about technical adjustment have risen to the political level. Within these debates, people's interest in theorizing and fully developing different reform models is not rooted in an attempt to exaggerate the degree to which they can be implemented in the present conditions, but rather in the need to consciously reestablish the social goals that the reforms aim to achieve. With regard to strategies of development, different objectives will lead to social struggles. If we want analyze China's options for the future, we need to analyze the primary and to secondary contradictions China faces today, the primary and secondary aspects of these contradictions, how these contradictions figure differently in domestic settings and internationally and the dynamics and possibilities for their transformation.

The current relationship between regions, between the city and the countryside, and the general uneven distribution of wealth mean that there is still much room for industrial transfer and upgrading, and urbanization and industrialization will continue in a relatively long process. With the financial crisis, a great amount of excess capacity appeared in China's productive industries, and as international markets have shrunk, the internal market is being cultivated. All in all I believe that the process of industrialization will not cease. I also think that China is in the process of ascending within the capitalist world system, not only in the immediate present, but for the next twenty years. Crises, setbacks and the intensification of social contradictions have not changed this trajectory within the system, but are, rather, its by-products.

Therefore I disagree with the prediction that China will collapse. I think China is in the process of rising. But this is not to agree with the developmentalist proposition that economic growth will resolve social contradictions—I believe that China's process of ascent will bring about the intensification of social contradictions. Although there have been discussions of and experiments with various development models and some partial policy adjustments, the basic mode of development will not change. The massive social transition brought about by urbanization, the development of manufacturing and the consequent conflicts and contradictions—especially with respect to regional relations and rural–urban relations—will not decrease.

In short, China will continue to rise within the world capitalist system, but economic development does not mean that contradictions will disappear on their own. The situation of social disparity will be around for a long time. Continued industrialization and the massive expansion of urban areas will increase demand for energy and other resources, and this will also lead to the sharpening of international conflicts. In fact, the integral relationship between economic growth and the accumulation of social contradictions has continually been a feature of capitalism. The period of rapid development of capitalism in the nineteenth and earlier half of the twentieth century was precisely a time of fierce class struggle in Europe, and a time of the worst international conflicts.

We need to study the respective characteristics of social conflict during periods of both rise and decline, and the difference between China and other newly emerging economies and Euro-American countries in terms of trajectories of change. Social conflict in China may intensify, not because the country is about to collapse, but because it is moving up in the world system. The sharpening of social conflict is precisely the result of this process.

This has been my view for some time. More than a decade ago, I stated this view when some raised the argument that China would collapse in the near future. Because China is rising, though there may be adjustments in some areas, its basic mode of development will not fundamentally change, and therefore it is inevitable that social and class contradictions will intensify. If we want to change this situation, then we need to discuss the question of how to change the mode of development. Without a change in orientation, the current situation cannot change. When discussing economic development, some people say that I'm optimistic; when discussing social conflicts and contradictions, some people say that I'm pessimistic. But actually, it is meaningless to employ "optimism" and "pessimism" this way. So-called "optimism" may well amount to "pessimism," and vice versa. Capital is powerful and the relationships between different interests are entangled in a complex web. Even if you point out the crises inherent in this model, without the emergence of a new situation a change in the structure is still quite far off.

On the other hand, global capitalism is characterized by uneven development, which gives the growth of certain regions special significance. For example, development in China, India, Brazil and some African countries has altered the unequal relationships in the international system and decreased the hegemonic status of Europe and the United States. Countries in Africa and Latin America have, up to this day, on the whole rather welcomed the new role played by China for the very reason that the rise of China has destabilized the old hegemonic structure. By the same logic, the development of peripheral regions within China facilitates more equal relationships between the countryside and the city and between regions. The current challenge is that the development of peripheral regions has a close relationship with industrial transfer. While this changes the old structure of uneven development, it does not necessitate a change in the mode of development.

Mao Zedong grasped the characteristics of twentieth-century imperialism—the contradiction between the First and Third World had risen to become the main contradiction, and the international division of labor brought about a change in the nature of class in the international field. With the international division of labor, disparity between classes and within the society as a whole has worsened in China. But these disparities are products of the international division of labor and, as such, aspects of larger systemic contradictions. Uneven development on both the international and domestic scales requires that we carefully analyze the main contradictions and their transformation.

A short time ago, in preparation for a discussion on political changes in China after the 1911 Revolution, I reread Mao Zedong's 1926 article on the peasant question and his 1936 article on the anti-Japanese war, and found that there was an important difference between the two. In the 1920s, the mainstream view was that the significance of war between states far over-shadowed the significance of internal civil wars—that is, class struggle. Today some people continue to hold this nationalist view. Mao Zedong disagreed with this and thought that the First World War proved that war between states paled in significance compared to internal domestic strug-gles. The October Revolution was the best example demonstrating that domestic struggles could determine international events. Mao thus empha-sized the importance of class struggle when he was engaged in the peasant movement in 1926. In the 1930s, in the midst of a global situation in which Japan's all-out invasion of China was imminent and the threat of interna-tional fascism much more serious, Mao's view changed. He came to believe that the contradiction had shifted from class struggle to conflicts between nations, and that therefore the Communist Party should engage not only in class struggle but also in building a united front. Thus, domestically, the national bourgeoisie and the landlord class were to be included in the united front. Internationally, capitalist countries engaged in fighting fascism also came to be included in the united front. Mao did not give up on class analy-sis but thought that the main contradiction had undergone a major shift within those particular historical conditions.

It is not this strategic analysis per se but this methodology that is still useful for explaining the rise of the Chinese economy. Chinese intellectu-als, on both the left and the right, have not successfully explained this issue. You asked the question of whether China could squeeze its way into the club of developed countries by following the old path of development. This is not an easy question to answer. First, the club of advanced capital-ist countries is premised on the unequal relationship between the global North and South. Why would China, which long suffered under the oppression of colonialism and imperialism and has traveled a socialist path for some time, want to squeeze into the club of the global ruling class? This should not be the goal of China's development. Instead, China's development should create an opportunity to change the unequal relation-ship between the North and the South.

Furthermore, the club of developed capitalist countries is an economic club, but also a political club. To enter this club, there is a "political test."

The political system in Russia has already undergone a transformation in accordance with the Western model, but it has yet to pass the bar according to Western standards and thus hasn't been able to join the club. China is different from the West in terms of its political and social system, and it is also an Asian country. No Western country really thinks that China could be a member of their club. Second, whether China can join the club depends not only on the situation in China, but also on the international situation. At the International North South Media Forum in Geneva (October 10 to 14, 2011), Indian economist Gopalan Balachandran argued that the scale of economic development of the BRIC countries is much smaller than that of developed countries. The West, however, has begun to greatly exaggerate the significance of the BRIC economies, with the goal of shirking the international obligations that Western countries should bear. While globalization has changed the earlier world structure such that the Three Worlds theory is no longer entirely adequate, the struggle between the First World and Third World countries or between the North and the South is still the major contradiction when it comes to issues of climate change, the energy problem and other negotiations regarding international obligations.

Of course, unlike before, this major contradiction unfolds around the issue of how to change the mode of development globally. The crisis of inequality in the world today has its roots in the North-South relationship and the structural inequality inherent in that relationship. There is not much doubt that China will become the world's largest economy in the next twenty to thirty years, but we must seriously consider the implications of this. There have been great changes in the international division of labor and the global economic structure. For example, the United States has the largest economy but is a debtor country. China is poor but a creditor country. Even if China's economy becomes the largest, the larger structural changes entailed with this shift might not be entirely beneficial to China.

The International North South Media Forum held this year in Geneva's International Conference Center focused on the BRICS countries. The first day focused on China, the second on Brazil, the third on India and the fourth on Russia and South Africa. (I participated during the first three.) Each country was linked with a theme according to this sequence. The theme for China was "the world's factory," the theme for Brazil was "the world's food basket" and the theme for India was "the world's office." These themes describe a new trend in the global division of labor, and China's industrialization really does fit into it in this fashion. Unlike other late-developing countries, China never experienced complete colonization, has a long agrarian tradition and has experience with autonomous development in the post–World War II period. Its economic structure is much more diverse than that of many developing countries. After independence, many former colonies still have economies with single-commodity specialization, based, for example, on coffee, sugar or oil. Some countries originally had a more diverse economy but have grown specialized with a speed exceeding that of the colonial period; Brazil and Argentina, for example, have become agriculture exporters within a very short period of time. Their agriculture is controlled by monopolistic seed companies and has become part of the global division of labor and subject to the global market. China's economy is comparatively diverse and a bit more stable and therefore would not immediately collapse during a crisis of the global market. But the moniker "world's factory" indicates a trend that is not necessarily beneficial to China.

Industrialization is necessary. But if this industrialization is connected with the new global division of labor, China will bear a greater cost compared with traditional industrialization in terms of the exhaustion of energy resources, the exploitation of cheap labor, damage to the environment and the loss of labor protections.

In the West, many people understand China's energy consumption, environmental problems, issues with migrant workers and the exploitation of cheap labor in the context of human rights and other international protocols but have never probed the relationship between these issues and the relocation of international industry. The relationship between China becoming the world's factory and the deindustrialization of the West should be obvious. Climate change, the energy issue, cheap labor and even the mechanisms of state oppression are all integral aspects of the new international division of labor. The transfer of global industry also entails the transfer of social contradictions to developing countries.

The international shift in industry and the change in international class relations are also very important for explaining social conflicts in China. Class struggle in the past was concentrated in labor-capital relations within each country. But transnational capital is very flexible and states have become its agents and committees. The increased mobility of capital and the transnationalization of production have brought about this change in the form of a contradiction between labor and capital. The relationship between the two is heavily shaped by the efforts of states to attract capital, and the conflict between them as such becomes a conflict between labor and the state. For example, labor unions are normally a product of labor-capital relations. But in China, it has become an issue between labor and the state. Under the conditions of global capitalism, analyzing social conflicts brought about by the international shift in class relations entails a new examination of the mechanisms of state repression. That is, unlike before, state repression is inextricably linked to shifts in industry and the new international division of labor. There is continuity in the form of state repression, but its content has undergone a major shift. Under these circumstances, analyzing the space of politics and the question of democracy becomes a new problem.

Let us return to the question of economic growth and the accumulation of social contradictions. China's ascendancy has strengthened the capacity of the state for controlling the intensity of social conflicts. The growth of the scale of the economy has also infused the entire society with a measure of confidence that the current situation will continue, thereby providing an element of stability. But if stability is increasingly linked with growth, it also implies a dangerous logic: Once the economy stops growing or if some new situation were to arise, the eruption of a political crisis would become unavoidable. Because of this, the more the state depends on growth for stability, the more difficult it is to change the growth model. In this sense, I think the aforementioned question concerning the direction of social change in China is a very urgent one.

What kind of international strategy should China adopt in the context of the international financial crisis? My own view is that we should search for an autonomous development strategy and break away from the division of labor imposed by capitalist hegemony. Without autonomy, there can be no strategy. But what constitutes "autonomy" under conditions of globalization has become a complicated question. Production, consumption, labor are all being internationalized. The type of autonomy nation-states could carve out under conditions associated with the Cold War is no longer possible. Therefore, there is a need to explore new forms of autonomy.

International strategy implies the methods for maintaining relations with the United States, Europe, Latin America and Africa as well as China's neighboring countries, and the maintenance of political capacity in a world dominated by capital. Theories of global justice from social democratic and liberal perspectives are quite vacuous and unable to provide substantial programs for action. Dependency theory and the theory of Three Worlds have also lost their explanatory power as general methods for analyzing the global situation. For example, China-Africa relations and China's relationship with Southeast Asian countries can no longer be explained within the framework of the Bandung Conference. Mao Zedong's Three Worlds theory was formed in the circumstances of the Cold War. Only with the opposition of two major camps could there be a middle ground in which nonsocialist countries in the Third World could form an anti-imperialist and antihegemonic united front with socialist countries. This situation no longer exists. But we should not ignore the inspiration that this theory can give us today.

Political cynicism and opportunism can only lead to the loss of autonomy. It is in the relationship between China and developed and developing countries that the issue of autonomy is most manifest. The weakening of autonomy has led to China's lack of a strong and flexible international strategy. In the past thirty years, the West has been at the center of all concerns, from the state to the field of knowledge. Sometimes the ensuing outlook has been pessimistic, at other times self-inflating; sometimes China is said to be a basket case, at other times it is said to be booming. After the beginning of the new century, there has been more of an air of self-congratulation, with some claiming that China is the creditor country and that therefore the United States would not dare to do us harm.

Now, with the United States making moves in the South China Sea, proponents of this view have discovered that China not only has a conflict of interest with the United States, but that there are also tensions in its relationships with neighboring countries. China's opportunism and self-interestedness has already produced a rather critical view toward China among various Third World countries. On the other hand, China's economic behavior has retained the influence of some practices from the earlier period. For example, unlike either Western companies or quick-profit-seeking private companies, Chinese state-owned enterprises in general have a long-term perspective and are usually welcome in Africa and Latin America. Not long ago an English director produced the documentary film *When China Met Africa* about Chinese relations with Zambia. I had a discussion with the director, and he agreed that Chinese state-owned enterprises are willing to invest in the local infrastructure, which has been long neglected by Europe and the United States, and that Chinese SOEs usually have long-term plans for returns. This is impossible for Western countries and their companies. The West already decided in the 1970s that investing in infrastructure in these areas is not feasible because the risks are too high. In these circumstances, the strategic relationship that China can forge with developing countries is a question worth thinking about.

TRENDS: Before the current international crisis, you had already discussed in some depth how contemporary capitalism is prone to crisis—for example, you have written about the contradictions inherent in globalization and neoliberalism.[1] You have pointed out in particular that the trend toward depoliticization created in these processes has led to an increasing crisis in equality.[2] Is there an internal logical connection between the crises that you previously discussed and the current financial, economic and even social and political crises faced by capitalism today?

WANG HUI: Neoliberal globalization and China's trend toward depoliticization have a logical relationship with the current financial and political crises of capitalism. First, in terms of the economic dimension, the entire capitalist system began its neoliberal turn in the late 1970s while the same trend began to appear in China in the mid-1980s, particularly after the launch of the urban reforms, deepened after 1989 and continued until the current global financial crisis. Second, in terms of the political sphere, neoliberalism has led to an important change in the meaning of politics and has broken down the earlier political situation. Almost without exception, politics in both socialist countries and in liberal democratic systems, particularly with regard to the kind of politics that centers on the state and the party, are undergoing crises. In the political sphere, these crises are mainly character-ized by a breakdown of representation. Because of this, different political party systems are all experiencing political crises.

A lack of representation is now a common feature in the political sphere. On November 18, 2011, I participated in a public dialogue and debate with the chairman of the German Social Democratic Party, Sigmar Gabriel, at the party's main office. I pointed out that, in spite of the great difference between China and the countries of Europe in terms of political systems, all of these countries not only face the same economic crisis, they also face a similar political crisis due to a breakdown in their political parties' capacity to represent the people. My basic viewpoint is that we must change the way in which we examine crises experienced by political institutions today.

The earlier type of political analysis is premised on an opposition between the two political systems—that is, an understanding of one system is premised on the other system. But in looking at the roots of the crisis of legitimacy, today's situation cannot be diagnosed in terms of the difference between one system and another. A diagnosis must be conducted within the context that different political systems are facing the shared problem of a breakdown in representation. The fact that the breakdown in representation is common to all political systems does not mean that the older opposition between the two social systems has disappeared, but rather that the global transformation has led to a change in the meaning of this opposition. At its root, the crisis in representation is a product of neoliberalism in the political sphere, in that it is a consequence of depoliticization. It has to do with the fundamental change in the structure of politics within the context of capitalism as a whole. Gabriel remarked that my placing Europe and China on the same platform for critique has surprised a lot of people, but this critique touched on the intellectual and political crisis in Europe.

TRENDS: Capitalism is facing a serious crisis, but it appears that the anticapitalist movement has lost its sense of direction since the 1970s and 1980s. After the radical changes in the Soviet Union and Eastern Europe, there has not been serious and comprehensive theoretical work on how to treat the history of traditional socialism, or how to treat the capitalist democratic system and its market system. As you said, the role of theory is extremely important. However, it seems that anticapitalist forces, from the movement against the Iraq War to today's Occupy Wall Street, do not know what they are opposed to and what they are struggling for. They are in a predicament in which they no longer believe in traditional socialism and yet their resistance is weak and ineffective within capitalist democracy and the market. You have been reflecting on these serious theoretical challenges faced by the left. How do you think anticapitalist movements can escape this predicament, and what is the alternative?

WANG HUI: It is impossible for the anticapitalist movement to fall into the model of traditional socialism based on the nation-state as a unit. We should have a clear understanding of this. This round of globalization, particularly the transnationalization of production, has made the possibility of reverting to the logic of the older state very small. The state is a space in which struggles unfold, and the issue of autonomy is manifested at the state level. If one observes the situation of countries in North Africa and the Middle East suffering from external interference, one can understand that the state issue is not at all inconsequential, contrary to what many have claimed. It is because of this that I have said we need to explore the issue of autonomy under the conditions of globalization.

Some changes have recently taken place in the anticapitalist movement. The Occupy Wall Street movement has truly raised the question of the systemic nature of the crisis, while at the same time it has displayed the weakness of lacking an effective strategy. We can sum up a few characteristics: First, after a series of movements aimed at reforming neoliberalism have been frustrated, a protest movement has emerged that opposes the system as such, a movement that has shown itself to be global and uneven. The globality is manifest in the fact that movements have appeared in the Middle East, North Africa, Latin America, Asia, the United States and Europe. The unevenness refers to the fact that these movements are related but are various in their forms, reflecting unevenness in their respective social, regional and economic-political-cultural conditions. For example, the movement in Egypt took place under the conditions of a high unemployment rate brought on by the global financial crisis, long-term and large-scale poverty and a high degree of corruption. These are long-standing and widespread phenomena common to many regions. But apart from these, Egypt's movement was also aimed at a political system that included decades of police dictatorship and the U.S.-Israeli order, as well as the existence of the Islamic movement. Its antisystemic nature has centered around these aspects. In Muslim regions, this antisystemic movement stimulated or released a religious energy, which, although not a new political force, contains the possibility of becoming a new political energy.

The reentrance of religion into the political sphere is found not only in the Arab world, but in all of Africa and Europe as well. China also faces a complex problem of religions, but the chief social contradiction is still economic and political. Through its long process of revolution and construction, China has forged a relatively independent and autonomous national economic system, and even after reforms aimed at opening the system have resulted in its becoming highly globalized, its relative independence (and internal unevenness) is still distinctly apparent. A few days ago, the Occupy Wall Street movement mobilized twenty to thirty thousand people to walk from New York to Washington, DC. This movement seems to be attempting to make explicit the relationship between capitalism's economic and political institutions. The rhetoric of opposition between the 99 percent and the 1 percent also implies a class element, but obviously the older model of class movements is not suitable for analyzing this movement. My own view is that we need to raise a conceptual question concerning the general direction in which the movement seeks to take its analysis of the systemic problem. At the same time, we must pay serious attention to the unevenness across the globe, between regions and within countries.

China is in the process of a large-scale industrialization and urbanization; rural–urban and class contradictions remain very important characteristics of the nation's social and economic landscape. To truly achieve the "five coordinations"[3] we must change the model of development, adjust the direction of reform and strengthen the ability of the society and state to shape a development strategy for China. With large-scale urbanization connected to industrialization and rural–urban relations linked to the formation of the new working class, it is crucial to consider how the rural–urban contradiction under the condition of massive urbanization can be resolved. As mentioned before, the expansion of the scale of China's economy is connected with the new global division of labor. Its profound dependence on energy consumption and on cheap labor cannot be explained singularly within China's own context but will undoubtedly lead to increasing internal conflicts. If China's position in the global division of labor does not change, the problems of social conflict and lack of equality cannot fundamentally be solved.

How can one forge an independent development strategy within a globalized system? Under the conditions of global capitalism and the global division of labor, we cannot have a breakthrough strategy if we forget the unique conditions pertaining to each society and its international positioning. In "On Protracted War," Mao states that victory in war entails three situations: that of the enemy, that of the self and that of the field. What is the situation of the enemy, what is our own situation and what is the objective condition of the field of struggle?[4] Only by comprehending the answers to these questions can we analyze what strategy should be adopted.

From this perspective, we first should analyze financial capitalism and the new global division of labor, and the international relations, regional relations, class relations and social relations that are produced by the new division of labor. Speaking of the competitors, are developed states able to reindustrialize themselves? If yes, what does that mean for us? If not, what kind of situation will emerge? Under conditions of crisis, what changes in political and military relations will occur? China is a developing country with very uneven development, and its regional relations are complex. What is the relationship between this unevenness and the sustainability of its development? China's coastal areas are more deeply impacted by the international crisis. Many industries have been moving inland. It is true that inland growth has helped in alleviating the crisis. The growth rates of Inner Mongolia and other regions now exceed that of coastal areas. This is an effect of uneven development. But with the transfer of industry, crisis has also reached these areas. The internal unevenness in China makes it more able to weather economic crisis than other smaller economies. The vast countryside and large rural population provide a space for crisis alleviation.

Philip Huang's analysis of Chongqing's land values highlights this. According to his analysis, there is little doubt that Chongqing's land prices will increase more quickly than wages. Many on the left may not like this analysis and may consider it supportive of a development model based on urbanization. But this analysis is based on China's developmental unevenness and has some significance for our methodology. This does not mean that regional imbalances can naturally ensure sustainability. I think we should undertake our analysis as Mao analyzed the war situation many years ago: Examine the scale and sustainability of China's development within the context of global capitalism and investigate the tendencies and development of its class and social contradictions. In this way, we can explain China's national situation and its development strategy.

TRENDS: You once mentioned a basic paradox regarding China's state capacity. On the one hand, compared with the governments of other countries, there is a wide recognition of the Chinese government's capacity. It has been demonstrated in the mobilization for disaster relief after the Wenchuan earthquake (on May 12, 2008), in the quick rollout of crisis relief plans after the financial crisis, in the successful hosting of the 2008 Olympics and in local governments' organizing capacity for development and for crisis management. These phenomena highlight the advantages of China's state capacity. On the other hand, various polls show that the public's level of satisfaction with the government is rather low. At times, government-citizen conflicts have become heated. People also have doubts about executive competence and corruption at various levels of government. The most critical question is whether these conflicts indicate a crisis in the government's legitimacy. What do you think?

WANG HUI: This is a question of legitimacy. Under the conditions of global capitalism, the core problem of the legitimacy crisis of a political system lies in the crisis of representation in party politics. In the global context, the danger facing political systems today is a change from one system in that there is no representation to another that also has no representation, with such an empty change serving only to legitimate a social process which in fact increases inequality. The so-called color revolutions present such a case. Superficially they entail democratization, but substantively they legitimate the most unreasonable social redistribution and wealth expropriation.

To overcome this political crisis, the real challenge is how to avoid the change from one system lacking representation to another. The essential requirement is re-politicization. This is a very acute and complex challenge. I think it is urgent that we articulate this problem theoretically, because many still do not understand how broadly and deeply the crisis of representation reaches and may believe that this problem does not exist in the West. To forge a space for real public discussion and to open up real political and theoretical debate is very important for China's political transformation. It is very difficult to have serious political discussions in the mass media. This situation is dangerous. The key is to let people understand the true nature and characteristics of the political crisis in global capitalism through discussions of autonomy.

Many observers have discussed the issue of China's state capacity. The real question is why, despite China's strong state capacity, the state is unable to overcome its crisis of legitimacy. State capacity is, first of all, the capacity of the state to respond to social needs. In this regard, China's state capacity is double-sided: It is very strong in certain exceptional circumstances and very tardy and slow in other circumstances. Recently Francis Fukuyama wrote that China's ability to respond to problems is not only stronger than that of its neighboring countries, but also that of many developed countries, including Japan, South Korea and many countries in Europe. In my debate with Gabriel, I noted that if a state's political system has a strong capacity to respond to problems, it indicates that the society contains elements of and a potential for democracy. But because our theories on democracy focus so intently on its political form, they have neglected these substantive potentials. However, how to develop these potentials into more institutionalized practices is unclear. If we can clearly delineate the theoretical and institutional conditions for the uncovering of these potentials, we may find a path toward democratic change. If a government can quickly respond to the demands of society, the political system has a potential for substantive democracy. The questions of how and to what degree to formulate and develop this potential, however, require concrete analysis.

Another aspect of state capacity is its ability to conduct political coordination—that is, its ability to coordinate various social interests and demands via public and administrative policies. Fukuyama, in his latest article, addressed the crisis in Western democracy by proposing a "democratic dictatorship, not a vetocracy."[5] Fukuyama and I are certainly different in terms of our views of history, but what he is actually pointing to in this piece has something in common with the points on political integration that I discussed in "Revolution, compromise and continuous innovation."[6] Conventionally, administrative power in the executive institution and the institutions of parliament and political parties are instruments for political coordination and integration. But when political representation breaks down, a state's capacity to engage in political coordination and integration is greatly reduced. Power is typically divided between the parliament, the judicial system and the administration, but with political parties' capacity to represent the people breaking down and with the increasing bureaucratization of governments and the crises within the judicial systems, states' ability to respond to social crisis declines. This is the basic characteristic of the contemporary political crisis.

TRENDS: You have more than once mentioned the importance of Mao Zedong's work as a theoretical resource for our analysis of the situation with regard to China and the world.

WANG HUI: This is an issue very relevant to your journal. Mao Zedong's work is one of the most important legacies of twentieth-century China. In terms of its influence on the West and the Third World movement, China has no other legacy that can surpass it. The well-known contemporary French philosopher Alain Badiou is a noted example of intellectual admiration for Mao's work. He has undertaken an in-depth analysis of Mao's texts, and his overall explication of the history of European philosophy accords with his explication of Mao's thought. In the late 1970s, Badiou wrote a booklet of commentary and response to a text on Hegel by the Beijing University professor Zhang Shiying, in which he developed his reading of Maoist dialectics.[7] According to the Italian scholar Alessandro Russo, that book marked an important turn in Badiou's intellectual trajectory and reflected the influence of the era on him. Due to the defeat of progressive forces after 1968, the entire theoretical scene, particularly leftist theory, has been characterized by political pessimism. But Alain Badiou's theory is marked by a kind of Maoist revolutionary optimism. That is, even at the time of the low tide, he still constructs a theory of history based on what Mao called "the enemy's logic"—"disruption, failure, more disruption, more failure"— and the logic of people's revolution that is "from victory to victory."

At the Twentieth-Century China Conference in Bologna in 2007, Badiou submitted a paper that gave a close reading of Mao Zedong's 1928 article "Why Is It That Red Political Power Can Exist in China?"[8] I was quite encouraged and inspired by the paper. In such difficult conditions, Mao had the unique insight to analyze how red political power could exist in China and propose that a single spark could start a prairie fire. His method of analysis concerning the existence of red political power is, in fact, exactly the same as his later analysis of how China would win the final victory in the war against Japan. He integrated three dimensions of analysis: military, philosophy and politics. Mao's military thought was never based purely on military strategy and tactics but was an integration of politics, philosophy and military strategy. The strategic thought expressed in "On Protracted War" represents both his philosophy expressed in the political field and his political thinking applied to the field of military strategy and tactics. How the two kinds of united front could come to be formed, whether they could be formed, whether a revolution within the imperialist world would break out—all of these are questions of strategy and analysis in the broadest sense, not merely questions of ordinary military tactics. All of these are combined. The important characteristic of Mao's thought is its orientation toward practice; it is always concerned with analyzing reality. Reality is not passive or static but a field where agency and objective conditions interact. In the analysis of reality, what we see is pulsing and shifting tendencies of various historical forces in interaction.

His proposition that a single spark could start a prairie fire has important methodological implications. Mao at that time was facing the "white terror" and a sharp disparity of power between revolutionary and counterrevolutionary forces. But within this situation, he developed an analysis of how Chinese red political power could exist in the revolutionary base areas of the countryside. This is an outstanding political analysis, and also something like a strategy manual for war. Mao upheld the righteousness of the revolution but was not blinded by this righteousness. Rather, he combined his sense of righteousness with strategic analysis. The small Red Army force later expanded rapidly within a short period of time. When the Red Army arrived in Northern Shaanxi, it numbered no more than a few thousand. But as early as 1936, Mao foresaw that Japan's aggression would inevitably lead to war, the coming of the world war and the basic trajectory of the War of Resistance against Japan. It would not have been possible to reach this height if Mao had not possessed a high degree of theoretical ability for abstraction and a holistic insight into the reality of social relations writ large.

When we initiated the new intellectual discussion just over ten years ago, it was purely academic. It was a lonely fight, and we were without political power, media power or even our own popular supporters. We aimed for intellectual discussion. Yet, even without having our own media platform, our critical standpoint still gained an audience. All manner of attacks, including media slander, did not prevent our critical outlook from spreading. Why is this? We need to form an objective but dynamic analysis concerning China's internal and external situation and draw theoretical and strategic lessons from this.

A number of Mao's concepts, such as building a united front in the time of war, the philosophy of "one dividing into two" and his explication of people's democracy, have all exerted a huge influence. Foucault's conceptualization of politics and power and Jameson's discussion of the Third World have both been influenced by Mao. On the right, Carl Schmitt's theory of the partisan and his political conceptualization of the enemy-friend distinction have this or that connection with Mao's military and political thought. The recent Occupy Wall Street movement is related to the Occupy University movement of the previous few years. With the development of the Internet, many have proposed anew the idea of an open university and have criticized the current university system. It is not clear whether these practices have any direct relationship to Mao's thought, but it is necessary to compare and analyze them. Mao provided explanations and proposed a set of analytical methods with which we can analyze the relationship between knowledge, power, politics and the capitalist economy, as well as its main social contradictions and principal social subjects.

In his response to me, Gabriel stated that the Western left has not really faced the questions I raised about equality and the breakdown of political representation. He said that when he had visited factories in the past, workers introduced him as a socialist; when he goes to factories now, workers introduce him only as a politician. A young social democrat told me that after the Cold War, the idea of socialism can no longer be mentioned. But if not toward socialism, then in what direction is social democracy aimed? In my discussion, I have pointed out two problematic tendencies: The first is to equate socialism and communism with the practices of state socialism in the past; the second is to treat the socialist practices of the past as a single entity and refuse to engage in a real political and historical analysis of these practices. In the European context, socialism is immediately equated with despotism and violent totalitarian rule. The whole tenor is negative. But socialism's legacy is rich and complex, and we must carry out a critical summation of it. The legacy of Mao Zedong's thought is both the object of our thinking and also a method we can use to reflect on his own political practices. It ought to be from this perspective that we revive his legacy.

Notes

Introduction

1   Lu Xun, "Fen – Wenhua pian zhi lun," in *Lu Xun quanji* vol. 1 (Beijing: Renmin wenxue chubanshe, 2005) 56–7, as translated by Jon Eugene von Kowallis in his *Warriors of the Spirit: Four Early Wenyan Essays by Lu Xun* (University of California, Berkeley: Institute of East Asian Studies, China Research Monographs, forthcoming).

2   *Lu Xun quanji* vol. 1, 47.

3   Ibid., 57.

4   Wang Hui, *Xiandai sixiang de xingqi* vol. 1, book 1 (Beijing: Sanlian shudian, 2004), 3.

1. Revolution and Negotiation

1   Wang Hui, "Depoliticized Politics: From East to West," in *The End of the Revolution: China and the Limits of Modernity* (New York: Verso, 2009), 3.

2   Zhang Taiyan, "Zheng chou Man lun" (Correct discourse on hatred of Manchus), in Zhang Nan and Wang Renzhi, eds., *Xinhai geming qian shinianjian shilun xuanji* (Selected essays from the ten years preceding the 1911 Revolution), vol. 1 (Beijing: Sanlian shudian, 1963), 98.

3   In 1948 the United Nations issued the Universal Declaration of Human Rights, declaring that "everyone has the right to a nationality," and marking the end of the Second World War as well as the triumph of the principle of nationalism. The ocean empire systems of Britain, France, Holland, Belgium and Japan gradually fell prey to nationalist movements, disintegrating one after another. The return in 1997 of Hong Kong and in 1999

of Macau to China marked the end of the old colonial system. However, the establishment of Special Administrative Regions of Hong Kong and Macau provides further indication of the continuity between empire and nation-state in China.

4   V. I. Lenin, "Address to the Second All-Russia Congress of Communist Organizations of the Peoples of the East," in *Collected Works*, 4th English ed. (Moscow: Progress Publishers, 1965), 159.

5   For Lenin's "discovery" of the 1911 Revolution, see Wang Hui, "The Politics of Imagining Asia," in *The Politics of Imagining Asia* (Cambridge; MA: Harvard University Press), 2011.

6   Translator's Note: The phrase "wuzu gonghe" is sometimes translated as "Five Races under One Union"; this, in my opinion, is vague and does not denote the notion of "republic" integral to this political design. The phrase "Republic of Five Nationalities" makes manifest the meaning of "republic" as different in terms of polity from the slogan of "Constitutionalism of Five Nationalities" proposed, at the time, by the constitutionalists. Replacing "races" with "nationalities," moreover, conveys the political demand of establishing separate nations made by Mongols, Uyghurs, Manchus, Han and Tibetans in their bid for political independence.

7   Zhongguo kexue yuan jindaishi yanjiusuo Zhonghua Minguo shizu (Chinese Academy of Sciences, Modern History Institute, Research Group on the History of Modern China), ed., *Zhonghua Minguo ziliao conggao: Dashiji* (Documents of the Republic of China: Major events), vol. 1 (Beijing: Zhonghua shuju, 1973), 53.

8   *Sun Zhongshan quanji* (The collected works of Sun Yat-sen), vol. 9, (Beijing: Zhonghua shuju, 1981), 114.

9   Yen Ching-hwang points out that "1. The Nanyang Chinese community was the center of the anti-Manchu revolution around 1908 and 1911; 2. Nanyang Chinese society was the place where most escaped revolutionaries took shelter; 3. Nanyang Chinese society made a lot of donations needed for revolutions" and so supported Sun Yat-sen's claim that "overseas Chinese are the mother of revolution." Though Yen's opinion is somewhat exaggerated, as he neglects the activities of Chinese revolutionaries in places such as Tokyo, North and South America and Hubei province, it does correctly characterize the strong influence of Southern and Southeast Asian Chinese in this stage of the Chinese revolution. Before the Wuchang Uprising, most uprisings during 1907 and 1908 were

organized along the route between Hanoi, Singapore and Hong Kong. Yen Ching-hwang, "Xinhai geming yu nanyang Huaren"(The Xinhai Revolution and Nanyang Chinese), in *Xinhai geming yu nanyang Huaren yantaohui lunwenji* (Seminar anthology of the Xinhai Revolution and Nanyang Chinese) (Taipei: Guoli zhengzhi daxue guoji guanxi zhongxin, 1986), 140.

10 In 1970s and 1980s, American revisionists ("the new left") held that the center of Chinese revolution was not overseas but in China. Such work included Joseph W. Esherick's study of reform and the 1911 Revolution in Hunan and Hubei and Mary B. Rankin's and Edward J. M. Rhoads's studies of revolutionaries in Shanghai and Zhejiang. These studies are consistent with studies of the 1911 Revolution produced within mainland China.

11 Yen Ching-hwang, "Xinhai geming yu nanyang Huaren," 417.

12 Lenin, "Democracy and Narodism in China," in *Collected Works*, 4th English ed., vol. 18 (Moscow: Progress Publishers, 1968), 164.

13 Lenin, "The Struggle of Parties in China," in *Collected Works*, 4th English ed., vol. 41 (Moscow: Progress Publishers, 1968), 281.

14 Lenin, "The Right of Nations to Self-Determination," in *Collected Works*, 4th English ed., vol. 20 (Moscow: Progress Publishers, 1964), 395.

15 Ibid., 396.

16 Ibid., 405–6.

17 Ibid., 407.

18 Ibid., 408.

19 Sun Zhongshan, "Zhonghua Minguo linshi da zongtong xuanyan shu" (Inaugural statement as provisional president of the Republic of China) in *Sun Zhongshan quanji* (Collected works of Sun Yat-sen), vol. 2 (Beijing: Zhonghua shuju, 1981), 2.

20 Chang An, "Qingmo minchu xianzheng shijiezhong de wuzu gonghe" (The "Republic of Five Nationalities" in the late Qing and early republican period), *Beida falü pinglun* (Peking University Law Review) 2, 2010; Yang Ang, "Qing di 'xunwei zhao shu' zai Zhonghua minzu tongyi shang de falü yiyi" (The legal implications of the Qing emperor's edict of abdication for the unity of the Chinese nation), *Huanqiu falü pinglun* (Global Legal Commentary) 33: 5, 2011, 8–25.

21 Murata Yujiro, "Sun Zhongshan yu xinhai geming shiqi de 'wuzu gonghe' lun" (Sun Yat-sen and the "Republic of Five Nationalities" in the 1911

Revolution), *Guangdong shehui kexue* (Social Science in Guangdong) 5, 2004.

22 Ibid.

23 "Menggu qiyi qingfang dang'an—Xuantong sannian shiyiyue chuqiri Menggu daibiao ji Nayantu deng zhi neige Yuan Shikai han" (Qing documents of the Mongolian Uprising: The letter of Mongol representatives and Nayentu to Yuan Shikai's cabinet on November 7 of Xuantong third year), in Chai Degeng, ed., *Xinhai geming ziliao congkan* (Materials on the 1911 Revolution), vol. 7, (Shanghai: Shanghai renmin chuban she, 1957), 298–9.

24 Ibid.

25 "Menggu wanggong Wu Tingfang han" (Letter from Mongolian princes to Wu Tingfang), in Shen Yulong, ed., *Jindai Zhongguo shiliao congkan* 1: 42, Taipei: Wenhai chubanshe, 1969, 901–5.

26 Ariga Nagao, "Geming shiqi tongzhiquan zhuanyi zhi benmo" (The full story of the transfer of power in the revolutionary age), in *Faxuehui zazhi* 1: 8, October 1913.

27 "Qing di xunwei" (Imperial Edict of Abdication of the Qing emperor) in Zhongguo dier lishi dang'an guan, ed., *Zhonghua minguo shi dang'an ziliao huibian* (Nanjing: Jiangsu renmin chubanshe, 1979), 217–18.

28 Lynn Struve, "The Inner Asian Factor in Early Qing China: Views and Issues from American Scholarship," *Saksaha: A Review of Manchu Studies*, 5, 2000, 2.

29 Peter C. Perdue, "Boundaries, Maps, and Movement: Chinese, Russian, and Mongolian Empires in Early Modern Central Eurasia," *International History Review*, 20: 2, June 1998, 263.

30 Mark Mancall, *Russia and China: Their Diplomatic Relations to 1728* (Cambridge, MA: Harvard University Press, 1968), 267–73.

31 Sun Yat-sen, "Zai Shanghai Zhongguo Guomindang benbu huiyi de yanshuo" (Speech at the conference of the Nationalist Party's Shanghai headquarters) (November 4, 1920), in *Sun Zhongshan quanji* (Collected works of Sun Yat-sen), vol. 5 (Beijing: Zhonghua shuju, 1981), 394.

32 For "super-parliament" and "super-president," see Chapter 5 of Zhang Yongle's *Jiubang xinzao: 1911–1927* (New invention of the old country: 1911–1927) (Beijing: Beijing daxue chubanshe, 2011), 150–66.

33 This contrasts with the system of the United States, where the presidential system gives parties a somewhat different role.

34 Sun Yat-sen, "Linshi da zongtong xuanyanshu" (Inauguration statement of provisional president) in *Sun Zhongshan quanji* (Collected works of Sun Yat-sen), vol. 1, 1.

35 Compare this with public choice theory, which applies classical economic liberalism's assumption of an economic agent (seeking to maximize his or her economic interest) to the political realm, treating executive authority as a realm in which information asymmetry allows officeholders to pursue their personal interests and rent seeking activities at the cost of taxpayers' interests. This type of public choice framework is often applied in criticisms of public power. In this and the liberal/Weberian perspectives, executive power is a power to be restricted and is usually portrayed negatively. See Wolfgang Seibel, "Beyond Bureaucracy: Public Administration as Political Integrator and Non-Weberian Thought in Germany," *Public Administration Review* 70: 5, 2010, 719.

36 For Kang Youwei's theory that "sovereignty lies in the state," see Chapter 3 of Zhang Youngle's *Jiubang xinzao* (New invention of an old country), 82–109.

37 Seibel, "Beyond Bureaucracy," 721.

38 Ibid., 720.

39 Ibid., 722.

40 Ibid., 722–4.

41 Mao Zedong, "Report on an Investigation of the Peasant Movement in Hunan," in *Selected Works of Mao Tse-tung*, vol. 1, (Beijing: Foreign Languages Press, 1965), 27.

42 Mao Zedong, "Analysis of the Classes in Chinese Society," in *Selected Works of Mao Tse-tung*, vol. 1, 13–19.

43 Wang Hui, *The End of the Revolution* (New York: Verso, 2009).

44 For the relations between the state and its citizens in the United States, please see Chaersi Taile (Charles Taylor), "Gongmin yu guojia zhijian de juli" (The distance between the citizens and the state) and my preface in Wang Hui and Chen Yangu, eds., *Wenhua yu gonggongxing* (Culture and publicness) (Beijing: Sanlian shudian, 1998), 199–220, 1–56.

2. The Transformation of Culture and Politics

1 This article is the first of a series by this author on the May Fourth Movement, and was presented at Stanford University (Feb. 27, 2009), New York University (Mar. 3, 2009) and as a keynote speech at the Moment and Methodology in Chinese Intellectual History conference at UC Berkeley (Apr. 3, 2009).

2 If we were to evaluate all May Fourth essays as a genre, Chen Duxiu's "Our

Final Awakening" would be the definitive contribution. Chen divided Sino-Western contact into seven stages from the late Ming dynasty to the May Fourth Movement, with the Self-Strengthening Movement occurring after the Opium War as the third stage, the Hundred Days' Reform the fourth, the 1911 Revolution the fifth and the cultural movement following the 1911 Revolution the sixth. Chen writes, "Could a republican polity truly establish itself here? Could constitutional politics be exercised without interference? In my view, the ultimate resolution to this sort of politics must wait until our people's final awakening. This is the seventh stage, or the period when the national constitution could be practiced." (Chen Duxiu, "Wu ren zui hou zhi juexing" (Our Final Awakening), *Qingnian zazhi* (Youth), 1: 6, Feb. 1916, 1–4). Many writers followed this viewpoint, but varied in their periodization. For example, Zuo Shunsheng argued, "The Chinese knowledge of the West [in the] first [stage] was of their powerful weapons and superb soldiers; the second stage was their industries, commerce and politics, and the third stage was about knowledge and thought, literature and other subjects. With regard to this progression, even though we could not clearly demarcate the chronology, in general we all agreed that the time before the Sino-Japanese War of 1894–5 was the first stage, the post-Sino-Japanese War the second stage, and the third stage did not start until the period around the May Fourth Movement." (Zuo Shunseng, "Zhongguo jindai sandu gaige yundong de jiantao: Wuxu, Xinhai, Wusi" in Zhou Yushan, ed., *Wusi lunji* (Taipei: Chengwen chubanshe, 1970), 681. On the eightieth anniversary of the May Fourth movement, Jin Yaoji reiterated the opinion he had first stated in *Cong chuantong dao xiandai* (From tradition to modernity) (Taipei: Shibao chubanshe, 1986), 161–6. He argued that the historical determination of the May Fourth Movement marked a watershed in Chinese modernization. Chinese modernization progressed from the Self-Strengthening Movement's level of "gadgets and technology" to the "institutional level" during the constitutional reform and 1911 Revolution, and finally to the level of the New Culture Movement's level of "thoughts and behavior." Jin Yaoji, "Wusi yu zhongguo de xiandaihua" (The May Fourth and Chinese modernization) in Hao Bin and Ouyang Zhesheng, eds., *Wusi yundong yu ershi shiji de Zhongguo* (Beijing: Shehui kexuewenxian chubanshe, 2001), 63–4.

3   Peng Ming, "Wusi yundong yu ershi shiji de zhongguo" (The May Fourth Movement and twentieth-century China) in Hao and Ouyang, *Wusi yundong yu ershi shiji de Zhongguo*, 23.

4   Liang Qichao suggested in *Inner Reflections on European Travels: The Great Chinese Responsibility toward World Civilization* that the Chinese "use Western civilization to expand our own, and use our civilization to ameliorate theirs, and together these will merge to create a new civilization." This view is quite different from that expressed in his *Discourse on the New Citizen.*

5   Cang Fu (Du Yaqvan), "Zhanhou dong xi wenming zhi tiaohe," *Dongfang zazhi* 14: 4, April 1917, 1–7.

6   Ibid.

7   Hu Zhide (Theodore Huters), "Yubo: 1910 nianjian de Zhongguo wenhua lunzhan" (Ripple effect: The Chinese cultural debate in the 1910s) in Hao and Ouyang, *Wusi yundong yu ershi shiji de Zhongguo*, 482.

8   Chen Duxiu, "Yi jiu yi liu nian," *Qingnian zazhi*, 1, 5, Jan. 1916, 1–4.

9   Chen Duxiu, "Eluosi geming yu woguomin zhi juewu" (The Russian Revolution and the enlightenment of our citizens), *Xin qingnian* (New Youth), 3: 2, Apr. 1917, 1–3.

10 Li Dazhao, "BOLSHEVISM de shengli" (The Victory of Bolshevism), *Xin qingnian* 5: 5, Nov. 1918, 442–8.

11 Gao Yihan, "Gonghe guojia yu qingnian zhi zijue," *Qingnian zazhi* 1: 1–3, Sep. 1915, 1–8 (issue 1), 1–6 (issue 2), 1– 8 (issue 3).

12 Gao Lao (Du Yaqvan), "Wuren jinhou zhi zijue," *Dongfang zazhi*, 12: 10, Oct. 1915, 1–4.

13 Chen Duxiu, "Wuren zuihou zhi juewo," *Qingnian zazhi*, 1: 6, Feb. 1916, 1–4.

14 Liu Shuya, "Ouzhou zhanzheng yu qingnian zhi juewu," *Xin qingnian*, 2: 2, Oct. 1916, 1–8.

15 Chen Duxiu, "Eluosi geming yu woguomin zhi juewu", *Xin qingnian*, 3: 2, Apr. 1917, 1–3.

16 Gao Lao, "Jinhou shiju zhi juewu," *Dongfang zazhi*, 14: 8, Aug. 1917, 1–5.

17 Xingyan (Zhang Shizuo), "Ouzhou zuijin sichao yu wuren zhi juewu," *Dongfang zazhi* 14: 12, Dec. 1917, 1–9.

18 Zhiyan (Chen Ouxin), "Ouzhan hou dongyang minzu zhi juewu yu yaoqiu," *Meizhou Pinglun* 2, Dec. 29, 1918.

19 Cang Fu, "Da zhan zhongjie hou guoren zhi juewu ruhe," *Dongfang zazhi* 16: 1, Jan. 1919, 1–8.

20 "Tongxun," *Qingnian zazhi* 1: 1, Sep. 1915, 1–2.

21 "She gao," *Qingnian zazhi* 1: 1, Sep. 1915, 1.

22 Chen Duxiu, "Tan zhengzhi," (Talking about politics), *Xin qingnian*, 8: 1, Sep. 1920, 1–9.

23   Chen Duxiu, "Tongxin (da Wang Shuqian)" (Correspondence: Answering Wang Shuqian), *Xin qingnian*, 2: 2, Sep. 1916, 1–3.

24   See the *Book of Changes* (*Yijing*), section 10 of the "Great Commentary" (*Da ẓhuan*): "Events have relationships, realized as patterns" (*Wu xiang ẓa, gu yue wen*). Richard Rutt, *The Book of Changes (Zhouyi)* (New York: Curzon, 2002), 429.

25   See *The Analects*, Book Nine: "Now that King Wen is gone, is not culture here invested in me?" (*Wen wang ji mo, wen buẓai ẓi hu?*). Edward Slingerland, *Analects: With Selections from Traditional Commentaries.* (Indianapolis: Hackett Publishing, 2003), 87.

26   Sun Zhonghan, "Zhi haiwai guomindang tongzhi han" in *Sun Zhongshan quanji*, vol. 5 (Beijing: Zhonghua shuju, 1985), 140.

27   This view was expressed by Vera Schwarcz in "Remapping May Fourth: Between Nationalism and Enlightenment," *Republican China*, 12: 1, 1986, 21–35; Li Zehou's "Qimeng yu jiuwang de shuangchong bianzou" (Enlightenment and salvation's double variation) in *Zhongguo xiandaishi lun* (Beijing: Dongfang chubanshe, 1987), first published in the first issue of *Zouxiang weilai* (1986), was also tremendously influential.

28   Benjamin I. Schwartz, "Notes on Conservatism in General and China in Particular," in Charlotte Furth, ed., *The Limits of Change: Essays on Conservative Alternatives in Republican China* (Cambridge, MA: Harvard University Press, 1976), 3–21.

29   Lin, Yu-sheng "Radical Iconoclasm in the May Fourth Period and the Future of Chinese Liberalism," in Benjamin Schwartz, *Reflections on the May Fourth Movement: A Symposium* (Cambridge, MA: Harvard University Press, 1973), 23–58. See also Lin, Yu-sheng *The Crisis of Chinese Consciousness: Radical Antitraditionalism in the May Fourth Era* (Madison: University of Wisconsin Press, 1979).

30   Maurice Meisner, "Cultural Iconoclasm, Nationalism, and Internationalism in the May Fourth Movement," in Benjamin Schwartz, *Reflections on the May Fourth Movement: A Symposium* (Cambridge, MA: Harvard University Press, 1973), 14–22.

31   Benjamin I. Schwartz, "Introduction," in *Reflections on the May Fourth Movement: A Symposium* (Cambridge, MA: Harvard University Press, 1973), 2.

32   Chen Duxiu, "Zhiwen 'dongfangzazhi' jizhe—'dongfang zazhi' yu fubi wenti," *Xin qingnian*, 5: 3, Sep. 1918.

33   Cang Fu, "Da 'xinqingnian' zazhi jizhe zhi zhiwen," *Dongfang ẓaẓhi*, 15: 12, Feb. 1918.

34 Chen Duxiu, "Zai zhiwen 'dongfang zazhi' jizhe," *Xin qingnian*, 6: 2, Feb. 1919.

35 Cang Fu, "Lun tongsu wen," *Dongfang zazhi*, 16: 12, 4–7.

36 In January 1920, *Eastern Miscellany* published "Our journal's hope," reiterating the mission of the journal. It stated, "The greatest responsibility of the journalistic world is to promote commentary. In order for commentary to be effective, first it must select its scope carefully. Second, it must be founded on a sound premise. Our journal believes that the hope for our country lies in society's self-awakening, and has nothing to do with those holding political power. Therefore from today we will focus mainly on discussions that might hasten the self-awakening of society, and not emphasize politics. Empty and baseless words would not help matters, but only increase the confusion in society." Pursuant to this declaration, the journal's social commentaries would favor practical problems and implementable solutions, such as those introduced in "On setting up cooperatives to promote domestic products" and "On welfare organizations." Jian Hu, "Ben zazhi zhi xiwang," *Dongfang zazhi*, 17: 1, Jan. 1920, 1–3.

37 The first issue of *Eastern Miscellany* edited by Du published a translation of "Letters from John Chinaman" by "Chinese anonymous," an article that sparked controversy in Europe. Its topic was the "clash of Eastern and Western civilizations"; aside from attempting to correct the West's misunderstanding of China (as well as China's misunderstanding of the West), it also attempted to explain the difference between the two civilizations. See "Songdong ouren zhi minglu" (The famous article that rankled Europeans), *Dongfang zazhi*, 8: 1, Feb. 1911, 6–10.

38 Cang Fu, "Dazhan zhongjie hou guoren zhi juewu ruhe," *Dongfang zazhi*, 16: 1, Jan. 1919, 1–8.

39 In 1900, Du founded a journal, *Yaquan zazhi*, that described scientific developments with an enlightenment slant. The journal pioneered a new approach to science education in the late Qing dynasty.

40 Jian Hu, "Benzhi zhi xiwang" (The hope of this journal), *Dongfang zazhi*, 17: 1, Jan. 1920, 1.

41 Eric Hobsbawm, *The Age of Extremes: A History of the World, 1914–1991* (New York: Pantheon, 1994).

42 *Indianapolis Star*, September 20, 1914, in Fred R. Shapiro, ed., *The Yale Book of Quotations* (New Haven: Yale University Press, 2006), 329.

43 At the invitation of President Li Yuanhong, Zhang Xun, the head of the military provincial leaders, entered the capital on June 14, 1917, to mediate

the dispute between the president's office and the parliament. Zhang later moved to restore the monarchy, however, and was ultimately vanquished by Premier Duan Qirui.

44 Mou xiren lai gao (A submission from an unknown Westerner), "Zuijin Ouzhou geguo zhi waijiao zhengce," (The recent diplomatic strategy of European countries), *Dongfang zazhi* 8: 2, Mar, 1911, 1–4.

45 Qian Zhixiu, "Yingwang you fa ji shi," *Dongfang zazhi* 11: 1, July 1, 1914, 44–6.

46 Cang Fu, "Geming zhanzheng" (Revolutionary war), *Dongfang zazhi* 8: 9, Nov. 1911, 1–3.

47 Cang Fu, "Jiexu zhuyi," *Dongfang zazhi* 11: 1, July 1, 1914, 1–3.

48 Shi Shuo, *Xizang wenming dong xiang fazhan shi* (The history of the eastern expansion of Tibetan civilization) (Chengdu: Sichuan renmin chubanshe, 1994), 427.

49 See "Zhong Ying Zang shi huiyi" (China-Britain conference on Tibet) in "Guonei da shi ji" (Important national news), *Qingnian zazhi* 1: 4, Dec. 1915, 3.

50 Kang Youwei, "Gonghe zhengti lun," and "Meng Zang aici," both in *Kang Youwei quanji*, vol. 10 (Beijing: Zhongguo renmin daxue chubanshe, 2007), 1–14.

51 Gao Lao, "Ouzhou da zhanzheng kaishi," *Dongfang zazhi* 11: 2, Aug. 1, 1914, 5–12.

52 Xu Jiaqing, "E meng jiaoshe zhi neirong," *Dongfang zazhi* 11: 2, Aug. 1, 1914, 15–18.

53 Cang Fu, "Da zhanzheng yu zhongguo," *Dongfang zazhi* 11: 3, Sep. 1, 1914, 1–7.

54 Fan Jiang, "Shi nian yilai shijie dashi zonglun" (A summary of world trends of the past ten years), *Dongfang zazhi* 9: 7, Jan. 1913, 1–8.

55 Cang Fu, "Da zhanzheng yu zhongguo" (The Great War and China), *Dongfang zazhi* 11: 3, Sep. 1, 1914, 1–7.

56 Qian Zhixiu, "Baizhong ren da tongmeng lun," *Dongfang zazhi* 11: 2, Aug. 1, 1914, 22–6.

57 Cang Fu, "Jiacha shi dong xi liangyang lun," (Curzon's Eastern and Western binary theory), *Dongfang zazhi* 8: 2, Mar. 1911, 5–7.

58 Xu Jiaqing, "Ouzhou hezhongguo lun (yi waijiao shibao)," *Dongfang zazhi* 12: 11, Nov. 1915, 1–4.

59 Liu Shuya, "Ouzhou zhanzheng yu qingnian zhi juewu," *Xin qingnian* 2: 2, Oct. 1, 1916, 1–8.

60   Ibid.

61   Lu Xun had strongly advocated for Haeckel's theory years before. In 1916 Ma Junwu published "Haeckel's Monism" (Heke'er zhi yi yuan zhexue) in *Xin qingnian* 2:2, Oct. 1, 1916, 1–3.

62   Liu Shuya, "Ouzhou zhanzheng yu qingnian zhi juexing" (The European war and youth's awakening), *Xin qingnian* 2: 2, Oct. 1, 1916, 1–8.

63   Ibid.

64   Zhang Xichen, "Ou ya liangzhou weilai zhi da zhanzheng," *Dongfang zazhi* 13: 1, Jan. 1916, 23–5.

65   Samuel Huntington, "The Clash of Civilizations?," *Foreign Affairs* 72: 3, 1993, 22–49.

66   Gu Xing, "Lun Zhongguo buneng pohuai zhongli" (On China's need to observe neutrality), *Dongfang zazhi*, no. 2 (Feb. 25, 1904), 27–29.

67   The inaugural issue was a special edition on the Russo-Japanese War, and the lead article, "On the effects of Sino-Japanese alliance or dissolution," proclaimed, "The recent Japanese resistance of Russia is a watershed event. The honor and disgrace of Europe and Asia, the victory and defeat of the yellow and white race, the strength and weakness of autocracy versus constitutionalism, all will be decided by this." Bie Shi, "Lun Zhong Ri fen he zhi guanxi." *Dongfang zazhi* 1, Jan. 25, 1904), 1–3. Other articles such as "On the great responsibility of China" and "Wishing for the rise of the yellow Race," emulated the American Monroe Doctrine and urged the Asian yellow race to resist the European-American white race. Xian Xiansheng, "Lun Zhongguo zeren zhi zhong," *Dongfang zazhi* 1, 3–5.

68   On the multiple nuances and transformations of the concept of Asia, see my article "The Politics of Imagining Asia" in Wang Hui, *The Politics of Imagining Asia* (Cambridge, MA: Harvard University Press, 2011), 10–62.

69   Gu Xing, "Manzhou shan hou wenti," *Dongfang zazhi* 2, Feb. 25, 1906, 21–9.

70   Ke Quan, "Lun ge guo dui xian shi lushun zhi yijian," (On other nations' opinion of present day Port Arthur [Lüshun]), *Dongfang zazhi* 5, May 25, 1904 (Guangxu 30), 79–82. The tenth issue of *Eastern Miscellany*, published on Oct. 25, 1906, printed an editorial from the August 2 issue of *Dagong bao*, "Chinese decline would not be Japan's gain" (Zhongguo shuailuo fei riben zhi fushuo) which also advocated the need for a Sino–Japanese-Korean alliance, but expressed great apprehension of Japan's "reliance on its military victory to blackmail China." See pages 231–3.

71   Xin Hua, "On Chinese loss of sovereignty," *Dongfang zazhi* 5, May 25, 1904), 82–6.

72   At this point the interpretation of the Russo-Japanese War turned from reading the event in terms of yellow race and Asian solidarity to considering it in terms of polity (that is, a triumph of constitutionalism over totalitarianism). The sixth issue of *Eastern Miscellany*, published on June 25, 1905), reprinted an article from August 18 of the same year in *Zhongwai ribao*, "On the prospect of constitutional rule in Japan's victory" (Lun ri sheng wei xianzheng zhi zhao"), 115–17. It used the Russo–Japanese War as a pretext for criticizing autocracy and encouraging Chinese constitutional reform.

73   Ru Peiyu, "Riben zhi diguo zhuyi" (Japan's imperialism) *Dongfang zazhi* 8: 4, May 1911, 16–18.

74   The related discussions were not limited to *Eastern Miscellany*; *Youth* also paid close attention to the topic. For instance in December 1915 the column "Important National Events" (Guonei da shi ji) of the fourth issue of volume 1 of *Youth* carried the piece "Bringing in the question of the treaty" (Yinru xieyue wenti) on this topic.

75   Shao You, "Zhanhou zhi zhongguo yu riben" (China and Japan after the war) translated from Japan's *Toho jiron*, *Dongfang zazhi* 14: 6, June, 1916 44–52.

76   *Eastern Miscellany* maintained a close scrutiny on the questions of Japanese Asian strategy and pan-Asianism. For instance, in 1917, the third issue of volume 14 printed articles translated by Jun Shi such as "Japanese thinking on the policy of Sino-Japanese rapprochement," (pp. 13–16) and "The Japanese presumption" (pp. 27–39). In the latter piece, the Japanese author clearly situated the problem of world peace and Eastern and Western civilizations as a point of observation. He not only equated Japanese pan-Asianism with the American Monroe Doctrine, but also explicitly declared that Japanese strategy toward China must coordinate with the Western powers; it must respect the pact between the powers but also "regard Japanese interest foremost, consider other powers as secondary, and the collaboration being guided by Japan as principle."

77   In January 1917, Hu Xueyu translated "Japan during the great European war" and analyzed in detail the alliances and oppositions that Japan had created during the war with the European nations. At the end, inspired by Britain, he argued that Japan did not harbor any designs on China. See *Dongfang zazhi* 14: 1, 9–15.

78 *Dongfang zazhi* 13: 5, May 1916, 16–18. Zhang commented, "The common ailment of Asians is to talk big and not prepare a realistic plan of action. Those who speak of pan-Asianism suffer from the same problem. For in order to unveil and call for such a large undertaking, one must have a preconceived plan, how to get rid of Euro-American influence, how to solidify the military, economic and administrative foundation in order to administer the Asian territory, and only then can this concept be carried out."

79 Gao Lao, "Shijie ren zhi shijie zhuyi," *Dongfang zazhi* 14: 12, 54–7.

80 In 1918, he published "On the benefits and costs of overseas immigration" (Lun yimin haiwai zhi li hai) (translated from *Shin Nihon*), which continued his discussion from "The impact of overseas immigration on our nation's economy and society." See *Dongfang zazhi* 15: 2, Feb. 1918, 44–9.

81 Translated from the Japanese journal *Ajia jiron* and published in *Eastern Miscellany* 15: 11, subtitled "New interpretation of Japanese Monroeism." Ukita had argued that this Asianism was a nonracist, supremely peaceful principle advocating autonomy for Asia. In May 1919, *Eastern Miscellany* printed Gao Yuan's "Pushy Asianism" (Duoduo yazhou zhuyi) in the column "Internal and External Times," (Nei wai shibao) strongly rebutting Ukita's "New Asianism" and pointing out that "New Asianism was nothing more than another name for 'Greater Japanism' " (see pp. 197–9). In the following issue, the sixth of the same volume, printed after the May Fourth student movement and featuring a picture of the student parade on the front, an article by Luo Luo titled "The imperialist and capitalist Japan" (Diguo zhuyi ziben zhuyi zhi Riben) was also published (see pp. 35–9).

82 Li Dazhao, "Da yaxiya zhuyi yu xin yaxiya zhuyi," *Guomin* 1: 2, Feb. 1, 1919.

83 Li Dazhao, "Zai lun xin yaxiya zhuyi," *Guomin* 2: 1, Nov. 1, 1919.

84 In October 1917, Jun Shi published "Asianism" ("Yaxiya zhuyi," translated from the Japanese journal *Ajia jiron*) in *Dongfang zazhi* 14: 10, supporting the concept of Asianism. His basic premise was that a Greater Asianism, along the concept of pan-Americanism, could be created by "merging and mediating between the Eastern and Western cultures" (see pp. 17–20).

85 Wu Tingfang (1842–1922) was an outstanding diplomat and legal scholar of the late Qing dynasty and early Republic. He was assigned to numerous diplomatic posts abroad in the late Qing era. After the 1911 Revolution he

was appointed minister of justice for the Nanjing provisional government and resigned when Yuan Shikai came to power. After the monarchical restoration he was appointed Minister of Foreign Affairs in the Duan Qirui government and became vice premier following a dispute between the president's office and the parliament in 1917. He later became foreign minister in Sun Yat-sen's government in the south.

86 Qian Zhixiu, "Wu Tingfang jun zhi zhong xi wenhua guan," *Dongfang zazhi*, 12:1 (Jan. 1915), 1–4. Wu unequivocally declared, "I daresay that Asia will improve the West with its culture. This is not my mockery but an honest opinion. The white race would benefit by learning from its colored comrades, and would learn from many places, such as India, China, Japan ..."

87 *Dongfang zazhi* 13: 12, Dec. 1916, 49–51.

88 Discussions on Tagore's Japanese visit lasted a long time; numerous correspondences took place from the war to the 1920s, when he arrived in China. For an interpretation of the war from a religious standpoint, please consult the translation by Bao Shaoyou in the Japanese journal *Chuokoron* of the long article "The European war and the question of religion in the world" (Ouzhou zhanzheng yu shijie zhi zongjiao wenti), *Dongfang zazhi* 14: 2, Feb. 1917, 17–29.

89 Tagore visited China in 1923 and 1929, and his visits not only became celebrated cultural events, but also triggered heated debates among various schools of intellectuals who had disparate reactions to his East–West civilization theory. Before his visit to China, Feng Youlan interviewed him in New York. This interview, titled "A conversation with India's Tagore (A comparison of the Eastern and Western civilizations)" (Yu Yindu Taiguer tanhua (Dong xii wenming zhi bijiao guan), was published in *Xin chao* 3: 1, Sep. 1921. At the same time, Yu Zhi's "A Critique of Tagore and Eastern and Western culture" ('Taige'er yu dong xi wenhua pipan') was published in *Dongfang zazhi* 18: 17, Sep. 1921, reviewing a Swiss philosopher's critique of Tagore's theory of the reconciliation of Eastern and Western civilizations. After Tagore's first visit to China, members of the Chinese Communist Party criticized Tagore's viewpoints. Chen Duxiu wrote "Tagore and Eastern and Western culture" (Taige'er yu dong xi wenhua) under the pen name of Shi An in *Zhongguo qingnian* 27, Apr. 1924; Qu Qiubai published "Tagore's view on nations and the East and West" (Taige'er de guojia guan yu dong xi fang) in *Xiangdao* 61, Apr. 1924. All critiqued Tagore's theory of Eastern and Western civilizations

from different perspectives. Two famous examples of a satire on Tagore's China visit are Lu Xun's "Fen: Lun zhaoxiang zhi lei" and "Huagai ji: Mashang zhi riji zhi er."

90 Shortly after taking over the editorship, Cang Fu published "The fundamental difference between Eastern and Western societies" (Dong xi yang shehui genben zhi chayi) (translated from the Japanese journal *Tayo*, authored by Dr. Toda). See *Dongfang zazhi* 8: 3, Apr. 1911, 1–6.

91 Qian Zhixiu, "Zheng jiguo zhuyi" (Correcting envy-nationalism), *Dongfang zazhi* 10: 4, Oct. 1, 1914, 1–4.

92 Chen Duxiu, "Wo zhi aiguo zhuyi," *Xin qingnian* 2: 2, Oct. 1, 1916, 1–6.

93 Du was greatly concerned with Yuan's attempt to restore the monarchy, as attested by his use of the pseudonym Gao Lao to publish *The Complete chronicle of the monarchical movement (Dizhi yundong zhi shimo,* Shangwu yinshu guan, 1923). The work drew heavily from the persistent observations he had made as editor of *Eastern Miscellany*.

94 Cang Fu, "Xiandai wenming zhi ruodian," *Dongfang zazhi* 9: 11, May, 1913, 1–6.

95 Cang Fu, "Zizhi zhi shangque," *Dongfang zazhi* 12: 2, Feb. 1915, 11–14.

96 Jia Yi, "Jianguo genben wenti," *Dongfang zazhi* 13: 3, Mar. 1916, 1–6.

97 Cang Fu, "Tianyi yu minyi" (Heaven's will and the people's will), *Dongfang zazhi* 13: 7, July, 1916, 1–4.

98 Cang Fu, "Jiquan yu fenquan" (Centralized power and shared power), *Dongfang zazhi* 13: 7, Jul. 1916, 5–10.

99 Cang Fu, "Zhonghua Minguo zhi qiantu" (The future of the Republic of China), *Dongfang zazhi* 8: 10, Apr. 1911, 1–6.

100 Qian Zhixiu, "Xunhuan zhengzhi" (Cyclical politics): "It has been five years since the Republic was established. During these five years, the political structure created unexpected new situations, and the protagonists were a crowded and varied bunch indeed. It is as if all had been useless. Look to the points of conflict in our political debates—people have not departed from the same three or so issues and the focus of political disputes involving the same three or so people. At the beginning [we moved from] cabinet rule to presidential rule, and not long after, [we returned] from presidential rule to cabinet rule." In order to extinguish the logic of cyclical politics, "[we must] be calm and be decisive. On the political system [one must] consider the national situation, and on the people [one must] observe before taking any action. If [one acted] in haste, it would produce a backlash, and that is why calm is needed. Once the political system has

been decided, then it should not be changed easily. When challenges arise, [one should] fight with full strength, and not put up a half-hearted attempt." *Dongfang zazhi* 13: 12, 1–6.

101 Aside from Cang Fu's discussions, other articles also discussed this topic. One of the future founders of the Youth Party, Chen Qitian, specifically authored essays on federalism in response to the relationship between central and local authorities after the Hongxian monarchical restoration. Chen Qitian, "Sheng zhi lun lue" (A short discussion on federalism) *Dongfang zazhi* 14: 1, Jan. 1917, 10–16.

102 Du Yaquan, "Jian zheng zhuyi" (Government reductionism), *Dongfang zazhi* 8: 1, Feb. 1911, 4–10.

103 Cang Fu, "Jiquan yu fen quan," *Dongfang zazhi* 13: 7, Jul. 1916, 5–10.

104 Ibid.

105 In March 1917, Du Yaquan (Gao Lao) published the lead article, "The boundary between the individual and the state," and argued for the necessity of "solidifying the position of the individual." He argued that "an individual has a substantial responsibility to the state" and opposed the "strengthening of the individual over the state" but also "strengthening the state to the disadvantage of individuals." "Geren yu guojia zhi jie shuo," *Dongfang zazhi* 14: 3, 1–5.

106 In "The concept of abolishing politics," Du wrote, "Today governments in all countries experience a structurally complex bureaucratic politics, and consider all affairs in society within the purview of politics. The governments have no boundaries and can do everything. Political power grows by the day, and governmental expenses increase; the power of the political institutions has become truly a concern of society." "Mie zheng zhuyi," *Dongfang zazhi* 8: 1, Feb. 1911, 4–10.

107 Cang Fu, "Lun gonghe zhezhong zhi" (On negotiated republicanism), *Dongfang zazhi* 8: 11, May 1911, 1–5.

108 Cang Fu, "Shinian yi lai Zhongguo zhengzhi tonglan—shang pian tong lun" (Overview of Chinese politics of the past ten years), *Dongfang zazhi* 9: 7, 1–2.

109 Cang Fu, "Lun minzhu lixian zhi zhengzhi zhuyi bu shi yu xianjin zhi shishi" (On the unsuitability of democratic constitutionalism and politics-centrism to today's situation), *Dongfang zazhi* 13: 9, Sep. 1916, 1–5.

110 Cang Fu wrote, "If citizens heavily favored politics-centrism, this would necessarily lead to the envy of neighboring countries and bring about diplomatic humiliation. Looking over our nation's recent development,

three revolutions took place in five years. Political reform has barely taken place and yet we have already lost our interests in Manchuria and Tibet. This should be a warning to those citizens who insist on politics-centrism." Ibid.

111 Cang Fu, "Lun zhengdang" (On political parties), *Dongfang zazhi* 8: 1, Feb. 1911, 10–14.

112 Ibid.

113 Xuan Lan, "Qingnian zhina dang yu qingnian tuerqi dang zhi bijiao lun" *Dongfang zazhi* 9: 6, Dec. 1912, 8–9.

114 Cang Fu, "Waijiao pu yan," *Dongfang zazhi*, 14:1 (Jan. 1917), 1–8.

115 Chen Duxiu, "Wuren zuihou zhi juewu" (Our final awakening), *Qingnian* 1: 6, Feb. 1916, 3.

116 Chen Duxiu, "Tong xin" (Correspondence), *Xin qingnian* 2: 1, Jan. 1, 1916, 3.

117 Chen Duxiu wrote, "The public attacks parliamentarians for two of their most egregious crimes: One is sabotage and the other is incompetency. By sabotage it is meant that they spend their time either clashing with the government or with each other, and by incompetency it is meant that they have never attempted to construct any business that would benefit the country or the people; these people have no concept of what a parliament should be. The only duty of the parliament is none other than to represent the people in supervising the administration to prevent illegal activities." "Sui gan lu (er)" (Ruminations pt. 2), *Xin qingnian* 4: 4, Apr. 15, 1018, 345.

118 Cang Fu, "Xiandai wenming zhi ruodian" (The failings of modern civilization), *Dongfang zazhi* 9: 11, May, 1913, 1–6.

119 Ibid.

120 Gao Lao, "Yanlun shili shi zhui zhi yuanyin" (The reason for the decline of power of seech), *Dongfang zazhi* 15: 12, Dec. 1918, 1–5.

121 Significantly, the modern political crisis could be resolved only through the remaking of political forces (such as reform of political parties) and through a national framework. A discussion on the redistribution of political power could not directly provide a solution. *Eastern Miscellany* made great strides in conducting political analyses but was unable to deliver a formula that could shape new political forces. While *New Youth* did not engage in direct discussions on polity and problems of political parties, it did launch the "New Culture Movement," which had a tremendous impact on the formation and reshaping of new political forces.

122 Cang Fu, "Waijiao pu yan" (Foreign affairs exposed), *Dongfang zazhi* 14: 1, Jan. 1917, 1–8.

123 Gao Lao, "Wuren jinhou zhi zijue" (My people's self-awakening in the future), *Dongfang zazhi* 12: 10, Oct. 1915, 1–4.

124 Cang Fu, "Xiandai wenming zhi ruodian," *Dongfang zazhi* 9: 11, May, 1913, 1–6.

125 Gao Lao, "Guojia zhuyi zhi kaolü" (Considering statism), *Dongfang zazhi* 15: 8, Aug. 1918, 4–9.

126 Cang Fu, "Jing de wenming yu dong de wenming" (Tranquil civilization and active civilization), *Dongfang zazhi* 13: 10, Oct. 1916.

127 In January 1915, Du advocated for "social-cooperativism." He believed that imperialism and pacifism occupied two extremes of Western political thought: "Statism's most extreme manifestation is the nonpacifist militarism or an ethnic imperialism. At the same time, the extreme aspect of pacifism is a nonstate cosmopolitanism, or socialism." In contrast, "China has been unified for a long time and isolated for thousands of years. Thus statism [in China] is not as developed as it is in Europe and pacifism is also less defined than theirs. As a result, we are not experienced when these two philosophies clash." He called for "social-cooperativism"—peaceful statism—or "national pacifism." See Cang Fu, "Shehui xieli zhuyi" (Social-cooperativism), *Dongfang zazhi* 12: 1, Jan. 1915, 1–6. "In looking at our country's present situation, an attempt to safeguard our nation's peace would evoke more unrest than safeguarding the world's peace. As a result, instilling peaceful statism would keep peace within the country, and indirectly safeguard peace in the world." Cooperativism's main thrust is that it acknowledges the difference between state, citizens and race "by recognizing that each nation must coexist in the world, and each could strive for prosperity and advancement."

128 Cang Fu, "Jing de wenming yu dong de wenming."

129 Qian Zhixiu, "Duoxing zhi guomin," *Dongfang zazhi* 13: 11, 1–6.

130 Yuan Sheng, "Xin jiu sixiang zhi chongtu" (The conflict between new and old thinking), *Dongfang zazhi* 13: 2, Feb. 1916, 1–5. Yuan Sheng wrote, "When scholars described the intellectual transformation of the times, they indicated three stages. The first was the nonconceptual stage, the second was the stage of criticism, and the third was the stage of knowledge creation. China today is moving from the stage of nonconceptualization to that of criticism ... The conflict between new and old

thinking existed on several fronts. This first was absolute respect for old things and proclivity for old customs, coupled with skepticism for and a wish to examine new concepts. The second was that the new thinkers who dared critique and analyze the sacred, thousands-year-old unassailable morality and social structures recognized that human beings have individual understanding of freedom ... The third was that the new thinkers could ascertain that mankind had such freedom because they possessed individual self-awakening. Because they pursued individual liberation, they recognized that human beings had independent characters ... The fourth was that the new thinkers who sought personal freedom must also seek freedom for their country. This was because they could not stop loving their society nor their nation. But the old thinkers were restricted by old traditions and did not understand what love is, therefore the manifestation [of the conflict] demonstrates one side to be dogmatic, the other critical; one side leaned on other people's strength, the other self-regulation; one side called for a merging, the other for analysis; one side used deduction, the other induction; one side was still, the other side active."

131 Cang Fu, "Zai lun xin jiu sixiang zhi chongtu" (Revisiting the conflict between new and old thinking), *Dongfang zazhi* 13: 4, Apr. 1916, 1–6.

132 Cang Fu, "Jing de wenming yu dong de wenming."

133 Cang Fu, "Xiandai wenming zhi ruodian" (Revisiting the conflict between old and new thinking), *Dongfang zazhi* 9: 11, May, 1913, 1–6.

134 Cang Fu, "Jing de wenming yu dong de wenming."

135 Cang Fu, "Lun sixiang zhan" (On the war of ideas), *Dongfang zazhi* 12: 3, Mar. 1915, 1–3. The author continued, "In this journalist's opinion, the cause of the current great European war is completely rooted in ideology. German Ottomanism, Russian Slavism and the English greater Britannia are all advantages anticipated by ideology."

136 Cang Fu, "Da zhan zhongjie hou guoren zhi juewu ruhe" (The state of our people's awakening after the Great War), *Dongfang zazhi* 16: 1, Jan. 1919, 1–8.

137 Max Weber, "Politics as a Vocation," in *From Max Weber: Essays in Sociology* (Routledge, 2009), 77.

138 Xun Zai, in "The Great War and the question of world peace" (translated in part from American Charles W. Eliot's original work), wrote, "What is a dictator? When the political power of the state falls into the hands of the ruler or a minority of politicians, and despite the existence of a

constitution and a parliament, the ruler's power reigns supreme and checks on governance do not exist. [Dictatorship] is when the great power of a state is manipulated by one or two people." See "Da zhanzheng yu shijie pinghe de wenti," *Dongfang zazhi* 15: 2, Feb. 1918, 11–18.

139 He continued, "What I am advocating today is not German national-ism. Even though the nationalism that is prevalent in the world is not as extreme as the German belief, its thrust does not go above rousing people and consolidating power in an effort to make an outward expan-sion. Thus it discriminates against others and extends one's own power. This leads to militarism, conspiracy and innumerable strategies that involve cheating people and sabotaging one another. However while these ideologies and strategies would obtain victory on the interna-tional stage, they were damaging to society." Gao Lao, "Guojia zhuyi zhi kaolü."

140 Cang Fu wrote, "Because the democratic experiment had been tested for only over one hundred years, there is still need for many improvements ... The recent strengthening of democratic nations is due to its intelligent polity. Its practitioners relied on statism to ameliorate the democratic prin-ciples of the state, which is truly the most accepted and appropriate ideology for this age." See "Weilai zhi shiju," *Dongfang zazhi* 14: 7, Jul. 1917, 1–6.

141 Cang Fu, "Zhen gonghe buneng yi wuli qiu zhi lun" (The thesis that true republicanism cannot be achieved by force), *Dongfang zazhi* 14: 9, Sep. 1917, 1–4.

142 Cang Fu wrote, "After the European war, nations in the world have shown signs of meltdown due to the interference of political parties and military strongmen. This will lead to the appearance of large alliances of several states." See "Weilai zhi shiju," *Dongfang zazhi* 14: 7, Jul. 1917, 1–6.

143 Xu Jiaqing, "Ershi shiji zhi zhengzhi wenti."

144 Peng Jinyi, "Ershi shiji zhi san da wenti" (The three great problems of the twentieth century), *Dongfang zazhi* 12: 3, 40–4.

145 Cang Fu, "Wuren jiang yi he fa zhiliao shehui zhi jibing hu?" (How do we cure social ills?), *Dongfang zazhi* 9: 8, Feb. 1913, 1–4.

146 Cang Fu, "Tuice Zhongguo shehui jianglai zhi bianqian" (Speculating about China's future social transformation), *Dongfang zazhi* 15: 1, Jan. 1918, 1–6.

147 Questions about "socialism and social policy" appeared as early as the June 1911 issue of *Eastern Miscellany*. The editor who succeeded Du,

Qian Zhixiu, had published a long essay titled "Socialism and social policy," in which he systematically described the rise of European social policies and suggested that China must implement them wholeheartedly without delay. (See "Shehuizhuyi yu shehui zhengce," *Dongfang zazhi* 8: 6, 1–10). Subsequent issues (such as 8: 12) also gave detailed accounts of European socialist parties, especially the German Socialist Party and the French Socialist Party.

148 Cang Fu, "Dazhan zhongjie hou guoren zhi juewu ruhe"

149 Ibid.

150 These new topics also emanated from Du's observations of wartime European society. In the early stage of the war, he pointed out, "When war starts, [people] in European nations band together. I am very astounded by the depth of their nationalist sentiment. But one sector of society, the labor class, held different convictions from the ruling class. They [the labor class] knew fully well that the spoils of victory would mostly go to the ruling class and little to them. Therefore they championed arms limitation and antiwar ideas, formed close ties with the same class in other countries to fight the ruling class in their own country. Their views were bound by class and not by nation, and therefore their nationalism was not as strong as their class conviction ... At the same time, their power could truly constrict European nationalism ... European nations might slowly realize the shortcomings of war."

151 Gao Lao, "Laodong zhengyi zhi jiejue fangfa" (The solution to labor disputes), *Dongfang zazhi* 15: 1, Jan. 1918, 13–22.

152 Cang Fu, "Laodong zhuyi" (Laborism), *Dongfang zazhi* 15: 8, Aug. 1918, 1–3.

153 Li Dazhao's "Shumin de shengli" (The common people's victory), Cai Yuanpei's "Laodong shensheng" and Tao Lugong's "Ouzhan yihou de zhengzhi" were all published under the group title of "Guanyu Ouzhan de yanshuo sanpian" in *Xin qingnian* 5: 5, Nov. 15, 1918, 436–41.

154 Gao Lao, "Ji ji euguo zhi jinzhuang" (Sequel to the chronicle on recent Russian conditions), *Dongfang zazhi* 15: 1, 37–42.

155 Cang Fu, "Duiyu weilai shijie zhi zhunbei ruhe," *Dongfang zazhi*, 15: 10 (Oct. 1918), 1–11.

156 Jun Shi, "Guoji sixiang yu fangzhi ce," *Dongfang zazhi* 16: 6, Jun. 1919, 1–10.

157 Cang Fu, "Zhongguo zhengzhi geming bu chengjiu ji shehui geming bu fasheng zhi yuanyin," *Dongfang zazhi* 16: 4, Apr. 1919, 1–7.

158 Gao Lao, "Zhongdeng jieji" (The middle class) (translated from the Japanese journal *Taiyo*), *Dongfang zazhi* 16: 6, Jun. 1919, 19–23.

159 Cang Fu, "Zhongguo zhengzhi geming bu chengjiu ji shehui geming bu fasheng zhi yuanyin."

160 Chen Duxiu, "Tan zhengzhi" (Talking about politics), *Xin qingnian* 8: 1, Sep. 1920, 1–9.

161 Cang Fu, "Zhengzhishang fenrao zhi yuanyin" (The reasons for political disturbances), *Dongfang zashi* 15: 2, Feb. 1918, 7–10.

162 Cang Fu, "Dazhan zhongjie hou guoren zhi juewu ruhe."

163 Cang Fu, "Zhanhou zhong xi wenming zhi tiaohe," *Dongfang zazhi* 14: 4, Apr. 1917, 1–7. Tolstoy's comments appear in English in "Letter to a Chinese Gentleman," *The Saturday Review* 102, December 1, 1906, 670.

164 Xingyan, "Ouzhou zuijin sichao yu wuren zhi juewu," *Dongfang zazhi* 14: 12, Dec. 1917, 1–9.

165 Gao Lao, "Maodun zhi tiaohe" (Mediating contradictions), *Dongfang zazhi* 15: 2, Feb. 1918, 1–6.

166 Zhang Dongsun, "Xian neng zhengzhi" (Politics of the able-minded), *Dongfang zazhi* 14: 11, 1–44.

167 Cang Fu, "Xin jiu sixiang zhi zhezhong," *Dongfang zazhi* 16: 9, Sep. 1919, 1–8.

168 Cang Fu, "Dazhan zhongjie hou guoren zhi juewu ruhe."

169 Cang Fu, "Xin jiu sixiang zhi zhezhong."

170 Ping Yi, "Zhong xi wenming zhi pingpan" (A critique of Chinese and Western civilizations), *Dongfang zazhi* 15: 6, 81–7.

171 Qian Zhixiu, "Gonglizhuyi yu xueshu," *Dongfang zazhi* 15: 6, Jun. 1918, 1–7.

172 Cang Fu, "Miluan zhi xiandai renxin," *Dongfang zazhi* 15: 4, Apr. 1918, 1–7.

173 Ibid.

174 Chen Duxiu, "Zhiwen 'dongfang zazi' jizhe — 'dongfan zazhi' yu jubi wenti."

175 Du concluded, "All those movements in the past had expected to create new forces to counter the old forces, but they only managed to attach themselves to these old forces and attempted to manipulate them. This led to the growing strength of the old forces, and to the total lack of any success on the part of the new forces. Their mistakes were first, they aimed to simply deploy the political aspect of social force without creating a basis on social life; second, they sought to expand power by the

manipulation of power politics, without tracing the root of power to the development of personal cultivation. Having either one of these two conditions would hamper the formation of power. As a result, new forces could not develop in such a manner." Cang Fu, "Zhongguo zhi xin sheng-ming" (China's new life), *Dongfang zazhi* 15: 7, Jul. 1918, 1–4.

3. From People's War to the War of International Alliance

1   This article is based on an interview of the author by Zhang Xiang. After several revisions it developed to its current form. Gao Jin translated and made contributions to this article.

2   Unless otherwise noted, "Korean War" in this article represents the Chinese term *Chaoxian zhanzheng*. In mainland China, *Chaoxian* is typically used to denote Korea (similar to *Choson*, the Korean term used in North Korea), while in Taiwan the term *Hanguo* (similar to the Korean term *Hanguk*, used in South Korea) is typically used.

3   The U.S. military forces ordered the minesweepers to only carry international swallow-tailed E signal flags, then the provisional Japanese "civil ensign," indicating that they were merchant or other civilian vessels. See Suzuki Hidetaka, "Chosen kaiiki ni shitsugeki shita Nihon tokubetsu sokaitai: Sono kikari to kage," *Senshi kenkyu nenpo* 8, March 2005, 26–46. Suzuki also listed international relations and domestic considerations as Yoshida's motivation to carry out the mining in secret: At the beginning of 1950, Dulles paid several visits to Japan and negotiated with Yoshida Shigeru about a potential peace treaty. In the sensitive situation before the signing of the peace treaty, Yoshida intended to avoid complications in international relations and was afraid of violating Article 9 of the Japanese constitution. See footnotes 26 and 27, which quote Okubo Takeo, *Uminari no hibi: Kakusareta sengoshi no danso* (Tokyo: Kaiyo mondai kenkyukai, 1978), 208–9, and James E. Auer, *The Postwar Rearmament of Japanese Maritime Forces, 1945–1971* (New York: Praeger Publishers, 1973), 84. Available at nids.go.jp (accessed October 28, 2013).

4   James E. Auer, *The Postwar Rearmament of Japanese Maritime Forces, 1945–1971*, 66.

5   Curtis A. Utz, "Assault from the Sea: The Amphibious Landing at Inchon," in Edward J. Marolda, ed., *The U.S. Navy in the Korean War* (Annapolis, MD: Naval Institute Press, 2007), 76.

6 At the ninth meeting of the Central People's Government Committee on September 5, 1950, Mao Zedong gave a speech entitled "The Korean War situation and our policy," saying that "The U.S. imperialists might try something reckless today. They are capable of anything. If they do something reckless and we are not prepared, that is not good. If we prepare we can counter them more easily." "When fighting begins, it may not be minor, but major. It may not be short, but long. It may not be a normal war, for it might involve atomic bombs. We must be fully prepared." "We should plan accordingly in the state budgetary estimate for 1951." *Mao Zedong wenji*, vol. 6 (Beijing: Renmin chuban she, 1999), 93–4.

7 See closing remarks by Mao Zedong in his "Closing Speech at the Second Session of the National Committee of the CPPCC, in *The Writings of Mao Zedong, 1949–1976*, vol. 1 (Armonk, NY: M.E. Sharpe, 1986), 111–5.

8 Mao Tse-tung, "Don't Hit Out in All Directions," in *Selected Works of Mao Tse-tung*, vol. 5 (Beijing: Foreign Languages Press, 1977), 33–6.

9 Jin Dongji, "Zhongguo renmin jiefangjun zhong de Chaoxian shi hui Chaoxian wenti xintan" (New explorations into the question of the return of Korean Divisions in the PLA to Korea), *Lishi yanjiu* (Historical studies) 6, 2006, 103–14.

10 Harry S. Truman: "Statement by the President on the Situation in Korea," June 27, 1950. Online by Gerhard Peters and John T. Woolley, *The American Presidency Project*. Available at presidency ucsb.edu/ (Accessed April 22, 2015).

11 Mao Zedong, "Zhongguo renmin zhiyuanjun yingdang he bixu ru Chao canzhan" (The Chinese People's Volunteer Army should and must enter Korea to join the war), *Mao Zedong wenji*, vol. 6, 103.

12 "Memorandum by the Director of the Central Intelligence Agency (Smith) to the President," *Foreign Relations of the United States: 1950 Korea*, vol. 7 (Washington: United States Government Printing Office, 1950), 1025–6.

13 Bruce Cumings, "From Containment to Regime Change and Back: How a Debacle in North Korea Stabilized Cold War Strategy for 40 Years," a paper for the conference "China in the Cold War Era" at the University of Bologna, September 13–15, 2007.

14 Junshi kexueyuan junshi lishisuo, ed., *Kang Mei yuan Chao zhanzhengshi (xiuding ban)* (History of the War to Resist U.S. Aggression and Aid Korea) (Beijing: Junshi kexue chubanshe, 2011), 303.

15 Zhou Enlai telegrammed Acheson to protest the invasion and strafing by U.S. military aircraft, and the UN to request sanctions against the United States. *Zhong Mei guanxi ẕiliao huibian*, vol. 2, book 1 (Beijing: Shijiezhishi chubanshe, 1960), 146–9.

16 See the text of the speech given by Wu Xiùquan at the United Nations Security Council on November 28, 1950, in Wu Hsiu-chuan, *People's China Stands for Peace* (New York: Committee for a Democratic Far Eastern Policy, Dec. 1950), 26, and *Zhong Mei guanxi ẕiliao huibian*, vol. 2, book 1, 309.

17 "Zhongguo renmin zhiyuanjun bixu yueguo sanbaxian zuozhan," *Mao Zedong wenji*, vol. 6, 114.

18 Pingchao Zhu, *Americans and Chinese at the Korean War Cease-Fire Negotiations, 1950–1953* (Lewiston, NY: Edwin Mellen Press, 2001), 22–5.

19 "The United States Representative at the United Nations (Austin) to the Secretary of State," *Foreign Relations of the United States: 1950 Korea*, vol. 7 (Washington: United States Government Printing Office, 1950), 1594–8.

20 *Mao Zedong wenji*, vol. 6, 93.

21 Mao Zedong, "Opening Speech of the Third Meeting of the First National Committee of the CPPCC," *The Writings of Mao Zedong*, vol. 1, 218–19.

22 "If Chinese forces could have helped defend the rear before the Inchon landing, this could have guaranteed the victory of the main force of the Korean People's Army at the front; after the Inchon landing the Chinese army could have established a defensive line at the 38th parallel and prevented the enemy from moving further north. By the beginning of October 1950, however, after the main force of KPA had been completely defeated and the 38th parallel already breached, the best opportunity for the Chinese army to enter the war in Korea had already passed." Shen Zhihua, "Nanyi zuochu de jueze" (A difficult decision), in Shen Zhihua, ed., *Yige daguo de jueqi yu bengkui* (The rise and collapse of a great power) (Beijing: Shehui kexue wenxian chubanshe, 2009), 845.

23 Glen D. Paige, *The Korean Decision–June 24–30, 1950* (New York: Free Press, 1968), pp. 218–9.

24 Warren R. Austin, "Peace and Security for the Future of Korea," *Department of State Bulletin* 23 (October 9, 1950), 579.

25 Michael Walzer, *Just and Unjust Wars* (New York: Basic Books, 2015), 115.

26 Mao, "Opening Speech of the Third Meeting of the First National Committee of the CPPCC," *The Writings of Mao Zedong*, vol. 1, 219.

27 Mao Zedong, "Talks at the Chengtu Conference, March 1958—(a) Talk of 20 March," in Stuart Schram, ed., *Chairman Mao Talks to the People* (New York: Pantheon, 1974), 109.

28 Mao Tse-tung "Problems of Strategy in China's Revolutionary War," *Selected Works of Mao Tse-tung*, vol. I (Beijing: Foreign Languages Press, 1965), 182.

29 Mao Tse-tung "Great Victories in Three Mass Movements," *Selected Works of Mao Tse-tung*, vol. V (Beijing: Foreign Languages Press, 1977), 62.

30 For example, Shen Zhihua argues that Stalin did not release to China any information in regard to the detailed content and plan of Soviet military actions in the Korean Peninsula. See Shen Zhihua *Mao, Stalin and the Korean War* (New York: Routledge, 2012). Ji Pomin asserts that the theory that China, Korea and the Soviet Union planned the war together should be put to rest: "The Korean War was planned by Stalin and Kim behind the back of China" and they only informed Mao on the eve of the war after all preparations had already been made. Ji further argues that Stalin was the most astute of the three leaders, for the Korean people were the ones fighting, and the Soviets would have much to gain if they won but would suffer only limited losses if they failed. China's interests were far more at stake. See Ji Pomin, "Jiaji zhong de fendou: Mao Zedong chubing yuan Chao de jiannan juece," *Xianggang chuanzhen* 41, June 9, 2011, 69–76.

31 For instance, Shen Zhihua argued that after the Sino-Soviet Treaty of Friendship, Alliance and Mutual Assistance was signed and the Soviet Union was forced to rescind most of the rights that it held in China, it might have been out of an effort to replace the ice-free port of Lüshun (Port Arthur) with another port on the Korean Peninsula and thus mitigate its losses in China that it changed its policy and supported the DPRK's attack on the South. See Chapter 3 in Shen Zhihua *Mao, Stalin and the Korean War*, and *Lengzhan zai Yazhou: Chaoxian zhanzheng yu Zhongguo chubing Chaoxian* (Beijing: Jiuzhou chubanshe, 2013), 133.

32 According to Ji Pomin, "Among Stalin's concerns was the problem of how to deal with the unruly and intractable Mao Zedong ... Through some measure of planning Stalin hoped to create a situation—a situation at a global scale—that could securely lock this just awoke 'lion of the East' into an iron cage of his own design." See Ji Pomin, "Jiaji zhong de fendou.

33 Zhang Wenmu, for instance, noting that Kissinger had called the Soviet Union "the biggest loser" in the Korean War, argued that both the Soviet Union and the United States were the biggest losers while China was the biggest winner. He emphasized that, as it rescinded its actual control of Northeast China, the Soviet Empire was again losing its foothold in this strategic border area. See Zhang Wenmu, *Quanqiu shiye zhong de Zhongguo guojia anquan zhanlüe* (A strategy for China's state security in a global perspective), vol. 2.2 (Jinan: Shandong renmin chubanshe, 2010), 720–60. Ji Pomin also considered the 156 Soviet aid projects in China the "trophy" won by China in the Korean War. See Ji, "Jiaji zhong de fendou," 69–76.

34 In *Mao Zedong, Sidalin yu chaoxian zhanzheng (Mao, Stalin and the Korean War)*, (Guangdong: Guangdong renmin chubanshe: 2003), Shen Zhihua argued that "[China] was mired in the enmity with the U.S. more deeply than was the Soviet Union because of the revolutionary impulse of Mao that was stirred up by the war" (p. 361) and that "China failed to alter its strategy at the right time [and stop at the 38th parallel]" (p. 359).

35 Zhang Wenmu emphasized that Mao conferred with Kim Il-sung's representative as early as May 1949 to discuss possible DPRK military action against South Korea and to analyze its possible consequences, including a possible scenario in which Japan entered the war. Mao clearly expressed his support: "You don't need to worry … When necessary, we will send Chinese soldiers quietly. They have black hair like the Korean soldiers and no one could tell the difference." For the telegram summarizing this meeting, which is the continuation of the Moscow Conference between Mao and Kim in March, see Shen Zhihua, ed., *Chaoxian zhanzheng: Eguo dang'anguan de jiemi wenjian* (The Korean War: Declassified documents from the Russian archives) (Taipei: Zhongyanyuan jindaishi yanjiusuo, 2003), 187–90. Zhang Wenmu also delineated a timeline of exchanges between Mao and Kim in regard to the pending war in May 1950: On May 13, Kim went to Beijing to convey to Mao that Stalin thought "North Korea could take action," and Mao requested "an explication by Comrade Georgi Filipov himself." On the next day Stalin telegrammed Mao that he "agreed to the proposal by the Koreans about unification" and that "this problem should ultimately be solved by Chinese and Korean comrades together." In light of the Soviet Union's clear show of support, Mao also expressed his willingness to support North Koreas's actions. See Zhang, *Quanqiu shiye zhong de Zhongguo guojia anquan zhanlüe*, pp. 634–6, 652–4.

36 Both Shen Zhihua, in *Lengzhan zai Yazhou*, and Ji Pomin, in *Jiaji zhong de fendou*, argued along these lines.

37 This letter to Gottwald was sent on August 27, 1950, and is now in the Russian State Archive of Socio-Political History (RGASPI) (Fund 558, Inventory 11, Work 62, Page 71–2). Shen Zhihua's translation of this telegram in *Lengzhan zai Yazhou* (pp. 53–4) is problematic in some places. Gao Jin wrote to the RGASPI for the original text and here I use her translation.

38 Ibid.

39 Dean Acheson; "Crisis in Asia—An Examination of U.S. Policy," *Department of State Bulletin*, XXII, No. 51, January 23, 1950, 114.

40 Ibid., 115.

41 "Our Answer to Acheson's Fabrications," in *Complete and Consolidate the Victory*, New China Library Series No. 1 (Beijing: Foreign Languages Press, 1950), 40.

42 Ibid. This quotation is attributed in the English version to Hu Qiaomu, but no such indication is present in the original version, which appeared in the January 21, 1950, edition of *Renmin ribao* (*People's Daily*). The article is known to have been drafted by Mao. See *Mao Zedong wenji*, vol. 6, 46.

43 Mao, "Zhongguo renmin zhiyuanjun yingdang he bixu ruchao canzhan" (The Chinese People's Volunteer Army should and must enter Korea to join the war), in *Mao Zedong wenji*, vol. 6, 103–4.

44 Mao Zedong "Jianjue zhanzai kang Mei yuan Chao baojiaweiguo de aiguo lichang shang" (Resolutely make the patriotic stand to resist U.S. aggression and aid Korea, protect our homes and defend the country), in *Mao Zedong wenji*, vol. 6, 110.

45 Mao, "Zhongguo renmin zhiyuanjun yingdang he bixu ru Chao canzhan", 104.

46 Ibid.

47 Mao Zedong, "Zhongguo renmin zhiyuanjun ru Chao zuozhan de fangzhen he bushu" (Guidelines and deployment for the Chinese People's Volunteer Army to fight in Korea), *Mao Zedong wenji*, vol. 6, 105–6.

48 Mao Zedong "Zai wendang kekao de jichu shang zhengqu yiqie keneng de shengli" (Make all possible efforts to achieve a stable and secure vitory), *Mao Zedong wenji*, vol. 6, 107–9.

49 After *The Origins of the Korean War*, vols. 1 and 2 (Princeton, NJ: Princeton University Press, 1981, 1990), Bruce Cumings has published a

large amount of research on the Korean War and discussed this issue from diverse perspectives. His most recent work is *The Korean War: A History* (New York: Modern Library, 2010).

50 A letter from the secretariat of the GMD to Chiang Kai-shek was outspoken in promising GMD support to Kim Ku and in its expectation that Kim would become a channel for future intervention in the peninsula. See "Zhongguo Guomindang mishuchu xiang Jiang Jieshi chengwen" (GMD party archive, Korean section, 016-26-5) in Shi Yuanhua and Jiang Jianzhong, eds., *Hanguo duli yundong yu Zhongguo guanxi biannianshi*, vol. 3 (Beijing: SSAP, 2012), 1505–6.

51 Kim Ku wrote in his memoir that he wished the Korean Provisional Government could be preserved but that, "saying that an American military government had already been installed in Seoul, the United States officials told us that they could not allow us to return in the official capacity of the government. Instead, we were only allowed to return as private individuals." See Kim Ku, Paekpom Ibchi: *The Autobiography of Kim Ku*, translated, annotated and introduced by Jongsoo Lee (Lanham, MD: University Press of America, 2000), 287.

52 In the case of Okinawa, Chiang Kai-shek eventually responded negatively to an inquiry made by Roosevelt. He apparently was aware of the American vision of postwar international structure and wished not to incur any further misgivings. See Wang Hui, "Liuqiu yu quyu zhixu de liangci jubian" (Okinawa and two great changes in the regional order), in *Dongxi zhijian de Xizang wenti* (The Tibetan question between East and West), (Beijing: Sanlian chucanshe, 2011), 207–60.

53 "The Acting Secretary of State to the Secretary of the Navy (Forrestal)," *FRUS 1945*, vol. 7, 882–3.

54 Cao Zhongping and Zhang Lianhuai, eds., *Dangdai Hanguo shi, 1945–2000* (A history of modern Korea, 1945–2000) (Tianjin: Nankai daxue chubanshe, 2005), 42.

55 Kang Man-gil, *A History of Contemporary Korea* (Folkstone, Kent, UK: Global Oriental, 2005), 184.

56 Cao and Zhang, *Dangdai Hanguo shi 1945–2000*, 60.

57 See Appendix II in Kim Ku, *The Autobiography of Kim Ku*, 325.

58 Ibid., 326.

59 Sergei Khrushchev, ed., *Memoirs of Nikita Khrushchev: Volume 2: Reformer, 1945–1964* (University Park, PA: Penn State University Press, 2006), 92.

60   See the Charter of the United Nations, Chapter 8 Article 53, Chapter 12 Article 77, and Chapter 17 Article 107 at un.org (accessed October 29, 2013).

61   Zhongyang dang'an guan, ed. *Zhonggong zhongyang wenjian xuanji*, vol. 7 (Beijing: Renmin chubanshe, 1983), 173, 289–90.

62   Mao Tse-tung, "Why Is It That Red Political Power Can Exist in China?" *Selected Works of Mao Tse-tung*, vol. 1, 63–72.

63   "Be Concerned with the Well-Being of the Masses, Pay Attention to Methods of Work," *Selected Works of Mao Tse-tung*, vol. 1, 147–52.

64   Wen Tiejun asserts that the industrialization process in the first Five Year Plan amounted to "Chinese industrialization controlled by the geopolitical strategic adjustments of two super countries and externally dominated by strategic foreign investment." See *Baci weiji* (Beijing: Dongfang chubanshe, 2012), 10–44. His argument was based on information in Shen Zhihua's article "Xin Zhongguo jianli chuqi Sulian duihua jingji yuanzhu de jiben qingkuang—laizi Zhongguo he Eguo de dang'an cailiao" (The basic situation of Soviet aid after New China was established: Archival materials from China and Russia), *Eluosi yanjiu* 1, 2001, 53–66; 2, 2001, 49–58.

65   Mao Tse-tung, "Order to the Chinese People's Volunteers," *Selected Works of Mao Tse-tung*, vol. 5, 43.

66   "The Commander in Chief, Far East (MacArthur) to the Department of the Army," in *Foreign Relations of the United States: 1950. Korea*, vol. VII, 1630–3.

67   Arthur Krock, "In the Nation: Recurrent Hazard of the Press Conference," *New York Times*, December 1, 1950, 24.

68   Appu K. Soman, *Double-Edged Sword: Nuclear Diplomacy in Unequal Conflicts: The United States and China, 1950–1958* (Westport, CI: Praeger, 2000), 58, 115–18.

69   Mao Tse-tung "The Situation and Our Policy after the Victory in the War of Resistance against Japan," *Selected Works of Mao Tse-tung*, vol. IV (Beijing: Foreign Languages Press, 1969), 21–2.

70   Mao Tse-tung "Talk with the American Correspondent Anna Louise Strong," *Selected Works of Mao Tse-tung*, vol. 4, 100.

71   Mao Tse Tung, "Problems of Strategy in China's Revolutionary War," in *Selected Works of Mao Tse-tung*, vol. 1, 179–254.

72   Ibid.

73   Ibid., 180.

74   Ibid.

4. The Crisis of Representation and Post-Party Politics

1 An earlier version of this article was published, in Chinese, in the January 2013 issue of *Beijing Cultural Review*. The author has expanded and revised some parts of the article for this book.

2 Debates and reflections on Bolshevism and its party structure also began in this period, but I do not have enough space to elaborate on this issue.

5. Two Kinds of New Poor and Their Future

1 Cai Yuanpei, "Laogong shensheng—zai qingzhu xieyueguo shengli dahui de yanshuo" (Laborers are sacred: A speech at the assembly celebrating the victory of the Allied Nations), *Beijing daxue rikan* (Beijing University Daily), November 27, 1918.

2 Translator's note: "Mr. Democracy" (De Xiansheng) and "Mr. Science" (Sai Xiansheng) were slogans popularized by intellectuals associated with *New Youth* magazine during the May Fourth period as forces capable of "saving China" from backwardness and poverty.

3 Jean Baudrillard, *Symbolic Exchange and Death* (Thousand Oaks, CA: Sage, 1993), 11.

4 Charles Taylor, "The Politics of Recognition," in *Multiculturalism: Examining the Politics of Recognition* ed., Amy Gutman (Princeton: Princeton University Press, 1994), 41.

5 Ibid., 26–39.

6 Peter Marsh, "Levelling Out: Emerging Markets and the New Industrial Revolution," Aug 27, 2012, at blogs.ft.com/beyond-brics (accessed January 20, 2015).

7 *Zhongguo shehui guanli chuangxin baogao* (Report on the innovation of China's social administration) (Beijing: Shehui kexue wenxian chubanshe, 2012).

8 Huang Zongzhi, "Chongxin renshi Zhongguo laodong renmin: Laodong fagui de lishi yanbian yu dangqian de feizhenggui jingji" (Another look at China's laboring people: Historical changes in labor regulations and the informal economy today), *Kaifang shidai* 5, 2003, 69.

9 National Bureau of Statistics of the People's Republic of China, "2013 national survey of rural migrant workers," May 12, 2014, at stats.gov.cn.

10 Beijing xing zai renjian wenhua fazhan zhongxin anquanmao daxuesheng zhiyuanzhe liudong fuwudui, "2011 nian jing, yu, hu, shen si chengshi

jianzhu gongren shengcun zhuangkuang diaocha baogao" (2011 survey report on the condition of construction workers in Beijing, Chongqing, Shanghai and Shenzhen) at wenku.baidu.com (accessed on January 20, 2015).

11 Pan Yi and Wu Jiongwenqian, "Yizhi laodong hetong de jianzhu mingong meng—2013 nian jianzhu gongren laodong hetong zhuangkuang diaocha" (A paper contract dream for migrant construction workers—2013 survey on the labor contract situation for migrant construction workers), *Nanfeng chuang* 3, 2014, 57.

12 Zygmunt Bauman, *Work, Consumerism and the New Poor* (Buckingham: Open University Press, 1998).

13 Cang Fu (Du Yaquan), "Zhongguo zhengzhi geming bu chengjiu ji shehui geming bu fasheng zhi yuanyin" (The reasons for the failure of China's political revolution and the lack of transformation of China's society), *Dongfang zazhi* 16: 4, April 1919, 1–7.

14 Karl Marx, "Manifesto of the Communist Party," in Karl Marx and Frederick Engels, *Karl Marx, Frederick Engels: Collected Works, vol. 6: 1845–1848* (New York: International Publishers, 1976), 493–4.

15 Karl Marx, "The German Ideology," in Karl Marx and Frederick Engels, *Karl Marx, Frederick Engels: Collected Works, vol. 5: 1845–1847* (New York: International Publishers, 1976), 202.

16 Lü Tu, *Zhongguo xin gongren: Mishi yu jueqi* (China's new working class: Loss and rise) (Beijing: Falü chubanshe, 2013), 11.

17 Ibid., 8–9.

18 Liu Mingkui and Tang Yuliang, eds., *Zhongguo jindai gongren jieji he gongren yundong* (The modern Chinese working class and the labor movement), vol. 1 (Beijing: Zhonggong zhongyang dangxiao chubanshe, 202), 1.

19 Li Jingjun, "Zhongguo gongren de zhuanxing zhengzhi" (The transitional politics of the Chinese working class), in Li Youmei, ed., *Dangdai Zhongguo shehui fenceng: Lilun yu shizheng* (Social stratification in contemporary China: Theory and evidence) (Beijing: Shehui kexue wenxian chubanshe, 2006), 57.

20 Karl Marx, *Capital*, vol. 1, in *Karl Marx, Frederick Engels: Collected Works*, vol. 35 (New York: International Publishers, 1996), 338. Translation amended.

21 E. P. Thompson, *The Making of the English Working Class* (New York: Vintage, 1966), 9, 11.

22 Lü Tu, *Zhongguo xin gongren*, 225–47.

23 Margaret Somers, "Class Formation and Capitalism: A Second Look at a Classic," *European Journal of Sociology* 37: 1, 1996, 194.

24 Li Jingjun, "Zhongguo gongren jieji de zhuanxing zhengzhi," in *Dangdai shehui fenceng: Lilun yu shizheng*, 61.

25 In 2003, the twenty-three-year-old university graduate Sun Zhigang was mistaken by local police in Guangzhou for a rural migrant worker and, upon his failure to produce an identification card, was arrested, detained and beaten to death. The case sparked widespread outrage and resulted in the abrogation of local authorities' power to detain migrants for lacking identification or a residence permit.

26 Wang Hui, "Gaizhi yu Zhongguo gongren jieji de lishi mingyun—Jiangsu Tongyu jituan gongsi gaizhi de diaocha baogao" (Restructuring and the historical fate of the Chinese working class—Report on the restructuring of the Jiangsu Tongyu group), in Wang Hui, *Quzhengzhihua de zhengzhi* (Depoliticized Politics) (Beijing: Sanlian shudian, 2008), 275–364.

27 "Constitution of the People's Republic of China (Adopted on December 4, 1982)," available at en.people.cn/constitution/constitution.html (accessed January 20, 2015).

28 The 2009 Tonggang incident in Jilin and the Han-Uyghur conflict in Shaoguan, Guangdong, which sparked off at least seventy-five further incidents in Xinjiang, are examples of this. The nature of the 2003 Baoma case in Harbin, the 2008 Weng'an incident in Guizhou and the Menglian incident in Yunnan, the 2009 Deng Yujiao incident in Hubei and the Shishou Incident is somewhat different. But the forms are similar in that they all began as concrete disputes over wages or conflicts between local workers and migrants and developed into protests against the government or the police.

29 "The trade unions arose out of capitalism as a means of developing the new class. Class is a concept which is evolved in struggle and development. There is no wall dividing one class from another. The workers and peasants are not separated by a Chinese Wall. How did man learn to form associations? First through the guild, and then according to different trades. Having become a class, the proletariat grew so strong that it took over the whole state machine, proclaimed war on the whole world and emerged victorious. The guilds and craft unions have now become backward institutions." V. I. Lenin, "Speech Delivered at the Third All-Russia

Trade Union Congress," April 7, 1920, in *Collected Works*, vol. 30 (Moscow: Progress Publishers, 1965), 512.

30 V. I. Lenin, "The Trade Unions, the Present Situation and Trotsky's Mistakes," in *Collected Works*, 4th English ed., vol. 32 (Moscow: Progress Publishers, 1965), 19–42.

31 Frederick Engels, "Engels to Theodor Cuno," in Karl Marx and Frederick Engels, *Karl Marx, Frederick Engels: Collected Works, vol. 44, 1870–73* (New York: International Publishers, 1989), 306–7.

32 Ibid., 306.

33 V. I. Lenin, "Report at the Second All-Russia Trade Union Congress," in *Collected Works*, 4th English ed., vol. 28 (Moscow: Progress Publishers, 1966), 418.

34 Karl Marx, "The Eighteenth Brumaire of Louis Bonaparte," in Karl Marx and Frederick Engels, *Karl Marx, Frederick Engels: Collected Works, vol. 11, 1851–53* (New York: International Publishers, 1979), 187–8.

35 Karl Marx, "Marx to Joseph Weydemeyer (March 5, 1852)" in Karl Marx and Frederick Engels, *Karl Marx, Frederick Engels: Collected Works, vol. 39, 1852–1855* (New York: International Publishers, 1983), 62–5.

36 V. I. Lenin, "The State and Revolution," in *Collected Works*, vol. 25, 421–2.

37 In the 1950s, with the promotion of socialist reform work, there emerged a discussion on whether the nature of governmental power in China was a people's democratic dictatorship or a proletarian dictatorship. It was argued that the former was the task of the new democratic revolution, which is to say the bourgeois democratic revolution, and that the latter was the task of the socialist revolution. But in order to prevent unnecessary worry from the democratic activists and the bourgeoisie, the 1954 constitution described the state as "a people's democratic state led by the working class and based on the alliance of workers and peasants." But in the constitutions formed in 1975 and 1978, the phrasing was changed to "a socialist state of the dictatorship of the proletariat led by the working class and based on the alliance of workers and peasants." The 1982 constitution changed it again to "a people's democratic dictatorship." The 1954 constitution clearly stated that there were five main categories of ownership of means of production, including capitalist ownership. The 1982 constitution is the product of the reform and opening of the country, and it once again permitted the existence of capitalist markets. As the earlier constitutions all emphasize the leadership of the proletariat and the alliance

between workers and peasants as the basis of the state, I refer to them as workers' states.

38 Lenin argued that " 'the alliance of the proletariat and the peasantry ... should not in any circumstances be understood as meaning the fusion of various classes, or of the parties of the proletariat and the peasantry ... Only if it pursues an unquestionably independent policy as vanguard of the revolution will the proletariat be able to split the peasantry away from the liberals, rid it of their influence, rally the peasantry behind it in the struggle and thus bring about an 'alliance' de facto—one that emerges and becomes effective, when and to the extent that the peasantry are conducting a revolutionary fight." V. I. Lenin, "The Assessment of the Russian Revolution," *Collected Works*, vol. 15, 57–8.

39 "The supreme principle of the dictatorship is the maintenance of the alliance between the proletariat and the peasantry in order that the proletariat may retain its leading role and its political power." V. I. Lenin, "Third Congress of the Communist International," in *Collected Works*, 4th English ed., vol. 32 (Moscow: Progress Publishers, 1965), 490.

40 "Insofar as different nations constitute a single state, Marxists will never, under any circumstances, advocate either the federal principle or decentralisation." V. I. Lenin, "Critical Remarks on the National Question" in *Collected Works*, vol. 20, 45–6.

41 Karl Marx, "General Rules and Administrative Regulations of the International Working Men's Association," in Karl Marx and Frederick Engels, *Karl Marx, Frederick Engels: Collected Works, vol. 23: 1871–1874* (New York: International Publishers, 1988), 3.

42 Karl Marx, "The Fourth Annual Report of the General Council of the International Working Men's Association," in Karl Marx and Frederick Engels, *Karl Marx, Frederick Engels: Collected Works, vol. 21: 1867–1870* (New York: International Publishers, 1985), 17.

6. Three Concepts of Equality

1 Eric Hobsbawn, *The Age of Extremes: A History of the World, 1914–1991* (New York: Pantheon Books, 1994), 4.

2 Cf. Pierre Rosanvallon, "What is a Democratic Society?" Paper for the Tenth Indira Gandhi Conference: An Indian Social Democracy, New Delhi, November, 2010.

3 The political reorganization of democratic systems is not a new

phenomenon. Conservative economist Robert Fogel divided modern American history into four "great awakenings": 1730, the period of the foundation of revolutionary thought; 1800 and shortly after it, when audacious reforms were passed, including the abolition of slavery; and 1890–1930, when social welfare and other pluralistic policies were enacted in order to combat inequality. Fogel's final "great awakening" was the so-called "spiritual reformation" (antimaterialistic) that began in the 1950s, "the period of religious reformation." I am not convinced by his discussion of this latter "great awakening" and of "post-modern equality," but this raises a methodological problem. That is, a given social organization responds to historically distinct phenomena of inequality. As has been the case previously, the ever more salient separation of democratic political forms from their social forms is the product of a political system that is not able to address conditions of inequality. Robert W. Fogel, *The Fourth Great Awakening and the Future of Egalitarianism* (Chicago: University of Chicago Press, 2000).

4   According to Polish sociologist Jacek Wasile wski analysis of elites in Russia and Eastern Europe between 1988 and 1993, one-third of civil servants were from the former elite classes. In the economic, political and cultural spheres, elites were even more prominent: 50.7 percent, 48.2 percent and 40.8 percent respectively Eighty-six percent of Russia's old elite class entered the new elite strata, while only 10 percent lost their original status. By 1996, Soviet-era bureaucrats constituted 75 percent of the presidential organization, 74 percent of government organization, and 61 percent of the economic elite. These statistics are taken from "Hou Sulian guojia shehui zhuanxing de jingshi—Feng Yujun boshi jiangtan" (Interview with Dr. Feng Yujun: On the transformation of society in post-Soviet countries), in *Guowai lilun dongtai (Foreign Theoretical Trends)*, March 2005, 3.

5   Rosanvallon, "What Is a Democratic Society?"

6   For example, Mouffe has made a trenchant critique of Rawls's theories of pluralism, political freedom and justice from a political perspective. See Chantal Mouffe, "The Limit of John Rawls' Pluralism," *Theoria*, March 2009, 1. See also "Deliberative Democracy or Agonistic Pluralism" (Vienna: Institute for Advanced Studies, 2000) and *The Democratic Paradox* (London: Verso, 2000).

7   Concerning these concepts and the relationships between them, see Amartya Sen, "Equality of What?" Tanner Lecture on Human Values,

delivered at Stanford University, May 22, 1979, available at tannerlectures. utah.edu, and Pierre Rosanvallon's "What Is a Democratic Society?" cited above.

8 A related discussion can be found in Claudia Pozzana and Alessandro Russo, "Continuity/Discontinuity: China's Place in the Contemporary World," *Critical Asian Studies* 43: 2, 2011, 272.

9 Fogel, *The Fourth Great Awakening*, 3.

10 Karl Marx, *Grundrisse: Foundations of the Critique of Political Economy*, trans. Martin Nicolaus (New York: Vintage Books, 1973), 241.

11 Ibid., 242.

12 Ibid., 245.

13 Ibid., 238.

14 Fogel, *The Fourth Great Awakening*, 6.

15 John Rawls, *A Theory of Justice* (Cambridge: Belknap Press, 1971), 54.

16 Ibid., 13–14.

17 Karl Marx, "Instructions for the Delegates of the Provisional General Council: The Different Questions," in *Karl Marx, Frederick Engels: Collected Works, vol. 20* (New York: International Publisher, 1984), 188–9.

18 Amartya Sen, "Equality of What?" 217–19.

19 Amartya Sen, *The Idea of Justice* (London, UK, and Cambridge, MA: Harvard University Press, 2009). Here the notion of justice is once again subjected to systematic analysis.

20 Amartya Sen, "Justice and the Global World," *Indigo* 4, Winter 2011, 24–35.

21 Amartya Sen, *Development as Freedom* (New York: Knopf, 1999).

22 Michael Walzer, *Spheres of Justice: A Defense of Pluralism and Equality* (New York: Basic Books, 1983), 11.

23 Karl Marx and Friedrich Engels, "Manifesto of the Communist Party," *The Marx-Engels Reader*, ed. Robert C. Tucker (New York: W. W. Norton, 1978), 491.

24 By way of clarification, we should add that equality of opportunity existed even in the socialist era. For example, a system of material incentives was introduced to stoke competition. This was—to use Mao's term—a "bourgeois right" Toward the end of the 1950s, village industries, as well as enterprises of various kinds, emerged in the countryside. These were regarded as proof that the divergence between city and country and between peasants and workers had been overcome. At the same time, however, socialist policy came to see the "bourgeois right" as facilitating

the emergence of a new hierarchy. For this reason egalitarian policy placed certain limitations on the bourgeois right but did not get rid of it entirely.

25 See Chapter 6 in Michel Albert, *Capitalism against Capitalism* (London: Whurr Publishers, 1993), 99–126. The rhine model was a model of development based on policies adopted by West Germany (the capital of which was then on the Rhine) during the postwar era.

26 Luonade Duoer (Ronald Dore) *Gupiao zibenzhuyi: Fuli zibenzhuyi (Ying Mei moshi vs. Ri De moshi) (Stock Market Capitalism: Welfare Capitalism: Japan and Germany versus the Anglo-Saxons)* (Beijing: Social Sciences Press, 2002), 10. See also Chapter 2, "A Society of Long-Term Commitments," in the English edition (Oxford: Oxford University Press, 2000), 23–48.

27 Song Lei, "Duoer de xiangchou yu riben xing shichang jingjide shenceng jiegou" (Dore's nostalgia and the deep structure of Japan's market economy), unpublished manuscript.

28 Cui Zhiyuan, "Angang xianfa yu hou Fute zhuyi" (The Angang Constitution and the post-Ford era) in *Dushu* 3, 1996.

29 Suicide among Foxconn workers is not a natural result of poor working conditions. It is the logical outcome of the abstraction of capitalist production and above all the complete reduction of factory and firm social *danwei* to mere mechanisms of production. Here the workers serve only as extended machines (rather than the machines operating as extensions of human beings), losing their position in the firm or social system. One thing is abundantly clear: *Danwei* in private enterprises are quite different from the original state *danwei*. They are hardly more than units of production, whereas the latter still retain their functions as complex mini societies alongside their function as factories.

30 Lin Huihuang, "Guatou zhengzhi yu Zhongguo jiceng minzhu" (The politics of oligarchy and China's democracy at the grass roots), *Wenhua zongheng*, April 2011.

7. The Equality of All Things and Trans-Sytemic Society

1 Maike'er Woerze (Michael Walzer), *Zhengyi zhu lingyu (Spheres of Justice: A Defense of Pluralism and Equality)* (Nanjing: Yilin chubanshe, 2002), 1.

2 Michael Walzer, *Spheres of Justice: A Defense of Pluralism and Equality* (New York: Basic Books, 1983), 3.

3 Ibid., 1.

4 Michael P. Levine, *Pantheism: A Non-Theistic Concept of Deity* (London: Routledge, 1994), 25.

5 Mao Zedong, *Mao Zedong zaoqi wengao* (Mao Zedong, early essays) (Changsha: Hunan Chubanshe. 1990), 194.

6 Mao Zedong, *Mao Zedong de qingnian shaonian shidai* (Mao Zedong's youth) (Beijing: Beijing Qingnian chubanshe, n.d.), 48.

7 Zhang Taiyan, "Qiwulun shi" (On the equality of all things), *Zhang Taiyan quanji*, vol. 6 (Shanghai: Shanghai renmin chubanshe, 1986), 4.

8 Karl Marx, "On the Jewish Question," *The Marx-Engels Reader*, ed. Robert C. Tucker (New York: W. W. Norton, 1978), 52.

9 A principle of equality is something that we evidently construct, but inequality is regarded as an eternal structure. And that is a characteristic (or weakness) shared by the chief modern theories of justice and equality. They don't emphasize the historicity of equality or inequality. For example, equality in the sense of the exchange of commodities is a feature only of a certain period in the history of human societies; it is not something essential to every human society.

10 Racist principles assume that inequality in outcome or exchange is due to racial difference. Before the French Revolution, in certain European countries, Jews were not only stigmatized but restricted from certain professions. The Jewish thinker Moses Mendelssohn (grandfather of the composer) complained that his son was only permitted to become a doctor, a businessman or a beggar. Some Central European countries divided Jews according to "use," allowing certain "useful" Jews special privileges and encouraging them to pay protection money to the government. Friedrich II of Prussia divided the Jews in his realm into four classes, with detailed laws governing the economic activities of the four categories. See Zhang Qianhong, "Cong 'Lun Youtairen wenti' kan Makesi de Youtai guan" (Marx's view of Jews as illustrated in "On the Jewish Question"), *Shijie lishi*, 2004, 6.

11 It is important to add some historical context here. Zhang Taiyan wrote "On the equality of things" during the gestation and outbreak of the Chinese Revolution. The complexity of his thought does not obscure the revolutionary flavor of his theorizing. Rawls's *Theory of Justice* was published in 1971, a product of the revolutionary atmosphere of the 1960s, which contributed to its radical quality. But Zhang Taiyan's radicalism is expressed in a negation of the system, whereas Rawls's radicalism

manifests in advocating for the reform of the system and the reconstitution of its legitimacy.

12 Maike'er Woerze (Michael Walzer), *Zhengyi zhu lingyu* (Spheres of Justice), 4.

13 Two important books deserve mention in this context: Peter Singer, *Animal Liberation: A New Ethics for Our Treatment of Animals* (London: Jonathan Cape, 1976); and Stephen R. L., C Lark *The Moral Status of Animals* (Oxford: Clarendon Press, 1977).

14 T. L. S. Sprigge, *The Importance of Subjectivity* (Oxford: Oxford University Press, 2011), 333.

15 Ibid.

16 In debates on the Jewish question during the mid-nineteenth century among Central European intellectuals, liberals considered ethnic identity to be an obstacle to Jewish liberation and took assimilation to be the precondition for ethnic equality. Within the Jewish community, the argument in favor of "group exodus" arose. Zionism, in this regard, is a response to liberal assimilationism. A critical issue, then, is that the concept of rights is closely bound with that of political community. The presupposition of a homogeneous subject initiates a process of separatism and antiassimilation.

17 On "regions" and "regions of national minorities" see my essay "Kua tixi shehui yu quyu zuowei fangfa" (Trans-systemic society and region as method) in *Dong xi zhi jian de Xizang wenti* (The Tibetan question between East and West) (Beijing: Sanlian Press, 2011), and my book *The Politics of Imagining Asia* (Cambridge, MA: Harvard University Press, 2011).

18 In the mid-nineteenth century, the Young Hegelians in Germany connected liberation and capability when discussing the liberation of the Jews. In *The German Ideology*, Marx addressed Bruno Bauer's identification of Jewish liberation with throwing off the shackles of religion. Bruno Bauer premised the liberation of Christians on the transformation of their Christian faith into "scientific critique." Likewise, Jewish liberation would entail a renunciation of Jewish religious identity—an argument tantamount to negating the question of Jewish liberation. In *On the Jewish Question*, Marx made a sharp critique of this viewpoint, aiming to liberate the Jewish question from the spiritual realm and place it within a political framework. "The criticism of this relation ceases to be theological criticism when the state ceases to maintain a theological attitude towards religion, that is, when it adopts the attitude of a state,

i.e., a political attitude. Criticism then becomes criticism of the political state." From the point of view of religion, Jews are only "Sabbath Jews." But within the secular framework, Jews are "everyday Jews," subject to various forms of secular oppression. "If we find in the country which has attained full political emancipation, that religion not only continues to exist but is fresh and vigorous, this is proof that the existence of religion is not at all opposed to the perfection of the state." Marx, "On the Jewish Question," 30–1.

19 For example, after experiencing a long period of preferential policies, a minority group will greet a policy of equal treatment with dissatisfaction. For example, Xinjiang recently made 7,000 civil service positions available, claiming that the policy was meant to address minority concerns. When the employment list included a substantial number of local Han people, however, some minority youths complained.

20 Karl Marx, "Critique of the Gotha Program," *Marx/Engels Selected Works*, vol. III (Moscow: Progress Publishers, 1970).

21 Actually, Balibar's suggestion that national borders should be subject to bilateral or multilateral mechanisms of adjustment is strikingly similar to the concept of "reciprocal borders" that I discussed in Volume II of *The Rise of Modern Chinese Thought*. I suggested there that the Chinese and Asian regional traditions could, under new historical traditions, be the model and inspiration for new regulatory mechanisms. Étienne Balibar, "What Is a Border?" In *Politics and the Other Scene*, trans. Christien Jones, James Swenson and Chris Turner (London: Verso, 2002), 85f; Étienne Balibar, *We, The People of Europe? Reflections on Transnational Citizenship*, trans. James Swenson (Princeton, NJ: Princeton University Press, 2004), 108–10.

22 Cf. Barry Sautman and Yan Hairong, "Demonising China: Pundits Get Its Role in Africa Wrong," *ON LINE opinion*, February 15, 2010, at onlineopinion.com. (Accessed on April 20, 2015).

23 Marcel Mauss, *Techniques, Technology and Civilization*, ed. Nathan Schlanger (New York: Berghahn Books, 2008), 58.

24 Cf. Wang Sifu (Stephan Feuchtwang), "Wenming de bijiao" (Comparing civilizations), trans. Liu Yuan et al., *Tantao* 1, 2009, 1.

25 Sung Yu, "Kanbujian de shequ: Yige Zhusanjiao yizu laogong qunti de shenghuo shi yanjiu" (Invisible communities: A study of the lives of migrant laborers in the Pearl River Delta), master's thesis, Minzu University of China, May 2011, 1–96.

26 Immanuel Kant, "To Perpetual Peace: A Philosophical Sketch," in *Perpetual Peace and Other Essays on Politics, History and Morals* (Indianapolis: Hackett Publishing Company, 1983), 108.

27 Fei Xiaotong, "Plurality and Unity in the Configuration of the Chinese People," Tanner Lecture on Human Values, delivered at the Chinese University of Hong Kong, November 15 and 17, 1988. Available at tanner-lectures.utah.edu.

Appendix

1 Wang Hui, *China's New Order* (Cambridge, MA: Harvard University Press, 2006).

2 Wang Hui, "Depoliticized Politics, From East to West," in *The End of the Revolution* (New York: Verso, 2011), 3–18.

3 Translator's note: Rural-urban development, regional development, socioeconomic development, harmony between humans and nature, and coordination between domestic development and international relations.

4 Mao Zedong, *Selected Works of Mao Tse-tung*, vol. 2 (Beijing: Foreign Languages Press, 1965), 113–94.

5 Francis Fukuyama, "Oh for a Democratic Dictatorship, Not a Vetocracy," *Financial Times*, Nov. 22, 2011.

6 "Geming, tuoxie yu lianxuxing de chuangzao," *Shehui guancha* 12, December 2011.

7 Alain Badiou, Joël Bellassen and Louis Mossot, *The Rational Kernel of the Hegelian Dialectic: Translations, Introductions and Commentary on a Text by Zhang Shiying*, ed. and trans. Tzuchien Tho (Melbourne: re-press, 2011). Available at re-press.org/book-files.

8 Alain Badiou, "People's War as a Political Concept," a paper for the "China in the Cold War Era" conference, University of Bologna, September 13–15, 2007.

Index